NEW SPIRITS

NEW SPIRITS

Americans in the Gilded Age, 1865–1905

Rebecca Edwards
Vassar College

New York Oxford
OXFORD UNIVERSITY PRESS
2006

Oxford University Press, Inc., publishes works that further Oxford University's
objective of excellence in research, scholarship, and education.

Oxford   New York
Auckland   Cape Town   Dar es Salaam   Hong Kong   Karachi
Kuala Lumpur   Madrid   Melbourne   Mexico City   Nairobi
New Delhi   Shanghai   Taipei   Toronto

With offices in
Argentina   Austria   Brazil   Chile   Czech Republic   France   Greece
Guatemala   Hungary   Italy   Japan   Poland   Portugal   Singapore
South Korea   Switzerland   Thailand   Turkey   Ukraine   Vietnam

Published by Oxford University Press, Inc.
198 Madison Avenue, New York, New York 10016
http://www.oup.com

Oxford is a registered trademark of Oxford University Press

Library of Congress Cataloging-in-Publication Data

Edwards, Rebecca, 1966–
   New spirits : Americans in the gilded age, 1865–1905 / by Rebecca Edwards.
     p. cm.
   Includes bibliographic references (p.) and index.
   ISBN-13: 978-0-19-514728-5 (acid-free paper)—ISBN-13: 978-0-19-514729-2 (pbk. : acid-free
paper)
   ISBN 0-19-514728-6 (acid-free paper)—ISBN 0-19-514729-4 (pbk. : acid-free paper)
     1. United States—History—1865–1921. 2. United States—Social conditions—1865–1918.

   I. Title.
   E661.E27 2006
   973.8—dc22

                                                                              2005047288

9 8 7 6 5 4 3 2

Printed in the United States of America
on acid-free paper

This is for Ben

Crees que la vida es incendio,
Que el progreso es erupción. . . .
Los Estados Unidos son potentes y grandes.
Cuando ellos se estremecen hay un
hondo temblor que pasa por las
vértebras enormes de los Andes.

—Rubén Darío, "A Roosevelt"

You think that life is fire,
That progress is eruption. . . .
The United States are powerful and grand.
When they stir, an earthquake shudders
Down the Andes' great spine.

TABLE OF CONTENTS

For a comprehensive timeline and a collection of images and documents relating to *New Spirits*, go to http://projects.vassar.edu/newspirits

Introduction:
Democratic Vistas

Ach! America! From the other end of the earth from where I came, America was a land of living hope, woven of dreams, aflame with longing and desire.
—ANZIA YEZIERSKA, "AMERICA AND I"

In the last half of the nineteenth century, a new United States emerged out of a crucible of fire. Literally as well as figuratively, fire shaped Americans' destinies. Fearsome prairie blazes scorched homesteads on the Plains. Workers in Andrew Carnegie's famous steel mills melted iron in Bessemer furnaces at 3,000 degrees, while day and night, refineries in Ohio and Pennsylvania burned off tall plumes of gasoline, a by-product of kerosene that no one yet knew how to use. Coal fires stoked the locomotives and steamships that began to dominate land and sea. Their fires sometimes raged out of control: steamboat explosions scalded workers and passengers, while stray sparks from railroads ignited barns and homes. An 1876 train wreck at Ashtabula, Ohio, burned dozens of people alive when a bridge collapsed under the Pacific Express. The explosive energy of miners' blasting powder was also danger-ous, trapping workers in underground infernos that killed as many as 200 in a single catastrophe. As Nevada silver miners chased the Comstock Lode deeper and deeper into the ground, temperatures in the shafts rose as high as 167 degrees.

Most dramatic of all were firestorms that raged around the Great Lakes, where clear-cut logging left miles of dry brush. The holocausts of 1871, described by terrified survivors as "tornadoes of fire," killed 1,500 people in Wisconsin alone. The heat was so intense that a wooded island a half-mile offshore in Lake Michigan burst into flames. Two decades later a similar

1

firestorm in Minnesota incinerated six towns in four hours. At Hinckley a heroic railroad crew saved 300 lives by running their train backward full-throttle to reach a pond beside the tracks. As roaring flames cracked the train windows, a black porter paced the aisles calming passengers and extinguishing sparks. When the engineer braked beside the pond everyone leaped from the cars and waded in. The engineer dragged with him the train's unconscious fireman, who had shoveled coal frantically to stoke the engine while his clothing burned. Neck-deep in water, the group waited for hours until the flames passed by. Two Chinese immigrants, terrified and apparently unable to understand English, stayed in their seats and burned with the train.

Americans in the growing cities suffered their own versions of such horrors. Two dramatic fires marked the beginning and end of the era in Chicago, where the Great Fire of 1871 destroyed most of the downtown and a 1903 blaze in the Iroquois Theater, a modern "fireproof" building, trapped and killed more than 600. (Engineers hastily explained that the frame of a building could be made fireproof but its occupants could not.) A swath of central Boston burned in 1876; the same happened to large portions of Seattle in 1889 and Baltimore in 1904, while flames engulfed much of San Francisco after the infamous earthquake of 1906. Urban tenement fires became such a well-known phenomenon that amusement parks on New York's Coney Island staged live spectacles called "Fire and Flames." The parks hired off-duty firemen and actors to battle the blazes, scream from windows, and flee out the doors.

Currier and Ives, "Night Scene at an American Railway Junction. Lightning Express, Flying Mail, and Owl Trains, 'On Time,'" 1876. Currier and Ives were among the nation's most popular lithographers in the late nineteenth century. Many of their images celebrated technological progress, especially the speed and power of steamboats and railroads and their ability to run through the night.
Source: Amon Carter Museum, Fort Worth, Texas.

"The Forest Fires in the West." In the autumn of 1871 immense fires swallowed
Peshtigo and other towns in Wisconsin and Michigan, after lumbermen left behind
miles of brush and dead wood that served as unintended kindling. Well over 2,000
people died, but the survivors' plight was overshadowed by almost simultaneous
news of another great fire: the famous blaze on October 9 that destroyed
downtown Chicago.
Source: *Harper's Weekly*, 2 December 1871.

(Fire later touched Coney Island in a real way when all three of its famous
parks—Dreamland, Luna Park, and Steeplechase—eventually succumbed to
accidental blazes.)

Some fires were set as intentional acts of protest in an era marked by sharp
social and economic conflicts. A group of female convicts in Georgia reacted
to sexual exploitation and abysmal living conditions by burning down the
Chattahoochee brickyard where they had been sent for hard labor. Striking
steelworkers at Homestead, Pennsylvania, lit up the night sky along the Mon-
ongahela River by torching the barges that had brought in an army of private
detectives. Anglo miners in Rock Springs, Wyoming, set fire to the cabins of
Chinese workers; when the occupants fled they threw them back inside to
burn, killing twenty-eight. And among 2,500 lynchings that occurred between
1885 and 1900, mobs burned at least twenty-three men and one woman at the
stake. The Civil War veteran Oliver Wendell Holmes famously wrote of his
generation that "in our youth our hearts were touched with fire." The same
was true for millions of Americans after the war's end—though their experiences were often less glorious than Holmes's memory of his war service. In
fact, the postwar world was almost as lethal as the war itself. During four
decades of clear-cut logging, more Americans died in forest fires than had

been killed at the Battle of Antietam. The number of employees, passengers, and bystanders killed by railroads in the same years probably approached 200,000—a figure not far distant from the sum of battlefield deaths for the Union and Confederacy combined.

As significant as it was, the Civil War was thus part of broader, even more sweeping transformations. Confederate surrender did not so much restore the old nation as create a new one, reshaped by not only the war but by economic and political changes that had begun earlier and had helped precipitate the conflict. With the Union preserved and slavery ended, many Americans hoped for the "new birth of freedom" Abraham Lincoln had called for in his Gettysburg Address. The great question of the postwar era was whether and how that promise would be fulfilled. What place would four million freedmen and freedwomen have in the new republic? What obligations did employers and employees have to each other in the rapidly growing economy? What was "free labor," and how free was it? How and how much should government stoke the mighty engines of industrial capitalism?

The restless Americans of this era experienced an array of profound confusions and dislocations. The rise of corporate capitalism had been underway before the Civil War, but after 1865 it took on new scale and geographic reach. Steamships ferried wheat, cigarettes, rubber, missionaries, immigrants, and tourists all over the globe. Millions of people said farewell to friends and kin in China, Russia, Mexico, Italy, and many other countries to seek their fortunes in America. Within the United States, individuals left the eastern seaboard for the frontier, the countryside for the towns, the towns for the cities, and together they made up mass migrations. Farmers' children headed to business school; the daughters and sons of slaves earned college diplomas and became teachers and insurance agents. Indian children left their parents' homes on reservations, entered boarding schools, and pursued careers as writers and doctors. The ideal of "separate spheres" for men and women began to fade; young women graduated from high school and even college, took jobs in the corporate world, and led great reform movements. If, as one historian writes, "the central dream of the modern world" is "the ability to escape the burden of the past," then Americans of the late nineteenth century embraced modernity with a passion.

Historians have long labeled the post–Civil War era "the Gilded Age," borrowing the title of an 1873 novel by Mark Twain and his friend Charles Dudley Warner. *The Gilded Age* satirized get-rich-quick schemes and corruption in Washington, and its title suggested that America glittered on the outside while it rotted at the core. In his notes for the novel, Twain wrote that gold rushes and railroad speculation had been "the worst things that ever befell Amer[ica]; they created the hunger for wealth when the Gr[eat] Civ[ilization] had just completed its youth & its ennobling WAR—strong, pure, clean, ambitious, impressionable—ready to make choice of a life-course." Troubled by corruption, Americans were even more shocked by postwar violence. The fires of economic and social transformation kindled conflicts over political power in the South and land in the West, while fierce clashes also broke out between labor and capital—including the first nationwide strikes—and among laborers themselves, especially those of different racial, ethnic, and religious back-grounds. These conflicts, described in Part III of this book, profoundly shaped the future course of U.S. history.

Yet the post–Civil War decades were also a time of enormous optimism for ordinary Americans. Walt Whitman suggested as much in his 1871 essay *Democratic Vistas*, capturing the hopes that arose in the wake of Union victory and accompanying amendments to the Constitution. Echoing Lincoln's call for a "new birth of freedom," Whitman proclaimed a "new spirit" in America's democratic experiment. Democracy, he argued, consisted of three related pro-jects. First, it was a set of political structures vesting authority in the people; in this sense American democracy had begun with the Revolution and continued with the Fifteenth Amendment enfranchising all men, irrespective of race. (Whitman predicted that within a generation women would also vote.) The second project was the advancement of "trade, finance, machinery, intercom-munications," which Whitman hoped would provide broad-ranging benefits. The old poet loved tramping around New York City talking to peddlers, housekeepers, trolley conductors, and dockworkers, and he wanted enterprise to serve them all.

Whitman's third project, which he believed had just begun, was democratic culture. "Did you, too, O friend," he asked, "suppose democracy was only for elections, for politics, and for a party name? I say democracy is only of use there that it may pass on and come to its flower and fruits . . . in religion, literature, colleges, and schools—democracy in all public and private life." Whitman called for a new American culture to complement the nation's political forms. Its "genius" would lie in the popular, the spiritual, and the scientific, and its goals would be to help each individual find truth and self-expression while strengthening ties of community and love. In dreaming this grand dream, Whitman was in good company. Freedmen and freedwomen, immigrants, students, workers, artists, intellectuals, and grassroots reformers believed post–Civil War America offered a chance to start anew.

What arose out of the ashes of the era's fires? To what extent were Whitman's dreams fulfilled? To the extent they were not, what intervened between dreams and reality? *New Spirits* seeks to answer those questions, capturing the optimism, doubts and conflicts of Americans in the postwar era. Whitman himself saw democracy as messy, unfinished, and too frequently thwarted. Like the authors of *The Gilded Age*, he deplored his country's "hol-lowness at heart" and obsession with money making. He worried about labor protests and criticized Americans for fawning over European culture rather than celebrating the freshness and diversity of their own. He deplored the stuffiness of a society he found overfed, self-righteous, and morally flabby, and he wondered where the United States was drifting. "In vain have we annex'd Texas, California, Alaska, and reached north for Canada and south for Cuba," he wrote. "It is as if we were somehow being endow'd with a vast and more and more thoroughly appointed body, and then left with little or no soul."

Whitman was right to be ambivalent. His United States combined modern technology with race hatred, eager consumerism with grinding poverty, greed with goodwill, humanitarian impulses with designs for economic empire. Between 1865 and 1905 Americans witnessed the first march on Washington, the first federal welfare programs, the first elections in which women and black men voted for president, and the first national park in the world. But the era that gave birth to such achievements—and to automobiles, telephones, and Coca-Cola—also ushered in new forms of discrimination and violence. The era in which Americans began organizing for world peace also brought the first major deployments of U.S. troops overseas. By 1900 the fires that raged at home had helped ignite conflagrations overseas. Among its other imperialist projects, the United States committed itself to occupation of the Philippines. Many soldiers there wondered why they were posted in a hostile landscape thousands of miles from home, battling guerrillas determined to control their own homeland.

It is critical to understand the United States of this past era, because we are its heirs. Much that is familiar about the United States that we know today emerged after the Civil War, both because of what Americans did in those decades and also because of the dreams they relinquished and the paths they did not take. To recapture the spirit of those pivotal years is to gain a better grasp of America's present as well as its past. For now, as when Whitman and Twain wrote, we live in fiery, conflicted times. Americans today are as proud of our country's achievements, as frustrated by materialism and shallowness, as outraged by corruption, and as troubled by injustice as Twain and Whitman were when they expressed their doubts and dreams. *New Spirits* maps a crucial piece of our past. I have sketched it for all those who are now setting out, in Whitman's words, to "write, as it were, upon things that exist not, and travel by maps yet unmade."

A FEW NOTES TO THE READER

New Spirits is a thematic treatment of the years between 1865 and 1905; insofar as possible it also relates events in chronological order. The aftermath of the Civil War appears in Chapter 1, for example, and the war of 1898 in Chapter 11. But the greater emphasis is on themes and patterns extending across the era. Part I focuses on politics and economics; Part II explores transformations in social relations and intellectual life; Part III describes conflicts wrought by the new order both at home and abroad. Thus, readers should expect, on occasion, to range from 1872 to 1903 and back within the space of a few pages. Those who would like to orient themselves to presidential administrations and other major events should refer to the timelines and other background materials at the New Spirits Web site: http://projects.vassar.edu/newspirits.

For reasons suggested in the introduction, I avoid using the term *Gilded Age* (except in the title, which accedes, for clarity's sake, to current usage). Historians have traditionally divided the years between 1865 and 1920 into two parts, the Gilded Age (roughly 1865 to 1890) and the Progressive Era (1890 to 1920 or thereabouts). The earlier period is generally portrayed as one of rapid economic growth with accompanying corruption, stagnation, and government paralysis, while in the latter decades citizens mobilized for reform. One of the goals of *New Spirits* is to challenge this dichotomy and place greater stress on continuities across the entire period. One can perhaps think of a "long Progressive Era" extending from the myriad initiatives of Reconstruction to those of the 1910s, and characterized throughout by economic and political integration, the building of nationwide networks for reform and protest, and use of government for new ends. Alternatively, one could consider the years between 1865 and 1905 a seedbed of ideas that achieved full growth in later decades. Such ideas ranged from tentative acceptance of Darwin's theory of evolution to the technological innovations that brought electricity and moving pictures, from federal civil rights legislation to the conception of homosexuality and heterosexuality as fixed orientations, from environmentalist ideas such as wildlife preservation to justifications for new patterns of U.S. intervention in the developing world. Though some emerging political proposals, like women's suffrage and the progressive income tax, did not reach fulfillment until the early 20th century or later, almost all the major ideas and thinkers of the Progressive Era had gained national prominence by 1900. In many ways, both positive and negative, the post–Civil War decades set the stage for the twentieth century.

New Spirits also draws connections among events in different regions of the country, since historians now see both the conquest of the West and the struggles of Reconstruction (which used to be set apart as a "southern story") as central facets of the nation's overall history. And while keeping its primary focus on the United States, *New Spirits* seeks to place that national history in the context of world affairs. Economic and cultural globalization, which commentators have recently "discovered," in fact stretches back through many decades—even centuries—of conflict and exchange. The origins of certain aspects of the modern global capitalist marketplace appear here, in the era when railroads and steamships began to roam the world and the American working classes began to arrive from Latin America, Asia, and eastern Europe as well as Africa and western Europe, making the United States a truly global society.

New Spirits is a synthesis that seeks to weave together the work of dozens of historians into a single narrative. I am thus deeply indebted to the scholarship upon which I have drawn. Readers are encouraged to trace those sources in the Further Reading lists at the ends of chapters, as well as to explore opportunities for further reading in both primary and secondary sources at the New Spirits Web site. Previous overviews of the era include Thomas C. Cochran and William Miller, *The Age of Enterprise* (New York, 1942), Samuel P. Hays, *The Response to Industrialism, 1885–1914* (Chicago, 1957; 2nd edition, 1995), Carl N. Degler, *The Age of the Economic Revolution, 1876–1900* (Glenview, IL, 1967), John Garraty, *The New Commonwealth, 1877–1890* (New York, 1968), Robert H. Wiebe, *The Search for Order, 1877–1920* (New York, 1967), Alan Trachtenberg, *The Incorporation of America* (New York, 1982), Nell Irvin Painter, *Standing at Armageddon: The United States, 1877–1919* (New York, 1987), and Sean Dennis Cashman, *America in the Gilded Age* (New York, 1984). The excellent articles in *The Gilded Age*, edited by Charles W. Calhoun (Wilmington, DE, 1996), are essential reading. For information on noted Americans, readers' first stop should be *American National Biography* (New York, 1999), edited by John A. Garraty and Mark C. Carnes. Its 24 volumes are a treasure trove. Neil Harris, Alan Trachtenberg, Leon Fink, John D. Buenker, and most recently Janette Greenwood in *The Gilded Age* (New York, 2003) have edited fine collections of primary documents from the era.

On the theme of fire, treated in the introduction, see Stephen Pyne, *Fire in America* (Princeton, NJ, 1982). The quote about "escaping the burdens of the past" is from James M. Jasper in *Restless Nation* (Chicago, 2000), p. 5. On Mark Twain and Walt Whitman see the biographies of both by Justin Kaplan, *Mr. Clemens and Mark Twain* (New York, 1966), *Mark Twain and His World* (New York, 1974), and *Walt Whitman, a Life* (New York, 1980), as well as Bryant Morey French, *Mark Twain and the Gilded Age* (Dallas, TX, 1965). Alan Trachtenberg also draws attention, in his book cited above, to Whitman's *Democratic Vistas*, though his reading of that text differs somewhat from mine.

I extend my deepest, most heartfelt thanks to all these scholars, as well as to the authors of the dozens of books named in the Further Reading lists, and to the astute critics who gave me advice on the book proposal for *New Spirits* and on parts or all of the manuscript. In addition to anonymous reviewers for Oxford University Press, they include Cindy S. Aron, Richard John, Lisa Materson, Robert Prasch, Reuel Schiller, and my Vassar colleagues Bob Brigham, Miriam Cohen, Clyde Griffen, Wendy Graham, Michael Hanagan, Jim Merrell, Deborah Dash Moore, and Leslie Offutt. I am immensely grateful to all of them for correcting mistakes and suggesting improvements that have made *New Spirits* a much better book than it would have been without their generous aid. Remaining errors are, of course, my own responsibility.

I am grateful to Oxford's developmental editor, Bruce Borland, who first suggested the project, and to June Kim, Peter Coveney, and Robert Miller, at Oxford, who have been a pleasure to work with. Deepest thanks go also to my Vassar research assistants, Liz Fletcher, David Greenstein, Diana Hebron, Mary Joyce, and Kathleen Pierce. I want to acknowledge, with particular appreciation and affection, the supportive and friendly atmosphere of the Vassar College History Department and the aid of its skillful administrator, Norma Torney, as well as financial support from the Vassar College Research Fund for photographic reproductions and permissions. Thanks also to the dedicated staff of Vassar College Library for their help, and in particular to Mark Christel and the ever-resourceful Kappa Waugh. I am also grateful to my parents, Robert and Verne Edwards, and my brother and sister-in-law Tim and Linglan Edwards for offering much-appreciated words of cheer in moments of confusion and woe.

Last but not least, many thanks to my son Ben, who would probably have preferred that Mama spend additional time playing with choo-choos rather than finishing a book, even one dedicated to him with love. To my husband, Mark Seidl, I owe everything else, which is a great deal indeed. He offered patient and insightful readings of the manuscript (including at least five drafts of Chapter 2) while living with considerable burdens and distractions as a result of the writing process. His love and support and the joy of our life together continue to make it all worthwhile.

PART I

THE WEDGE

Three years after the Civil War an itinerant journalist living in San Francisco ventured some predictions about the transcontinental rail line that would soon connect California to New York. In "What the Railroad Will Bring Us," Henry George developed the arguments he later presented in *Progress and Poverty*, a book that went through more than a hundred editions in the twenty years after its publication in 1879. *Progress and Poverty* shocked readers by challenging their belief in progress. The author observed that railroads, economic growth, and industrialization held out the hope of prosperity for everyone, but they delivered to only part of the population. George had watched rents escalate in San Francisco while more and more local people became wage workers in factory and service jobs. Unlike other observers, he saw that these were not temporary or marginal side effects but an integral part of the nation's economic transformation. "Widespread destitution is found in the midst of the greatest abundance," he observed. "Where population is densest, wealth greatest, and the machinery of production and exchange most highly developed—there we find the deepest poverty, the sharpest struggle for existence."

George hastened to note that economic growth *did* bring wealth to many Americans. The problem, he argued, was that the new forces "do not act upon the social fabric from underneath, as was for a long time hoped and believed, but strike it at a point intermediate between top and bottom. It is as though an immense wedge were being forced, not underneath society, but through society.

Those who are above the point of separation are elevated, but those who are below are crushed down." George noted that these problems had arisen in monarchies and democracies, high-tariff and free-trade countries. He concluded that they were structural to capitalism, especially in its emerging corporate form. The new economy, George predicted, would destroy traditional agriculture, trades, and crafts and "make sharper the contrast between the House of Have and the House of Want."

The extent to which one accepts Henry George's critique depends on how one defines "Have" and "Want." Was the measure of "Have" the ability to put money in the bank? If so, then in George's lifetime the Wants far outnumbered the Haves. If the prospect of home ownership was the measure, then the numbers looked better, putting perhaps half above the wedge. Was it freedom from hard physical labor? More Americans rose above the wedge. Was it the ability to be one's own boss? Many more fell below it. The enjoyment of more consumer products, including more variety on the table? More above. In a global economy, though, poverty among workers overseas might need to be counted in the totals. And it was even more daunting to try to measure the development of democracy, cultural achievement, and spiritual growth. Capitalism promised *material* progress. Even if it delivered that to every person on the globe, other measures remained in question.

Part I of *New Spirits* turns first to the material, exploring the transformations wrought in the nineteenth-century United States by revolutions in technology, finance, and economic policy. Controversy over the role of government, especially in helping distribute economic risks and rewards, had helped precipitate the Civil War, and it remained a critical issue of the postwar decades. This, along with the many legacies of the war itself, is the subject of Chapter 1. Chapter 2 explores the speed and reach of telegraphs, railroads, and steamships and the more general impact of the rise of fossil fuels. Chapter 3 examines the world of work as experienced by those below and above Henry George's "wedge." Chapter 4 considers some of the ways in which Americans used, debated, deplored, and celebrated the power of money. Was the United States, as many critics charged, becoming a money-obsessed society? What were the benefits and pitfalls of rapid material progress? Were traditional values being displaced, and if so, was that a cause for celebration or for mourning?

CHAPTER 1

━━⊱✦⊰━━

An Uneasy Peace

What is freedom? Is it the bare privilege of not being chained?
. . . If this is all, then freedom is a bitter mockery, a cruel
delusion.

—CONGRESSMAN JAMES A. GARFIELD

On New Year's Day, 1863, on a Union-controlled island off the coast of South
Carolina, Colonel Thomas W. Higginson bore witness to a great human
triumph. For weeks he had been drilling the First South Carolina Volunteers
(Colored) as they prepared to join the Union Army, but to recognize President
Lincoln's final Proclamation of Emancipation, which went into effect on
January 1, camp commanders declared a holiday. Former slaves gathered
from miles around to hear a local preacher read the executive order that made
them officially free. "The very moment the speaker had ceased," Higginson
reported, "and just as I took and waved the flag, . . . there suddenly arose close
beside the platform a strong male voice (but rather cracked and elderly) into
which two women's voices instantly blended." The assembly broke into an
impassioned verse of "My country 'tis of thee, sweet land of liberty, of thee I
sing!" "I never saw anything so electric," Higginson wrote. "It made all other
words cheap; it seemed the choked voice of a race at last unloosed. . . . Art
could not have dreamed of a tribute to the day of jubilee that should be
so affecting; history will not believe it." Against all odds, the aspirations of a
people in bondage and of the U.S. government had converged. Higginson's
soldiers would henceforth fight for a freedom President Lincoln had ruled
to be rightfully theirs.

Ironically, the men and women gathered at Camp Saxton were among only
a handful whom Lincoln's proclamation actually liberated. Many thousands
had already escaped and freed themselves in the chaos of war; millions still
lived in parts of the Confederacy that U.S. forces had not conquered. Lincoln,
in his capacity as commander in chief, had issued the proclamation as a

11

military measure to punish seceded states, and for the time being it left slavery intact in Union border states such as Maryland and Kentucky. Not until 1865 did the Thirteenth Amendment officially abolish slavery nation-wide and Union troops enforce that measure with victory on the battlefield. Nonetheless, those who attended the celebration in South Carolina had good reason to hope that Lincoln's proclamation marked the beginning of the end. When the United States fully ceased to practice slavery two years later, the trend toward New World abolition became unmistakable. Spain would sustain slavery in Cuba for only another decade, while Brazil, the last holdout, abolished the institution in 1882.

Immense as this transformation was, it was only one of several great revolutions, both national and global, carried forward by the American Civil War. A new United States, led by the victorious North and West, consolidated its boundaries from Atlantic to Pacific and emerged as a continental behemoth. Republican leaders in Washington worked to secure unrestricted internal flow of products and labor, while America's immense domestic market became the envy of the world. Leaders of both Union and Confederacy had, like their forerunners in the early republic, fretted over the prospect of European intervention in the war, but after Union victory the tables turned: British leaders listened anxiously as the U.S. Congress, flush with victory, debated whether to ask Britain to hand over Canada. Acknowledging that it owed reparations because Confederate raiders such as the CSS *Alabama* had been built in English shipyards, Britain submitted to international arbitration and paid the United States $15.5 million. After the war relations between the United States and the great powers of Europe would never be the same.

At the same time, almost every aspect of American culture was reshaped by the Civil War. Veterans' writings brought a hard edge to journalism and literature in what one scholar calls "the chastening of American prose style." Colonel J. W. De Forest of Connecticut was still in the army when he published one of the first works of American realism, *Miss Ravenel's Conversion from Secession to Loyalty* (1867). The author bluntly depicted battlefield carnage, and he refused to punish bad characters and reward good ones, as Victorian convention required. Ambrose Bierce, a Union veteran who suffered recurring nightmares and trauma from his war experiences, also built his fiction around scenes he had witnessed: dead men's faces being eaten by pigs and a soldier writhing in the dirt after a shell removed the top of his skull. One of Bierce's favorite sayings was "nothing matters." His fellow Union veteran Robert Ingersoll, who in 1863 had declined to reenlist because he could "bear no more bloodshed and mutilation," became the country's most prominent *agnostic*, a word that entered general usage after the war. Immense crowds flocked to hear Ingersoll hail Union victory and question the existence of God.

So when eighteen-year-old Isaac Moses Perski, a Russian Jew fleeing the czar's military draft, landed in New York in 1882, it is not surprising that one of his first purchases was a picture book about the U.S. Civil War. Perski could see the war's legacy all around him in the city where he settled. Slavery was dead; African Americans in New York, as elsewhere, were building new institutions, founding churches and businesses, and creating nationwide networks

TABLE 1.1 A growing urban population.

	1860	1870	1880	1890	1900
U.S. Population	31,444,000	38,558,000	50,156,000	62,947,000	75,995,000
Urban Population	6,217,000	9,902,000	14,130,000	22,106,000	30,160,000
Percent Urban	19.8	25.7	28.2	35.1	39.7
Percent Rural	80.2	74.3	71.8	64.9	60.3

While the majority of Americans still lived in rural areas (defined by the census as places with 2,500 or fewer inhabitants), the urban population increased spectacularly after the Civil War. By the turn of the century, 38 American cities had passed the 100,000 mark of population, and more than 66 percent of northeasterners lived in urban areas. Note that during each decade, the U.S. population as a whole grew between 20 and 30 percent. Figures in the table above have been rounded to the nearest thousand.
Source: Robert G. Barrows, "Urbanizing America," in Charles W. Calhoun, ed., The Gilded Age *(Wilmington, DE, 1996), 93, 95.*

of advocacy and mutual aid. The war had helped create New York's first millionaire class and fill the burgeoning tenement wards. In fact, the war had helped build New York itself. In all parts of the country, urbanization accelerated rapidly during the 1860s and 1870s. By the time Perski arrived more than half of northeasterners lived in urban areas, and New York's population had recently surpassed one million. By 1900 it would double again.

While the former Confederacy remained in turmoil, Perski saw plenty of scars on the human landscape of the North. Thousands of veterans suffered lingering effects of wounds and wartime illnesses ranging from dysentery to syphilis. The Union alone counted more than 20,000 amputees. Contemporary testimony suggests that alcoholism rose sharply in both North and South after soldiers returned home. Perski, like many others, undoubtedly saw veterans stumbling out of saloons at midday after drinking up their pension checks. Confronted by an antiliquor reformer, one veteran scoffed that "we men of blood and iron, who have seen death in every shape and color without flinching, . . . we want something stronger than water, tea, or coffee." Many veterans dosed themselves with opiates, vast quantities of which had been administered in wartime hospitals. Though a majority of the era's morphine users were women addicted through doctors' prescriptions, morphine took the nickname "soldier's joy," while hypodermic drug use became known among pharmacists as "army disease."

The war deaths of more than 1.5 percent of the nation's population—630,000 soldiers and perhaps 30,000 civilians—provoked major social upheavals. In the devastated war generation thousands of young women gave up hope of marriage or remarriage. Thrown into desperation by the loss of a breadwinner, many war widows went looking for work, and their plight was so obvious that it helped establish women's right to earn a living by their own labor. Thousands of women pursued careers as teachers and nurses, while others went into reform and foreign mission work. "The exigencies and inspirations of the great civil war," wrote one missionary journal in 1879, "were the best of preparations. They evoked from the heart and brain of

American women undertakings of national significance, and gave us, for the first time in our history, some adequate consciousness of our power."

The women's temperance campaign, one of the largest grassroots movements of the 1870s and 1880s, was partly a response to postwar conditions. The United States had seen considerable temperance activity before the war, but the plight of alcoholic veterans, as well as women's new prominence as reformers, intensified the campaign. Joining a wave of spontaneous local protests in the decade after the war, some women entered saloons to pray and sing; others circulated petitions asking officials to withhold licenses from liquor dealers. The national Woman's Christian Temperance Union (WCTU) coalesced in 1873, claiming more than a million members by its peak in the late 1880s. Under the guidance of its charismatic leader, Frances Willard, after 1879 WCTU members founded kindergartens, soup kitchens, free lunch rooms, and libraries; advocated prison reform and public health measures; endorsed an eight-hour day for workers; and denounced domestic violence. Willard also advocated women's suffrage, and when Republicans resisted the temperance agenda she persuaded the WCTU to back the Prohibition Party, taking women directly into partisan politics. In adopting this strategy, Willard drew on the

Thomas Nast, "New York in a few years from now. View from the harbor." With rapid urban growth, property owners began to build up as well as out, aided by technological innovations such as elevators and structural steel beams. Chicago played a leading role in the trend, with the architect Louis Sullivan designing some of the first acclaimed "skyscrapers." Sullivan became disillusioned with the priorities of his corporate clients, whose key interest was not architectural purity but increased rental income from their valuable downtown real estate.
Source: *Harper's Weekly*, 27 August, 1881.

Hester Street, New York City, 1898. Immigrant neighborhoods such as this one on Manhattan's Lower East Side had a vibrant street life, and visiting native-born Americans found it unsettling to hear predominantly Yiddish, Italian, Chinese, and other languages rather than English. Here, a photographer for one of New York's premier commercial studios has included a U.S. flag in the background. He thus reminds viewers that the bazaar—made familiar to Americans through travel sketches and world's fair representations of Asia and the Middle East—has arrived in the United States.
Source: Museum of the City of New York. The Byron Collection.

legacy of antislavery. Her father had been a Wisconsin legislator whose Free Soil Party had once, in the 1850s, "held the balance of power" on the question of slavery in the federal territories. For a decade Willard's party strove to win the same kind of power.

The war experiences of one woman, Clara Barton, helped prompt the United States to accept new international standards for human rights. Early in the war forty-year-old Barton volunteered as a nurse in the Army's desperately understaffed field hospitals. She later remembered staunching wounds with corn husks when bandages ran out. At Fredericksburg, she recalled, she had to "wring the blood from the bottom of my clothing, before I could step, for the weight about my feet." After the war Barton traveled to Europe, where she met founders of the Red Cross and other humanitarian organizations. By 1881 she and her allies in the United States had established the American

Red Cross, and a year later she won a related victory: due to her almost single-handed lobbying Congress ratified the 1864 Geneva Convention, agreeing to uphold international standards for treatment of wounded soldiers and prisoners of war. Through the Red Cross Barton aided victims of natural and human-made disasters across the United States, including forest fires, floods, tornadoes, hurricanes, and yellow fever epidemics in the South. By the 1890s the American Red Cross began work overseas, supplying relief during a Russian famine and aiding refugees after the massacre of Armenians in Turkey. Barton became an outspoken leader of the international peace movement.

The Union and Confederacy had trained three million men to fight, and not all of them went home to live peacefully. The weapons of war were widely in evidence in the late 1860s and 1870s. With government permission, discharged veterans from both sides of the conflict took their sidearms home with them, and at the same time cheap handguns proliferated as patents expired on the famous Colt and Smith & Wesson revolvers. Shop windows displayed pistols with names such as Czar and Dictator, and in the decade after the war guns replaced knives and poison as the weapon of choice for both murder and suicide. Sensationalist newspapers exaggerated the threat posed by violent crime, but the headlines were right about the depredations of the country's most notorious ex-soldiers. Frank and Jesse James had been Confederate raiders in Missouri's vicious guerilla war. Using the railroads for mobility and surprise, they robbed a West Virginia bank in 1866, a Kentucky bank two years later, and a Missouri train in 1876. Jesse James, who never officially surrendered to the Union, was finally shot dead in 1882, the same year Isaac Perski landed in New York.

New arrivals like Perski, then, found a country no longer at war but also not quite at peace. The war had wrought immense violence and grief. It had accelerated economic changes that would transform the postwar world. It had encouraged women to take on new public roles, and it had brought about many other profound changes in society and culture. It had, perhaps most importantly, ended slavery, but the Republicans who had united to achieve that goal found they could not reach agreement on the postwar role of freedmen in politics and the economy. Despite four grueling years of military conflict, antebellum disputes over the extent and legitimacy of government power had been only partially resolved.

NEW GOVERNMENT POWERS

The Civil War reorganized political and economic power within the United States. While the cotton-rich South continued to produce the country's leading export crop, in the aftermath of the war it temporarily lost control over its destiny. Reconstruction, the reincorporation of ex-Confederate states into the nation, was a messy and conflicted process. Two very different Republican presidents—Abraham Lincoln until his assassination in April 1865 and Andrew Johnson afterward—both sought lenient terms for the reentry of

Southern states and the political rehabilitation of ex-rebels. Congressional Republicans proposed, on the contrary, a sweeping transformation of Southern society aimed at protecting freedmen's rights. For about two years after the war's end, presidential leadership held sway, but within months of their military defeat several Southern states passed laws that shocked Northerners with their defiance. Mississippi's Black Codes, for example, did not quite reinstate slavery, but the legislature devised mechanisms by which freedmen and freedwomen could be forcibly indentured for long periods, beaten, deprived of pay if they protested, and have their children taken away to serve other masters. At the same time President Johnson's stubborn resistance to Congressional proposals, as well as the copious pardons he granted wealthy ex-Confederates, prompted a legislative revolt. Congress nearly impeached Johnson in February 1868, and though the attempt failed, afterward Congress took the lead in setting policy.

The Union war hero Ulysses S. Grant, elected to the presidency in 1868, lent his stature to help Congressional Radicals implement a vigorous program for reshaping the South and the nation, lasting roughly from 1868 to 1875. The landmark Fourteenth Amendment, ratified in 1868, established the primacy of federal over state citizenship, declaring that no state could "deprive any person of life, liberty, or property without due process of law." For the first time, after the amendment's ratification the U.S. Constitution defined what it meant to be a U.S. citizen and asserted the federal government's authority to protect all Americans' rights from infringement by a state. Two years later the Fifteenth Amendment granted voting rights to men of all races, sending hundreds of thousands of freedmen to the polls. Congress accompanied these amendments with a series of other measures. The 1875 Civil Rights Act and Judiciary Act, for example, asserted sweeping federal powers. Though the Supreme Court constricted or struck down many of these statutes, they left a powerful legacy to which future reformers would return again and again.

In fact, though historians sometimes describe the late nineteenth century as an era of laissez-faire, when government was weak, that notion would have baffled both Unionists and ex-Confederates. Advocates of laissez-faire responded to what they saw, at the time, as a strong central government that was exercising vastly expanded powers. Emancipation and Union victory had consolidated a new, nonslaveholding nation. Postwar Republicans, who remained the ruling party for a decade, took an attitude toward government more like that of today's Democrats than today's Republicans. (We will explore in Chapter 10, how the parties began to change places in the 1890s.) In the South Republican state governments created boards of health to battle yellow fever and provide free smallpox vaccinations. City governments installed streetlights and sewage systems, and for the first time southern states and localities funded public schools in which all children could receive an elementary education. Enrollments quadrupled in the space of a few years, and a few schools—such as New Orleans' public schools and Kentucky's private Berea Literary Institute—were even racially integrated. Missouri's new public school system taught more than 280,000 students by 1870 and won nationwide praise.

With definitions of citizenship hotly debated during Reconstruction, women's suffrage emerged for the first time as a subject of serious national debate. In the campaigns to ratify the Fourteenth and Fifteenth Amendments, suffragists pressed hard to include voting rights for women. Though the effort failed, a number of suffragists tried to vote in the election of 1872, hoping to persuade judges that the language of the new Fourteenth Amendment included women as full citizens. In *Minor v. Happersett* (1875) the U.S. Supreme Court decisively rejected this interpretation. However, though women had to wait until 1920 to win a constitutional amendment for full suffrage nationwide, the movement won important postwar victories. Wyoming and Utah territories gave women full suffrage in 1869 and 1870, respectively. Many other states and municipalities granted women partial ballots on temperance and school matters or gave suffrage to widows and independent women who paid taxes. Many suffrage advocates, male and female, supported such measures in the context of Reconstruction, though not always because they viewed a broader franchise in positive terms. "If we give Negroes, and Chinamen, and everything else, a right to vote," asked one disgruntled man in California, "why in the name of God don't you give [women] equal rights?" On the other hand, suffragist Olympia Brown argued that enfranchising African-American men met the needs of only half of former slaves: Black women, she declared, "need the ballot more than anyone in the world."

While Americans began acclimating themselves to the idea of women's suffrage, other revolutionary political changes took place in the growing cities. Sanitary engineering emerged in the late 1870s after New York City led the way with the nation's first comprehensive health code. Though rapid growth overwhelmed urban planners, most cities tried to enforce architectural safety codes. City dwellers began to expect paved sidewalks where they could wait under gas or electric streetlamps for trolleys that would carry them to and from the business districts and residential suburbs. Mayors and city councils established thousands of playgrounds and public parks. New York's Central Park was the largest and most famous, but by the turn of the century Boston, Philadelphia, Chicago, and St. Louis each boasted more than 2,000 landscaped acres. An approving British visitor reported that "no country in the world" had "such extensive and delightful public parks and pleasure-grounds."

State governments across the country undertook a flurry of activism. Almost all recognized married women's right to claim their own wages, which had previously been the property of husbands. Pressured by the WCTU and other temperance groups, many states restricted the sale of liquor, and several banned it outright. Some legislatures began to regulate other key industries, appointing mine inspectors and dairy boards. Iowa, Illinois, Wisconsin, and Minnesota sought to end unscrupulous railroad dealings and even regulated shipping rates. By the mid-1880s Massachusetts had capped the workday at ten hours for women and children, restricted unsafe food and drugs, and imposed state oversight of banks, insurance companies, and utilities. In the 1870s and 1880s the courts allowed most of these regulations to stand.

At the federal level even more radical changes were afoot. Near the war's end Congress had created the first federal social welfare agency, the

Freedmen's Bureau, which mediated legal disputes in the ex-Confederacy, set up more than 2,500 schools, and provided food and shelter to thousands of destitute freedpeople and Anglos. Though Congress cut off the bureau's funding after only a few years, other new agencies remained. The National Weather Service began keeping systematic records and delivering public forecasts. The postal service expanded steadily, culminating in the 1890s with rural free delivery, which brought mail directly to every home and business in the nation. The Department of Agriculture, created during the war, set up a nationwide network of experiment stations and extension services whose employees hybridized plants and advised farmers on crop rotation, fertilizers, and control of insects and disease. Through the wartime Morrill Act, Congress transferred thousands of federal acres to the states for public universities, placing particular emphasis on the education of women and working-class men. The act created or expanded an array of leading educational institutions ranging from the University of California to Cornell.

In the meantime the laboratories of the U.S. Marine Hospital Service brought major advances in bacteriology. The U.S. Geological Survey, founded in 1879, sent expeditions out to map the far corners of the continent and precipitated discoveries in geology and paleontology. In doing so it employed some of the era's most brilliant and unconventional thinkers, including the naturalist John Wesley Powell, philosopher Charles Peirce, and sociologist Frank Lester Ward. Americans were even prouder of the U.S. Life-Saving Service (LSS), whose heroic deeds won attention in the popular press. The service had existed before the Civil War but like many other federal agencies had been grossly underfunded, relying mainly on volunteers. In the 1870s Congress expanded and professionalized the service, ushering in its heyday. Stationed along the coastlines, LSS employees burned flares in bad weather to warn navigators away from dangerous shores, and during raging storms they undertook dramatic rescues by lifeboat and towline. Between 1871 and 1915, when the LSS merged with the Coast Guard, its surfmen saved more than 178,000 lives.

A host of new federal programs, like the Freedmen's Bureau, traced their origins directly to the war itself. Pensions for Union veterans, far more exten-sive than any provided in previous American wars, supported not only dis-abled veterans but also widows, orphans, and even dependent mothers and sisters of the Union dead. By 1890, with most veterans reaching their sixties and seventies, a Republican-led Congress extended pensions to all living men who had served the Union cause. (Some southern states emulated the program with smaller pensions for ex-Confederate soldiers.) Pensions kept thousands of families out of poverty, and though opponents criticized the system as bureaucratic and corrupt, it served as an early, tentative step in the direction of Social Security. Branches of the U.S. National Soldiers Home also sprang up to care for the most disabled men. Showcases of Union pride, they featured state-of-the-art medical care, libraries, and telegraph offices. Outside its gates each home attracted a cluster of saloons, painful reminders of the war's psychic toll, but the institutions' beautifully landscaped grounds became popular picnic sites for tourists. At the home outside Dayton, Ohio, visitors could stroll through acres of gardens and admire two scenic lakes, a grotto, and an aviary.

Such aid to Union veterans won widespread public support, as Republican politicians well knew. A marker of the pension system's prestige was an 1893 suggestion by none other than the editor of *Confederate Veteran* magazine that similar pensions be provided to former slaves. (He took it for granted that the federal government would never offer pensions to ex-Confederate rebels.) Such a move, he wrote, would honor the "plantation darky" and bring funds into the cash-starved South. Sadly, the editor's idea was never adopted, but his proposal suggested the extent to which even ex-Confederates grudgingly accepted new federal government activities, as well as the demise of slavery. One radical reformer wrote that she and her fellow abolitionists, looking back on the coming of emancipation, had realized "the tremendous power of the political lever within their own grasp." Such women and men expected continued federal leadership in the building of a progressive nation.

For all these reasons, the Civil War cast a shadow across American politics long after Reconstruction's end. The 1880 presidential campaign featured no fewer than four former Union generals, running on the Republican, Democratic, Prohibition, and Greenback-Labor tickets. Editorials and campaign speeches dwelled constantly on the war and its consequences. Across the country veterans in uniform marched in torchlight campaign parades. Republican candidates made pilgrimages to giant reunion camps organized by the powerful Union veterans' association, the Grand Army of the Republic. Even the symbols of the political parties echoed wartime interests. In 1870 *Harper's* cartoonist Thomas Nast began drawing the Democratic party as a kicking donkey, a symbol of the rebellious South. In 1876 he added the elephant, an animal with a proverbially long memory, to represent Republicans' fixation on Union victory.

Despite an array of positive initiatives during Reconstruction, some postwar uses of government power offered ambiguous or even ominous signs for the future. Many observers worried about the immense power of parties in an era of sharp political division. Campaigns were hard-fought and exhausting, especially in swing states such as Ohio and New York, and very close margins of victory prompted fraud and high-pressure tactics as each party struggled for advantage. Spokesmen stressed their parties' achievements and ideals, associating an array of their policies with national pride (or for southern Democrats, regional pride) as well as prosperity and the protection of family life. But as Reconstruction faltered, many citizens viewed such claims with increasing skepticism. The pitfalls of the "spoils system"—in which most officeholders were partisan appointees who kicked back a portion of their salaries to party coffers—became increasingly clear.

While Republicans boasted privately about winning Indiana through the liberal use of "soap" (bribes and semilegal uses of campaign funds), political machines in the rapidly growing cities won an equally bad reputation. Machine politicians made illicit deals with private contractors for gaslight, water, and trolley services and the construction of parks and roads. Though urban machines reached their apex near the end of the nineteenth century,

New York's Tammany Hall, named after the building in which it rented head-quarters, was already infamous by the time of the Civil War. William Marcy Tweed, Tammany's flagrantly corrupt boss, was exposed, convicted, and imprisoned in 1871. He left behind an infamous courthouse, finished the next year, whose projected cost had been $250,000 but whose actual price tag exceeded $12.5 million. The excesses of partisanship, both at the national and urban levels, led many Americans in search of new political institutions, ranging from nonpartisan associations to civil service laws that would clean up politics and usher in a new round of reforms.

In Washington Republicans worked closely with business interests, and one of their first and foremost goals was to provide plentiful capital and cheap labor for economic growth. By 1872 Congress had subsidized transcontinental railroads with grants of a staggering 100 million public acres and $64 million in tax incentives and direct aid. State and local governments vied to offer rail-roads their own subsidies, and dozens of railroad companies lobbied (and bribed) for government funds. They then built competing and overextended lines, a result of the industry's hybrid public/private structure and the increasingly fierce competition that resulted from the large number of private companies involved. Many of the postwar era's most famous scandals resulted from unsavory deals between legislators and railroads, including the Crédit Mobilier affair that brought shame to Congress and the second Grant administration and (as we shall see in Chapter 2) the financial collapse that triggered nationwide depression in 1873.

Republicans undertook an array of other probusiness initiatives, most notably the implementation of high protective tariffs. The tariff, first instituted in the 1790s as a revenue measure, required foreign manufacturers to pay a tax for the privilege of selling goods in the United States. In the antebellum decades northern mill owners had argued for much steeper "protective" tariffs that would shield U.S. industries against overseas competition. Representatives from agricultural areas, especially the South, had blocked them, since tariffs on manufactured goods would not help growers get a higher price for their crops but would raise prices when farmers went shopping. Up until the Civil War the South used its political clout to dampen high-tariff enthusiasm, with South Carolina even threatening to secede over tariff policy in 1832.

After the South left the Union, Congress promptly instituted higher tariffs and kept them in place for most of the rest of the century. Tariff rates were crafted to serve both economic and political ends, protecting not only manu-factured goods such as textiles, steel, tin, and iron but also certain agricultural products, including sugar and wool, that were linked to critical constituencies in swing states. What the tariffs did *not* cover was cotton and wheat, the great export crops so critical to Southern and Western farmers—a fact that eventu-ally set these voters at odds with Republicans. Tariffs brought in the bulk of federal revenue during the postwar decades, earning more than $2.1 billion in the 1880s alone. That income paid off the massive Union war debt with remarkable speed. Incredibly, two decades after the war's end the U.S. Treasury was running in the black and accruing large annual surpluses.

Today the benefits of free trade are axiomatic to American economists, who argue that developing nations harm themselves by adopting tariffs. That was not true of the United States, whose industries grew spectacularly behind the tariff barrier. Real gross domestic product rose an average of more than 4 percent a year for decades after the Civil War. While many factors led to the high growth rate, tariffs played a key role. Protected industries such as sheep ranching and steel were among the fastest-growing sectors, and the entire western sugar-beet industry was launched with the help of a tariff on sugar. American-born cane planters in Hawai'i and Cuba, in fact, worked desperately for annexation so they could be classed as domestic producers and obtain the same advantage.

Much controversy ensued over who benefited from these developments. Republicans claimed tariffs helped workers, and, indeed, high tariffs did create new industries and protect jobs from moving overseas. However, the argument that tariffs would keep American wages high proved false. By the 1880s economic reformers argued that most tariff benefits went to major industrialists, who could mark up prices in the absence of foreign competition, keep wages low, and hold on to the resulting profits themselves. It gradually became clear that tariffs had helped create the giant corporations that were beginning to overshadow the economic landscape while raising wages little, if at all. Even leading high-tariff advocates, such as Pennsylvania Congressman William "Pig Iron" Kelley, began to admit as much. Kelley's daughter Florence, studying economics in Germany in 1884, wrote home arguing that laws to cap the workday at eight hours would help workers more than tariffs did. Politicians in the United States (like their German counterparts) were slow to accept such advice, but William Kelley read his daughter's letter into the *Congressional Record* and declared that he agreed.

In the meantime, as the examples of Hawai'i and Cuba suggested, aspirations for global power emerged from the Republicans' economic program. William Seward, secretary of state from 1861 to 1869 under Presidents Lincoln and Johnson, developed a sweeping vision of overseas power that has resonated in U.S. foreign policy ever since. While European strategists believed political conquest led to increased trade, Seward argued the reverse. He wanted America to achieve "commercial ascendancy" and let political power follow in its wake. In pursuit of this goal Seward initiated talks with China to ensure an open market for American products and for Chinese immigrants, a source of cheap labor, to enter the United States. Coveting Asian and Latin American markets, Seward advocated the purchase of overseas sites for naval ports and coaling stations. Faced with opposition at home, he won only two acquisitions: tiny Midway (an uninhabited Pacific island) and Alaska, purchased from Russia in 1867. Seward, however, accurately predicted that the United States would eventually control Hawai'i, the Virgin Islands, and the Philippines, as well as additional Pacific and Caribbean territories and a Panama Canal that American engineers would construct. By the turn of the twentieth century, Republican policy makers would follow Seward's roadmap in exactly this direction.

THE STRUGGLE FOR CONTROL OF THE SOUTH

In the 1870s many Americans rejected Seward's imperial proposals, perhaps because they implied further military operations at a time when the nation was exhausted by war. A more immediate development was the militarization of domestic politics. One of federal and state authorities' chief objectives was to maintain public order, and after the Civil War they did so through military force, more quickly and on a far wider scale than they had before. Cities developed professional urban police forces, while the federal government established the Secret Service in 1865 and the National Guard in 1877. As we shall see in a later chapter, armories for the latter sprang up all over the North during the depression of the 1870s, not to guard against foreign invasion but to protect property in case of upheaval at home.

Nowhere was government force wielded more dramatically than in the former Confederacy, a point demonstrated by the ultimate outcome of an 1876 labor conflict in coastal South Carolina. On big rice plantations along the Combahee River, freedmen walked off the job to protest sharp reductions in their wages, as well as some employers' custom of paying in "scrip" that could be used only at the planter's own store. Amid mass meetings and parades the black community united behind the protest, and local employers were forced to pay higher wages or let rice rot in the field. The strike worked, in part, because South Carolina's Reconstruction government declined to intervene on landowners' behalf. Prominent Republicans, such as the black Union veteran Robert Smalls, crisscrossed the region calming tensions, but the state refused to send militiamen to force striking workers back to the fields. When a delegation of planters demanded that the governor ask for federal troops, he refused. State leaders simply allowed the power struggle to play out between workers and employers themselves, and federal authorities concurred. Privately, some were amused at the spectacle of South Carolina's elite, who had just instigated a war to defend "states' rights," pleading for federal troops to police their plantations.

Though rice plantations extended farther down the coast into Georgia, the Combahee strike stopped abruptly at the state border. The reason was that in Georgia, ex-Confederate Democrats had seized political power, largely excluded blacks from voting, and made it clear they would suppress any labor activity. When Georgia rice workers threatened to join the strike, planters informed them that "a company of soldiers was ready at a moment's notice in Savannah, to cross the river, and sweep out of the plantation all disaffected negroes, not only there, but if necessary troops would scour the entire Savannah Swamp." "This was strictly true," reported one planter, "and had the desired effect." The lesson was not lost on conservative South Carolinians. While the Combahee strike was still going on, the Democrat Wade Hampton, a wealthy planter and ex-Confederate general, launched a race for the South Carolina governorship. During his campaign vigilantes assassinated several Republican politicians, murdered thirty black militiamen in Aiken County, and assaulted and intimidated would-be voters. Election results were

Group of freedpeople near the canal, Richmond, Virginia, April 1865. This informal portrait was taken just after the Confederate capital fell to U.S. forces by John Reekie (studio of Alexander Gardner). Most African Americans were living in hardship amid the Confederacy's collapse, but their freedom was now secure.
Source: Library of Congress, Washington, DC.

nonetheless so close that they remained in dispute until March 1877. During those months the presidential election between Rutherford B. Hayes and Samuel B. Tilden also remained undecided, since in three southern states (Florida and Louisiana as well as South Carolina) both Republicans and resurgent Democrats had sent electors. In negotiations over the presidency South Carolina Democrats agreed to accept Hayes, the Republican, in exchange for getting Hampton as governor. Hampton quickly implemented the kinds of

Atlanta University, graduating class of 1903, a portrait of achievement in the four decades since Emancipation. All the graduates in this picture were "Negro" according to prevailing racial definitions.
Source: Atlanta University Photographs, Robert W. Woodruff Library of the Atlanta University Center, Atlanta, Georgia.

measures that had secured Georgia planters' power: restrictions on black voting rights, steep cuts in landowners' taxes, and repeal of fair-labor laws.

Such struggles for power raged across the former Confederacy, so much so that the Civil War can hardly be said to have ended in 1865. In the immediate aftermath of defeat, white mobs led deadly assaults on freedmen and freed-women in cities such as Memphis, New Orleans, Norfolk, Charleston, and Atlanta. For the next decade pitched battles like the one at Combahee raged all over the South. Some ex-Confederates used artillery pieces they had hidden away; there were dozens of large-scale episodes of terror and a much larger number of local crimes carried out by loosely organized groups such as the Ku Klux Klan and Knights of the White Camellia. Freedmen's teachers were beaten and shot. Leaders among the freedmen were burned alive in their homes. There was little doubt of the motive when a woman in Henry County, Georgia—the wife of a black Union veteran and Republican leader—was gang-raped at gunpoint by a group of Confederate veterans, one of whom was still on crutches from war wounds.

By the mid-1870s such violence was largely internal to the South, with less and less federal intercession on freedmen's behalf. Republicans, so willing to use force in other contexts, were losing their will to intervene in the South. Events in the village of Colfax, Louisiana, provided a dramatic illustration of the trend. By 1873 Louisiana's Republican party had splintered into factions, unable to cope with the increasing violence of Democrats who refused to accept the state government's legitimacy. One Republican had been dragged from his bed and beheaded. Another had opened a New Orleans newspaper and found his own obituary, submitted by enemies as a warning. Faced with such threats, Republican leaders in Colfax Parish fled and abandoned local black farmers to a wave of vigilantism. Several dozen families trekked to town, dug trenches, and prepared to defend themselves. At dawn on Easter Sunday, armed Democratic vigilantes gave the farmers thirty minutes to send their wives and children away. Then they attacked, using men on horseback and an artillery piece concealed across the river. When sixty men retreated inside the courthouse the attackers set it on fire and shot everyone who emerged. Then they marched forty prisoners into the woods and shot them dead. One elderly black man survived under the pile of bodies, later leading investigators to the site.

The Colfax Massacre provoked national outrage, as had atrocity after atrocity in the years after the war. Federal investigators arrived two days after the slaughter, conducted a thorough investigation, and indicted 98 men under a recent civil rights statute, but only three were convicted. Then, in the critical case of *U.S. v. Cruikshank* (1876), the Supreme Court overturned even those three convictions. The justices ruled that the Fourteenth Amendment could only prevent a *state* from violating its citizens' rights; it had no power over individuals, even when they organized themselves into private armies to seize political control. Through *Cruikshank* and a series of related decisions the Court gutted almost all the laws that Congress had designed in the aftermath of the war to protect civil rights. While the justices were doing so, self-styled "white supremacists" reclaimed control of the South, state by state. "The white people in Louisiana are better armed and equipped now than during the war," one freedman testified to Congress in 1880. "They have a better standing army now in the State of Louisiana than was ever known."

Most white northerners were as disinclined as the Supreme Court to intervene. Few savored the prospect of continued military intervention, and only a small minority had ever been deeply committed to equal rights for freedmen. A year and a half after Colfax, when Grant sent troops to halt a Democratic coup in Louisiana, northern editors widely denounced the move. Distinguished abolitionists were booed when they spoke in Boston in defense of Grant's action. Such men, wrote the *New York Times* dismissively, "represent ideas in regard to the South which the majority of the Republican Party have outgrown." Key voters were becoming—as we shall see—intensely conscious of their own labor troubles in the North and West, and their yearnings turned from social justice to social order.

Declining support for Reconstruction reflected the waning of Radicalism and the rise of Liberal Republicanism, a name made famous by Horace Greeley's presidential campaign, as a "Liberal Republican," against President Grant in 1872. Though Grant won an overwhelming victory, liberal ideas were on the rise in the decade that followed. Influential proponents included editors such as E. L. Godkin of *The Nation* and George W. Curtis of *Harper's Weekly*. They were not "liberal" in the sense the word is used today in the United States. Rather, they championed the virtues of laissez faire and market economics. They mistrusted many uses of government power, critiquing Reconstruction policies, high tariffs, and the "spoils system."

Liberal Republicans responded in the 1870s to what they saw as increasing corruption, and they also reacted to two challenges that arose in the wake of the war. First, wage workers' organizations nationwide began in 1865 to call for laws limiting the workday to eight hours. Liberal Republicans argued that such laws would violate rights of contract and property; though they denied taking sides between labor and capital, their arguments served the purpose of protecting business interests from regulation. Second, Liberal Republicans attacked southern Reconstruction governments as illegitimate, run by "trashy whites and ignorant negroes," as Godkin put it, a libel that endured for decades afterward. Editors such as Godkin and Curtis cheered when Reconstruction governments were driven out by conservative southern Democrats, and they urged northerners to abandon the defense of freedmen's voting rights. Both North and South, they argued, should be "governed through the part of the community that embodies the intelligence and the capital."

Public hostility to the achievements of southern Republicans was also driven by profound disappointment with the economic and political outcomes of emancipation. Few in the North wanted the postwar South to become a region of subsistence peasants; its export crops were far too crucial to the national economy. Thus, reconstructing the South meant transforming ex-slaves into wage laborers on the big plantations that produced cotton, sugar, and other cash crops. Few former slaves saw this as a full measure of freedom. Emancipation for them meant autonomy and a life as different from slavery as possible. Rejecting gang labor in cotton fields, many freedmen in rural areas built cabins in the woods where they could hunt and fish, keep pigs or a cow, and grow crops for their own use. Yet because Reconstruction leaders did so little to help freedmen gain access to land, most were eventually pushed back into the cash economy, toiling for others (usually whites) at low wages. "A deep misunderstanding," one historian observes, "caused the authors of Reconstruction to offer with a great flourish a gift that the freedmen did not want [that is, wage labor on plantations], and to interpret as perversity or racial incapacity the latters' refusal to accept the gift with gratitude."

The 1874 funeral of U.S. Senator Charles Sumner, a passionate advocate of justice for freedmen even on his deathbed, marked the eclipse of the Republicans' progressive wing. Not coincidentally, the party as a whole found itself on the defensive and its federal majority increasingly thin. After 1870 all the southern states had representatives seated in Congress again for the first time since 1860, and over the next decade increasing numbers of the new congressmen were ex-Confederate Democrats. Close votes and bitter wrangling resulted, and Democrats began to set their sights on the White House. Their presidential candidate, Samuel Tilden, nearly won in the contested election of 1876. Eight years later Grover Cleveland became the first Democrat to win the White House since James Buchanan in 1856. His victory marked a decisive end to Republican dominance in Washington.

Republicans across the South succumbed, in the meantime, to defeat and despair. Such was the fate of Mississippi Governor Adelbert Ames, a former Union general from Maine. Faced with violence on a horrific scale in 1875, Ames called for federal troops, but the Grant administration, mindful of the shifting tide of northern public opinion, refused to send aid. Unable to stem the bloodbath and warned by advisers that Democrats were planning fresh episodes of terror, Ames told his allies not to resist. Intimidation, violence, and fraud did their work, and Mississippi's Republican majority turned into a Democratic margin of 30,000 votes. "A revolution has taken place—by force of arms," wrote Ames, "and a race are to be disfranchised—they are to be returned to a condition of servitude." "The war," Mississippi's last Republican congressman said in anguish, "was fought in vain."

Southern conservatives often claimed that they sought to reduce the size and scope of government and implement laissez faire, goals that won the admiration of Liberal Republicans. To some extent this was true: southern Democrats did slash property taxes and cut an array of Reconstruction programs and services. But in other ways southern state governments remained quite powerful. As in the North, the question was not so much what powers government had but whose interests it served. After Reconstruction ended southern governments served the interests of economic elites. Despite their criticisms of Republican corruption, in most cases they continued to offer bonds and tax incentives to railroads, and they brokered deals as eagerly as some of their predecessors. "You are mistaken," one Democrat wrote a northern colleague, "if you suppose that all the evils . . . result from the carpetbaggers and negroes. The Democrats are leagued with them when anything is proposed that promises to pay."

The most notorious example was the convict lease system, a monstrous public/private hybrid that flourished across the South between 1880 and the early twentieth century. Through it, legislatures authorized state courts to loan out thousands of convicts—mostly blacks, but also some working-class whites and in Texas many Mexicans—to private firms that paid a fee for their labor and promised to feed, clothe, and shelter them. At the system's peak, Alabama received 73 percent of all its state revenue from convict leasing. Set to work in mines and turpentine camps, leased convicts endured extraordinary brutality. In a typical Mississippi camp they slaved from 4:30 A.M. until after sundown, "as long as it is light enough for a guard to see how to shoot." At night they were crammed into stifling boxcars or locked in open stockades. Before the 1890s female convicts were often chained in bunks with male strangers. Severe beatings were routine; few inmates left without permanent scars, and episodes of torture and murder provoked brief, futile bursts of public indignation. Overwork, scurvy, and typhoid killed as many as 5 percent of all leased convicts per year, escalating to three times that level during particularly disease-prone summers.

The convict lease system made a few well-connected insiders extremely rich. Among them was U.S. Senator Joseph Brown, the ex-Confederate governor of Georgia. Brown's Raccoon Mountain Coalmine employed convict laborers, courtesy of the state of Georgia, at a cost of $15 per worker per year. Brown, who netted $98,000 annually from Raccoon Mountain alone, was soon a millionaire. Among African Americans his notorious site inspired the folksong "Joe Brown's Coal Mine": "Sez that's the train I leave here on, / Sez I'm bound to that sundown job." Defenders of convict lease called it a small-government measure, one that saved taxpayer dollars by reducing the need to maintain prisons. But viewed from another angle convict lease was a massive appropriation of government power for private ends on a scale few could have imagined in the days of slavery. Joe Brown's business, based literally on a captive labor force, in many ways mirrored the northern railroad industry, in which federal and state subsidies stimulated enterprise while helping insiders amass spectacular fortunes through the use of public funds. But Brown's coal mines brought the nation far less economic good at high human cost.

Thus, conservatives who denounced excessive government made vigorous use of government themselves, and political power was central to the very creation of the economic conditions that would soon call forth demands for government to do more to protect the weak and regulate the strong. The late nineteenth century has been called an era of private excess, when the absence of government as a moderating force allowed the growth of great corporations and vast disparities in wealth and power. But extremes also came about in part because government power *was* used on behalf of specific interests. At the same time many new government ventures arose that can be viewed today only as positive: financial aid to war refugees, pensions to elderly veterans, heroic rescues of shipwrecked passengers, scientific discoveries, city safety codes, and the establishment of beautiful parks and playgrounds. Most of all, the United States had preserved its existence and freed millions of enslaved people from bondage. Even after Reconstruction ended, the legacy of those acts endured.

FREEDMEN AND THE POSTWAR ECONOMY

One of the central challenges facing freedmen and freedwomen after emancipation was shared by Americans generally: how could one best get ahead in an economy that required mobility, flexibility, and very hard work? By any measure, freedmen's accomplishments in the decades after the war were impressive. In the Yazoo Delta of Mississippi, only a few years after slaves there had been tortured to death for conspiring to join the Union Army, freedmen were clearing forests, selling lumber, and saving money. Some, such as

William Toler, learned to read and write, purchased land, and passed along prosperous farms to their sons and daughters. The freedman and Union veteran Isaiah Montgomery launched an even more ambitious project in the delta during the 1880s. When the railroad came through he purchased 840 acres to create the town of Mound Bayou. Its African-American residents soon owned 30,000 acres surrounding the town, which supported a bank, railroad station, and cotton-oil mill. Mayor Montgomery proudly noted that in his town "a black man could run *for* sheriff instead of *from* the sheriff." Almost everyone could read and write, and the town later produced a number of distinguished civil rights advocates. (More than a century later Mound Bayou students still score significantly above average on state literacy exams.)

In rural areas compromises between the desires of landowners and freedmen led to the development of sharecropping, through which a landowner and a tenant family split the proceeds of the tenant's crop. The most successful sharecroppers saved money to become landowners themselves, though with crop prices spiraling downward this proved difficult. A northern journalist reported from Alabama in 1880 that "I met a woman who lived a few miles from Talladega, and she showed me $98, the receipts from her own little

"In the Cotton Field," photograph by A. W. Moller, Thomas County, Georgia, circa 1895. This man and woman are probably sharecroppers or tenants. Like millions of poor Americans, amid the plummeting agricultural prices and global economic depression of the 1890s, they were probably laboring hard just to scrape by.
Source: Vanishing Georgia Collection, Georgia Archives.

African-American woman working in domestic service, Norwalk, Connecticut, with the six children in her care, circa 1900. The children carry books and toys; the painted backdrop indicates that this is a studio portrait.
Source: Connecticut Historical Society, Hertford.

cotton patch, and, said she, 'I plowed, and I sowed, and I hoed every lick of it myself, and I picked it, and got it baled and sold it too.' This is no extraordinary case. I met everywhere in the neighborhood of Talledega women not only able but willing to do more than a man's work, if by it they could send their children to school." But for rural blacks economic success was achieved against enormous odds. They were barred by custom, if not by law, from high-paying jobs, business loans, mortgages, and land purchases. In 1883 Mississippi counted 19 black-owned country stores, but this was out of a total of 2,248.

The greatest opportunities lay in the growing cities, where boosters proclaimed that a "New South" would rise from the old. Even before the war's end many refugees moved to urban locales, and after Reconstruction ended some turned to the rail networks to seek better prospects in other parts of the country. During the hard years between 1878 and 1881 as many as 50,000 southern African-Americans moved west. About 68,000 went north in the 1870s, a figure that reached 185,000 by the 1890s and accelerated from there through the Great Migration of the 1910s. Before 1900, however, the vast majority of journeys took place within the South. Mobility and dislocation, hallmarks of black life in America ever since African survivors of the Middle Passage had arrived in the British colonies, endured in new forms. Thousands of men and women undertook long journeys in search of work and to get back home to visit or care for kin. After emancipation Annie Burton, who began life as a slave on an

Alabama plantation, moved into town with her mother and sisters to attend school. She cooked for families in Macon and Atlanta, Georgia, and then found a job in New England by responding to a magazine advertisement. She returned to the South frequently to care for ill relatives and to adopt her nephew after his mother died. At various times she operated restaurants in Massachusetts and Florida and a boardinghouse in Rhode Island.

A small, prosperous black elite emerged in the wake of the war, and networks of black lawyers, real estate brokers, and other professionals developed to serve their own communities. Even a single institution could make an enormous difference in the growth of the black middle class. The Freedmen's Hospital in Washington, D.C., for example, run by the Department of the Interior, was one of a tiny number of hospitals in the United States that trained African-American doctors; its interns went on to practice medicine all over the country. Dr. Daniel Hale Williams, the hospital's surgeon-in-chief, set up a nursing school and in 1893 performed the nation's first successful open-heart surgery. In the meantime, young men and women earned degrees from new universities such as Howard, Fisk, and Atlanta and carved out niches in the professional world. By the turn of the century (as we shall see in Chapter 10) a new generation of black leaders emerged, whom the scholar and civil rights leader W. E. B. DuBois would call "the talented tenth" and "the exceptional men."

Yet prosperous blacks felt, just as keenly as the working class, the many impediments created for them by a race-conscious society. The prevailing code defined race both by color—brown, black, yellow, and white—and by nationality, and the consequences varied for groups designated by terms such as *Nordic* and *Hebrew*. The U.S. Immigration Commission, for example, designated southern Italians as an "Iberic" people with defined racial characteristics: "excitable, impulsive, highly imaginative, impracticable," they supposedly had trouble adapting "to highly organized society." But in color terms Italian immigrants were usually defined as white, permitted by both law and custom to live in white neighborhoods, attend white schools, and take jobs blacks were denied. By contrast, prejudices of color and nationality worked in tandem against blacks: whether designated as Africans, Negroes, blacks, or "coloreds," and whether prosperous or poor, they were assigned to the bottom tiers of the racial hierarchy. In addition, the overwhelming majority still lived in the South, where the majority of whites defined themselves as "Anglo-Saxon" or sometimes "Teutonic" and claimed superiority to such "lesser" whites as the Irish, Italians, and French Canadians. The divide between Anglos and African Americans, then, was exceptionally stark and persistent.

Denied the right to locate in white neighborhoods, African Americans in southern cities too often lived in cramped and filthy slums such as "the Bottoms" along polluted Cripple Creek in Knoxville, Tennessee, a neighborhood of "rickety shacks clustered on stilts." The vast majority of the post-emancipation generation found themselves below the economic wedge described by Henry George, trapped in low-wage jobs or tenant contracts out of which it was very difficult to climb. Booker T. Washington, born a slave in Virginia in 1856 and educated at the Hampton Institute, spoke for millions of such farmers and laborers when he called for "industrial education," training that would help working-class youth get decent skilled jobs. In the two decades after 1881, when he assumed leadership of Alabama's Tuskegee Institute, Washington was the nation's most prominent black leader. He preached hard work, thrift, and respectability and argued that self-help would bring just rewards. "My experience," he wrote in his autobiography, "is that there is something in human nature which always makes an individual recognize and reward merit, no matter under what color of skin merit is found."

The career of African-American writer Charles Chesnutt offered a counterpoint to Washington's optimism. Chesnutt, a grocer's son who grew up in North Carolina, got a good education and began teaching at an early age. He reported the comment of an Anglo clerk when one of his friends called Chesnutt a gentleman: "Well he's a nigger; and with me a nigger is a nigger, and nothing in the world can make him anything else but a nigger." Chesnutt found this to be "the opinion of the South on the 'Negro question.'" Very light-skinned, Chesnutt wrestled with the dilemma of whether he should pass himself as Anglo. "I am as white as any of them," he wrote angrily in his diary at age seventeen, but Chesnutt chose to identify himself as black. "I *will* live down the prejudice, I *will* crush it out," he vowed. "I *will* show to the world that a man may spring from a race of slaves, and yet far excel many of the boasted ruling race." For a decade Chesnutt produced subtle, accomplished fiction, but he was forced to give up his writing career in 1905 and return to law clerking, since demand for his fiction was insufficient to support his family. In that same year Thomas Dixon's pathologically racist novel *The Clansman*—basis for the later film *Birth of a Nation*—became a nationwide best-seller. It revised the history of Reconstruction to depict freedmen and their northern allies menacing white womanhood, while the Ku Klux Klan rode to the rescue as noble avengers.

Chesnutt captured some of the complexities of African Americans' struggles after emancipation in his story "The Doll," which recounts the dilemma of Tom Taylor, a barber who has moved north. When a political convention meets in town, one of Taylor's customers turns out to be an ex-Confederate colonel who long ago murdered Taylor's father in a dispute over the sexual molestation of Tom's sister. For decades the barber has dreamed of revenge, but with his razor at the colonel's throat he looks around at the employees who depend on him. "One was sending a son to college; another was buying a home. The unmarried one was in his spare hours studying a profession." If he murders the colonel all will lose their jobs and be thrown into poverty. Tom himself will lose his access to prominent white citizens whom he has often asked for help on behalf of those in need. Still anguishing over what to do, Tom looks up and sees the doll his little daughter has asked him to repair, hanging beside his mirror, and he decisively swallows his rage. "His own father had died in defense of his daughter; he must live to protect his own." Tom thus pins his dreams on the next generation, but to do so he has to let his father's murderer walk free. In describing the barber's dilemma, Chesnutt captured something essential about how African Americans entered the post-Reconstruction world, carrying burdens of justice denied.

Yet some of the other challenges blacks faced were not different in kind than those of other Americans, though blacks experienced the dislocations of the postwar years with particular intensity. Looking back from the vantage point of the 1930s, W. E. B. DuBois criticized Americans' tendency to think of emancipation and southern Reconstruction as events segregated from the rest of U.S. history. "The most magnificent drama in the last thousand years," he wrote, "is the transportation of ten million human beings out of the dark beauty of their mother continent into the new-found Eldorado of the West. They descended into Hell; and in the third century they arose from the dead. . . . It was an upheaval of humanity like the Reformation and the French Revolution." The struggles of freedmen and freedwomen, DuBois argued, were central to the history of America's labor movement, its economic modernization, and its politics, culture, and religious faith. To claim otherwise was to be "blind and led by the blind."

African Americans shared with other Americans a postwar world of rest-lessness, mobility, and risk. Freedom itself brought the impulse to move along and seek new opportunities, to seek lost relatives or leave behind terrible memories. At the same time the postwar economy transformed the landscape of the South and the nation, pushing and pulling even those with the strongest ties to their old communities and to the land. As thousands of former slaves left the plantations and moved to towns, they found there a crucial new insti-tution: the railroad station. Folk and blues ballads soon found in the railroad a symbol of restlessness and disconnection. "When a woman gets the blues," went one famous line, "she goes to her room and hides; When a man gets the blues, he catches a freight train and rides." Being on the road brought blues of its own: "I'm a broken-hearted bachelor, travelin' through this wide world all alone, It's the railroad for my pillow, this jungle is my happy home." Other songs spoke of the difficulties of traveling poor:

> Mmmm—please help me win my fare,
> Cause I'm a travelin' man, boys I can't stay here.
>
> I said "Looka hyah engineer, can I ride your train?"
> He said, "Look here you oughta know this train ain't mine an' you askin' me in vain."

Blacks were not the only ones who found their lives marked by traveling, searching, and longing for home. A tremendous economic upheaval in the postwar years set the conditions not only for the hopes and struggles of freedmen and freedwomen, but for those of all Americans.

FOR FURTHER READING

Thomas Higginson's memoirs can be found in *Army Life in a Black Regiment* (New York, 1984 [1869]), and Isaac Perski's story is in Tony Horwitz, *Confederates in the Attic* (New York, 1998). On veterans see the Surgeon General's Office, *Medical and Surgical History of the War of the Rebellion* (Washington, DC, 1888), Richard Severo and Lewis Milford, *The Wages of War* (New York, 1989), Eric T. Dean, Jr., *Shook Over Hell* (Cambridge, MA, 1997), and T. J. Stiles, *Jesse James* (New York, 2002). On veterans' services see Patrick J. Kelly, *Creating a National Home* (Cambridge, MA, 1997), and Theda Skocpol, *Protecting Soldiers and Mothers* (Cambridge, MA, 1992), though I take a somewhat more optimistic view than Skocpol of the pension system's legacy. On guns and violence I rely on Donald B. Webster, Jr., *Suicide Specials* (Harrisburg, PA, 1958), and Eric H. Monkkonen, *Murder in New York City* (Berkeley, CA, 2001). Consider also the last chapter of Michael A. Bellesiles's provocative book, *Arming America* (New York, 2000).

On the war's cultural and religious impact see Edmund Wilson, *Patriotic Gore* (New York, 1962), and Susan Jacoby, *Freethinkers* (New York, 2004). For the impact on women see Jeannie Attie, *Patriotic Toil* (Ithaca, NY, 1998), Elizabeth B. Pryor, *Clara Barton* (Philadelphia, 1987), and for the WCTU, Ruth Bordin, *Woman and Temperance*, 2nd ed. (New Brunswick, NJ, 1990), and Barbara L. Epstein, *The Politics of Domesticity* (Middletown, CT, 1980). On suffrage see Ellen Carol DuBois, *Feminism and Suffrage* (Ithaca, NY, 1978), and in the West, Rebecca J. Mead, *How the Vote Was Won* (New York, 2004).

For Reconstruction in the South my main source is Eric Foner's *Reconstruction, 1863–1877* (New York, 1988). On the Combahee strike see Foner's *Nothing but Freedom* (Baton Rouge, LA, 1983), and on Colfax, Ted Tunnell, *Crucible of Reconstruction* (Baton Rouge, LA, 1984). Also helpful are Philip D. Curtin, *The Rise and Fall of the Plantation Complex* (Cambridge, MA, 1990), Howard N. Rabinowitz, *Race Relations in the Urban South, 1865–1890* (New York, 1978), and the essays in *Divided Houses*, edited by Catherine Clinton and Nina Silber (New York, 1992).

For politics and government at the national level see Morton Keller's classic account *Affairs of State* (Cambridge, MA, 1977). On Seward see Walter LaFeber, *The American Search for Opportunity* (New York, 1993), which is volume four of the Cambridge History of American Foreign Relations. On partisan politics see H. Wayne Morgan's readable *From Hayes to McKinley* (Syracuse, NY, 1969), Robert W. Cherny, *American Politics in the Gilded Age, 1868–1900* (Wheeling, IL, 1997), and Rebecca Edwards, *Angels in the Machinery* (New York, 1997). For a broad view of Whig and Republican state-building see John Gerring, *Party Ideologies in America, 1828–1996* (Cambridge, 1998). On federal activism in the economy there are two immensely helpful books by Richard F. Bensel, *Yankee Leviathan* (New York, 1990), and *The Political Economy of American Industrialization, 1877–1900* (Cambridge, 2000). For an alternative perspective on protective tariffs see Alfred E. Eckes, Jr., *Opening America's Market* (Chapel Hill, NC, 1995), and Dana Frank, *Buy American* (Boston, 1999). On "Pig Iron" Kelley and his daughter see Kathryn Kish Sklar, *Florence Kelley and the Nation's Work* (New Haven, CT, 1995).

On new government powers see, in addition to Keller and Bensel, William R. Brock, *Investigation and Responsibility* (Cambridge, 1984), Ballard C. Campbell, *The Growth of American Government* (Bloomington, IN, 1995), and Walter I. Trattner, *From Poor Law to Welfare State* (New York, 1974). Howard S. Miller discusses the USGS in "The Political Economy of Science," in *Nineteenth-Century American Science*, edited by George H. Daniels (Evanston, IL, 1972), pp. 95–114, as does Thomas G. Manning in *Government in Science* (Lexington, KY, 1967). On the Freedmen's Bureau see Barry A. Crouch, *The Freedmen's Bureau and Black Texans* (Austin, TX, 1992), and *The Freedmen's Bureau and Reconstruction*, edited by Paul A. Cimbala and Randall M. Miller (New York, 1999). On city government see John C. Teaford, *The Unheralded Triumph: City Government in America, 1870–1900* (Baltimore, 1983), and Stanley K. Schultz, *Constructing Urban Cultures* (Philadelphia, 1989). As a starting point on urban machines see Terence J. McDonald's wonderful introduction to his edition of William L. Riordon's *Plunkitt of Tammany Hall* (Boston, 1994).

On northerners' fading support for Reconstruction see, in addition to Foner, David W. Blight, *Race and Reunion* (Cambridge, MA, 2001), Heather Cox Richardson, *The Death of Reconstruction* (Cambridge, MA, 2001), and Nancy Cohen, *The Reconstruction of American Liberalism, 1865–1914* (Chapel Hill, NC, 2002). Thomas A. Guglielmo offers a useful analysis of systems of racial categorization in *White on Arrival* (New York, 2003). On the South after Reconstruction see Edward L. Ayers, *The Promise of the New South* (New York, 1992), and Barbara Fields' brilliant essay, "Ideology and Race in American

History," in *Region, Race, and Reconstruction*, edited by J. Morgan Kousser (New York, 1982). The quotation about the "deep misunderstanding" between Reconstruction policy makers and freedpeople is from Fields' essay, page 166.

On labor during Reconstruction see also Julie Saville, *The Work of Reconstruction* (New York, 1994). For Republican policies in one Southern city see Lawrence L. Hartzell, "The Exploration of Freedom in Black Petersburg, Virginia, 1865–1902," in *The Edge of the South*, edited by Edward L. Ayers and John C. Willis (Charlottesville, VA, 1991), 134–156. There is a burgeoning literature on convict lease, including Alexander C. Lichtenstein, *Twice the Work of Free Labor* (London, 1996), Matthew J. Mancini, *One Dies, Get Another* (Columbia, SC, 1996), and Martha Myers, *Race, Labor, and Punishment in the New South* (Columbus, OH 1998). On Booker T. Washington's life and thought, Fitzhugh Brundage provides an excellent brief overview in his edition of Washington's autobiography, *Up from Slavery* (Boston, 2003).

On African-American experiences see also John Hope Franklin, *From Slavery to Freedom*, 8th edition (New York, 2000), as well as Leon F. Litwack's two extraordinarily rich accounts, *Been in the Storm So Long* (New York, 1979) and *Trouble in Mind* (New York, 1998), and for a brief overview, Leslie H. Fishel, Jr., "The African-American Experience," in Charles W. Calhoun, ed., *The Gilded Age* (Wilmington, DE, 1996). Also see Darlene Clark Hine et al., *The African-American Odyssey*, 2nd ed. (Upper Saddle River, NJ, 2003), Hine's *A Shining Thread of Hope* (New York, 1998), Dorothy Sterling, *We Are Your Sisters* (New York, 1984), and Tera Hunter, *To 'Joy My Freedom* (Cambridge, MA, 1998). On the Yazoo Delta see John C. Willis, *Forgotten Time* (Charlottesville, VA, 2000). Willard B. Gatewood examines the black elite in *Aristocrats of Color* (Bloomington, IN, 1990); on its rise in Washington, D.C., especially, see Jacqueline M. Moore, *Leading the Race* (Charlottesville, VA, 1999). W. E. B. DuBois reflected on African-American history in *Black Reconstruction in America, 1860–1880* (New York, 1935). On the blues see Paul Oliver, *Blues Fell This Morning*, 2nd ed. (New York, 1990), and Alan Lomax, *The Land Where the Blues Began* (New York, 1993).

CHAPTER 2

Reach

Corporation. n. An ingenious device for obtaining individual profit without individual responsibility.
—AMBROSE BIERCE, *THE DEVIL'S DICTIONARY*

In the fall of 1883 dozens of buffalo hunters bought supplies for the season and trekked out to the Dakotas and Montana to slaughter America's last great bison herd. To their astonishment, it had vanished. In the previous three years hunters had already, without realizing it, exterminated so many bison that there were no substantial numbers left. Construction of the transcontinental railroad, linking Sacramento to Omaha and points east, had divided the Plains buffalo into two great herds north and south of the tracks. The southern herd had been hunted to near-extinction in the late 1870s; now the northern was gone as well. Strips of tough, supple bison hide made excellent belts for Eastern industrial machines, and the slow animals were easy targets for modern weapons. The hunter Orlando Brown killed 5,700 bison in the first two months of 1876 alone, firing his .50-caliber rifle so many times that he went deaf in one ear. Taking only hides, hunters such as Brown left skinned carcasses rotting across the Plains.

In one of the first pieces of legislation proposed to protect wildlife, Congress tried in 1874 to prohibit the killing of female bison by non-Indians, hoping this measure would allow the species to reproduce. But the Grant administration had an incentive for extermination: removal of Plains Indians, who depended on bison for tools, food, shelter, and clothing. In the 1867 Treaty of Medicine Lodge, for example, the government had pledged that Comanche, Kiowa, Southern Cheyenne, and Arapaho could hunt south of the Arkansas River "so long as the buffalo may range thereon in such numbers as to justify the chase." Few officials openly said so, but many agreed with an army officer who advised a visitor to "kill every buffalo you can. Every buffalo dead is an Indian gone." Grant pocket-vetoed the bison protection bill. In the next decade six million bison vanished, with such horrific speed that native peoples believed the animals had hidden themselves underground.

During the same winters when the last remnants of the northern herd fell, shoppers in Chicago and New York City discovered fresh oranges on the shelves of their grocery stores. Chinese farm workers in California had boxed the fruit in a much-admired style called the China pack: "every wrapper smooth, not a wrinkle," as one citrus grower described it, "and the tissue triangled to a point on top so that when the box was opened it was something to display." Fresh fruit in winter began as an expensive luxury, but boxcars soon arrived with larger cargoes, and Florida and California "sunshine fruit" became a national marvel. Walt Whitman waxed rhapsodic over the fragrance of orange blossoms, mailed to him from Florida amid winter snows. He called it tangible proof of American progress. By 1891 California railroads were shipping out 302 million pounds of fruit a year.

The rotting bison carcasses in Montana and winter oranges in Chicago were directly related phenomena, both manifestations of a nationwide economic revolution. In the name of progress, bison and Indians had to make way for rail cars that could whisk oranges to customers across the continent. In the post–Civil War years economic enterprise achieved new scale and reach, linking producers and consumers in a breathtaking set of transformations. Networks of communication and transportation—telegraphs, railroads, and steamships—laid the foundations for this revolution, which relied more than anything else on harnessing the power of fossil fuels. The process was a global one that disproportionately benefited the large and resource-rich United States. Within two decades of 1865, the outlines of a modern global economy had emerged, and within it U.S. corporations exercised new and formidable power.

PALEOTECHNOLOGY

If one could isolate a single transformative economic factor in the last half of the nineteenth century, it would be the development of fossil fuels. The physical energy of animals, humans, wood, and water came to be replaced by coal-fired steam engines and soon by petroleum and coal-powered electricity. So essential was the shift that critic Lewis Mumford, looking back from the vantage point of the 1930s, characterized the mid- to late nineteenth century as the dawn of the "Paleotechnic Era." His phrase highlighted the use of coal and oil, two natural resources created in the distant geological past. (Mumford, an advocate of renewable energy, also hinted with the prefix "paleo-" that an economy based on fossil fuel was hopelessly retrograde). By the 1850s improved steam engines were already becoming more cost-effective than water in many applications. While as late as 1890 almost half of New England's manufacturing energy still came from water, steam engines could be taken to inland areas without prime sites along falling rivers and streams. In the meantime, natural gas and artificial gas, extracted from coal, had come into widespread use by the 1850s for urban lighting. The development of kerosene from crude oil, which began in western Pennsylvania and Ohio just before the start of the Civil War, soon offered a rival source of heat and light. Petroleum drilling and refining had become a booming industry by the 1880s.

Railroads and fossil fuels brought urbanization and industry to every region of the country. Though parts of the South remained overwhelmingly rural, ports such as Norfolk and Houston expanded and so did inland rail hubs like Atlanta and Louisville, as well as the steel city of Birmingham, Alabama. In the West, refining and smelting centers like Denver gained similar size and clout, while San Francisco became a dominant presence on the Pacific coast. Paleotechnology, however, wrought an especially dramatic transformation in the Mid-Atlantic and Midwest. Before the Civil War, American manufacturing had been largely concentrated in New England's water-powered textile mills, but afterward an extensive industrial heartland developed, with the three corners of its triangle located roughly in Lynn, Massachusetts; Wilmington, Delaware; and Chicago. Rich coal deposits made Pennsylvania the nation's leading state in manufacturing and helped build the great steel mills of Pittsburgh, Buffalo, and Cleveland. Towns like Trenton, New Jersey, and Schenectady, New York, grew into busy manufacturing centers, while in addition to its steel cities along Lake Erie, Ohio boasted major hubs such as Akron, Cincinnati, and Dayton. By 1900, industrial production in the United States exceeded the *combined* output of Britain, Germany, and France.

No place better exemplified the rise of Paleotechnology than Chicago, which in the forty years after 1860 grew from a small city of 30,000 to a metropolis of two million. The city benefited from nearby deposits of bituminous coal, and while early Chicagoans relied largely on wood for heat and whale oil for light, these soon gave way to coal, coal gas, and kerosene. By the 1880s bright, steady, coal-fired electricity became a major energy source for streetlamps and commercial lighting. In 1893 tourists gasped at the sight of thousands of electric bulbs outlining the elegant buildings of the Chicago World's Fair against the evening sky. Electric trolleys ferried fair visitors and rush-hour commuters around the Loop and out to the suburbs. A decade later the city's electric company had 30,000 private customers, and Chicago's inhabitants were using, per capita, 4.3 tons of coal per year.

Steam power had its most dramatic impact on transportation. In the 1830s the fastest form of inland transport had been the canal boat, pulled by plodding mules. Canals froze in winter, their walls collapsed in heavy rains, and they suffered frequent blockages from fallen trees. Furthermore, canals had to run near rivers or other water sources and could not extend into the arid regions of the West. Dirt roads were worse: rocky, muddy, and cratered, they were often impassable after spring rains. Thus, in Chicago, as elsewhere, railroads played an especially central role in the paleotechnic order. The city's phenomenal growth was largely a result of its aggressive development as a rail hub: By the 1890s 4 percent of all railroad tracks in the *world* terminated in Chicago. Steam locomotives not only moved goods and people much faster than canals and wagon paths, but engineers could also lay railroad tracks over rugged terrain, even deserts, and span wide rivers with bridges. Nimble small-gauge tracks soon carried passengers and freight through spectacular passes in the Rockies. Locomotives could run day and night, through searing heat, high winds, thunderstorms, droughts, and blizzards. They carried immense loads for long distances with no biological need for rest.

Railroads, then, facilitated commerce over vast geographic spaces. Measured in travel time, the distance between New York and Chicago fell steadily across the era from a length of many days to a mere eighteen hours in 1905. A journey from New York to San Francisco—which a half-century earlier had required either months of rugged overland trekking or a sail around Cape Horn—now took eighty-two hours. In order to support complex operations over broad swaths of territory, railroad companies pioneered many of the structures and practices of corporate capitalism. Their managers worked out new methods of finance, management, accounting, and labor relations. Railroads

Guthrie Cotton Depot, Texas, undated. Workers pose atop immense bales of cotton, compressed in steam-powered cotton presses and loaded for shipment. While an array of raw materials and products traveled by rail and steamship, cotton remained the country's leading export in dollar value from the 1840s to the 1920s.
Source: Library of Congress.

"Observation End of the *Pennsylvania Limited* on Horseshoe Curve" (detail), east slope of the Alleghenies, circa 1893. With the railroad revolution people as well as goods moved from place to place more efficiently than ever before. William H. Rau, a photographer for the Pennsylvania Railroad, halted the train to take this publicity shot of elite passengers enjoying the view on the company's premier line.
Source: American Premier Underwriters, Inc., Library Company of Pennsylvania, Philadelphia.

dominated the New York Stock Exchange for decades, attracting the bulk of European investment in the United States. Everywhere, Americans acknowledged steam power and "the roads" as catalysts of geographic expansion and economic growth. An Illinois woman remarked that without a railroad her town would have "neither telegraph, nor schoolhouse, nor anything."

The power of fossil fuels arose in human contexts, and its influence on the economy depended to a large extent on political decisions. As we saw in Chapter 1, Union victory and Republican economic policies set the stage for industrialization, and simultaneous events in other nations worked toward similar ends. Canada attained dominion status within the British Empire in 1867, and in the same year France withdrew its claim over Mexico. Thus, America's two nearest neighbors gained an autonomy from Europe that brought them more tightly into the economic orbit of the United States. A year later advocates of modernization in Japan deposed the last shogun and set their country on the path toward industrial development. Then, in an 1870–1871 war the crushing defeat of France by a combined force of German states reshaped Europe's political landscape. Strong and unified, Germany would soon become the continent's leading empire, competing head-to-head with Britain around the globe. In all these countries a new generation of government leaders strove to harness paleotechnology and out-compete national rivals. Meanwhile, observers around the world were shocked by the Paris Commune of 1871, in which French radicals protested government paralysis and the threatened return of monarchy. The Communards burned buildings and assassinated the archbishop of Paris; after the rebellion was suppressed the government ruthlessly executed 20,000 Parisians. The Commune raised a hysterical fear of "communism" that influenced for decades afterward political debate in every industrializing nation. It reinforced many Americans' conviction that, as Liberal Republicans argued, social order was a more urgent concern than social justice, and political power should be limited to the educated, property-holding classes.

Political and technological developments thus influenced each other, and in the United States as elsewhere government policies shaped the forms that paleotechnology took. The corporation itself, as a legal entity in the modern sense, was an invention of government. Over the course of the nineteenth century state legislatures gradually gave up the task of chartering corporations only for special public purposes, and by the 1870s anyone could create a corporation for almost any purpose without a legislative act. At the same time, Congress and the federal courts worked to create an unimpeded nationwide market in goods, services, and labor. North Carolina, in an 1879 Supreme Court ruling, was not allowed to require out-of-state insurance companies to deposit funds with the state as security for residents who bought policies. A Virginia law that charged licensing fees to out-of-state manufacturers was likewise struck down the following year. In *Munn v. Illinois* (1877) the Supreme Court did allow states to regulate grain-elevator operators (and by implication railroads) because those businesses were "clothed in the public interest," but in doing so the Court implied that any businesses *not* so clothed were out of bounds for regulation. Thus, as telegraphs and railroads bound the continent together, government policies not only facilitated their construction but set sweeping new conditions for the business and trade they carried on.

The impact of paleotechnology was as apparent in traditional sectors such as agriculture as it was in heavy industry. Steam-powered grain threshers, corn huskers, sugar mills, cotton presses, and dairy cream separators appeared, manufactured by companies including McCormick and Deere in steam-powered plants and brought to the hinterlands by rail. In the 1830s twenty bushels of wheat (roughly one acre's yield) had taken more than sixty hours of human labor to grow; by the late 1880s and 1890s the same yield took less than four hours. A midwestern farmer no longer bagged his wheat in burlap sacks clearly identifiable as his own product and liable to rot as it waited for shipment by wagon or barge. Instead, he sent it by rail to a steam-powered grain elevator in Chicago or another hub. The process rearranged economic relationships at every point along the path from farmer to consumer. It benefited large-scale processors such as the Pillsbury Company of Minneapolis, which bought great quantities of wheat at discount and shipped out mass-market products. Small-town mills could not compete. By the 1880s affluent shoppers in the cities and suburbs were beginning to think of Pillsbury and Gold Medal as synonymous with flour. Quaker Oats, Campbell's Soup, Hershey's Chocolate, and Heinz Ketchup arrived through similar large-scale manufacturing and marketing strategies.

Few industries showed more clearly than meat packing the stunning reach of paleotechnical capitalism. Railroads began shipping live cattle and hogs to feedlots for fattening, then to centralized slaughtering facilities. (Frequent suffocation and injuries in these mass shipments prompted a long battle by the Humane Society against cruelty to livestock.) The ranching firm of Miller and Lux, which created a 1.25-million-acre empire in California, Nevada, and Oregon, sent its cattle to San Francisco's Butchertown. Chicago's Union Stockyards became a meat packing capital in the 1870s, killing and processing more than a million hogs a year for pork and side products. Visiting British author Rudyard Kipling found the process disturbing. He described how on the slaughterhouse floor the hogs' "full-voiced shriek became a sputter, and then a fall as of heavy tropical rain." Hogs and cattle died at a rate of five per minute. "The blood ran in muttering gutters," Kipling reported. "There was no place for hand or foot that was not coated with thicknesses of dried blood, and the stench of it in the nostrils bred fear." While eastern shoppers were at first reluctant to purchase meat that had not been locally slaughtered, companies such as Swift and Armour ruthlessly undercut smaller competitors. In market after market they offered astonishingly cheap meat, pricing their products below cost if necessary until customers made the switch.

While paleotechnology standardized and mechanized the deaths of millions of animals, it also built up heavy industries, most prominently steel. The career of Andrew Carnegie suggested many of the complexities of this process. As a young immigrant from Scotland, Carnegie moved with his family to Pittsburgh, where he ingratiated himself with leaders of the Pennsylvania Railroad as an errand boy. Rising through the ranks, Carnegie worked his way into the steel industry by borrowing British technologies such as the Bessemer process as well as brokering deals for railroad rebates via his Pennsylvania connections. Carnegie shrewdly chose to enter the steel business just after policy makers erected a tariff barrier to block competing imports. Most of all, Carnegie watched the bottom line. He made innovative use of cost accounting to keep close track of expenses. He mercilessly slashed labor costs. On occasion, he tore down recently built factories and built them over from the ground up, calculating that increased efficiency would make it worth his while. Carnegie maddened his shareholders by refusing to pay dividends for years at a stretch, insisting instead on plowing profits back into the enterprise. He was fond of quoting the dictum of his frugal Scottish mother: "Watch the pennies, and the pounds will take care of themselves."

It was appropriate that John D. Rockefeller, whose Standard Oil Company dealt in fossil fuel itself, built an even bigger corporate empire. Like Swift and Armour, Rockefeller sold his products at below cost until he bankrupted competitors, a practice that became notorious as "predatory pricing." By 1880 Standard Oil controlled nine-tenths of the national market in refined oil, and its size allowed Rockefeller to demand, in turn, deep rebates from railroads for shipping in bulk. The former refiner George Rice told investigators that Standard Oil had driven him into bankruptcy through secret deals, predatory pricing, and collusion with the railroads. It was, Rice said, "a very sad, bitter, and ruinous experience for me." The scale of Rockefeller's empire can be measured by the companies that emerged from its court-ordered breakup after 1911: they included the roots of today's ExxonMobil, Amoco, Chevron, Sunoco, *and* Conoco.

As Rockefeller's maneuvers showed, powerful capitalists were no fans of marketplace competition; in this realm they gave only lip service to Liberal Republicans' ideal of laissez faire. Instead, they strove to lessen and block rivalries by gobbling up competitors, divvying up markets, and cooperating through secret financial deals. After experimenting for years with various unenforceable "gentlemen's agreements" and pools, major corporations turned in the 1880s to the trust, a legal invention through which multiple firms deposited stock in an umbrella entity. The Standard Oil Trust led the way in 1882, followed within five years by trusts in linseed oil, sugar, whiskey, salt, and many other products. The resulting vast corporations began to dominate key sectors of the economy.

If in retrospect the transition appears orderly and inevitable, it was not. Though many Americans have seen photographs of the celebratory "golden spike" being driven in 1869 at the site of the first transcontinental link in Utah, few know the instructive story of the second transcontinental line, the Northern Pacific, which eventually ran from Minneapolis to Seattle. Despite an unprecedented federal grant of sixty million acres—over half of all the land Congress gave to railroads before 1871—the line proved very difficult to build. Banking legend Jay Cooke, who had become a national hero by helping manage the Union's finances during the Civil War, over-extended himself selling risky bonds and illegally mortgaging government-granted property. The collapse of his firm in 1873 not only bankrupted the railroad but helped trigger a severe depression. Cooke's successor, Henry Villard, completed the rail line a decade later, but the effort broke his health. He lost control of the Northern Pacific to rivals, who then competed ruinously with newer roads. Before Villard's death in 1900, the Northern Pacific had gone bankrupt a second time, and the region's rail lines faced a crisis of overbuilding.

The replacement of Plains bison with millions of range cattle was an equally messy process. In the cattle bonanza of the early 1880s, giant ranching companies invested millions of dollars in ventures that stretched hundreds of miles. By 1884 they had turned loose twenty million cattle in the inland West. The cattle kings wanted large-scale, rationalized, efficient production, but they did not get it. Even the toughest cattle could not cope with the Great Plains' extremes of heat and cold, and a series of brutal winters on the Plains—so shocking that they introduced the term *blizzard* to Americans in its modern usage—starved and froze millions of cows and calves. As they migrated in search of food and warmth, the cattle bumped against barbed wire fences that marked human property lines. Along fences where the bodies piled up, settlers later walked long distances on top of nothing but bones. Some cattlemen went bankrupt, while others were too revolted to stay in the business. "I wanted no more of it," a Montana rancher remembered later. "I never wanted to own again an animal that I could not feed or shelter."

Farming in the arid West proved equally problematic. In the immediate postwar years the Great Plains had seemed well-watered. Not understanding the twenty-year cycle of rising and falling precipitation in Kansas, Nebraska, and the Dakotas, settlers concluded that their arrival was causing rainfall to increase. Both western promoters and scientific experts enthusiastically proclaimed that "rain follows the plow." Some believed sod-breaking itself released moisture into the air, while one Harvard professor proposed that steel railroad tracks had a magnetic effect on cloud formation. "Rain follows the plow" was an astonishing and disastrous display of optimistic thinking. In the late 1880s the rain cycle shifted, and the resulting drought left thousands of farmers stranded. Homesteaders and their families were not the only ones caught out. Large bonanza farms, similar in structure to the great cattle companies, had set up operation in areas such as South Dakota's Red River Valley and planted thousands of acres of wheat. Drought and debt broke up most of these farms within a decade. The first round of corporate farming in the arid West, like the first attempts at corporate ranching, ended with spectacular disaster. The novelist O. E. Rolvaag, a Norwegian immigrant who worked for several years as a farmhand in the Dakotas, summed up his view of the process in the title of a chapter of his grim novel *Giants in the Earth*: "The Great Plain Drinks the Blood of Christian Men and Is Satisfied."

Despite catastrophic defeats and disasters, the incorporators forged ahead. Before railroad-builders had established themselves securely in the West, they were already reaching southward into Mexico. Railroads, again, served as catalysts for other forms of development, and in the early 1870s they demanded the same kinds of concessions from Mexico's government that they sought from their own. Mexico's Liberal leaders were, in fact, busily breaking up communal and church landholdings and seeking to modernize the economy, but President Sebastian Lerdo de Tejada thought the New York, Pennsylvania, and Texas railroad magnates asked too much, especially since they insisted on getting grants of Mexican land rather than bonds or cash. After Lerdo won reelection in 1875, private U.S. interests secretly sent weapons and $500,000 to the losing presidential candidate, Porfirio Díaz, who was so eager to promote development that his followers won the nickname "Railroaders." Díaz engineered a coup the following year.

Díaz's three decades of rule were some of the friendliest in Mexican history for U.S. corporate investment. The Mexican railroads that U.S. companies built, owned, and operated rarely served the interests of Mexican passengers or linked Mexican cities to one another. Rather, they were designed to ship raw materials from south to north and from the interior to the coasts. Each project solicited per-mile land concessions from Mexico—helpfully provided by the Díaz government—and each led investors to pursue further ventures south of the border. The results were staggering. By 1896 American investors owned 80 percent of Mexico's railroad stocks and bonds. A decade later foreigners owned one-third of all the country's land, with Americans accounting for three-quarters of the total. Texas Oil had claimed four million acres for exploration and drilling. Phelps-Dodge oversaw a lucrative cross-border empire in copper mining, and the Guggenheim Company supervised mining and smelting operations in gold, iron, copper, and zinc. Around Monterrey U.S. companies vied with Italian and British competitors to exploit fabulous silver deposits. Other U.S. companies ran huge coffee, sugar, henequen, and rubber plantations.

These enterprises benefited enormously from the policy, pursued by both Díaz and his predecessors, of dispossessing traditional Indian communities and breaking up landholdings for private sale. Many poor Mexicans uprooted by this process became wage laborers in corporate enterprises; for thousands, migration to northern Mexico and across the border in search of work became a way of life. Mexican workers faced relentless discrimination, as companies openly differentiated the "American wage" from the "Mexican wage" and reserved high-status jobs for U.S. nationals. At the Batopilas mine in the Sierra Madre, for example, an American supervisor earned $18,000 a year, an assistant electrician $1,500, and a Mexican miner about $75. Farmers uprooted from their land, however, had few options other than working on ranches, sugar beet farms, or railroad gangs. Northern Mexico developed a distinctive economy in the shadow of the United States. The people of Sonora, known as "Mexican Yankees" to their countrymen farther south, began to play baseball and adopt words such as *picher* and *cacher* (as well as the curse *sanabich*) into their vocabulary.

Thus, ordinary Mexicans as well as Americans were swept up in continental transfers of products and capital, and Mexico became a model for American business expansion and corporate investment, during the twentieth century and beyond, in many other parts of the world. Copper and rubber from Mexico joined the stream of commerce along with Montana cattle, Wisconsin ice, Georgia cotton, Cuban sugar, and Brazilian coffee. Such tangible products were not the only ones exchanged. By the 1890s prosperous residents of Mexico City could open savings accounts at offshoots of several American banks, and many bought insurance policies from firms such as New York Mutual Life.

Already, by this time, dozens of U.S. corporations fit the modern definition of *multinational*. The pioneer was Singer Sewing Machine, which had exported its popular machines a decade before the Civil War, sent agents abroad during the war years, and by 1868 operated a factory in Scotland. A decade later Singer had sales headquarters in six European capitals as well as South Africa and New Zealand. Singer managers experimented early with global marketing and sales. They advertised their sewing machine as "The Great Civilizer" and boasted of serving the "Hindoo mother," the "dark-eyed Mexican Senorita," "Ireland's fair-skinned Nora," the "sturdy German matron," and the "flaxen-haired Russian peasant girl." The company's foreign agents negotiated the complexities of the caste system in India, and in China they hosted free sewing schools, hoping students would become future customers.

Other manufacturers followed similar patterns of growth: Seeking markets abroad, they soon found it profitable (partly because of tariff barriers) to manufacture in those countries rather than at home. By the mid-1880s producers of farm machinery, locomotives, elevators, typewriters, and pharmaceuticals had substantial sales in Europe and elsewhere. Four dozen U.S. corporations had factories in Canada. Bell Telephone had subsidiaries in Europe, Latin America, and Asia. Edison was exporting electric lights to countries as far away as Chile and Japan. Standard Oil, the behemoth of them all, was competing head-to-head in foreign markets with refiners of Russian and Middle Eastern oil. George Eastman of Eastman Kodak, which by the end of the decade sold cameras from Shanghai to St. Petersburg, remarked that foreign sales cushioned the ups and downs of the U.S. marketplace: they helped "distribute our eggs and pad the basket." For Eastman and many other corporate titans, the pile of eggs was already growing very high.

REDEFINING SPACE AND TIME

Railroads and steamships carried not only fruit, meat, and sewing machines, but also people with dreams of prosperity. Carlos Córdoba's journey began after his father's death, when he became an apprentice in his uncle's blacksmith shop near the border between Sonora and Arizona. There he learned to use the latest American machine tools, and at age fifteen he crossed the border and found a maintenance job at a copper mine. For Michael Daunis, a Lithuanian farmer's son, the journey began with letters from a cousin in the United States who reported (falsely, it turned out) that he was getting rich. The cousin sent a transatlantic ticket, and Michael left, expecting to return in a few years and buy "the biggest farm in the village." Ellen O'Grady's travels also began with kin: two sisters working in New York City paid her passage from Ireland. For Chen Yixi of Langmei village in southeast China, the journey began with famine and a ravaging civil war that left his family destitute. The teenaged Yixi headed for the United States, where he ended up in Seattle for almost four decades.

Like 40 percent of U.S. immigrants during the late nineteenth century, two of these migrants eventually went home. Carlos Córdoba returned to his childhood village with a sewing machine and stove for his mother. Chen Yixi returned triumphantly to China as a wealthy entrepreneur. Michael Daunis and Ellen O'Grady, like the other three-fifths of new arrivals, ended up living and dying in the United States. Their journeys show how quickly global transportation became a direct consumer product, available to people abroad as well as within the United States. Paleotechnology made it far cheaper and quicker to cross an ocean or continent. With the advent of steamships the cost of a transatlantic or transpacific trip fell to $50 and sometimes half as much. At steamship offices in most major U.S. cities, workers could buy tickets to send back to family and friends. Labor recruiters also went abroad to offer contracts for work in the United States, with the cost of passage built in. Better communication provided incentives to go, since reliable mail and telegraph service allowed family and friends to keep in touch and even wire money. Those who said goodbye could also expect to come home for a visit. More and more immigrants lived in the manner of Antonia Peralta, the wife of Arizona mineworker Santiago Aguirre. Nine times Peralta trekked to her home village in Mexico so she could be with her mother as she gave birth to the couple's nine children.

In an era of transcontinental roaming the origins of immigrants shifted from western European destinations such as Ireland and Germany to southern and eastern Europe, Asia, and Latin America. The United States was by no means the sole destination. Thousands of English and Welsh workers headed for Canada, Australia, and New Zealand, and many manual laborers left southern Italy for other parts of Europe and Argentina, with only a third choosing North America. Chinese migrants moved to Southeast Asia in large numbers before turning to the United States and Australia. But the United States was a major beneficiary whose arrivals came from every point on the compass. As one historian observes, "the American working class formed out of four great diasporas—from Europe, Africa, Asia, and Mexico." With Chinese and Latinos

TABLE 2.1 Sources of immigrants to the United States, 1866–1900.

Country or Region of Origin	Number of Arrivals	Percentage of U.S. Immigrants
Germany	3,230,720	24.7
Ireland	1,720,188	13.0
Scandinavia	1,380,676	10.4
Britain	1,986,745	15.0
Austria-Hungary	1,026,296	7.7
Italy	1,023,238	7.7
Canada	900,103	6.8
Russia	759,739	5.7
China	239,730	1.8

Chinese immigrants are almost certainly undercounted. Most Mexicans in the United States were native born, but census takers did not ask citizens to identify themselves by Hispanic origin until 1930. The number of Americans who identified themselves as having been born in Latin America rose from 38,315 in 1860 to 137,458 in 1900; this number doubled by 1910.

Sources: Roger Daniels, "The Immigrant Experience in the Gilded Age," in The Gilded Age, ed. Charles W. Calhoun (Wilmington, DE, 1996), 65–67; U.S. Census Bureau.

arriving in substantial numbers after the Civil War, Americans became a truly global people.

Not all migrants came willingly. Around the world, paleotechnology pushed people off the land and out of traditional trades, forcing them toward the industrial core. Small-scale farming proved vulnerable to capital intensification and consolidation of landholdings by powerful elites. European tailors and blacksmiths found their crafts undermined by cheaper factory-made goods, while eastern European Jews, who had long held a distinctive place as artisans and middlemen, found their livelihoods undermined by urbanization and new networks of shipping and trade. In Poland the arrival of Singer sewing machines drew rural women into clothing factories well before they traveled to the United States to take up similar work. Government policies played a powerful role in these changes. By raising import duties, for example, the McKinley tariff of 1890 virtually destroyed the thriving tin industry of Wales. U.S. manufacturers quickly recruited unemployed Welsh tin workers to emigrate and work for them.

Even migrants with noneconomic motives, such as Russian Jews seeking refuge from religious persecution, depended on the infrastructures of steam power: while it was railroads that displaced Jews from their prescribed economic niche, it was also railroads that enabled Jews to flee remote inland locations and reach Germany's ports, gateways to America. A Russian Jewish lullaby promised material plenty as well as religious freedom to those who undertook the journey:

> Your daddy's in America, little son of mine,
> But you are just a child now, so hush and go to sleep.
> America is for everyone, they say it's the greatest piece of luck
> For Jews, it's a garden of Eden, a rare and precious place.
> People there eat challah in the middle of the week.

As the song suggested, almost all immigrants came to America looking for economic opportunity. In doing so they changed their customs, languages, and sometimes even their names. At age twelve Spyridon Demopoulos was chosen by the elders of his Greek village to go to the United States; arriving in Maryland, he took the name Stephen Demas and worked his way up in the restaurant and laundry business, eventually bringing over three siblings. Min Chung of China became Billy Ford, a labor boss in the Nevada borax mines. He and his California-born wife, Loy Lee (Lily Sue), had seven children: Timothy, James, Rose, Bessie, Lillian, Alice, and George Washington.

On opposite sides of the globe, the factors that drove emigration in Ireland and southeast China were strikingly similar. Both were poverty-stricken agricultural regions swept up in Britain's expanding empire. Ireland had been a British colony for centuries, while China had recently been forced through gunboat diplomacy to trade with Britain on unfavorable terms. Both Ireland and South China suffered overcrowding on the land and massive crop failures. These catastrophes were exacerbated by British policies that dictated the export of grain from starving Ireland and the import of opium to China. Ireland's Great Famine left an estimated 1.1 to 1.5 million dead, and combined with the emigration of 2.1 million cut the island's population by a third. A decade later South China endured the extraordinary upheaval of the Taiping Rebellion, a civil war sparked by economic dislocation and exposure to Christian missionary ideas. The resulting struggle left twenty million people dead. Faced with such catastrophes, both the Irish and southern Chinese were drawn from their homelands into international manufacture and trade. Having traveled halfway around the globe in opposite directions, Irish and Chinese railroad gangs met face to face in America when the Central Pacific (employing Chinese) and Union Pacific (employing Irish) joined up in 1869.

Millions of people took on transnational identities, viewing themselves as, for example, Chinese and American or Italian and Argentine. They subscribed to newspapers from their home countries and switched back and forth from English to their own languages. Their gamble was double or nothing. If they were lucky they might end up fitting in comfortably on two continents, lifting themselves out of poverty and sharing prosperity with kin at home and abroad. If they were unlucky, illness, death, or prolonged separation might leave them or their families stranded. In California prominent Chinese merchants' wives told a visitor they were terrified that they would "die among strangers." Suey Hin, a successful San Francisco madam, had a more ambiguous view. She liked the United States but told a visitor she had returned to Hong Kong three times and hoped to go back permanently. "I am too old to be an American," she said. "If I were younger, I would be one."

Immigrants most often took jobs on the bottom rungs of the economic ladder. A few specialized in work they had done at home, but most, like the Chinese who started laundries and restaurants, carved out niches based on whatever work was available and allowed. Sweatshop garment production, so prominent in New York City, was already familiar to many European immigrants, but Syrians chose itinerant peddling simply because it required little overhead. In a pattern typical of many cities, Jewish men in Poughkeepsie, New York, tended to become tailors, an Old World holdover, while Irishmen found work as teamsters, carpenters, and policemen, jobs few had held at home. To a large extent immigrants took on the economic roles in the Northeast, Midwest, and West that African Americans occupied in the South. (In 1890 the populations of seven ex-Confederate states remained more than 98 percent native born.) In comparison to immigrants, though, native-born blacks had a more difficult struggle to purchase homes, move up the employment ladder, and secure better prospects for the next generation. Even in a northern industrial city such as Poughkeepsie, overt discrimination excluded blacks from most occupations and relegated them to the lowest-paying jobs as waiters, butlers, cooks, and maids.

Immigrants were an enormous asset to the American economy, which exercised its strongest pull during boom years. In effect, the United States skimmed off able-bodied and talented breadwinners from other countries, kept them during their peak productivity, and sent them home when they could no longer work. If the United States served as something of a safety valve for desperate immigrants, the reverse was also true. During severe depressions millions of foreign-born workers returned to their homelands, exporting their poverty and easing unemployment pressures in the United States. Investigating in the early twentieth century, Italian officials were distressed to find that steamships were not only taking prime Italian workers to America but were also bringing home thousands with injuries and illnesses, including tuberculosis. Since the United States offered no social safety net, the elderly also tended to return home when they could no longer earn a living. Touring Greece in the twentieth century, the author Wallace Stegner found coffeehouses filled with "gnarled, durable old men" who greeted American visitors in fluent English. "They tell you that they have spent many years in America. They wonder if you know their cousin Joe Kosmos in Joliet, Illinois, or if by chance you come from Paterson, New Jersey, or Denver, Colorado, places they have lived and have friends."

The benefits of migration were obvious: opportunities for migrants, cheap labor for employers, and flexibility and adaptability for both groups. Many of the costs fell into categories that economists, then and now, tend not to measure. Most notable, perhaps, were the tremendous stresses it placed on family life. Thousands of fathers never saw their newborn infants, meeting them only when they were older children or never at all. Occasionally a migrant husband just vanished, leaving a spouse who never knew whether she had been widowed or abandoned. Long years of loneliness sometimes contributed to adultery and divorce, and lack of proximity to kin brought an array of other problems. In Texas, where young Louisa Rollfing lived with her husband August, distance from her beloved mother in Germany contributed to tragedy. When her first baby was born prematurely she had difficulty nursing and could not find an older woman to give her advice. "I did not have any experience," she later wrote. "Maybe he could have been saved if I had Mother near me." Instead, the baby died. Conversely, many women in South China counted themselves lucky to have a husband's income from overseas while they enjoyed extended periods of freedom from patriarchal control. The restless search for work and opportunity both strengthened women's rights and weakened family ties.

While immigrants journeyed to and fro in cheap, unpleasant steerage berths, affluent Americans made use of new high-end transportation offering unprecedented luxury and speed. The New York Central, advertising a trip of only twenty hours from New York to Chicago, billed itself as the "fastest train in the world." On its premier service in the 1890s, the Pennsylvania Railroad featured not only mahogany dining cars and sleepers but a library, barber, stenographer, and stock reports three times a day. Even before the Civil War railroads had begun to build and promote resorts, tempting well-to-do Americans to participate in a ritual newly described as "vacationing." In postwar decades the practice grew exponentially. Wealthy Manhattanites could get to the spa at White Sulphur Springs, Virginia, for $28, or to a great camp in the Adirondacks for $50. Philadelphians could reach Cape May, New Jersey, nonstop in three hours. Many of the great names of the American travel industry—from Lake Tahoe to Palm Beach, Florida—became fashionable destinations. By 1900 railroads offered direct service to national parks in the West, which they played a role in developing. Even rural and working-class

Americans shared some of the fun. Few had the money or leisure for extended tours, but through "excursion trains" an occasional summer Sunday at the state fair or the beach became accessible to millions.

Meanwhile, wealthy adventurers turned their attention overseas as travel to Europe and the Holy Land became cheaper, faster, safer, and more comfortable. Some travelers came home with their prejudices confirmed. "I felt as never before," declared one visitor to England, "the unspeakable superiority of America." But ease of travel and communication also stimulated cross-fertilization of ideas. Jane Addams got the inspiration for Hull House in London; the antilynching advocate Ida B. Wells funded her work through lectures to sympathetic Britons. Almost every major American artist sojourned in Paris, bringing the American art world fully into Europe's orbit. Scholars in many fields studied on the Continent or in England. The pioneer mathematician J. Willard Gibbs took his advanced degrees in Germany, and though his

"From Sicily," 1905. Cheaper, faster transportation led to more fluid patterns of immigration as well as increased numbers of migrants. Many, such as these new arrivals, came as single men or left wives and children at home, hoping to work in America for a few years and either send for their families or return home with their savings. Lewis Wickes Hine took this photograph as part of a series at Ellis Island in New York. Hine, who went on to a celebrated career as a photojournalist, hoped to instill in native-born Americans the same admiration for new immigrants they had for the Pilgrims.
Source: George Eastman House, Rochester, New York.

Mexican-American ranch family, Mora Valley, New Mexico Territory, 1895. Note the leather boots on the baby's feet: this family perhaps has aspirations for their young son.
Source: Photographic Archives, Palace of the Governors, Museum of New Mexico, Santa Fe, New Mexico.

later papers were published in Connecticut, almost no Americans had the training to comprehend them. Major social thinkers such as Florence Kelley and W. E. B. DuBois also undertook postgraduate study in Germany. In a very different field of learning, Americans in London around 1870 first encountered the practice and the phrase "living in drag."

For the Boston intellectual Henry Adams, son of the U.S. ambassador to Britain during the Civil War, extended travels in Europe prompted perceptive comparisons with conditions in his homeland. Having visited the great museums and cathedrals of Europe, Adams stood and pondered the operations of an electric dynamo at the 1893 Chicago World's Fair. The influence of the Virgin Mary and of Christianity, Adams wrote, was being eclipsed by American enterprise, enormously powerful but bereft of spirituality. "At the Louvre and at Chartres," Adams wrote, speaking of religious faith, "was the highest energy ever known to man, the creator of four-fifths of his noblest art, exercising vastly more attraction over the human mind than all the steam-engines and dynamos ever dreamed of; and yet this energy was unknown to the American mind." Americans, Adams wrote with foreboding, "felt a railway train as power." Walt Whitman expressed a more optimistic version of the same view in "To a Locomotive in Winter":

Type of the modern—emblem of motion and power—pulse of the continent . . .
By day thy warning ringing bell to sound its notes,
By night thy silent signal lamps to swing.
Fierce-throated beauty!
Roll through my chant with all thy lawless music, thy swinging lamps at night,
Thy madly-whistled laughter, echoing, rumbling like an earthquake, rousing all,
Law of thyself complete, thine own track firmly holding, . . .
Thy trills of shrieks by rocks and hills return'd,
Launch'd o'er the prairies wide, across the lakes,
To the free skies unpent and glad and strong.

Whitman's enthusiasm was widely shared. For the first time in human history an ordinary person could cross an ocean in two weeks with reasonable safety, and the continent of North America in half that time. In 1889 millions of Americans followed the progress of the twenty-two-year-old stunt reporter Nellie Bly, who set out to beat the fictional record set in Jules Verne's *Around the World in Eighty Days*. Bly traveled by rail and steamship from New York to London, Paris, and Italy; through the Suez Canal to Sri Lanka, Singapore, Hong Kong, and Yokohama; and across the Pacific. A special train dispatched by her sponsors at the *New York World* then whisked her from San Francisco to Manhattan for a record journey of seventy-two days, six hours, and eleven minutes. "Father Time Outdone!" trumpeted the *World*, proclaiming a "new age of lightning travel." The editors glossed over the inconvenient fact that Bly's achievement depended largely on British steamships, a British-built canal, and the well-maintained ports of the British Empire. Instead, they hailed Bly as an American success story, a "chic and pert" young woman who had shown that global speed and reach could be enjoyed by any American who traveled first class.

Bly's trip revealed as much about news as it did about transportation. The managers of the *World* funded her journey because they knew she would write lively telegraph dispatches that would reach home quickly, fueling sales. Global communication had become, by the time of Bly's trip, nearly instantaneous. Telegraph lines connected every continent; a reliable message could get from London to New York in only ten minutes and from Bombay in ninety. The news business had already been exploring the advantages of this system for years. In 1871, in a stunt not unlike Bly's, the *New York Herald* had sent their reporter Henry Stanley to the Congo to "find" the English explorer David Livingstone. (Livingstone was unaware that he was lost.) The significance of the trip had been again not so much the outcome but the search itself. Stanley's vivid dispatches made it to the coast to be telegraphed back for sensational and lucrative headlines.

To a large extent the Civil War fostered Americans' insatiable demand for information, which papers like the *Herald* and *World* worked to sustain. "Each magazine and periodical," observed a reporter in 1893, "now runs a neck-and-neck race to capture the first and freshest news. . . . Priority in catching a current event is the overwhelming aim." Paper and printing costs fell steadily, and simple presses became available at prices many individuals could afford. Visitors to San Francisco could sample an array of ethnic newspapers, ranging from *União Portuguesa* to *Slavenska Čitaonica*. African-American "race papers" became a potent tool for discussion and organization, culminating by the turn of the century in papers of nationwide circulation and distinction such as the *Chicago Defender*. Meanwhile, mass-market papers such as the *New York World* boasted circulations in the hundreds of thousands. Like other corporations they sought profits on high volume and razor-thin margins, bolstering sales through celebrity coverage and aggressive advertising campaigns.

Information thus became a major industry in itself, just as critical as railroads to the expanding networks of administration and commerce. Western Union telegraph company, which like Rockefeller's Standard Oil succeeded in absorbing rival firms and establishing an effective nationwide monopoly, operated on a staggering scale: by 1900 it counted 22,900 offices in the United States and carried sixty-three million messages a year. The telegraph helped transform financial markets, sending stock and futures quotes, bond prices, and shipping news humming along the wires. Since before the Civil War most of America's major financiers, such as J. P. Morgan and J. and W. Seligman, had arrived with European connections, backed by substantial capital from Britain, Belgium, and other financial centers. In the postwar years rapid communication made it increasingly easy to sustain those connections and move money around the world.

Along with the telegraph, the postal service also played a critical but under-recognized role in the transformation of news and commerce. Officials in the U.S. Railway Mail Service, created in 1869, found creative ways to deliver mail quickly using night trains and having postal workers sort mail in transit. While the expensive telegraph was used largely by businesses, almost all Americans benefited from cheap, reliable mail. "The post office is the visible form of the Federal Government to every community and to every citizen," declared the postmaster general in 1890. "Its hand is the only one that touches the local life, the social interests, and business concern of every neighborhood." Through Railway Mail, as well as subsidies to the railroads over which it traveled, the U.S. government gave a tremendous boost to economic growth. Banks, businesses, and customers mailed millions of checks, drafts, bills of exchange, and other instruments of credit, which by the 1880s made up more than 90 percent of all bank receipts. Cheap bulk mailing rates, introduced in the mid-1880s, stimulated the rise of mail-order catalogs and magazines, which, as we shall see in Chapter 4, became channels for mass consumer culture.

By the 1880s telegraphs also channeled every kind of news, and one small-town Michigan editor complained bitterly about the result. There had been a severe forest fire nearby, he wrote, but nothing about it came over the wires; instead, the telegraph brought "a full account of the flood in Shanghai, a massacre in Calcutta, a sailor fight in Bombay, hard frosts in Siberia, a missionary banquet in Madagascar, [and] the price of kangaroo leather from Borneo." The editor, one of a handful who bucked the trend, told readers he was canceling his telegraph service and would henceforth report only local news. Before people had adjusted to a cacophony of reports from around the globe, innovators were promising to bring even more, faster. In 1899 the *New York*

Herald followed the America's Cup race through a wireless radio broadcast, transmitted by inventor Enrico Marconi from steamships near the racing yachts. In 1903 Marconi opened the first commercial wireless service on Cape Cod, and the era of radio broadcasting was born.

The economic revolution flooded Americans with information and promoted the expectation that they should act on what they learned, whether through motives of charity, education, entertainment, or profit. Watching the hustle and bustle of shipping, selling, and shopping that came with economic transformation, many Americans experienced an accelerating rush in the pace of life. Newcomers shared the impression, especially when they disembarked in a metropolis such as New York. In his autobiographical novel *The Rise of David Levinsky*, Abraham Cahan described his character's disorientation after making the Atlantic voyage: "The active life of the great strange city made me feel like one abandoned in the midst of a jungle." Levinsky was struck by the "preoccupied faces and hurried step," "the scurry and hustle." One of the first English phrases he learned from his landlady was "hurry up." The noted pianist Ignace Paderewski, visiting from Poland in 1891, remembered in Chicago "an atmosphere of intense competition, of continuous effort, and of speed—speed, speed, even then."

Medical experts soon warned that the pace of information and travel was exerting great psychological pressure. They noted that it was much more stressful to receive stock market updates five times a day than it was to check them once a week, even though one could profit from the extra information. In *American Nervousness* (1881) Dr. George Beard warned of an epidemic of neurasthenia brought about by the need for punctuality. "We are under constant strain, mostly unconscious," Beard argued, "oftentimes in sleeping as well as in waking hours, to get somewhere or do something at some definite moment." He identified the five sources of neuresthenia as "steam power, the periodical press, the telegraph, the sciences, and the mental activity of women." Unfortunately, the exact symptoms of the resulting malady remained unclear. Doctors suggested that neuresthenia might be implicated in almost every kind of complaint, including baldness, hay fever, skin rashes, headaches, insomnia, sexual dysfunction, hot flashes, and alcoholism. Authors such as Beard seemed proud of neuresthenia, a "distinguished" illness made "possible by a new and productive country." Others were not so sure. Writers such as Kate Chopin in *The Awakening* and Edith Wharton in *House of Mirth* used neuresthenic characters to critique American society and its status- and money-centered values.

The illness Beard diagnosed was, he and many others assumed, a problem of the affluent classes. The drive for efficiency and speed was equally obvious, however, to railroad and telegraph workers and anyone whose job depended on those networks, including wholesalers and traveling salesmen. A Cincinnati paper worried that *commuters*—a new term in Americans' vocabulary—had to bend their lives to fit train schedules. Commuters enjoyed suburban life in more relaxing surroundings than the city could offer, but they lost much of that repose as they rushed to catch the 7:03. "The longer a man is a commuter," the editor worried, "the more he grows to be a living timetable."

In fact, railroads altered the reckoning of time itself. Before the 1880s American cities and towns operated on their own local times. Savannah, Georgia, for example, operated a half-hour ahead of Atlanta time. This system wreaked havoc on railroad schedules and passengers—or, to put it another way, rapid intercity transit created confusion where before there had been little or none. At the behest of a zealous manager who advocated standardized time, a group of major railroads announced in 1883 that they were dividing the nation into four zones—Eastern, Central, Mountain, and Pacific—and setting standard times for the operation of trains. Despite sporadic protests, usually from cities and towns that experienced a dramatic clock shift, most Americans accepted railroad time as a matter of convenience and progress. On Sunday, November 18, 1883, "the day of two noons," clock-keepers all over the country changed their clocks to reflect the new system. The *Washington Post* observed, with only slight exaggeration, that it was a revolution "scarcely second to the reformation of the calendar by Julius Caesar."

In moments like these, Americans came to understand the implications of paleotechnical capitalism in fits and starts, as people do in any revolution. Even when the consequences of the new economy arrived at a precise moment—as they did at noon on that November Sunday—they often seemed inevitable or unstoppable. The paleotechnical era, a creation of human invention and of myriad decisions by voters, policy makers, financiers, and businessmen, arrived like a mandate from nature itself. Andrew Carnegie perhaps expressed the attitude best in his famous essay "Wealth." "The conditions of human life have not only been changed, but revolutionized," he declared. "Whether the change be for good or for ill, it is upon us, beyond our power to alter, and therefore, to be accepted and made the best of. It is a waste of time," he added impatiently, "to criticize the inevitable."

The educational reformer John Dewey, writing in 1899, took an optimistic view of progress for reasons rather different from Carnegie's. In the economic revolution that was occurring, Dewey wrote, "the face of the earth is making over, even as to its physical forms; political boundaries are wiped out and moved about; . . . population is hurriedly gathered into cities from the ends of the earth; habits of living are altered with startling abruptness and thoroughness; the search for the truths of nature is infinitely stimulated." He observed that information, like wheat, now moved from place to place more fluidly and in larger quantities than ever before. "Knowledge is no longer an immobile solid; it has been liquefied. It is actively moving in all the currents of society." Even morality and religious faith were undergoing change, and so were the traits that parents should teach their children. Just as Carnegie thought it a waste of time to lament the loss of traditions—in the modern world, after all, who wanted to light their homes with whale oil?—Dewey thought it "useless to bemoan the departure of the good old days of children's modesty, reverence and implicit obedience." Instead, Dewey identified other virtues that Americans could nurture to make the new order serve the cause of democracy. "We must recognize our compensations," he wrote, "—the increase in toleration, in breadth of social judgment, the larger acquaintance with human nature, . . . greater accuracy of adaptation to differing personalities." Through his work at a model school attached to the University of Chicago, Dewey was already seeking forms of education that would combine discipline with independence, manual skill with intellectual exploration. He hoped to imbue each student with "the spirit of service and . . . the instruments of effective self-direction."

Like many thinkers of his day, Dewey combined enthusiasm for progress with an attempt to preserve the best of what he saw fading away. He appreciated the ways in which children had traditionally learned from their parents, contributing to the productive work of the household while they mastered a skill such as carpentry or candle making. Dewey's model school thus engaged both boys and girls in sewing, cooking, and shop work, hoping to instill responsibility and love of craft. In this, Dewey's school was not so different from Booker T. Washington's Tuskegee Institute, which taught blacksmithing, tin making, sewing, and other industrial arts. They sought, in a world of coal-fired locomotives, Bessemer furnaces, and far-flung corporate enterprise, to sustain some of the virtues of local production and craftsmanship.

Dewey, Washington, and their counterparts recognized that they were preparing young Americans for revolutionary journeys—journeys from the farms to the big city, from region to region, and even from continent to continent and into a future world that would challenge the expectations and dreams of their grandparents' day. Dewey emphasized the link between work and education because he understood that the transformation of labor lay at the heart of the journeys his students would undertake. But though he insisted that the corporate and industrial workplace depended, at root, on the old "household and neighborhood" systems of production, most of his students would enter employments of a very different type. The world of work for both the prosperous and the struggling poor was changing as radically as any other sector of life in America.

FOR FURTHER READING

On bison see Andrew C. Isenberg, *The Destruction of the Bison* (Cambridge, 2000), and Richard White, "Animals and Enterprise," in *The Oxford History of the American West*, edited by Clyde A. Milner II et al. (New York, 1994), pp. 237–74. On the citrus industry see Steven Stoll, *The Fruits of Natural Advantage* (Berkeley, CA, 1998), and Robert V. Hine and John Mack Faragher, *The American West* (New Haven, CT, 2000). Critical throughout this chapter is William Cronon's breathtaking exploration of Chicago's relationship to its western economic hinterlands, *Nature's Metropolis* (New York, 1991). For fossil fuel use see David Nye, *Consuming Power* (Cambridge, MA, 1998), and Harold Platt, *The Electric City* (Chicago, 1991). My analysis of Lewis Mumford's *Technics and Civilization* is indebted to Richard White, *The Organic Machine* (New York, 1995). For railroads I rely on another book by White, *"It's Your Misfortune and None of My Own"* (Norman, OK, 1991), and on Carlos A. Schwantes, *The Pacific Northwest*, 2nd ed. (Lincoln, NE, 1996), as well as John F. Stover, *American Railroads*, 2nd ed. (Chicago, 1997). For a history of Miller and Lux see David Igler, *Industrial Cowboys* (Berkeley, CA, 2001). On agriculture see Fred A. Shannon, *The Farmer's Last Frontier* (New York, 1945).

On consolidation of the infrastructure see George L. Anderson, "Banks, Mails, and Rails, 1880–1915," in *The Frontier Challenge*, edited by John G. Clark (Lawrence, KS, 1971), as well as Morton Keller, *Affairs of State*, Richard Bensel, *The Political Economy of*

American Industrialization, and Edward L. Ayers, *Promise of the New South*, all cited in Chapter 1. On the information revolution see Richard R. John, "Recasting the Information Infrastructure for the Industrial Age," in *A Nation Transformed by Information*, edited by Alfred D. Chandler, Jr., and James W. Cortada (New York, 2000), pp. 55–105; Wayne E. Fuller, "The Populists and the Post Office," *Agricultural History* 65 (1991): 1–16; Richard A. Schwarzlose, *The Nation's Newsbrokers* (Evanston, IL, 1989); Sally M. Miller, ed., *The Ethnic Press in the United States* (Westport, CT, 1987); Tom Standage, *The Victorian Internet* (New York, 1999); Susan J. Douglas, *Inventing American Broadcasting, 1899–1922* (Baltimore, 1987); and for a sweeping global perspective on technology, Daniel R. Headrick, *Tentacles of Progress* (New York, 1988). A helpful overview of industrialization and its impact in the United States is Walter Licht, *Industrializing America* (Baltimore MD, 1995).

The best biography of Carnegie is Joseph Frazier Wall, *Andrew Carnegie* (New York, 1970). For Rockefeller see Ron Chernow, *Titan* (New York, 1998). On the rise of corporate management the classic source is Alfred E. Chandler's *The Visible Hand* (Cambridge, MA, 1977). For an international perspective on these developments see E. J. Hobsbawm, *The Age of Empire, 1875–1914* (New York, 1987). On U.S. investment in Mexico I have drawn largely on John Mason Hart's study *Empire and Revolution* (Berkeley, CA, 2002). See also Ramón Eduardo Ruíz, *The People of Sonora and Yankee Capitalists* (Tucson, 1988), Matt S. Meier and Feliciano Ribera, *Mexican Americans/American Mexicans* (New York, 1993), and Linda S. Gordon, *The Great Arizona Orphan Abduction* (Cambridge, MA, 1999). The quote about the construction of the American working class out of "four great diasporas" comes from Gordon's book, p. 48. On the rise of multinational companies I have depended on Emily S. Rosenberg, *Spreading the American Dream* (New York, 1982), and especially on Mira Wilkins, *The Emergence of Multinational Enterprise* (Cambridge, MA, 1970). On the Singer Company see Robert Bruce Davies, *Peacefully Working to Conquer the World* (New York, 1976).

The best overviews of immigration are Roger Daniels, *Coming to America* (New York, 1990), Walter T. K. Nugent, *Crossings* (Bloomington, IN, 1992), Mark Wyman, *Round-Trip to America* (Ithaca, NY, 1993), and Bruce M. Stave, *From the Old Country* (Hanover, NH, 1999). On specific immigrant groups see Donna R. Gabaccia, *Italy's Many Diasporas* (Seattle, 2000); Hasia R. Diner, *Erin's Daughters in America* (Baltimore, 1983), and Kerby A. Miller, *Emigrants and Exiles* (New York, 1985), both on the Irish; on Asian immigrants, Madeline Hsu, *Dreaming of Gold, Dreaming of Home* (Stanford, CA, 2000), Ronald Takaki, *Strangers from a Different Shore* (Boston, 1989), and Judy Yung, *Unbound Voices* (Berkeley, CA, 1999); on Jews, Hasia R. Diner, *A New Promised Land* (New York, 2003). Stegner's memoir of visiting Greece is in his introduction to Zeese Papanikolas, *Buried Unsung* (Salt Lake City, 1982). On Poughkeepsie see Clyde Griffen and Sally Griffen, *Natives and Newcomers* (Cambridge, MA, 1978).

Cindy S. Aron looks at tourism and vacations in *Working at Play* (New York, 1999); see also Earl Pomeroy, *In Search of the Golden West* (New York, 1957). On transatlantic intellectual and political connections see Daniel T. Rodgers, *Atlantic Crossings* (Cambridge, MA, 1998). For neuresthenia I rely on Tom Lutz, *American Nervousness, 1903* (Ithaca, NY, 1991), and for railroad time on Ian R. Bartky, *Selling the True Time* (Stanford, CA, 2000). I am also grateful to David Greenstein for his research paper "From Sunshine to Smokestacks: Practicality and the Adoption of Railroad Standard Time," History 367, Vassar College, May 2003.

CHAPTER 3

Work

Go west, young man, and grow up with the country.
—HORACE GREELEY, 1853

Our young men can no longer go west; they must go up or down.
—HENRY DEMAREST LLOYD, 1884

The most dangerous job on a nineteenth-century railroad belonged to the brakeman. Half a mile before a train reached its station, each brakeman climbed a ladder to the top of a car, turned a braking wheel, and then crossed to another car to repeat the maneuver. Since no crew could do this in perfect unison, the cars jolted. Brakemen often suffered crushed hands and arms, especially in windy, rainy, or icy weather, and many fell to their deaths. On the Illinois Central Railroad between 1874 and 1884, one out of every twenty trainmen suffered death or disabling injury; among brakemen the rate was one in seven. Switchmen, who linked up cars in the switchyard, suffered almost as much risk. A widespread measure of job experience was for a switchman to show a potential employer that he had one or more missing fingers.

Management decisions had a great deal to do with these appalling odds. Railroad companies saw little incentive to improve safety, and, in fact, to cut costs they began in the 1870s and 1880s to require brakemen to halt four, five, or six cars rather than two, upping the accident rate. State governments had trouble enforcing standards across state lines, and railroad companies worked strenuously to block safety bills in legislatures. Federal regulations were nonexistent until the Railroad Safety Appliance Act of 1893, which finally required the use of air brakes. George Westinghouse had invented these brakes back in 1869, after seeing the wreckage of a spectacular crash, but he had not been able to persuade many executives to spend money adopting them. The act, by requiring use of the new brakes, promptly reduced the accident rate by 60 percent, bringing the U.S. industry in line with its European counterparts.

Thus, railroads mastered the business of *go* long before they committed themselves to *stop*. The same might be said of American enterprise generally in the late nineteenth century. The United States was a gambler's paradise, holding out the allure of jobs, money, and mobility but filled with mortal dangers for working-class women and men. Like the railroads that helped drive its growth, the country's economy astonished onlookers with its power and pace. Except during years of severe depression, manufacturers could boast faster production, higher outputs, and larger exports and domestic sales almost every year. Between 1870 and 1910 jobs in the chemical, oil, and rubber industries grew by an astounding 1,900 percent, in iron and steel by 1,200 percent, and in railroads sixfold. Service jobs also burgeoned, with the country counting five times more barbers and hairdressers and laundry workers by the end of the era than at the start. The dynamic economy drew not only men and women from abroad and rural Americans to the cities but also women from the domestic sphere. By the turn of the century, one of every five women in the country was working for pay.

Amid this extraordinary growth business and political leaders put few brakes on the system. Like railroadmen, coal and hard-rock miners in the United States died at triple the rates of their European counterparts, who were protected by safety legislation. By one estimate, one quarter of the immigrant men working the most dangerous jobs in Pennsylvania steel mills suffered death or disabling injuries. Other tasks killed men slowly. Smelter workers—and everyone who lived downwind of their operations—endured constant exposure to sulfur fumes, arsenic, and lead. Well into the twentieth century blast furnace operators averaged a seventy-seven-hour work week. An English visitor to Pennsylvania's mills was stunned by what he saw. He wrote that "the 'bosses' drive the men to an extent that the employers would never dream of attempting at home."

In addition, government activism had not extended to the provision of social safety nets or requirements that employers provide them. There was no legal minimum wage. Workmen's compensation, unemployment benefits, and Social Security (except for Union veterans' pensions) were unknown for the working class. Employer health coverage and paid vacations were extreme rarities; state regulation of working hours and child labor had only just begun, and the economy suffered massive, sudden depressions that lasted for years. Injuries on the job, unemployment, and chronic poverty were familiar problems to large swaths of the population. Industrialization left a human wreckage that affluent Americans tended to dismiss as the inevitable price of progress. Workers bore the consequences for the lack of regulatory brakes, just as brakemen paid the toll for employers' less-than-satisfactory control over their speeding trains.

Nowhere was the line between Henry George's "House of Have" and "House of Want" more clear than in the world of work. The line between "blue collar" and "white collar" was to a large extent forged in the post–Civil War era, and even a skilled, relatively well-paid blue-collar worker, such as a brakeman, could with a single misstep become bedridden or leave behind a widow and orphans. But the changing economy also created many jobs that fell in between the broad categories defined by blue and white collars: typist, department store clerk, traveling salesman, telegraph operator, and even professional baseball player. The new economy excelled in creating middlemen (and middlewomen) of various kinds, and even groups of Americans who held the same job often did not agree on whether they worked in production, management, or service, much less on whether they should join a union. The intensely hierarchical structure of the modern corporation encouraged many low-paid office workers to identify with management, while some independent merchants and businessmen, finding their autonomy threatened by voracious monopolies, forged ties with the labor movement. As it reorganized trade and finance, then, the economic revolution rearranged Americans' identities as workers and their understanding of what they did on the job.

BLUE COLLARS AND APRONS

The idea that most workers would earn a regular hourly wage or salary, paid by an employer, was itself an innovation of the late nineteenth century.

Logger breaking a jam, upper Midwest, undated. Loggers used river currents to carry lumber to the nearest trading centers, but huge piles of logs sometimes jammed up under pressure from the tons of lumber that lay behind. Breaking jams was dangerous business, and many loggers lost their lives. The wire in this picture may indicate that the logger is setting dynamite or attaching a line to a team of horses onshore, hoping to loosen the obstruction.
Source: Wisconsin Historical Society, Madison.

The Suffolk Mine, San Miguel County, Colorado, undated. Workers pose with
their tools at the opening to the mineshaft. Much industry, especially in the West,
focused on the exploitation of natural resources.
Source: Colorado Historical Society, Denver (20004574).

Pre–Civil War Americans had expected most people to become independent
craftsmen, shopkeepers, businessmen, or farmers, an ideal that in the early
republic had undergirded confidence in the independence and virtue of
the citizenry. Permanent paid employment was widely derided as "wage
slavery." Over the course of the post–Civil War decades, however, debate over
the legitimacy of wage work faded. For most workers the key issues came to
be not the fact that they were wage earners but whether they enjoyed decent
hours and working conditions and whether they could live comfortably on
their pay.

Immigrants often remarked on the ruthless pace of labor in the United
States. The young radical Emma Goldman, who had worked for a Russian
glove manufacturer since age thirteen, found a New York factory "large,
bright, and airy" by comparison, but she observed that "the work here was

harder. . . . The iron discipline forbade free movement." Goldman was shocked to find that she could not use the bathroom without permission. Her workday, with no breaks except a half-hour lunch, seemed "endless." Watching an Italian railroad construction gang, which started each morning at 5 A.M., an observer wrote that "they work like bulls, like slaves, like prisoners." "Here you do not have any free time!" exclaimed one recent arrival. "Everyone works like hell," reported an exhausted Finn. Paul Siu, a Chicago laundryman, recalled how thrilled he had been to leave southern China. "If I had known beforehand that this is the way I would have to toil, I would never have come here," he told an interviewer. "Now I am here, I begin to feel America is work, work, work."

A key trend in manufacturing was the use of "operatives," unskilled workers whose tasks were separated into component parts by white-collar managers. In the making of everything from coffins to chocolates, traditions of craftsmanship eroded, and more and more workers repeated single, rote tasks. A light bulb maker might, for example, spend day after day inserting thousands of filaments into thousands of bulbs, while women at adjacent tables flared and sealed the wires, used exhaust machines to create vacuums inside the bulbs, and tested the finished product against a metal plate with electric current running through it, receiving a mild shock with each touch, at the rate of thirty-three bulbs per minute. Even at a brassworks in Connecticut, which relied on skilled brass molders, unskilled female operatives constituted half the workforce; they attached labels and packed products for shipping. Operatives did not necessarily work in factories. Many labored at home, where children could join them in finishing piecework, paid by the item rather than the hour. Wherever it was done, such unskilled work required long days of concentrated effort at the fastest possible pace in order to make a living. After touring a Chicago tenement, reformer Jane Addams was haunted by the memory of "a little girl of four who pulled out basting threads hour by hour, sitting on a stool at the feet of her Bohemian mother, a little bunch of human misery."

Women—notably African-American and immigrant women—did a great deal of the lowest-paid and most difficult labor in the economy, and for most of them this work was not a particularly liberating experience. In the 1870s the most common employment was as a maid or housekeeper, and judging by domestic workers' high turnover rates and eagerness to enter other fields, it was a less-than-satisfying job. Live-in housekeepers, who remained on call twenty-four hours a day, found the demands placed on them especially relentless, and for black women reminiscent of slavery. Low pay and disrespectful or abusive treatment were common complaints. "I feel like a slave on account of the way I am treated," one housekeeper told an interviewer. In Kansas and Minnesota female factory workers told the same story: they had left domestic work because it was "dirty," "nasty," and "degrading." The growing economy offered women an increasing range of alternatives. In 1870 about 1.5 million women worked for wages, 67 percent in domestic service; by 1910 a staggering 6.3 million women were earning wages, but less than 40 percent were in domestic service. Outside the South, where African-American women were excluded from nondomestic jobs, middle-class employers complained of a "servant problem." Servants, in other words, were finding better opportunities in other fields.

Jobs in manufacturing carried their own hardships. The young reformer Eva McDonald of Minnesota, disguising herself as a worker to investigate for the *St. Paul Globe*, documented the choking air and dim light in which women toiled in local woolen mills. Employers knew that women, like non-English speaking immigrants, could be isolated and intimidated more easily than men. Labor investigator Leonora Barry documented a host of abuses suffered by women in the textile industry, from starvation wages to sexual harassment. Many told her they would be fired if they complained, and they thought labor organizing was futile. "Through long years of endurance," Barry wrote, "they have acquired, as a sort of second nature, the habit of submission and acceptance without question of any terms offered them, with the pessimistic view of life in which they see no hope."

Mechanized steam laundries, which employed 125,000 people by the turn of the century, became a focus of journalistic exposés because they embodied all that was wrong with industrialism. Laundry employees, the vast majority of whom were black and immigrant women and Chinese men, endured extreme heat and harsh chemicals. Foul wash-water pouring over arms and legs caused swelling and skin ulcers. In *The Long Day* (1905), the undercover journalist Dorothy Richardson described her forays into housekeeping, box making, and crafting artificial flowers, but she found laundry work the most grueling of all. Richardson's protagonist (a stand-in for herself) is horrified to find that during the summer rush, with heaps of sheets and towels coming in from hotels, her crew works on Saturdays till 1 A.M. A coworker tells with a grin the story of her missing hand:

> I was clean done out, one Saturday night, and I jist couldn't see no more; and first thing I know—Wo-o-ow! And that hand went right straight clean into the rollers. And I was jist tired, that's all. I didn't have nothing to drink all that day, excepting pop; but the boss he swore I was drunk, and he made the foreman swear the same thing, and so I didn't try to get no damages. They sent me to the horspital, and they offered me my old job back again; but I jist got up my spunk and says if they can't pay me some damages, and goes and swears I was drunk when I didn't have nothing but rotten pop, I says, I can up and go someplace else and get my four dollars a week.

Richardson's heroine sticks to the job for several weeks and wins a promotion, but a foreman warns her not to take the new job because the boss reserves it for his sexual prey.

As Richardson discovered to her dismay, the American workforce was ruthlessly sex-segregated. Women earned half or less of men's wages on the still widespread supposition that as wives or daughters, women only needed pocket money while men provided the "real" income for their families. Except among African Americans, the majority of female workers outside the home were unmarried, but many were key breadwinners, and the wages of many independent women could not keep them above the poverty line. The

Table 3.1 Two household budgets in New York City, 1905.

Seamstress

INCOME

Mrs. M., sewing, 14 weeks, avg. $5.00 a week	$70.00
Mrs. M., sewing, 38 weeks, avg. $3.00 a week	114.00
Girl, 13, earned in summer	14.00
Mother, extra work	20.50
St. Vincent de Paul Society, grocery tickets	26.00
St. Vincent de Paul Society, shoes	4.00
Charity Organization Society, for rent	11.50
Total income:	$260.00

EXPENDITURES

Food	$130.00
Rent	92.75
Clothing	18.00
Fuel	13.00
Medicine	1.00
Moving expenses	3.00
Sundries	2.25
Total expenditures:	$260.00

Glassworker

INCOME

Man, 51 1/2 weeks at $14.00 (3 holidays deducted)	$721.00
Woman, for janitor services	132.00
Boy (15), 22 weeks at $3.50, 25 weeks at $4.00	177.00
Gift from landlord at Christmas	10.00
Total income:	$1,040.00

EXPENDITURES (TCSH)

Food, $10 a week, including lunch money	$520.00
Rent	132.00
Clothing	85.00
Light and fuel	48.50
Insurance, .60 a week	31.20
Newspapers, .11 a week	5.72
Union dues	6.00
Drink for man, $3 a week	156.00
Medical attendance	27.00
Church	13.00
Recreation for father and oldest boy	10.00
Sundries	5.58
Total expenditures:	$1,040.00

The seamstress and her daughter lived in dire circumstances, though the mother did manage to keep her child in school. They scraped by with aid from two charitable organizations, which required the mother as an independent woman to show proof that she was "respectable" and deserving of aid. The glassworker and his family enjoyed a considerably higher standard of living (note that the main breadwinner belonged to a trade union). But Louise Bolard More, the researcher who compiled this data, was clearly aware of the unequal distribution of rewards between men and women in the glassworker's household.
Source: Thomas J. Schlereth, Victorian America *(New York, 1991), 80–81.*

investigator Helen Campbell reviewed the budget of one widow and her daughter in New York who had fallen on hard times after the death of the husband and father. The widow had suffered a debilitating fever and now the two were scraping by on the daughter's pay of $23 a month. After $10 rent and the cost of coal and transportation to and from work downtown, mother and daughter were living on 24¢ a day. "I've had no shoes in two years," the mother told Campbell. "I patch the ones I got then with one of my husband's old coats, and keep along."

Urban areas offered a gamut of opportunities for wage work. Cincinnati, a typically diverse city, boasted more than 1,600 different small and medium-sized firms that processed meat, lumber, and tobacco and manufactured beer, liquor, baked goods, clothing, books, carriages, clothes, and tools. Though workers in some of these enterprises enjoyed relative freedom to practice a craft, even they were vulnerable to seasonal slumps. The factories of Haverhill, Massachusetts, made only women's summer shoes, purchased by consumers primarily in the spring. "January, February, March and April we are rushed to death," a local worker reported, but summer and fall brought waves of layoffs. Furniture workers in Grand Rapids, Michigan, worked seventy-hour weeks in the high season but faced months of unemployment with little saved from wages of $1.75 a day. Thus, even skilled workers in boom times experienced a paradox: as a business prospered its workers often did not. Managers resorted to deskilling and cyclical layoffs to slash costs while pressuring workers to increase their pace and efficiency.

Low as urban wages were, they usually exceeded those in rural areas. Western cowboys, for example, despite their mythic status as rugged frontier individualists, were for the most part poorly paid wage-workers for large cattle corporations. Cowboys in the Texas Panhandle actually struck for higher wages in 1883, though employers moved quickly to suppress the revolt. In the same state skilled *tasinques* came over from Mexico in spring and late summer for two rounds of sheep-shearing; a Mexican-born *pastor* (shepherd), working in isolation in the mountains, might tend 2,000 sheep for as little as $8 a month. Three million people worked for hire on farms, including more than 600,000 women, most of whom were black southerners. A South Carolina plowhand might earn as little as 20¢ a day, paid partly in cornmeal, bacon, and credit at an employer's store. In California, by contrast, Chinese wheelbarrow crews earned up to $4 a day reclaiming farmland from the swamps of the Sacramento-San Joaquin Delta. But the work was so brutal and dangerous that employers testified no Anglo would do it. Some survivors became tenant farmers on the reclaimed land. By 1900 two-thirds of all Americans in agriculture were not the yeoman landowners of Thomas Jefferson's dream but share-croppers, tenants, or workers for hire.

Faced with high risks, farmers and workmen in many industries formed mutual benefit associations (*mutualistas* for Latinos) that pooled members' contributions and used them to support the widows and orphans of any who died. Other forms of solidarity skirted the law: hard-rock miners looked the other way when fellow workers tucked ore into their boots, and investigators in Cripple Creek, Colorado, guessed that a quarter of all miners engaged in

Chinese workers on an onion seed farm, Santa Clara County, California, undated. Asian immigrants played critical roles in California agriculture, but due to racial animosity and legal restrictions they most often worked as wage laborers or tenants, finding it difficult to obtain their own land.
Source: Title Insurance and Trust Photograph Collection, Department of Special Collections, University of Southern California Library, on behalf of the USC Specialized Libraries and Archival Collections.

this practice of "high-grading." Employers considered it theft, but miners argued that they were just closing the gap between what they were owed and what the company paid. On a less militant level, textile workers sometimes chipped in coins when a woman's pay was docked for breaking a needle or talking on the job. Department store clerks developed informal systems to distribute commissions fairly. Once a worker made her daily "stint"—an agreed-upon income from commissions—she would move to a corner to clean shelves or fold clothes, giving others a chance to make their share. Clerks who tried to grab all the commissions found themselves shunned.

More organized resistance to deskilling, low wages, and bad working conditions proved to be an uphill battle. Labor unions tried two strategies in the late nineteenth century. The first was broad-based organizing, bringing together workers in different jobs and trades, sometimes even across lines of gender and race, into associations such as the Knights of Labor. The second

Ole Johnson family, Round Valley, Custer County, Nebraska, 1886. Only immigrants who arrived with significant savings, such as this Norwegian family, could pay for rail tickets to the inland West and purchase land and farm equipment. But despite their relative advantages, those who sought to farm the Plains often endured prolonged periods of deprivation and hardship. Solomon D. Butcher, who recorded this image, returned in 1904 to photograph the same family in front of their new white two-story clapboard farmhouse. Like many Plains families, the Johnsons probably converted their old sod house into a barn.
Source: Nebraska Historical Society.

strategy was to build craft-based trade unions, usually limited to skilled men in a single job, such as carpenters or brakemen. Neither avenue proved fully successful. Among the structural problems faced by unions were the sheer size of the United States, the scale of enterprise, and the diversity of the workforce. As we shall see in Chapter 9, ethnic, religious, and racial animosities among workers, and especially antagonism toward Chinese immigrants and African Americans, proved particularly divisive. At peak in 1886 the Knights of Labor unionized almost 10 percent of the nation's nonagricultural workers, a stunning achievement that nonetheless quickly collapsed due in part to problems of scale and organization. Craft unions, reaching a later peak around the turn of the century through the leadership of the American Federation of Labor, counted about two million members. But they did so, in part, by excluding unskilled workers and women.

Perhaps the biggest losers in the changing economy were skilled craftsmen. Traditionally proud and independent, craftsmen had once asserted their right to frequent holidays and leisurely lunches over a pint of beer, alternating periods of intense work with spells of relaxation. The post–Civil War era brought less leisure, less control over workplace conditions, and simply fewer skilled jobs. One of the culminating defeats occurred in 1892 at Homestead, Pennsylvania, the last union holdout in Andrew Carnegie's steel empire. At issue was not so much wages or hours but the very existence of the Amalgamated Association of Iron and Steel Workers, with whom Carnegie officials refused to negotiate a new contract. In one of the most infamous and bitter lock-outs of the century, Carnegie's deputy, Henry Clay Frick (with the aid of 300 Pinkerton detectives and the Pennsylvania militia), succeeded in crushing the union. Carnegie was then free to bring in new technologies that shunted aside highly paid craftsmen.

Even some celebrities, such as professional ballplayers, found themselves as stymied at the bargaining table as the Amalgamated union had been at Homestead. With baseball flourishing in the 1880s, team owners of the dominant National League (NL) had introduced a $2,000 salary cap, ensuring that owners rather than star players kept most of the game's profits. They followed this with an infamous "reserve clause" under which players had no control over their contracts and no chance to achieve what is now called free agency. Like many factories of the day, the NL introduced a complex system of fines levied against players' salaries for offenses ranging from absence caused by injuries to "lacking zeal." For players the last straw was the establishment of salary categories designed to slash pay even more. As a spokesman for the players put it, the issue was whether they were skilled, independent craftsmen or simply team owners' "chattel."

Already organized in a secret Brotherhood of Professional Base Ball Players, a majority of aggrieved players refused to sign for the 1890 season. Instead, they found financial backers for their own Players' League, with eight teams of top talent. In the Players' League there was no reserve clause or "sale" of players. It was a grand experiment in player-managed baseball, but it did not last. Though attendance was higher at Players' games, both leagues lost money in the first year. Faced with uncertain financial backing and intimidation from NL owners, the new league collapsed after one season. The National League emerged from this conflict with virtually absolute control over wages and working conditions, reaching a shared agreement on these matters with the emerging American League after a brief rivalry between 1900 and 1903.

The rise and fall of the Players' League highlighted many of the challenges facing workers in the post–Civil War economy. Whole new industries arose in which the rules of employment were fluid and contested. Baseball managers and players, for example, fought over whether the men on the field were essentially blue-collar workers, doing skilled manual labor, or whether baseball was "brainwork" that required professional recognition. With managers aggressively slashing costs and pressing advantage, many employees yearned, like the baseball Brotherhood, to assert their independence and resist being robbed of power and pride on the job. Yet in the complex new economy, it was increasingly hard for workers in many arenas to become their own bosses—as the failure of the Players' League showed. Just as unions disappeared from Homestead's steel mills for decades, baseball owners and players went back to occupying different realms, and the reserve clause remained in place for more than a century.

WHITE COLLARS AND SHIRTWAISTS

By no means all workers lost ground in the economy of the post–Civil War years. Thousands of rural workers got off the farm and earned better pay in the growing towns and cities. Unmarried women took up opportunities in teaching and clerical work, and thousands of working-class men found a place among the ranks of salesmen, middlemen, and managers. Their experiences raised questions about which jobs lay above and below Henry George's wedge. Many emerging forms of employment were not managerial or supervisory, but they also required no hard physical labor—and despite all protests to the contrary, the stigma of sweat ran deep. A stenographer might spend her day doing tasks just as routinized as the average factory worker's, and she was just as unlikely to move up the corporate ladder into management ranks. But men and women who dressed smartly in the morning and came home clean at the end of the day could count themselves upwardly mobile. "All want to crowd into employments deemed genteel," the Massachusetts reformer Lydia Child observed, "that do not soil the clothes or the hands." After interviewing telegraph operators, one writer described what they liked about their job: it did not "soil their dresses" or "keep them in a standing posture," and it placed them in "a social position not inferior to that of a teacher or governess." Telegraphers also earned $10 a week, the equivalent of better-paid nurses and teachers and four times more than a factory operative.

The contrasts among emerging forms of work were nowhere sharper than in Troy, New York, which by the 1880s carried the proud name of Collar City U.S.A. The nation's leading producer of cuffs and collars for men's shirts, Troy employed 8,000 female operatives who ran collar-making machines and washed, starched, and ironed the products for sale. Thousands of other women took in collars as piecework to sew details such as buttonholes and trim. The products manufactured by Troy women served men of a different class. Crisp detachable collars were becoming standard wear for businessmen and professionals, who earned sufficient income to afford a fresh collar each morning, attaching it to the same shirt several days in a row to save on laundry. Troy's famous product soon came to define them: in contrast to denim-shirted workers who sweated for their bread, these were "white-collar" men.

Servers and customers at a Chicago restaurant, 1895. Many sectors of the service industry moved from the domestic space of the private home into public venues ranging from steam laundries to commercial boarding houses. In the burgeoning cities restaurants like this one catered to increasing numbers of single men and those with no place to cook at home.
Source: Chicago Historical Society.

Such workers began in this era to coalesce as a recognized class, albeit one with many layers and complications. The term *middle class* first appeared in the *Century Dictionary* in 1889, and men of that class began to speak of making a career rather than finding a job. Most often native-born Anglo Protestants, they lived in towns or in suburbs outside the burgeoning cities. C. W. Post marketed his famous breakfast drink, Postum, to these growing ranks of "brainworkers." Post, addressing widespread job anxieties in his advertisements, warned that drinking coffee would "reduce your work time, kill your energy, push you into the big crowd of mongrels, deaden what thoroughbred blood you may have and neutralize all your efforts to make money and fame." He recommended that middle-class men and women choose Postum instead. (Despite his dire warnings, Post himself was often seen sipping a cup of coffee.)

Some of the most dramatic areas of growth were in professional occupations. Lawyers had traditionally trained by reading in a law office, like an apprentice to a craft, but the increasing need for specialized training, notably in high-status fields such as corporate law, was reflected in the rapid proliferation of law schools. In medicine lay healers and midwives found themselves

Telephone linesmen, Black River Falls, Wisconsin, circa 1899–1903. Tools and work uniforms often appear in studio portraits from the era as well as photographs taken on the job.
Source: Photograph by Charles Van Schaick. Wisconsin Historical Society, Madison.

marginalized or banned from practice altogether by state legislatures, and male doctors with M.D. degrees and state licenses became the norm. New professional societies brought together specialists in such fields as neurology, dermatology, orthopedics, and pediatrics. By 1900 the nation had thirty-eight schools of pharmacy and forty-seven of dentistry, while veterinarians began to offer specialized care to farm animals and pets. In the 1880s scholars and professionals could already join national associations of chemists, foresters, geologists, and statisticians. The rise of engineering was especially spectacular, with the number of professionals employed in the field leaping 586 percent between 1870 and 1900, forcing U.S. census-takers to begin differentiating civil engineers, electrical engineers, and those in other fields. Many new professional groups vigorously defended their privileges. The American Medical Association, for example, fought various plans to provide free government medical care in the 1890s, arguing that only doctors in private practice could give quality care. And for many years the association refused to admit women, even if they had graduated from an accredited medical school.

A far larger number of Americans entered white-collar ranks as business managers and corporate employees. Traveling salesmen, or "drummers" (who drummed up sales), became familiar figures in small towns and country stores, where they tried to persuade merchants to carry their companies' products and offered ideas for effective display. By the 1880s John Patterson, the founder of National Cash Register, was already promoting commission sales as a "scientific" profession, providing salesmen with handbooks explaining how to approach customers, demonstrate products, and close a deal. Arch Trawick, a young Tennessee drummer in the 1890s, recalled years later the thrill of his first tour. "I am traveling on the railroad," he wrote. "I buy a new suit; have grown a full set of whiskers, very imposing. I have a derby hat, a white vest, an ascot tie and patent leather shoes; carry a neatly folded umbrella, ride the bus [electric streetcar] from the depot to the hotel, 25 cents round trip, the hotel porter handles my bags. I am now a full fledged Commercial Traveler."

Among the elite and professional classes there was considerable doubt as to whether a drummer, clerk, or typist counted as "one of us." These workers themselves, however, generally saw the class wedge as falling below them. Tens of thousands of successful men were now earning salaries in complex bureaucracies, hoping to climb through the ranks. They ranged from insurance agents to wholesalers and included, in the higher ranks, experts in the developing fields of corporate accounting, finance, and advertising. At the same time, "management" was coming to be defined as a standard set of skills, irrespective of any particular service or product. The Wharton School at the University of Pennsylvania offered the first undergraduate business degrees in the 1880s, and other universities soon followed suit, while in the first decade of the twentieth century Harvard pioneered the M.B.A.

Corporate managers expected blue-collar workers to provide the hands and themselves the heads. In comparison to their counterparts in Europe, U.S. companies developed an especially wide gap between the work of white-collar managers and that of employees on the shop floor. America's distinctive corporate pattern emerged over several decades, and it was both a result and a cause of the weakness of labor unions. In the pre–Civil War era, for instance, U.S. cotton-spinning companies faced less pressure than did their English counterparts to preserve jobs; they were therefore freer to cut labor costs by using high-quality cotton that broke less often. That choice led, in turn, to further mechanization and greater management power. Industrial workers (and often agricultural workers, as well) often complained that they were merely "an appendage of a machine." This was especially true in the United States, and in tandem with the benefits of the immense domestic market, it helped build the country's industries into some of the largest and most profitable enterprises in the world. But it also created a management class notably insulated from those beneath them in the hierarchy, less sensitive to employees' needs and experiences. In later eras, as a result, many U.S. corporations proved to be less flexible and adaptable to changing circumstances than their rivals overseas.

The drive to professionalize had a different effect on government than on private business. In one of the major achievements of the late nineteenth century, Liberal Republican reformers succeeded in beginning to replace the "spoils system" of appointments with civil service. They launched the process after President James Garfield was shot to death in 1881, allegedly by a disappointed office-seeker. (In fact, the killer was mentally ill, but reformers made shrewd use of the tragedy to promote legislation.) The Pendleton Act, passed two years later, established a basic structure for civil service and applied it to 10 percent of federal jobs. By 1897 civil service rules applied to half of federal positions, and many state and local governments had followed suit. Some politicians protested, with justification, that the system took jobs from working-class men and handed them to the college-educated elite. But the civil service also buffered government from partisan maneuvering, and over time it increased fairness and expertise in administration. Both were sorely needed. The cost of collecting tariff revenues at U.S. customs houses, a notorious site of corruption and spoils, was four or five times higher than that of European equivalents.

Government also offered new work opportunities for women, 6,000 of whom were working in federal offices by 1900, in addition to hundreds of local postmistresses and others in state, city, and county jobs. By the 1890s almost half the applicants who passed the U.S. civil service examination were women, and though supervisors reserved higher-paid jobs for men, many women worked in the lower ranks in government departments. This novel situation precipitated a series of changes in the previously all-male workspace. Some men saw women as intruders, while middle-class women found their reputations at risk when they worked among male strangers. Female clerks, for example, lodged complaints about messenger boys who smoked, cursed, and refused to take off their hats in front of ladies.

The growth of the public school system was a crucial source of jobs for women. By 1900 the country's schools employed almost half a million teachers, more than 70 percent of them female. Teaching had become women's work, so much so that a third of all native-born American women in this era may at some point have taught school. Teaching was one of the few jobs open to educated African-American women, and though the work was invariably in segregated schools, black teachers served as distinguished community leaders and in some cases national spokeswomen for the race. Along with teaching, nursing joined the trend toward professionalization, though female nurses still struggled in this era to win respect and decent pay. Other women struck out on their own, running shops and businesses. A visitor to Tampa, Florida, in the late 1880s could meet the female editors of both the *Guardian* and *Daily Times*, patronize a female-owned bookstore and grocery, and then visit more traditional women's enterprises such as millinery shops and boardinghouses. Tampa residents could also refresh themselves at Mrs. Hirst's Ice Cream Parlor and transact business with a female teller at the local bank. All these jobs were reserved for white native-born women, with African-American and Afro-Cuban women segregated in domestic service, laundry, and the higher-paid but grueling jobs in Tampa's cigar-making factories.

In the growing cities the corporate office symbolized many of the innovations of the age, and it had from the start both male and female employees. By 1900 more than a quarter of a million women worked as typists, stenographers, filing clerks, and switchboard operators. Like telegraphy, such employment was "respectable" and offered relatively good pay. From managers' perspective women filled important niches far down in the corporate hierarchy. Typists and clerks could handle burgeoning stacks of paperwork with the aid of an array of new equipment: typewriters, adding machines, dictation machines, carbon paper and mimeographs, and vertical filing cabinets. As this system emerged the definitions of *clerk* and *secretary* changed. Such employees were no longer young men just starting out who expected to move up into management after a few years. Instead, women, who could be paid half as much as men, began to seem "naturally" suited for dead-end secretarial jobs, allegedly because they were more patient than men, were more willing to take orders, and had more dextrous fingers. Thus, the "typewriter girl," dressed in a crisp shirtwaist and dark skirt, became a fixture on the corporate landscape.

Young clerical workers reported mixed experiences on the job. Effie Jones, who moved from Iowa to Chicago in 1890, took stenography courses and obtained work with an import company. She found the job not onerous and Chicago's downtown exhilarating. "[My] office is very nice," she wrote home, "and I have a nice desk right by the window. We are opposite the Post Office and I amuse myself looking at the people who are always around." Jones enjoyed far greater independence than did her counterparts who worked for larger corporations. Stenographer-typists at the Sears Roebuck Company worked in vast rooms of 150 employees and received their assignments through impersonal graphaphone cylinders. Sears kept careful track of their productivity and punished lateness and unnecessary talking, much as Macy's did. Though the Illinois Bureau of Labor Statistics calculated a young woman's minimal living cost at $312 a year in 1892, Sears started its typists at $208. To add insult to injury, Sears employees were evaluated on manners and deportment, and entering a saloon was grounds for dismissal. Thus, Chicago clerical workers who typed and filed for Sears, Montgomery Ward, and McCormick Reaper had much in common with those companies' blue-collar employees, also subject to low wages and strict workplace discipline.

Yet for young women especially, office work represented exciting opportunities. In a famous speech in 1892, suffragist Elizabeth Cady Stanton appealed for women's voting rights on the basis of the new range of women's paid labor. "Machinery has taken the labors of woman as well as man on its tireless shoulders," she observed. "The loom and the spinning wheel are but dreams of the past; the pen, the brush, the easel, the chisel, have taken their places, while the hopes and ambitions of women are essentially changed." Women needed equal rights, Stanton argued, because the economy's liberating power was accompanied by great risks. "The talk of sheltering woman from the fierce storms of life is the sheerest mockery. They beat on her from every point of the compass, just as they do on man, and with more fatal results, for he has been trained to protect himself, to resist, to conquer." Stanton argued that each woman should be "arbiter of her own destiny," raised to "use all her faculties for her own safety and happiness." Such an appeal would have been almost inconceivable a century earlier, when far fewer women had worked for wages, but by the turn of the twentieth century, women's paid employment persuaded increasing numbers that they needed equal political rights.

The spectacle of men and women working together in the same office still disturbed some observers. As late as 1900 the *Ladies' Home Journal* warned that secretarial jobs put too much strain on the female brain and could result in nervous collapse. In a perhaps subconscious effort to ease fears of the unfamiliar, corporate offices took on many of the trappings of the middle-class home. Executive suites featured fireplaces, chandeliers, expensive carpets, and other markers of domesticity. But these offices echoed the decor of exclusive gentlemen's clubs even more than that of the home, reflecting and perpetuating divisions of both gender and class. In his novel *The Cliff-Dwellers* Henry Fuller described how the Chicago office of the Massachusetts Brass Company displayed the tangible markers of its financial success. In its tenth-floor suite with extensive views, visitors waited to confer with executives in a "parlor" with a fancy glass door and velvet upholstered seats. Good taste was evident in "the harmonious tinting of the walls, in the padded leather backs of the swivel chairs, in the polished brightness of the cherry desktops." The office gave "quite a new impression of the possible luxury of business."

Like Fuller's fictional company, the grandest enterprises housed white-collar employees in skyscrapers whose design celebrated in tangible form the "vertical vision" of the emerging professional class. With the nine-story Montauk Block (1882) and the Home Insurance Building two years later, Chicago launched a national trend toward spare, soaring, multistory offices. The most famous of the city's architects, Louis Sullivan, incorporated large windows into his designs, providing office workers with much-needed light for typing and filing. He explained his architectural decisions with the famous dictum "form follows function." Sullivan also sought to combine masculine and feminine principles, with special emphasis on the former. Reacting to the flowery excesses of Victorian decor, he called for "manliness" in commercial design. The appeal of a steel-framed skyscraper, Sullivan suggested, lay in its "element of loftiness, in the suggestion of slenderness and aspiration." Its builder's message was, "I shall do as I please with my own." (Though hailed for his innovations, Sullivan became disillusioned with his corporate clientele, whose priority was not architectural purity but efficiency and rental income.)

The lives of men at the top of the corporate hierarchy, who implemented their "vertical vision" in business, seem at first glance to have been worlds away from that of immigrant and working-class employees. Yet for both groups, in different ways, "America was work, work, work." John D. Rockefeller, Sr., made it a point to be the first to arrive at his workplace each morning and last to leave at night. He worked all morning on his wedding day (as did President Grover Cleveland) and even after retirement was noted for his restlessness and attention to detail. J. P. Morgan lamented "the wear and tear" on his body and psyche of his compulsion to "do everything myself or personally supervise everything done." It was more than an idle complaint: Morgan exhausted everyone around him and eventually worked himself into a nervous breakdown. Henry Clay Frick of Carnegie Steel, when he was stabbed in the chest by a would-be assassin who broke into his office, famously wrapped the wound in a bandage and stayed at his desk until the end of the day. Of course, most of the titans eventually bought yachts, joined country clubs, and enjoyed substantial leisure (to the extent their hard-driving personalities allowed them to relax). But they understood the importance of continuing to *appear* to work hard. Even at the pinnacle of achievement—perhaps especially there—men flaunted the national work ethic at their peril. Andrew Carnegie endured enormous public criticism and damage to his reputation when he went fishing in Scotland during the clash at Homestead. George Pullman, who had flamboyant tastes, met the same storm of outrage when he skipped out of Chicago during a strike against his company. (Public anger redoubled when a judge, improperly influenced by Pullman's allies, imposed no fine for the magnate's failure to answer a subpoena.)

Men such as Frick and Rockefeller, on the other hand, understood that Americans knew and respected hard work. Success, the advice books preached to both rich and poor, was the result of "determined will, industry, perseverance, economy, and good habits." In an economy based on "free labor" and competition, hard work was one of the few accepted bases for the legitimacy of wealth. The fundamental insight of reformers such as Henry George, in fact, was to call that legitimacy into question. They did so by questioning whether it was really "industry" and "good habits" that got some men to the top while others sweated and failed.

Why did Americans work so hard and accept such risks and dangers in the marketplace? Each individual was, of course, constrained by the opportunities available, and those who made it to the top, from Carnegie to P. T. Barnum, were only too happy to write books crediting their own hard work and intelligence for their success. On the other hand, hundreds of thousands of dissatisfied farmers and working-class Americans sharply critiqued the economic system, as we shall see in a later chapter, but their struggles to change it met with less than full success. Divisions in the labor force hampered solidarity. Many working-class youths, if able to free themselves from the stigma of manual labor, identified their interests with those of white-collar managers. And the geographic and economic fluidity of the United States encouraged all in the belief that hardship might be temporary. In a mobile, boom-and-bust economy, many a laborer wiped the sweat from his brow and hoped fervently that things would get better next month or next year, when he had saved enough to move on. Hamlin Garland captured this dogged faith in his short story "Under the Lion's Paw," about a midwestern farmer and his wife (who bore considerable resemblance to Garland's parents). "Haskins worked like a fiend, and his wife, like the heroic woman that she was, bore also uncomplainingly the most terrible burdens," Garland wrote. "They rose early and toiled without intermission till the darkness fell on the plain. . . . No slave in the Roman galleys could have toiled so frightfully and lived, for this man thought himself a free man." Farmer Haskins and John D. Rockefeller, Sr., might have recognized each other as kindred American souls.

Americans' hard work was driven not only by material necessity but by a host of less tangible desires and perceptions. The workforce included millions of former slaves and children of slaves as well as new arrivals from around the globe; their work in the new economy, however difficult, looked to many like a positive opportunity in comparison with the hardships of the past. At the same time, rural youths moved to the cities, and while they worked hard they used their spare hours to revel in the pleasures of urban life, from amusement parks to baseball games. An expanding array of mass-market goods also offered the promise of "material progress" in concrete forms. In short, Americans' relationship with money was changing. Consumer culture held out enticements that promised—or seemed to promise—that the sweat, the risk, and the long hours on the job might all be worthwhile.

FOR FURTHER READING

On the changing structures of American business, see Walter Licht, *Industrializing America* (Baltimore, 1995), influential throughout this chapter, and also William Lazonick, *Competitive Advantage on the Shop Floor* (Cambridge, MA, 1990), Philip Scranton, *Endless Novelty* (Princeton, NJ, 1997), and Alfred Chandler's *Visible Hand*, cited in Chapter 2. On the dangers of work, see Licht's *Working for the Railroad* (Princeton, NJ, 1983), and John Stover, *American Railroads*, 2nd ed. (Chicago, 1997). Lawrence B. Glickman traces debates over "wage slavery" in *A Living Wage* (Ithaca, NY, 1997).

On the working class two key books by David Montgomery are *The Fall of the House of Labor* (Cambridge, 1987), and *Citizen Worker* (Cambridge, 1993). For an overview, the American Social History Project's *Who Built America?* (New York, 1989) is broad-ranging and readable. On mining and steel I depend on, respectively, Mark Wyman, *Hard Rock Epic* (Berkeley, CA, 1979), and David Brody, *Steelworkers in America* (Cambridge, MA, 1960). On dockworkers see Eric Arnesen, *Waterfront Workers of New Orleans* (New York, 1991). On Homestead see Paul Krause, *The Battle for Homestead, 1880–1892* (Pittsburgh, 1992), and David P. Demarest, ed., *The River Ran Red* (Pittsburgh, 1992). On Latinos see Richard G. del Castillo, *La Familia* (Notre Dame, IN, 1984), and Arnoldo DeLeón, *The Tejano Community, 1836–1900* (Albuquerque, NM, 1982). On immigrant experiences see the books on immigration cited in Chapter 2.

For women's employment a key source is Julie A. Matthaei, *An Economic History of Women in America* (New York, 1982). See also Arwen P. Mohun, *Steam Laundries* (Baltimore, 1999); on Italian immigrant women, Miriam Cohen, *Workshop to Office* (Ithaca, NY, 1992); and on domestic service, three books: David M. Katzman, *Seven Days a Week* (New York, 1978), Faye Dudden, *Serving Women* (Middletown, CT, 1983), and Susan Strasser, *Never Done* (New York, 1982). On Eva McDonald's investigation of factory conditions see Elizabeth Faue, *Writing the Wrongs* (Ithaca, NY, 2002). On store clerking see Susan Porter Benson, *Counter Cultures* (Urbana, IL, 1986), and on Troy, New York, Carole Turbin, *Working Women of Collar City* (Urbana, IL, 1992).

On ranching and farming see Richard White, "Animals and Enterprise," cited in Chapter 2; Fred A. Shannon, *The Farmer's Last Frontier* (New York, 1945), and for the Chinese in California, Suchen Chan, *This Bittersweet Soil* (Berkeley, CA, 1986). Baseball and football are covered in Steven A. Riess, *Sport in Industrial America, 1850–1920* (Wheeling, IL, 1995). For the baseball Players' League I have relied in addition on Michael Dimmitt Magidson, " 'The Greatest Move in the History of the National Game': The Players' League of 1890," senior history thesis, Vassar College, 2000.

For white-collar workers see Barton J. Bledstein, *The Culture of Professionalism* (New York, 1976), Stuart M. Blumin, *The Emergence of the Middle Class* (Cambridge, 1989), and on the culture of salesmanship Walter A. Friedman's *Birth of a Salesman* (Cambridge, MA, 2004). For women's work in key industries see Thomas C. Jepsen, *My Sisters Telegraphic* (Athens, OH, 2000), Lisa M. Fine, *The Souls of the Skyscraper* (Philadelphia, 1990), Venus Green, *Race on the Line* (Durham, NC, 2001), and Stephen H. Norwood, *Labor's Flaming Youth* (Urbana, IL, 1990).

For civil service and government work see Ari S. Hoogenboom, "Spoilsmen and Reformers," in *The Gilded Age*, edited by H. Wayne Morgan (Syracuse, NY, 1963), pp. 69–90, and Cindy S. Aron, *Ladies and Gentlemen of the Civil Service* (New York, 1987). Nancy A. Hewitt covers women's work in Tampa in *Southern Discomfort* (Urbana, IL, 2001), and Angel Kwolek-Folland analyzes the corporate office in *Engendering Business* (Baltimore, MD, 1994). A discussion of "vertical vision" appears in David Shi, *Facing Facts* (New York, 1994), a book helpful to me here and elsewhere in its coverage of the rise of realism and modernism in the arts.

CHAPTER 4

⟶⟶◆⟵⟵

Money

As I know them, there are few millionaires, very few indeed,
who are clear of the sin of having made beggars.
—ANDREW CARNEGIE, "WEALTH"

For the Lakota Sioux the Black Hills are the world's sacred center, the heart of lands their great-grandfathers fought for and won. As early as the 1840s some Lakota knew that the hills' streams glittered with a mineral that was eagerly sought. They kept the secret for decades, but in the 1870s rumors spread nationwide about "gold in the hills." Prospectors invaded Dakota Territory, encouraged by editors and boosters and driven by desperation in the midst of a severe economic depression. The army, upholding a U.S. treaty with the Lakota, forcibly removed as many prospectors as it could, but more and more arrived. Some came in the middle of winter, hoping blizzards and subzero temperatures would hamper the army's efforts to police Indian lands. One persistent gold seeker was ejected five times in seven months.

While temporarily protecting treaty rights, the Grant administration pressured the Lakota to sell the Black Hills, arguing that it could not stop the hordes of gold seekers for long. Indian leaders refused. Chief Sitting Bull contemptuously proposed getting a scale and digging up soil to "sell it by the pound"—which, he knew, was exactly what prospectors were doing. When negotiations broke off in 1875, federal officials instructed the army to stop defending Sioux lands. Prospectors surged in to stake claims and build the mining camps of Deadwood and Lead. The Lakota angrily withdrew northward; on isolated claims dead miners were found with arrows through their hearts. Sitting Bull and other chiefs declined to relocate to a proposed reservation, pointing out that less than a decade earlier the United States had promised they could live forever in the Black Hills. A few Lakota who did settle on the new reservation found conditions so wretched that they abandoned it. The resulting stand-off led to the Battle of the Little Big Horn in 1876, the death of George Armstrong Custer, and the Lakota's dispossession from their land.

In the meantime prospectors found what they came for, but few of them got rich. A man working alone could pan a few flakes from the streambeds, but these were just the eroded edges of an immense 480-foot-wide underground vein of gold. Extracting that wealth required the latest equipment and engineering know-how. Investors from California and elsewhere, led by railroad magnate George Hearst, were the ones who built and profited from the Black Hills' gigantic Homestake Mine. By 1880 it produced more than a million dollars worth of gold per year, and by 1900 four times more, enabling the lead investor to pass on a stupendous fortune to his son William Randolph Hearst. The 2,200 men who actually mined Homestake—immigrants from Britain, Ireland, Scandinavia, Serbia, Turkey, Russia, and elsewhere—worked seven days a week for less than $3 a day.

The seizure of the Black Hills was one of a long series of nineteenth-century gold rushes, starting in California with the "'49ers" and ending with the Klondike strike of 1898. Other minerals also provoked rushes. Copper and zinc, for example, came into great demand for industrial applications, and Nevada's Comstock Lode yielded such a flood of silver that it altered world silver prices and helped keep the Union afloat during the Civil War. But gold was the great bonanza prize, a metal of extraordinary economic and political significance. In one specific way it was *the* American metal: with the United States on the gold standard, it underpinned the nation's money supply. In a literal sense Homestake miners dug money out of the ground.

The fabulous and corrupting power of money was late nineteenth-century Americans' great obsession. Women who tried to woo wealthy men were "golddiggers." A person with a gold tooth had a "California smile." In a broader sense, from the icy streams of Dakota Territory to the plush executive offices of Standard Oil, men bent their energies to the search for dollars. Government monetary policy, finance, enterprise, speculation, and new extremes of wealth and poverty all proved critical topics of national debate. In the same decades an expanding consumer culture generated new ideas about savings and debt. Material progress enticed Americans to offset hard work and thrift with a new devotion to comfort, leisure, and pleasure seeking.

WALL STREET AND WASHINGTON

The gold standard established many key conditions of the nineteenth-century economy. To pay the enormous cost of the Civil War the Union had printed paper dollars, popularly known as greenbacks, that could not be exchanged for a fixed amount of gold from the Treasury. Greenbacks were actually banknotes issued by designated private banks, but they were backed by U.S. bonds that the banks purchased and on which they received interest (at a hefty profit). This system, skillfully managed during the war, played a significant role in Union victory. But most Republicans viewed the circulation of millions of greenbacks, unsupported by equal reserves of gold, as inflationary and "unnatural," a temporary expedient that ought to end after the war. Thus, Congress pulled millions of greenbacks out of circulation and by 1879 placed the United States on the gold standard. This meant that the U.S. Treasury and the "national banks"—private banks with a special relationship to the Treasury—held, in theory, enough gold to match all the dollar bills in circulation. At the federal subtreasury window in New York after 1879, anyone could exchange a U.S. banknote for its equivalent in gold coin. Investors in Treasury bonds could collect interest and principal the same way.

This system had several critical flaws. By destroying millions of greenbacks Republicans sharply contracted the money supply at a time when the economy was growing, a policy few economists today would endorse. The national banks, privately owned and run for profit, enjoyed special privileges but were under no obligation to issue notes. They often had little incentive to do so, and between 1882 and 1891 the number of banknotes in circulation declined by half. Lack of money played a role in the era's severe deflation, a long, steep decline in wholesale and consumer prices that discouraged borrowing because it kept interest rates high, wreaking tremendous hardship. On the gold standard money was tight for ordinary people. This was especially true in the West and South because national bank reserves remained concentrated in the northeastern industrial core. Interest rates on farm and home mortgages, for example, averaged below 5 percent on the island of Manhattan, 8 percent in Louisiana, and more than 12 percent in western Kansas.

In the South, where the Confederacy's collapse destroyed old banking networks, cotton farmers could go years without seeing a dollar. Many owed the entire value of each year's crop to landlords and local store owners, whose extensions of credit often forced them, in turn, to do without much cash. The shrinking money supply placed severe pressure on debtors. A farmer, merchant, or home buyer who borrowed $500 had to pay back that loan plus interest in dollars that were worth more and more. In the same decades prices fell precipitously, and industrial workers experienced sharp, repeated wage cuts. Not surprisingly, many protested a monetary system that enriched bankers and investors at the expense of those who grew wheat and cotton and crafted steel and textiles. Republican policies, they argued, impoverished these producers while enriching men who shuffled papers or lived on accumulated wealth.

During the depression of the 1870s, midwestern critics organized the Greenback Labor Party, which at peak won more than a million votes and fourteen seats in Congress. Greenbackers sought a return to the Civil War system of issuing more paper dollars and unhitching them from the gold supply. They denied that gold had any special value: government, they asserted, had the right to define money as it chose. As one Greenbacker argued, "Gold is not money until coined, and made money according to the law. . . . Paper is equally money, when conditioned and issued according to the law." Paper dollars, by this view, could be issued on the nation's whole wealth—land, labor, and capital—rather than just its reserves of one metal. An increased money supply would create wealth in turn by giving borrowers access to cash and loans on easier terms.

Gold-seekers crossing Chilkoot Pass to access the Klondike during the mining rush of 1898. At the top of the pass prospectors left Alaska and entered Canada. One person who *did* get rich from the gold rush was the operator of this electric line, which helped lift travelers over the pass.
Source: Photograph by E. A. Hegg. University Archives, The Bancroft Library, University of California, Berkeley.

In the twentieth century the federal government accepted the Greenbackers' central idea, and today Americans use paper dollars marked "United States of America—This Note Is Legal Tender for All Debts" without expecting to exchange them for gold at a government window. During economic crises the Federal Reserve lowers interest rates in an attempt to make credit (that is, money) easier to obtain and to stimulate economic activity, a policy Greenbackers would have understood and approved. At the time, however, Greenbackism was viewed as a shocking heresy by the financial and political establishment and millions who followed their lead. The eastern press depicted Greenbackers as "wild-eyed fanatics" and pirates. The Greenbackers won some victories, especially at the state level, but on their key issue, the federal definition of money, they never came close to winning power.

Ironically, financiers and officials in Washington had an acute understanding of the perils of the existing system. The Treasury faced the daunting task of keeping a "safe" level of at least $100 million in gold coin and bullion on

Aftermath of the Watermelon Festival, Rocky Ford, Colorado, undated. Whether they grew peaches or forged steel, residents of American towns and cities developed new rituals to advertise products and celebrate local pride. From county fairs to world expositions, states and communities vied to build "corn palaces," silver statues, and other exhibits made from local resources. When they attracted crowds of tourists, festivals like this one could become lucrative enterprises in themselves.
Source: Colorado Historical Society, Denver (10028835).

hand at all times, in case a panic caused thousands of note-holders to suddenly demand gold. But European investors were a powerful force in the U.S. economy: interest on their loans flowed steadily out of the United States, often in the form of gold. During periodic depressions European lenders called in as much gold as they could get to stabilize their own finances, and ships filled with gold left New York for London and the Continent. During such wild moments of panic, the gold standard became virtually unmanageable.

Most spectacular was the crisis of 1893, when the nation's gold reserves dropped sharply and kept on dropping. Banks failed, depositors lost their savings, the Treasury's gold reserve plunged, and it took President Grover Cleveland three years to stabilize the situation with extensive help from J. P. Morgan and August Belmont. These private financiers sold the government $65.1 million worth of gold coin in exchange for $62.3 million in bonds, which they turned around and resold through their extensive personal networks at a profit of $1.5 million (not counting interest on the bonds). The deal was risky, but as the dominant American financier, Morgan was forced to act since collapse of the gold standard would have been catastrophic for the whole U.S. economy. Watching maneuvers like this, foreigners marveled that the United States managed to stay afloat. "God is good to his little children, to drunken men, and to the people of the United States," said one observer, "or they would have gone to eternal smash long ere this."

The country maintained its unwieldy and unfair monetary system for two main reasons. The first was financial: all of western Europe was on the gold standard, and until 1900 the United States was a net borrower of European money. The British and Dutch investors who bought railroad stock and western land did not want currency fluctuations to devalue their holdings. Keeping the United States on the gold standard gave dollars a fixed value against pounds, francs, and marks (or at least everyone thought so until the crisis of World War I, but that is a story for another book). The gold standard thus boosted European confidence and brought much-needed capital into the United States, but at a high price for American wage workers and farmers. During the depressions of the 1870s and 1890s unemployment soared, wages plunged, and no federal policies ameliorated the situation. Even in boom periods farmers struggled to make mortgage payments due to deflation and falling crop prices, and thousands watched as homes and land they had partly paid for were seized by lenders for nonpayment. The system operated much like those of many Latin American and African nations today, where governments enforce domestic misery in order to meet the demands of foreign investors and the World Bank. The United States' immense domestic market and diverse economy, however, to some extent helped offset the disadvantages.

The second reason the United States adhered to the gold standard was political. Reformers such as the Greenbackers (and later the People's Party, as we shall see in Chapter 10) did not have enough power to change the monetary system, but they looked threatening enough that even doubtful conservatives rallied to defend the status quo. The climactic fight was the presidential campaign of 1896. Democrat William Jennings Bryan was the first major-party candidate to run against the gold standard, though he advocated not greenback dollars but the more limited goal of coining silver as well as gold, fixing the ratio at sixteen to one. Bryan's opponent, Republican William McKinley, had remarked in the past on the advantages of bimetallism, but as a candidate backed by northeastern capital he toed the gold-standard line. Gold, Republicans claimed, was the only sound and honorable form of money, and they labeled advocates of "free silver" as anarchists and thieves.

In retrospect, it seems unlikely that Democrats' cautious proposal for a bimetallic system would have produced the desired effect. And since most financiers and businessmen backed the gold standard, the Republicans' promise to restore business confidence when they took office was something of a self-fulfilling prophecy. But Bryan eloquently expressed the grievances of millions of Americans disadvantaged by the gold standard, especially rural people in the South and West who had come to hate the northeastern "money power." In a famous speech Bryan reminded urban middle-class voters where true value lay:

> You come to us and tell us that the great cities are in favor of the gold standard; we reply that the great cities rest upon our broad and fertile prairies. Burn down your cities and leave our farms, and your cities will spring up again as if by magic; but destroy our farms and the grass will grow in the streets of every city in the country. . . . We answer the demand for a gold standard by saying . . . : You shall not press down upon the brow of labor this crown of thorns, you shall not crucify mankind upon a cross of gold.

In the midst of a severe depression that had begun on the Democrats' watch, McKinley won. The currency issue then faded through an accident of fate most fortunate for the Republicans: immense gold strikes in the Klondike, South Africa, and Australia boosted the world's gold supply and saved the system for another forty years.

Republicans may have clung to their gold creed in part because other financial assets were becoming less and less tangible. Capital, traditionally held in the form of land and slaves, took on a new array of abstract forms, prompting an exuberant era of risk and speculation. Stocks, which had once held a fixed par value, now fluctuated in price. On the New York Stock Exchange, which had settled into its permanent home in 1865, an investor with inside connections could buy $50,000 worth of stock on margin for a down-payment of only $5,000. He might end up either rich or ruined, owing the remaining $45,000 of the price and more besides. Unscrupulous corporate directors created and manipulated secret hoards of stock, diluting the value of the certificates in general circulation. Brokers peddled stocks for nonexistent mines, while ranching companies listed as assets the theoretical offspring of uncounted cattle wandering on the Plains. Even an honest chief executive could rarely tell how much he or his company was worth on any given day. The scale and complexity of the financial system made simple answers obsolete.

Thus, the line between investment and speculation blurred, and the success of a new class of financiers and corporate managers came to depend on shrewd manipulations of numbers. Successful men (and a very few women) had to master cost accounting and excel at deal making on a grand scale. Many importers profited by grossly undervaluing products such as bananas to get them through foreign and U.S. customs barriers at minimal cost and then revaluing them far higher for sale in the United States. Theodore Dreiser described some of the new financial maneuvers in his novel *The Financier*, based on the life of streetcar magnate Charles Yerkes. "He knew instinctively what could be done with a given sum of money," Dreiser wrote, "how as cash it could be deposited in one place, and yet as credit and the basis of moving checks, used in not one but many other places at the same time." Often such transactions were illegal but secret; sometimes there were no laws on the books that could be applied.

Most bewildering to many observers was the growing trade in commodity futures, in which buyers purchased contracts for cotton or hogs to be delivered at an agreed-upon date. Futures were designed to help companies manage and predict costs. Michigan cereal manufacturers such as Kellogg's and Post could, for example, buy wheat, oat, and barley futures in January for crops that would mature in September. They then knew in advance what they would pay for key ingredients in Grape-Nuts and Shredded Wheat. Companies paid a premium for this guarantee, but they preferred predictability over lower cost. Designed for such uses, futures markets quickly took on a speculative life of their own. By the mid-1880s brokers on Chicago's Board of Trade were exchanging contracts for twenty times more wheat than actually passed through the city in a given year. Savvy dealers "cornered" markets, secretly buying up contracts until they controlled a product and could command exorbitant prices. As early as 1868 a Chicago observer reported "three [corners] on wheat, two on corn, one on oats, and one attempted on rye." The novelist Frank Norris used the famous Leiter Corner of 1896 as the basis for his novel *The Pit*. With each corner grain prices fluctuated wildly, and prices ceased to bear any relation to quality or supply. The spectacle outraged farmers, who with falling crop prices were watching their own fortunes fail. Why, they asked, should farmers fall deep into debt while brokers gambled and got rich on a crop they never saw? Even the railroad magnate James J. Hill complained that the nation's financial markets focused not on building tangible wealth but on "selling sheaves of printed securities."

In their novel *The Gilded Age* Mark Twain and Charles Dudley Warner poked fun at Americans' speculative urges through the character of Colonel Mulberry Sellers, a hapless Kentuckian who tried to make money by raising mules, lobbying for a railroad to run through his property, and selling a patent medicine called The Infallible Imperial Oriental Optic Liniment and Salvation for Sore Eyes. Despite repeated failures, Sellers greeted each new idea and swindle with the exclamation, "There's millions in it!" (A group of Colorado prospectors honored the character by naming their Leadville site the Colonel Sellers Mine. It turned out, remarkably, to have millions in it.) Sellers, with his fatal ability to draw others into disastrous schemes, was instantly recognizable to Americans in 1873. "Everyone knows Mulberry Sellers at once," wrote the *New York Tribune*, "and recognizes in him his next door neighbor, his chum at college, his wife's uncle—the one that ruined the family." Twain and Warner were hardly alone in criticizing Americans' attitude toward money. Ministers warned of the perils of greed. Advice books cautioned (somewhat in the face of facts) that speculation was the antithesis of the hard work that truly made men rich. Reformers denounced government's lack of control over speculation, and after the crisis of the 1890s, many Americans looked back on the previous decades with a critical eye. No less conservative a figure than Republican President William Howard Taft remarked in the 1910s that "for thirty years we had an enormous material expansion in this country, in which we all forgot ourselves in the enthusiasm of expanding our natural resources and in making ourselves the richest nation on earth."

At the time, however, critics seemed outnumbered by those seeking to strike it rich. Immigrants from China and Poland came looking for what they called "Gold Mountain." Gambling houses in San Francisco's Chinatown posted large signs promising "riches ever flowing." An African-American author argued that freedom would come "when we [blacks] have more bank and railroad stock." Boys read Horatio Alger's stories about urchins who worked their way up from rags to riches, and young men studied success manuals called *Pushing to the Front* and *The Way to Win*. Crowds flocked to hear the Baptist minister Russell Conwell give his famous address "Acres of Diamonds," which he supposedly delivered more than 5,000 times. "I say you ought to be rich; you have no right to be poor," Conwell thundered. "Money is power; money has power, and for a man to say 'I do not want money,' is to say, 'I do not wish to do any good to my fellow man.'" "There is not a poor person in the United States," Conwell claimed, "who was not made poor by his own shortcomings."

Like Conwell, many commentators assured men that if they suffered financial ruin it was the result of their own flaws, even as they acknowledged steep odds against success. The author of *Onward to Fame and Fortune* warned readers that only three out of every hundred American business ventures succeeded. But despite this daunting estimate he told those who failed they could blame only themselves; they were obviously "lacking in tact, economy, judgment and persistence." Samuel Smiles echoed the sentiment in four books that sold more than one million copies each, with the titles *Self-Help*, *Character*, *Thrift*, and *Duty*. Published between 1860 and 1881, they promised to guide young men through the competitive world of work, which Smiles and other authors described as a violent "battle of life." A man of insufficient boldness, authors advised, "must expect not only to be outstripped but knocked, crushed, and trampled underfoot in the rush and roar of the nineteenth century."

Following this creed to its conclusion, some unemployed and bankrupt men became alcoholics, deserted their families in shame, or even committed suicide. Tens of thousands who were desperate to overcome a debilitating addiction to alcohol chose a more positive course of action, but one that aptly represented Americans' obsession with money and especially gold. The famous Keeley Cure, promoted by the former Civil War surgeon Leslie Keeley, consisted of doses of a mysterious compound called Bichloride of Gold. The drink actually contained little or no gold, but it had powerful symbolic appeal. Its name was a "concession," one observer remarked, "to the prevailing materialism." Bichloride of Gold supposedly purged the body and ended alcohol cravings, and it apparently did help some patients, though whether this was due to other secret ingredients or the power of optimism only the inventor knew. In any case, the product proved valuable for Keeley himself. He made bundles of money on the Keeley Cure and retired to a mansion in Los Angeles, where he died a millionaire.

CONSUMER APPETITES

With the rise of mass consumer culture, Americans devoted themselves to spending money as well as making it. One of the things they bought most frequently was information, including reams of advertisements and advice about what they should buy. With developments in printing and chromolithography as well as new bulk mailing rates, newspapers and magazines found that advertisements could subsidize much of their production cost, enabling them to lower subscription prices and achieve mass circulations. The 10¢ magazines *Munsey's* and *McClure's* became so famous for the appeal of their illustrations and ads that writers complained they were just filling gaps between the pictures. The magazine that innovated most brilliantly was *The Ladies' Home Journal*, which in the 1880s built an unheard-of circulation of more than 500,000 at a price of 5¢ and in 1903 became the first magazine to reach a million subscribers. *Journal* readers eagerly awaited columns such as "Heart to Heart Talks" as well as diet and fashion news, sheet music, and glimpses into the homes of the famous, all with pages of illustrations. The diary of Mary Dodge Woodward, a widow homesteading with two grown sons and a daughter in Dakota Territory, suggested how important such publications became. "We have all been reading nearly the whole day long," she recorded one winter Saturday. "I have read *Harper's Monthly*, 'Easy Chair' and all. Walter takes the Fargo papers and the *Weekly Wisconsin*; I take the *Examiner*; Katie, the *Ladies' Home Journal*; and Fred, my baby, the *Police Gazette* [a racy sports and 'true crime' magazine]." She added in February that "without material to read we could not live here."

Advances in printing also brought an array of illustrated books, posters, and trade cards at decreasing prices, and by the 1890s Sunday color comics. The Irish tenement boy featured in one of the most popular comics, F. J. Outcault's "Yellow Kid," was a special hit with working-class readers. There was a national craze for stereographs, in which viewers placed a double-image card in a stereoscope and got a three-dimensional effect. Stereograph sets offered photographs of world landmarks, steamships, labor-saving machines, and engineering marvels. "Do you wish to travel around the world and not leave your own household?" asked the president of the National Photographic Association as early as 1871. "Photography will give you hill, valley, mountain, plain and river, city and hamlet, and the inhabitants, too, of every nation, placing all before you for your examination."

Like advertisers, wholesalers used the rail and telegraph networks to build nationwide marketing networks. "Commercial travelers are more numerous today than ever before," noted a candy-makers' trade journal in 1875. "No firm can get along without them." By the early 1890s America's traveling sales force had expanded to more than 60,000, with top sellers earning $2,000 or more per year. In the same years Barnum & Bailey's Circus used the railroads to build a sophisticated multimillion-dollar enterprise. They designed special trains to transport lions, elephants, and circus performers, and their advance cars crisscrossed the nation on regular train routes according to a carefully orchestrated schedule. Employees on the advance cars contracted for supplies, took out advertisements in local newspapers, created and distributed handbills, and arranged "excursion trains" to bring folks from outlying areas. The company spent as much as $128,000 a year just on its brightly colored posters.

With their pace of life accelerating, Americans were captivated by a host of convenience products. After 1889 Eastman Kodak offered hand-held cameras loaded with film that could be mailed intact for processing. "You press the button," Kodak promised, "we do the rest." The Gillette safety razor with disposable blades arrived in 1895. Meanwhile James Buchanan Duke had pioneered the 5¢ cigarette pack. Though wealthy men still savored hand-rolled cigars and rural folk chewed tobacco, time-pressed urban consumers increasingly chose premade cigarettes, easy to carry and quick to smoke. By the 1890s housekeepers opened their pantry doors and reached for Jell-O, while Aunt Jemima mixes offered tempting shortcuts at breakfast time. Aunt Jemima herself made an appearance at the Chicago World's Fair. The company hired

Nancy Green, a freedwoman working as the cook for an elite Chicago family, to dress in a bandanna and apron and cook and dispense pancakes to fairgoers, showing how good they tasted "right out of the box." In creating the character of Aunt Jemima, the company harked back to the mythic values of the antebellum South: a slower pace of life, rural hospitality, and attentive service by allegedly cheerful slaves. In this and many areas of consumer culture, manufacturers evoked nostalgia in order to persuade customers to accept the new.

Aunt Jemima won quick success because customers were already accustomed by this point to other processed foods. Even poor tenants in the rural South used canned meat, vegetables, and fruit. Condensed milk, invented in the 1850s, had been a staple of Union soldiers' rations, giving veterans a taste for it in their coffee. Out on the range cowboys celebrated the product with a witty song:

Carnation milk, best in the land,
Comes to the table in a little red can;
No teats to pull, no hay to pitch,
Just punch a hole in the son of a bitch.

By the 1890s some products succeeded largely on the basis of clever packaging. Uneeda Biscuit sold ten million packages a month not by claiming their soda cracker tasted better than the competition's but by touting its humorous name and portable airtight package. The company's slogan, "Lest you forget, we say it yet, Uneeda Biscuit," proved so popular that a host of less successful imitators followed, including Uwanta Beer and *Ureada Magazine*.

Some of the most popular products offered consumers energy to compete in the economy from which the products themselves sprang. With Americans' hurried, striving attitude, the use of depressants such as alcohol was widely frowned on, but stimulants of all kinds became increasingly popular. By 1900 the United States bought almost half the world's coffee crop; the average American used almost twelve pounds a year. Both industrial operatives and "brainworkers" found coffee allowed them to work longer and harder on fewer calories, especially with sugar stirred in. Sharecroppers were as likely to drink it as Pittsburgh steel executives. "Families whose aggregate incomes do not amount to three dollars a week," wrote one southern observer, "will rather let their youngsters run barefoot" than give up coffee. Living with her traditional Dakota mother on the Yankton reservation, young Zitkala-Sa remembered making coffee over an open fire as a key ritual of hospitality.

Sugar also took on mass-market forms with the introduction of such all-American treats as chewing gum, Cracker Jack, and Tootsie Rolls. Chocolate, once an elite indulgence, became a popular mainstay. At the Chicago World's Fair caramel magnate Milton Hershey purchased a collection of German chocolate-making machines and soon introduced Americans to the nickel chocolate bar. One of Hershey's by-products, cocoa bean shells, was rich in the stimulant theobromine, and he began selling it to the makers of another famous pick-me-up, Coca-Cola. Invented by an Atlanta doctor in 1886 and licensed for bottling in the 1890s, Coca-Cola was made by a closely guarded secret recipe. But the company's lavish ad campaigns left no doubt about its stimulating effects as a "Brain Tonic" that would "Renew and Refresh."

Thus, the economic transformations that hurt many Americans as workers helped them as consumers: deflation and mass production slashed prices and delivered an ever larger and more enticing range of consumer goods. The cost of food dropped, and on the whole Americans enjoyed wider variety on the table than they had in the past. One undercover journalist working in a Chicago department store was astonished at how a low-paid clerk comforted herself when she had a headache. Fed up with weeks of scrimping, the young woman marched to the department store's restaurant and splurged on 25¢ worth of Swiss cheese sandwiches, coffee, chocolate ice cream, and plum pudding with wine sauce. Observing such exuberant purchases—especially the popularity of cheap beef shipped in from the West—the German sociologist Werner Sombart famously wrote that the hopes of socialists were dashed on "the reefs of roast beef and apple pie." In other words, Americans identified themselves increasingly as consumers rather than as workers. Struggling families put up with loss of craft pride, grueling hours, and risky conditions on the job in order to sit down for steak on Saturday night.

Mass consumer culture had clear democratic tendencies, offering the promise of material comfort and pleasure to anyone who could raise the cash.

"Let the advertising agents take charge of the Bartholdi Business, and the money will be raised without delay." In the early 1880s French citizens raised money to present to the United States the immense sculpture "Liberty Enlightening the World," by Frederic-Auguste Bartholdi. American fundraising to build the pedestal took considerably longer, proving something of an embarrassment until publisher Joseph Pulitzer ran a high-profile campaign in the *New York World* and secured the needed $100,000. While fundraising efforts were still struggling, cartoonist Frederick Opper, in his humor magazine, offered this wry suggestion.
Source: *Puck*, 1 April 1885, p. 80.

"Liberty Feeding the World," trade card for Sea Foam Wafers printed by Holmes
& Coutts, circa 1890. Many companies, selling products that ranged from kerosene
to sewing thread to the crackers pictured here, used the Statue of Liberty in their
advertisements.
Source: Courtesy the Winterthur Library: Joseph Downs Collection of Manuscripts and Printed Ephemera.

Macy's advertisements promised "goods suitable for the millionaire at prices
in reach of the millions," and many former luxury items did drop in price and
become widely available. At the 1876 Philadelphia Exposition wealthy tourists
bought individual bananas wrapped in tinfoil; two decades later a dime
bought a large bunch at new chain groceries such as A&P, Grand Union, and
Kroger. (One family of poor immigrants played a prank on a greenhorn relative by serving her a banana, which she had never seen before. After watching
her struggle to eat it with a knife and fork, the onlookers burst out laughing
and showed her how to remove the peel.) Similarly, the tradition of Christmas
cards—inspired by an antebellum craze for St. Valentine's Day cards—began
in the 1880s with expensive and fashionable cards offered by the lithographer
Louis Prang. By the 1890s cheap imported cards enabled many Americans to
take up the custom.

   In fact, holidays and special occasions were a major focus of consumer
culture. Births and weddings acquired long lists of consumer "must-haves"
for the properly outfitted baby or bride. Funeral rituals were increasingly
complex, involving the purchase of fancy caskets, memory books, mourning
clothes, and stationery. Christmas became more and more a celebration of
material abundance, marked by trees, stockings, and gifts. The cartoonist
Thomas Nast drew the first modern Santa Claus during the Civil War, and

Macy's introduced its famous Christmas display windows in 1874. Within a decade Santa's arrival with presents defined the holiday for millions of American children. At the same time Easter became an important time to buy new ready-made clothes, carrying forward in new ways the traditions summed up by the old Irish adage, "for Christmas, food and drink; for Easter, new clothes." In New York by the 1880s, afternoon parades of churchgoers in their spring dresses and bonnets became an urban public spectacle, a sort of informal fashion show. Clothing retailers quickly incorporated it into a pre-holiday marketing blitz.

As these examples suggest, mass consumer culture did not prompt Americans to reshape their identities completely, but instead to interpret old traditions in new ways. While many Christians feared rising commercialism was undermining faith, others saw no contradiction. "Went to town looking for Easter cards and buying myself a dress," wrote one New York woman in 1881, "and then went to Bible class and heard a lovely lecture from Dr. Hall on the resurrection." Networks of trade and advertising might even advance the gospel cause. One religious writer urged "the Christian business men of America" to "make the marketplace as sacred as the church." Christian retailing was on its way to becoming a major industry by the 1880s. Customers could choose an increasing array of Bibles, filled with color illustrations and informative articles about the coins, plants, and customs of Bible times. The Gospel Trumpet Company of Indiana (precursor to today's Warner Press) offered postcards, tracts, and inspirational mottoes for sale through independent agents.

Consumer culture could reinforce other traditional identities, for example, the affirmation of manhood. Attending sports events, as we shall see in the next chapter, became an important form of male bonding across class lines. And while saloons and taverns were increasingly owned by large commercial breweries, they nonetheless carried on the tradition of the tavern, serving as informal working men's clubs. Surrounded by colorful advertisements as they enjoyed mass-market Budweisers, working men confirmed bonds of class and masculinity. Saloons also sustained the ethnic identities of Irish, Germans, Italians, Russian Jews, and other recent immigrants. In large cities merchants and grocers competed to help immigrants maintain and celebrate their distinctive cultures, offering everything from kosher and ethnic foods to fireworks for the Chinese New Year.

While saloons and Chinese groceries looked disreputable to native-born Protestants, urban department stores became celebrated sites for the fulfillment of middle-class material desires. A. T. Stewart began the trend during the Civil War with his large New York emporium. The Philadelphia merchant John Wanamaker learned a great deal from the 1876 exposition in his city, winning customers through museumlike exhibits, concerts, and lectures as well as fantastic window displays. (Frank Baum, the author of *The Wizard of Oz*, was a professional display artist in Chicago whose belief that people loved to be deceived helped to inspire the novel.) Department stores offered personal services ranging from credit accounts to free delivery. Stores in New York's department store district, christened the Ladies' Mile, vied to attract middle-class women by offering ladies' lounges, tea rooms, and indoor play-grounds, encouraging women to bring friends and children and linger all day. Macy's, Wanamaker's, and Marshall Fields installed elevators and electric lights when they were still novelties. This fascinated the public and gave stores an aura of public service. In theory, at least, any American could walk in and stroll the aisles, enjoying a store's amenities without spending a dime.

But the commercial space of department stores was not quite like a public park or town hall. Managers quickly realized that their profits came from con-sumers who made multiple purchases, and they discouraged the poor from entering while avidly seeking customers with discretionary income. A tasteful mannequin or window tableau encouraged such women and men to buy on impulse once they had entered the magical world of the store. Managers also quickly comprehended the "Diderot effect," in which buying one item pre-cipitates further purchases. The acquisition of a suburban home, for example, required not only furniture and carpets but drapes, linens, lithographs to decorate the walls, bookcases (which needed books and knick-knacks to cover their shelves), and perhaps a gazebo and croquet set for the backyard.

Merchants and advertisers, then, made it their specific goal to entice people to buy products they did not need or had not thought they needed. Depart-ment stores experimented with dazzling displays through the use of vibrant colors and glittering lights. They placed items on open tables to be touched and admired, and they suggested that particular items were not just products but affirmations of a buyer's respectability, religious faith, or love of home and children. The big retailers did this so effectively that a few respectable middle-class women, lost in the fantasy world of the department store, began to steal. In a series of well-publicized trials, women from prosperous families confessed that they could not stop themselves from roaming department stores and engaging in repeated shoplifting. The phenomenon seemed to have no precedent. Why should a well-to-do woman choose to shoplift? Puzzled by the impulse, doctors labeled it *kleptomania*.

Well before 1900, then, the supposedly natural laws of supply and demand were turned on their head in the consumer marketplace, just as they were in the abstract world of futures markets and stock exchanges. "The time to advertise is all the time," declared John Wanamaker. "Without advertising," wrote Frank Baum, "the modern merchant sinks into oblivion." Advertisers launched sophisticated campaigns to familiarize Americans with such pro-ducts as the W. L. Douglas $3 Shoe for Gentlemen, the $8 American Typewriter, and medicines such as Lydia Pinkham's Vegetable Compound ("for female complaints—from a woman who knows"). Ads plastered city sidewalks, build-ings, and barns. Edward Bellamy commented on the phenomenon in his famous utopian novel *Looking Backward*. Waking up back in 1887 after dreaming of a pristine ad-free future in the year 2000, Bellamy's protagonist is revolted by all the ads he sees on a Boston street. "The walls of the buildings, the windows, the broadsides of the newspapers in every hand, the very pavements, every-thing in fact in sight, except the sky, were covered with the appeals."

While products begged to get bought through advertising, one journalist observed in 1876 that money was "shouting itself hoarse in the effort to get itself loaned." "On credit" became a more and more common way to buy, whether one was a farmer assembling bare necessities or an urban lady choosing to splurge. Though commentators constantly warned Americans about the dangers of going into debt, no admonishment stemmed the tide of loans and installment purchases. Asked how she balanced her family's meager budget, one German-American woman wrote in 1882 that "I buy everything on credit until I get no more, then I go to another store and do the same there." "Borax stores," so named because they could clean you out, offered high-interest purchases to the urban poor, and pawn shops and loan sharks did a thriving business. "We Trust the People" was the motto of Bell's Easy Payment Store in Chicago, though it accompanied its expression of faith in humanity with very high interest rates.

By the late 1880s the level of private debt in the United States became a political issue, though no attempt had yet been made to measure it statistically. Various economic reformers claimed Americans were deeply in debt, perhaps to the tune of $25 or $30 billion. Conservatives protested that such figures were far too high; one business leader estimated $6 billion, and others thought less. In response, Congress directed census-takers to collect data for the first time on private debt. Robert Porter, the 1890 census director, warned in his final report that he had probably missed billions of dollars in informal loans, but the figure he produced was stunning: at minimum, private debt in the United States totaled more than $11 *trillion*. Americans, in other words, were 300 times more deeply in debt than even the most radical critics had expected. It was a dramatic example of the direction in which Americans were heading in the new economy and their lack of awareness about the extent of that change.

THE PROBLEM OF PECUNIARY STANDARDS

The total of $11 trillion worth of private debt flew in the face of some of Americans' most deeply held convictions in the 1890s. Many commentators continued to declare that debt was shameful and should be avoided at any cost. They linked thrift and savings to the much-admired traits of hard work and self-control, without which no man could succeed. At the same time, women's highest calling was said to be the nurturance of noncommercial values: domesticity, faith, self-sacrifice, and charity. Among the many things Americans were buying were millions of copies of books such as Louisa May Alcott's *Little Women*, published in 1869, with its story of how frugal, benevolent Marmee and her four daughters spend Christmas morning sharing their gifts and holiday breakfast with poorer neighbors. Catherine Beecher and Harriet Beecher Stowe's best-selling guide *The American Woman's Home*, published one year later, urged Christian women to practice "self-denying benevolence." Beecher and Stowe condemned the "mind that is worldly, living mainly to seek its own pleasures instead of living to please God." As late as 1875 Abraham Lincoln's son Robert managed to get his mother, Mary Todd Lincoln, committed to an insane asylum in part by demonstrating that she purchased things she did not need.

If this was the standard of sanity, then Americans' mental health was in serious trouble. In his brilliant book *The Theory of the Leisure Class*, published in 1899, the Wisconsin-born sociologist Thorstein Veblen satirized Americans' acquisitive practices. Veblen coined a number of apt phrases that have remained in circulation ever since. Practitioners of "pecuniary emulation," he argued, spent money to mimic the habits of wealthier people. A "pecuniary standard of living" was based on sheer freedom to indulge in waste rather than in taste, comfort, education, or moral improvement. Veblen observed that people often suffered great discomfort and inconvenience to vacation in the "right" way or hold the "right" kind of social event. The beauty of a silver spoon or a manicured lawn, Veblen proposed, might lie less in the object itself than in what it signified: the power to command someone else's labor to keep the spoon polished and the lawn mowed, or the leisure to do it oneself.

Most famous of all was Veblen's concept of "conspicuous consumption." He argued that particular types of carriages, clothing, or even diseases (such as gout from rich eating) served to demonstrate social position. Whether it was real estate in the city's best neighborhood or tickets to the opera, such a social marker enabled people to establish "invidious distinctions" between themselves and those lower on the social scale. Veblen observed that fashionable dresses were heavy and restrictive, hampering the ability of women who wore them to move around or even breathe. Their design, he concluded, was meant to "testify to the wearer's exemption from or incapacity for all vulgarly productive employment." In other words, ultratight corsets and heavy brocades advertised a woman's status as a lady of leisure and by extension her husband's or father's ability to pay for her to do nothing at all.

No one exemplified Veblen's analysis more clearly than Alva Smith Vanderbilt, an Alabama belle who married a second-generation heir to a great shipping fortune. Though a lady of leisure, Alva hardly did nothing: she had a burning ambition for social glory, but she and her family were shunned as "new money" by Caroline Astor, arbiter of the New York elite. Alva took revenge by engaging the famous architect Richard Morris Hunt to design an extravagant mansion on Fifth Avenue, complete with turrets and flying buttresses. With all New York curious to peek inside, Alva announced that a housewarming costume ball would be held on a Monday evening—the night Mrs. Astor traditionally received callers at her home. The Astors' daughter, who loved to dance, pleaded desperately with her parents to recognize the Vanderbilts so she would receive an invitation. Her mother relented, paid a social call to the Vanderbilts, and promptly received her daughter's wish. Alva had broken the power of Mrs. Astor's "Four Hundred" (supposedly the number of people who could fit in the Astor ballroom) and opened New York society to money, old or new.

The party that followed astounded the nation. Having spent $3 million on the house (roughly equivalent to $43 million today) the Vanderbilts lavished another quarter-million on food, music, and decorations for the ball. Among the guests was Alva's sister-in-law Alice, dressed as The Electric Light in an evening gown fitted with gas jets that periodically spouted flames. Other guests appeared as famous royal figures, including Elizabeth I of England and

Louis XV of France. The host and hostess dressed as the duc de Guise and a Venetian princess, and their mansion featured bronze sculptures that had once belonged to Marie Antoinette. Clearly, among the most flamboyant faction of America's rich, democratic pride was giving way to "pecuniary emulation" of European monarchs and aristocrats.

Not surprisingly, with events such as the Vanderbilt ball receiving sensational coverage in the newspapers, the getting and spending of money became a central theme in the work of American fiction writers as well as a topic of research for social scientists such as Thorstein Veblen. The relationship of women to money was especially fascinating, as writers and readers made the transition from romanticism to more realistic treatments of American life. William Dean Howells's *The Rise of Silas Lapham* described the efforts of a Vermont paint manufacturer and his wife and daughters to break into Boston society. The Laphams shed their country virtues of honesty and compassion as they attempt to rise in society—thus, in fact, sinking morally until they come to their senses. Henry James's *Portrait of a Lady*, meanwhile, told the story of Isabel Archer, an heiress who travels through Europe with her sophisticated aunt and becomes entangled in others' financial intrigues. Lily Bart, the heroine of Edith Wharton's *The House of Mirth*, is a memorable "hothouse flower" from a wealthy family who is devoted to material comfort and unable to prioritize love over money. By the time Wharton wrote *The House of Mirth*, American writers were also exploring the underside of the class structure. Stephen Crane's *Maggie, a Girl of the Streets* offered a landmark portrait of life in New York's slums, tracing the descent of a young girl from abuse and seduction into prostitution and suicide. Theodore Dreiser's *Sister Carrie* was even more controversial because its heroine does not die. Instead, young Carrie Meeber conducts lucrative affairs with a string of well-to-do men and ends up a Broadway star.

Chastity in jeopardy was not the only moral problem posed by material standards. To many observers the goals of businessmen, financiers, and speculators seemed at odds with human decency and the collective good. Grain speculators rejoiced in bad harvests. Speculators on the volatile New York Coffee Exchange were thrilled in 1899 when Brazil went under quarantine during an outbreak of bubonic plague. Anger mounted at the way individuals and corporations used great wealth to purchase influence, and many writers explored money's impact on civic life as well as individual character. Twain and Warner's *The Gilded Age* launched a cottage industry in novels about Washington corruption, including Henry Adams's *Democracy*, Hamlin Garland's *A Spoil of Office*, and a host of lesser-known entries. Fictional exposés of collusion between corporations and urban political machines were also popular. The machinations of streetcar companies inspired such diverse treatments as Howells's *A Hazard of New Fortunes* and Dreiser's *The Financier*. "The misapplication of public money has become the great crime of the age," intones a judge in Dreiser's novel. "If not promptly and firmly checked, it will ultimately destroy our institutions. When a republic becomes honeycombed with corruption its vitality is gone." But the judge himself is an appointee of Philadelphia's Republican ring, and he reaches the verdict his bosses demand.

Novelists produced an array of broad critiques of industrialization and corporate power, ranging from Rebecca Harding Davis's *Life in the Iron Mills* in 1861 to Upton Sinclair's famous indictment of Chicago meatpacking companies, *The Jungle*, in 1906. Frank Norris's *The Octopus* condemned the stranglehold railroads maintained over California's economy, a theme María Amparo Ruiz de Burton had explored some years earlier in *The Squatter and the Don*. By the 1890s nonfiction treatments also gained prominence. Henry Demarest Lloyd's *Wealth Against Commonwealth* pointed out that assets were concentrating in the hands of a few. Ida Tarbell offered a scathing account of Rockefeller's rise to power in *The History of the Standard Oil Company*, while Lincoln Steffens condemned urban machines in his famous tract *The Shame of the Cities*. Magazines such as *Arena* and *McClure's* made their reputations on article-length investigations. By the turn of the century, critiquing American business had become an industry itself.

Seeking to sustain nonmaterial values amidst great wealth, some of the most powerful titans dismissed the Vanderbilts as nouveau riche and strove to give away large sums of money—while simultaneously defending how they had gotten it. Even before he created his famous charitable foundations, John D. Rockefeller, Sr., gave great sums to the Baptist Church, the temperance movement, and various projects for medicine and education. Rockefeller also kept his pocket full of dimes to give away to children, keenly aware of the public relations value of all largesse. Most overt in his efforts to develop an ethics of wealth was Andrew Carnegie, who was tormented as a young man by the belief that he had sacrificed religious principles for financial gain. Carnegie tried to reconcile the two, arguing that a rich man's money was a public trust he must spend for the common good. Such a man, Carnegie wrote, should strive to "set an example of modest, unostentatious living, shunning display or extravagance; to provide moderately for the legitimate wants of those dependent on him; and after doing so, to consider all surplus revenues . . . simply as trust funds." He must spend his riches in the way "best calculated to produce the most beneficial results for the community." If a wealthy man failed to follow such a course, Carnegie proposed that the government levy a 100-percent estate tax. He followed his own advice by founding an array of charitable and reform institutions.

While one of the country's richest men mulled over the proper disposition of money, commentators lamented what they saw as dramatic new extremes of both wealth and poverty. Amid furious debate over inequalities of wealth, few hard facts were available until the 1890 census, which on this as on other questions unleashed a storm of controversy. The economist George K. Holmes summarized what census-takers found: 71 percent of the nation's private wealth belonged to 9 percent of the population, while 91 percent of the population held the other 29 percent. Conditioned, like most Americans of his day, to believe that industrialization was promoting widespread prosperity, Holmes could scarcely believe these numbers. "This result seems almost incredible," he wrote. He reluctantly concluded that "the concentration of wealth has probably gone too far" and warned that "the problem that is to vex the coming ages of the republic is already clearly manifest."

Holmes's figures were in line with those of historians today, who estimate that in the post–Civil War decades roughly 27 percent of America's private wealth belonged to the top 1 percent of households and 49 percent to the top 5 percent. Expressed in quintiles (dividing the entire population into five groups of equal size), this meant that 87 percent of private wealth belonged to the richest fifth, 11 percent to the next fifth, 2 percent to the next fifth, and virtually none to the rest. Wealth had, in fact, been highly concentrated since the colonial era; the greatest increase in inequality had occurred in the three decades before the Civil War, when industrialization began. But extremes of wealth and poverty were increasingly noticeable to Americans in the late nineteenth century, perhaps because wealth took new forms (stocks and bonds rather than land and slaves) and because of the high visibility of a new class of multimillionaires. This tiny group constituted less than one-third of 1 percent of the U.S. population in 1900, but they owned about one-sixth of all the nation's private wealth.

At the same time Americans could see all around them signs of great poverty and economic desperation, even starvation. In towns and cities across the country, women's relief organizations geared up each winter to feed and shelter the destitute. In the depression of 1873, one Massachusetts editor reported the "pitiful and miserable sight which we have seen night after night in front of the fruit and vegetable stands. . . . A drove of poverty-stricken children, often girls, clad only in one or two ragged and dirty garments down on their hands and knees in the gutters, greedily picking out of the mud and dirt and eating the bits of spoiled and decaying fruit which have been thrown away." Visiting New York, the Chinese diplomat Lin Shu was shocked by juxtapositions of luxury and homelessness. They reminded him of a line by the classical poet Du Fu: " 'Crimson mansions reek of wine and meat, while on the road lie frozen bones. Rich and poor but a foot apart; sorrows too hard to relate.' " "New York is the most prosperous city in the world, and also the bleakest," Lin Shu wrote. "I look at the slums of New York and think with a sigh that socialism cannot be avoided."

Extremes of wealth and poverty, then, were visible well beyond the pages of the *Political Science Quarterly* with Holmes's statistical charts. And the pain of poverty was made all the keener by lavish displays in grocery and department stores and mail-order catalogs. It was bad enough to be poor while millions in the professional and business classes prospered; it was even worse to see what they had, temptingly laid out in the pages of the Sears catalog and in Macy's windows. The ultimate insult was a grotesque display like Alva Vanderbilt's party. During the terrible depression of the 1870s, the financier August Belmont threw his daughter a debutante ball "more splendid than the famous one given the previous year in London by the Prince of Wales." And increasing numbers of American heiresses began to marry European noblemen. The years between 1874 and 1911 brought 115 such weddings, including 72 between American heiresses and British peers. For noblemen such marriages brought a much-needed lift to declining financial fortunes in the industrial era. For heiresses these unions were the logical result of the quest for status: in the United States a title was the only thing money could *not* buy.

American onlookers were both fascinated and outraged. "Of what account is it," demanded *Life* in 1889, "that Thomas Jefferson perspired, and our forefathers fought and bled in the Revolution to be quit of titles and class distinctions?" The Populist orator Mary Lease accused the elite of auctioning off their daughters: "Once we made it our boast that this nation was not founded upon any class distinction," she declared, but now the super-rich were "selling our children to titled debauchees." Newspapers anxiously calculated the sums flowing overseas with every match between a daughter of Goulds, Pfizers, or Vanderbilts and a British duke or earl. "American Dollars the Prop of Europe's Tottering Aristocracy," blared the *New York World*. "The millions belong in America," declared the equally populist *New York Journal*, which printed caricatures of puny British fops marrying tall, athletic American brides.

The phenomenon of the titled match reached its apex with the infamous wedding of eighteen-year-old Consuelo Vanderbilt, daughter of the ambitious Alva who had bested Mrs. Astor. Alva had named her daughter in honor of a friend, an heiress of Cuban-American descent who had married Britain's Viscount Mandeville. Little Consuelo was groomed to marry a nobleman as well, and though she longed to go to college and inconveniently fell in love with a plebian suitor, her mother got her way. In November 1895 Consuelo Vanderbilt, her eyes red from hours of crying, married the ninth duke of Marlborough. The fashionable Fifth Avenue church was buried in roses and orchids, and the wedding featured a symphony orchestra and a sixty-voice choir. Amid one of the bleakest years of a global depression, *Vogue* devoted pages to describing Consuelo's wedding dress, her diamond tiara, and her trousseau. In a move that appalled traditional arbiters of taste, wedding gifts were put on display at the reception, accompanied by social cards so guests could see who had spent what. (Consuelo eventually got the last laugh. After her husband cheated on her repeatedly and ridiculed the array of charities to which she devoted herself, she separated from him in 1906, won a divorce in 1920, and remarried happily to a Frenchman. In a lively memoir, *The Glitter and the Gold*, she later depicted her unhappy life in England.)

A decade after Consuelo boarded a steamship for London as the new duchess of Marlborough, the novelist Henry James returned to the United States at age 62 following two decades as a European exile. James, like Consuelo, was struck by the contrasts between cultures on either side of the Atlantic, and he struggled to come to terms with the new United States in an extended essay called *The American Scene*. Sitting in a popular theater in New York's Bowery district, James concentrated less on the melodrama than on people in the audience—Americans of many ethnic and national backgrounds, all sitting companionably together in a way, James recognized, that "we had not dreamed of in my day." Pondering the presence of Greeks, Italians, Germans, Irish, and many other European immigrants, James reflected that he had toured their home countries and knew the beautiful landscapes and rich legacies of literature and culture that flourished there. Why, then, had these people come to America? What did they find here? He watched peddlers moving up and down the aisles selling treats to the audience. He pondered the variety of candies that many in the audience (including himself) were happily munching. "These almost 'high-class' luxuries," he observed, "circulating in such a company, were sort of a supreme symbol of the promoted state of the aspirant to American conditions." Immigrants, James suggested, had "been promoted, more or less at a bound, to the habitual use of chocolate creams."

Thus, James captured in a brilliant passage many of the ironies of American consumer culture. For the past twenty years, while he had been admiring historical treasures in London, Berlin, and Florence, working-class Europeans had been streaming into the United States. All hoped to partake of what James called "a sense of material ease"—the tangible goods Werner Sombart referred to when he described great reefs of beef dashing the little ship of American socialism. Millions of Americans ate roast beef and chocolate creams. Those who did not—yet—labored on in hopes that their children and grandchildren would. Having come to a place where money was the measure, they would earn it, save it, spend it. But, James wondered, would they keep their religious faith? What would they remember and treasure from the cultures of their childhood? Would they build a great civilization in America? Would they pass down any values other than material ones? In other countries, James observed, "the wage-earners, the toilers of old . . . were known by the wealth of their songs." "Has it been given to the American people," he wondered, "to be known by the number of their candies?"

FOR FURTHER READING

On gold rushes see William S. Greever, *The Bonanza West* (Norman, OK, 1963). In addition to key works cited in previous chapters, especially Bensel's *Political Economy* and Cronon's *Nature's Metropolis*, three books are central to this chapter. They are William Leach's sweeping history of the rise of consumer culture, *Land of Desire* (New York, 1993), Judy Hilkey's study of success manuals, *Character is Capital* (Chapel Hill, NC), and Thomas J. Schlereth's overview of daily life and material culture, *Victorian America* (New York, 1991). On consumerism and domesticity Ellen Garvey, *The Adman in the Parlor* (New York, 1996) is also helpful. See also the essays in *Consuming Visions*, edited by Simon J. Bronner (New York, 1989). On money questions in politics see, in addition to Bensel's book above, Gretchen Ritter, *Goldbugs and Greenbacks* (Cambridge, 1997), Milton Friedman, "The Crime of 1873," *Journal of Political Economy* 98 (1990): 1159–94, and Stanley L. Jones, *The Presidential Election of 1896* (Madison, WI, 1964).

An enduring overview of the social impact of industrialization is Thomas C. Cochran and William Miller, *The Age of Enterprise* (New York, 1942); see also Walter Licht, *Industrializing America*, cited in Chapter 2. On Barnum and Bailey's business strategy see Janet M. Davis, *The Circus Age* (Chapel Hill, NC, 2002), and on the selling of Aunt Jemima, Grace Hale, *Making Whiteness* (New York, 1998). On stereographs and photography see Peter Bacon Hales, "American Views and the Romance of Modernization," in *Photography in Nineteenth Century America*, edited by Martha A. Sandweiss (Fort Worth, TX, 1991). Leigh Eric Schmidt looks at holidays in *Consumer Rites* (Princeton, NJ, 1995); on religion and consumer culture see Colleen McDannell, *Material Christianity* (New Haven, CT, 1995), and on the saloon, Madelon Powers, *Faces Along the Bar* (Chicago, 1998). H. Wayne Morgan discusses the Keeley cure in *Drugs in America* (Syracuse, NY, 1981). For Americans' diverse experiences with consumer culture see also passages from David S. Cohen, ed., *America, The Dream of My Life* (New Brunswick, NJ, 1990), Daniel S. Boorstin, *The Americans* (New York, 1973), and Elaine S. Abelson's wonderful study of department store shoplifting, *When Ladies Go A-Thieving* (New York, 1989). Histories of two peppy products are Pendergrast, *Uncommon Grounds* (New York, 1999—on coffee, of course), and Joël G. Brenner, *The Emperors of Chocolate* (New York, 2000).

On the super-rich, Gail MacColl and Carol McD. Wallace's book *To Marry an English Lord* (New York, 1989) is both well-researched and fun. For more scholarly treatments see Eric Homberger, *Mrs. Astor's New York* (New Haven, CT, 2002), and Sven Beckert, *The Monied Metropolis* (Cambridge, 2001). I rely also here on Ellen Adams, " 'Noble Husbands and Republican Wives': American Perceptions of International Marriages, 1874–1911," senior history thesis, Vassar College, 1998. On broader critiques of consumption see Michael Barton, "The Victorian Jeremiad," in *Consuming Visions*, cited above, pp. 55–71. On Werner Sombart see, in addition to Glickman's *A Living Wage*, cited earlier, Eric Foner, "Why Is There No Socialism in the United States?" *History Workshop* 17 (Spring 1984): 57–80.

On debt and credit I am, well, very much indebted to Lendol G. Calder's detailed history, *Financing the American Dream* (Princeton, NJ, 1999). On measures of wealth I depend on Carole Shammas, "A New Look at Long-Term Trends in Wealth Inequality in the United States," *American Historical Review* 98 (1993): 412–31, and Jeffrey G. Williamson and Peter H. Lindert, *American Inequality* (New York, 1980). The views of Chinese visitors to the United States are documented in *Land Without Ghosts*, edited by R. David Arkush and Leo O. Lee (Berkeley, CA, 1989).

PART II

THE EXCHANGE

For a young woman of the 1880s who needed a job, one of the best opportunities was to become a telephone operator—a "hello girl." The pay was fairly good, up to $6 a week, and working conditions were not dangerous. Managers still hired boys to work nights, so the hours as well as the nature of the work rendered it respectable, equivalent to becoming a "saleslady or schoolteacher," as one St. Louis operator phrased it. Hello girls wore big headsets and sat side by side facing the walls of the exchange room, scanning panels that held operating keys, connecting holes, transmitters, and receivers. Each operator served a specific set of subscribers (in the 1880s usually between 50 and 80). Whenever one rang, a metal flap dropped to indicate service was desired. The operator connected to the line in question, asked whom the caller wanted to speak to, and routed the call. After 1900 operators began to handle much higher volumes of calls, making their work frantic and stressful. But in the early years the pace was manageable as long as a worker kept her attention focused on her panel and refrained from talking to others in the room.

We can think of the telephone exchange as a metaphor for the rearrangement of Americans' identities in the late nineteenth century. Sitting elbow to elbow with fellow operators wearing their headphones, a hello girl had less connection to them than she did to subscribers sitting in their homes several miles away. The transformed economy disconnected and reconnected individuals. Mass-market magazines, products, and associations created new communities made up not of people in a particular town or county but of bicyclists, ragtime aficianados, baseball fans, and users of Pear's Soap. Political interest groups, from wildlife advocates to women's suffragists, played key roles in developing national networks, as did advertisers, mail-order houses, and young people who developed an exuberant sense of generational identity. Even Americans' sense of geography got rearranged. Villagers with a railroad station might find themselves more tightly connected to stations down the line, reachable in ten or fifteen minutes, than they were to closer towns accessible only by dirt roads. With Chicago newspapers arriving on the morning train, residents of Davenport, Iowa, might know more about doings in that city than in their own state capital.

Economic growth and dislocation, especially the "reach" of transportation and communication lines, disrupted old identities and encouraged Americans to reshape their ideas and beliefs. Part II of *New Spirits* examines four realms in which these sweeping rearrangements occurred. Chapter 5 looks at the lives and hopes of young Americans, born during and after the Civil War, who grew up in a world sharply different from that of their parents' generation. Chapter 6 considers sexuality and family life, while Chapter 7 outlines developments in science and medicine. Chapter 8 looks at changing institutions and ideas in the world of religious faith. In all these social and cultural realms, as well as in the political and economic arenas, Americans adapted old ways to accommodate the new.

CHAPTER 5

Youth

The form of the dreams for beauty and righteousness changes
with each generation, . . . and it is always difficult for the
fathers to understand the sons.

—JANE ADDAMS, *THE SPIRIT OF YOUTH*
AND THE CITY STREETS

Between 1853 and 1893 the New York Children's Aid Society shipped more
than 84,000 working-class children out of New York City and placed them
with small town and farm families across America. The society's famous
"Orphan Trains" were misnamed, since most of the resettled children had at
least one living parent and many had two. Some had been born out of wedlock. The parents of thousands of others faced unemployment, prolonged illness, desertion, the death of a spouse, or another family catastrophe that led
them to give up children to prevent them from starving. Organizers of the
Orphan Trains expressed utter confidence in their mission. They believed that
big cities exercised a corrupting influence, especially in the poor immigrant
wards, and that rural life was wholesome. They assumed native-born Protestants had a right (even a duty) to convert immigrant Catholic children, and
they argued that hard work on a farm would benefit "orphans" as much as it
did the families who took them in.

Thus, at rail depots across the country, excited crowds gathered to watch
society agents disembark with shipments of children ranging from toddlers to
teens. The society generally asked civic leaders to find families with good reputations and keep track of new arrivals, but hundreds of children were handed
off to bystanders on impulse, and in the absence of paperwork some changed
hands multiple times. Efforts to check on the children's welfare were haphaz-
ard. Pressured by critics, society officers acknowledged in the 1890s that in
parts of the country they had no clue as to the whereabouts of one of every ten
children they had placed.

Predictably, results varied wildly. Hundreds, perhaps thousands, of children endured abuse and cruelty. One teenager placed in Missouri found herself virtually enslaved, as her foster "mother" conspired to get her pregnant by one of the family sons, hoping shame would keep the girl in her power. A much larger number of children were clothed and fed but received little affection, finding themselves treated like hired hands. "They never touched me or said they loved me," one man remembered of his adoptive parents. "Think what that does to you. . . . They weren't mean, they were cold." Many children tried secretly to keep in touch with their birth families. Some ran away. Others, however, became beloved members of their new families. When birth parents tracked down children and came to claim them, some refused to go. After being forcibly returned to her birth father, one nine-year-old girl wrote wistfully of the Nebraska farm where she had been placed. "I had a nice room, good meals, taking lunch out to the men out in the fields. . . . For three short years, I had love." Many children who stayed in their placements got a good education and grew up to be teachers, businessmen, civic leaders, and even a governor of Colorado. One of the luckiest, a boy raised in Indiana who went on to attend Yale, wrote that he would "ever acknowledge with gratitude that the Children's Aid Society has been the instrument of my elevation."

The children on the Orphan Trains were apt representatives of their generation, young Americans born between about 1860 and 1900. Millions of these young people ended up far from the world of their parents, culturally and in many cases geographically, and were swept up in a vast lottery with high risks and potential rewards. Americans had always been a young, restless, and mobile people, and this was strikingly true after the Civil War. The war itself divided Americans into three loose age groups: one that had parented the war generation, one that fought the war, and one that came of age or arrived in the country after it was over. The war profoundly marked survivors of the middle generation. Those who came afterward were shaped in turn by the sense of having missed a great revolution, yet it was they who grew up wrestling most directly with its consequences.

Whether by choice or necessity, young Americans of the late nineteenth century proved notably mobile and independent minded. Lured by urban employment and excitements, hundreds of thousands lived far from the supervision of kin. Many who lived with their parents wrestled over what kind of work they should pursue, how much education they needed, and, if they were female, whether they should work outside the home. Participants in an exuberant mass consumer culture, young Americans began to enjoy a range of activities and institutions—from basketball teams to urban dance halls—designed largely for them. In an era of wrenching discontinuities, young people were often best-positioned to adapt to the new, and in doing so they helped invent modern youth culture.

OUTSIDERS

Young people from the working classes took some of the most dramatic journeys of the post–Civil War era. A common strategy for advancement was for parents to invest in the next generation, selecting a promising child and paying for education or, in the case of immigrants, passage to America. Parents and siblings accepted a future of hardship and pinned their hopes on these children, sisters, and brothers. Those left at home sometimes bitterly resented their lot; those singled out for opportunity could feel guilt and intense pressure to succeed. The writer Hamlin Garland, returning to his family's farm for a visit, was oppressed by the sense that "my own career was disloyal, something built upon the privations of my sister . . . and mother." Even at best, the process of adapting created chasms between the experiences of young and old. In a Lower East Side theater, one Yiddish-speaking woman confided to a stranger that "'I like to talk about the old country, . . . and some day I think I go back; but my children make fun of me and call me 'Dutchman.' Here the father chirped in: 'Yes,' they say, 'What hell good the old country? This here the United States.' "

In comparison to other working-class youths, native-born Anglo farm children had easiest access to business colleges and professional jobs in the towns and cities. Hamlin Garland became one of the most famous spokesmen for such farm boys, thousands of whom made the trek to cities in search of opportunity. Born in Wisconsin in 1860, Garland did years of backbreaking agricultural work in Iowa and the Dakotas while becoming angry at farmers' increasing poverty and the hardships of rural life. He grieved for his mother, worn from toil. "I bled, inwardly, every time I looked at her," he recalled. "Why should this suffering be?" Garland got a college education and moved east to become a teacher and writer. His early fiction captured the grim realities of midwestern farm life, most powerfully in the 1891 collection *Main-Traveled Roads*. With his income Garland proudly bought his parents a comfortable cottage in a Wisconsin town so they could abandon their bleak farm on the Plains. He reported that the effect on his mother was "almost miraculous."

In contrast to Anglo farmers' children, African-American youths faced perhaps the sharpest gap between dreams and realities. Those born after about 1860 were the first free generation, with little or no memory of slavery, and their elders hoped they would enjoy previously unimagined opportunities. Observers in the South reported a widespread and fervent quest for literacy in the wake of emancipation. "A negro riding on a loaded wagon," reported a Freedmen's Bureau officer, "or sitting on a hack waiting for a train, or by the cabin door, is often seen book in hand. . . . A group on the platform of a depot, after carefully conning an old spelling book, resolves itself into a class." Young freedmen and freedwomen poured into schools founded by philanthropists, Reconstruction governments, and literate freedmen, while dedicated northerners journeyed South to serve as teachers. Laura Towne of Philadelphia settled in the Sea Islands of South Carolina and taught there until her death in 1901. Ohio-born Lucie Stanton Day, who in 1850 had become the first black woman to graduate from an American college, headed to Mississippi. She wrote simply, "I desire the elevation of my race." Day taught in the South for the next thirty-two years.

The spirit of emancipation also manifested itself in the lives of young people such as Ella Shepherd, whose mother had once nearly drowned herself and her baby in despair over their bondage. In the early 1870s Shepherd made her

Edward J. Steichen, self-portrait, 1901. Steichen, born in Luxembourg in 1879, emigrated to Milwaukee with his family when he was two. As a young artist he experimented with both painting and photography, and he later became an influential designer in the advertising industry. This image is gum bichromate: Steichen has taken a photograph depicting himself with palette and brush and then altered it through brushwork. Using up-to-date technology to create a work of art reminiscent of paintings by the Old Masters of Europe, Steichen suggests that he is an artist poised between old and new worlds.
Source: The J. Paul Getty Museum, Los Angeles.

way to Fisk University in Nashville, Tennessee, founded in the heyday of Reconstruction, but by the time she arrived the school faced closure from lack of funds. Advised by an abolitionist teacher, a group of students created the Jubilee Singers to raise money through concert tours. Transcribing slave music in ways Anglo audiences could appreciate, Ella Shepherd created the first nationally recognized versions of such spirituals as "Swing Low, Sweet Chariot" and "Steal Away to Jesus." The Jubilee Singers toured the Northeast, finishing with a triumphant concert for President Grant in Washington. Over the next five years they traveled twice to Europe, sightseeing in Geneva and Mainz and performing before Queen Victoria in London. Their income saved Fisk and built the university's imposing Jubilee Hall.

By the 1890s the postwar generation began to exercise broad leadership, and their activism culminated, as we shall see in Chapter 10, with the creation of twentieth-century civil-rights groups. W. E. B. DuBois, born in Massachusetts in 1868 and educated at Harvard, predicted in 1903 that "the problem of the twentieth century would be the problem of the color line." He urged African Americans who had gained an advanced education and material

Henry Ossawa Tanner, *The Banjo Lesson*, 1893. Tanner, born in Pittsburgh in 1859 to parents who were prominent in civil rights advocacy and the AME church, Tanner studied with leading American art teachers such as Thomas Eakins. He became disillusioned with discrimination in the United States, however, and in the 1890s moved to Europe, spending most of the rest of his life in Paris. The elderly man in this painting is not teaching his pupil old-fashioned strumming, as we might expect, but the new style of the 1880s and 1890s, in which players plucked upward and picked out individual notes. The new style disassociated banjo playing from minstrelsy and other stigmatized forms, freeing players of all races to use the banjo in popular music. Tanner's painting suggests not only a climate of optimism and new beginnings for young African Americans, but also for their elders.
Source: Hampton University Museum, Hampton, Virginia.

prosperity to use their influence on behalf of the race as a whole. DuBois described this group as the "talented tenth," and the challenges they faced were revealed by the fraction DuBois chose. Far less than 10 percent of black teenagers completed high school, while native-born Anglos educated a "talented fourth" to this level. The collective material wealth of whites was also vastly greater. In 1890 one African-American editor estimated that the twenty richest black men in Baltimore, many of whom had started out as caulkers and stevedores, were together worth about $500,000. The wealthiest handful of black families in the District of Columbia were worth about $100,000 each. They were successful, yes, but by the standards of the new Anglo millionaire class, such fortunes were modest indeed.

For poor blacks living in rural parts of the South, the legacies of slavery proved to be a powerful obstacle even to the most ambitious. Ned Cobb, a son of Alabama sharecroppers, grew up determined to escape poverty and live differently than his abusive father. "Slavery just taught the colored man to take what come and live for today," Cobb observed. "My daddy was a free man but in his acts he was a slave. Didn't look ahead to profit hisself in nothing that he done." Cobb had watched white men cheat his father out of all his land and savings, twice. He guessed that his father's reasoning was "it weren't no use in climbing, . . . if they was going to take everything you worked for when you got too high." Cobb himself worked his way up from hauling logs and loading fertilizer to tenant farming and eventually land ownership. He was not alone: the 1900 census estimated that one-fifth of black farmers in the former Confederacy owned their land. Yet later in life, when Cobb defended Alabama sharecroppers' rights to form a union, he was convicted on trumped-up charges and spent twelve years in jail.

Young men like Cobb found that most whites expected subservience and refused to sell them land or hire them for better-paying jobs. Grossly unequal segregated schools also hindered advancement. After the fading of Reconstruction, the best most black youngsters in the South could hope for was the basic "three Rs" in a poorly funded, understaffed primary school. Over and over Anglo editors and politicians declared that "education spoiled a good field hand" and that "what the Negro needed" was not books but "manual toil." Asked why black education roused such opposition, a professor at the University of Mississippi gave a frank response: "because the white people want to 'keep the negro in his place,' and educated people have a way of making their own places and their own terms." The level of state funding for education bore out his point. In 1900 the seventeen ex-Confederate and border states had an average of six black high schools each.

Young people adopted a variety of strategies for coping with this injustice. Most tried to learn at least enough to read contracts and sign their names. The parents of some, such as Ned Cobb's father, judged this to be all they needed. But when Lee Lincoln, another sharecropper's son, got a job on the Louisville and Nashville Railroad, the job taught him that "a man's got to have schooling to get anywheres." Studying place names and product labels on his lunch breaks, Lincoln paid a white man 50¢ per lesson to teach him at night. He soon won a promotion. Those unhappy with the state of southern public education sometimes founded private academies. All over the South black students sought professional skills and upward mobility at colleges and universities such as Morehouse, Spellman, and Fisk.

Black southerners were not the only ones who had to overcome segregation, both informal and formal. From 1860 onward California schools were segregated, with the state legislature authorizing school boards to deny funds to any school that admitted "non-White" students, whether black, Indian, Asian, or in some cases Mexican. Segregation was a special affront to assimilated Americans such as Mary Tape, who had been raised by missionaries in China and married a Chinese-American teamster. When their daughter was denied entry to San Francisco's public schools, Mary Tape wrote a bitter letter to a local paper. "It seems no matter how a Chinese may live and dress so long as you know they [are] Chinese. Then they are hated as one. There is not any right or justice for them." In rural parts of the state, education for Mexican children was virtually nonexistent until the 1880s. Growers then found they needed to form community schools in order to attract and keep laborers. The practice spread, suggesting that Mexican farmworkers placed a high value on education for their children.

For American Indians school carried distinctive meanings. All through the post–Civil War decades, as native peoples were relocated to reservations, Anglo reformers engaged in an unprecedented campaign to enroll reservation children in federally funded boarding schools. By the late 1880s Congress appropriated more than a million dollars a year to Indian education, turning over much of the money to private missionary groups. Whether public or private, almost all Indian schools had the same goal: to obliterate "barbaric" cultures and languages and turn the rising generation into English-speaking Christians. Boarding schools were the favored option, since day schools did not remove students from kin and traditional ways. The most famous was Pennsylvania's Carlisle School, founded by the U.S. Army Lieutenant Richard H. Pratt. Pratt began his educational career teaching Cheyenne and Kiowa military prisoners; when he sought placements after his students' release, state universities refused to admit them. Pratt then persuaded the federal government to fund his school. By 1895 Carlisle was one of 157 Indian boarding schools operating in the United States, with a total attendance of more than 15,000.

Like the New York children shipped out on Orphan Trains, Indian students took bewildering journeys that wrenched them from their cultures. (In fact, many of the Indians *were* orphans, often the first selected when reluctant tribes faced pressure to enroll.) Going to school required considerable courage. "When I had reached young manhood the warpath for the Lakota was a thing of the past," recalled a man named Ota K'te. "So I could not prove that I was a brave and would fight to protect my home and land. . . . When I went East to Carlisle School, I thought I was going there to die. . . . I could think of white people wanting little Lakota children for no other reason than to kill them, but I thought, here is my chance to prove that I can die bravely." For almost all Indians boarding school began traumatically, with harsh scrubbing, uncomfortable new clothes, and the symbolic cutting of long hair. Language differences were a painful barrier. Much of the daily routine focused on farm tasks for boys and sewing and laundry for girls. Lessons were often dull and, by design, completely disconnected from Indian history and life ways. Use of corporal punishment was a shock, since most Indians thought it both cruel and cowardly to strike a child. Zitkala-Sa described boarding school as an "iron routine" that transformed her into a "dumb sick brute . . . one of many little animals driven by a herder."

Yet Zitkala-Sa's reaction to school, like that of many other students, was complex. Having begged her widowed mother to let her go away in the first place, she found herself equally restless after coming home. She returned to school, eventually graduated from college, and became a teacher and writer in English. The Apache student Asa Daklugie denounced Carlisle as "a vicious and hostile world that we both hated and feared," yet he met his future wife and many friends there and reported moments of intense intellectual excitement. He remembered when one of his favorite teachers "opened a big book to show me Arizona, and for the first time in my life I saw a map. I was fascinated. When she showed me mountains and rivers I could tell their names in my language. . . . She let me take that geography book to the dormitory and Frank Mangus and I almost wore it out."

Resistance to enrollment ran high on many reservations, especially where schools were coercive and the student death rate from diseases was high. Some young people, such as Samuel Blue of the South Carolina Catawbas, quietly rejected Western education and chose instead to apprentice themselves to elders in the traditional way, carrying on their peoples' languages, history, and spiritual practices. Boarding school, on the other hand, brought wildly varied results. One Carlisle graduate, Reginald Oshkosh, went home and used his education to help his Menominee people defend their lands from government encroachment, yet two other Menominee children, desperate to escape a Wisconsin boarding school, ran away and froze to death in a blizzard.

For those who survived, boarding school offered a window onto how Anglos lived and thought and sometimes tools for self-defense. While he was still at Carlisle, Patrick Miguel, the son of a Quechan chief in Arizona, wrote back to the Indian agent in English, warning that he knew about the agent's abuses and would report him if he did not stop. When he returned to Arizona, Miguel helped his people win limited self-rule. Other graduates filed suits over land rights, petroleum rights, and treaty violations. Having studied with students from many different tribes, some built upon those networks to create cross-tribal advocacy groups. In doing so they laid the foundations for a native renaissance in the twentieth century, in which Indians would forcefully defy the assumption that they were "a vanishing race" unfit to adapt to the modern world and thus destined for extinction.

One of the most celebrated voices of the rising generation was Ohiyesa, a Santee Sioux born in 1858, who earned a medical degree and became Dr. Charles Eastman. Young Ohiyesa struggled to resolve a conflict between generations of his elders. His grandmother maintained the old ways and warned against Anglo education, but his father, a Protestant convert, wanted for his son "the wisdom of the white man." "We have entered upon this life, and there is no going back," he advised the boy. "All of the white man's children must go to school, but those who study best and longest need not work with their hands after that, for they can work with their minds." Ohiyesa took the observation to heart. After graduating from Boston University's School of Medicine, he took a post at Pine Ridge, South Dakota, one of the poorest reservations in the country. Eastman found much to respect and learn from Anglo culture, but he never accepted the claim that traditional Indian ways were inferior. At Pine Ridge he worked side by side with elder healers, winning their trust and respect.

Eastman married an Anglo wife, Elaine Goodale, a teacher who had come to Pine Ridge in 1886 to serve the Oglala Sioux and had published several essays on Indian rights. A few years later, when they exposed a scandal that had defrauded Pine Ridge residents of more than $10,000, the Eastmans were forced out by the corrupt local agent. Charles wrote later that he was "disillusioned and disgusted" by the incident, which made him realize "the helplessness of the best-equipped Indians to secure a fair deal for their people. Later experience, both my own and that of others, has confirmed me in this view." Charles carried his medical practice to St. Paul and New England while Elaine raised their six children, but the couple did not give up their advocacy. They spent two years in Washington, where Charles lobbied for recognition of Indian land claims. And with Elaine's collaboration and support, Charles wrote a series of acclaimed memoirs, beginning with *An Indian Boyhood*. On the frontispiece of some of his books, Charles chose to appear as Ohiyesa, in traditional native dress.

The life of Anzia Yezierska reflected similar creativity in new circumstances. Born in a Polish village in 1885, Yezierska immigrated with her family to New York's Lower East Side when she was a young teenager. In the autobiographical novel *Bread Givers* she described her stormy conflicts with her Old World father, a Talmudic scholar who, unlike most immigrant Jews, clung to the old ways, expecting to be supported by his wife and daughters so he could devote himself to prayer and study. "Heaven and the next world were only for men," as his daughter summarized his views. "Women had no brains for the study of God's Torah, but they could be the servants of men who studied the Torah. Only if they cooked for the men, and washed for the men, and didn't nag or curse . . . then, maybe, they could push themselves into Heaven with the men, to wait on them there." The fiercely independent Anzia rejected this role. She left home at seventeen and supported herself as a garment worker until winning recognition as a writer.

Inflecting her prose with the rhythms of Yiddish, Yezierska vividly described the experiences of young foreign-born Americans caught between their parents' traditions and the novelties of American life. In "When Lovers Dream" she told the story of an immigrant girl who falls in love with a second-generation Jewish medical student but loses him because his family despises her poverty. In perhaps her greatest story, "Children of Loneliness," Yezierska related the torments of Rachel Ravinsky, a college-educated immigrant who returns to her parents' cramped, filthy East Side apartment and finds herself torn between love and shame. "I have broken away from the old world; I'm through with it," Rachel thinks. "I must hope for no help. . . . I'm one of the millions of immigrant children, children of loneliness, wandering between worlds that are at once too old and too new to live in."

Yezierska described her fiction as an effort to "build a bridge of understanding between the American-born and myself," a project carried on by many other immigrants in less public ways. One of them was Suey Hin, born in Shandong in northern China and sold by her family at age five. "My people were poor," she said. "Two baby girls had been left exposed—that is, to die, you know. They were born after me and my father said often, 'She is too many.'" Brought from Hong Kong to San Francisco, Suey Hin was raised with a half-dozen other girls and at age twelve sold into prostitution. A local laundryman fell in love with her, and for eight years both saved to buy her freedom. But soon after they succeeded and married, the husband died. Suey Hin returned to prostitution, becoming by the 1890s a prosperous madam. She resolved to return to her hometown in China—but not to contact her parents. Instead, poignantly, she sought out the place where baby girls were left to die. There she found an infant whom she brought back to California and raised as her daughter. Suey Hin told an interviewer that her daughter was a "good girl": she would never work as a prostitute. She would grow up as a proud American, living the respectable life that Suey Hin herself had not been able to achieve.

INSIDERS

While working-class and immigrant youth were crossing great divides, the world of Anglo privilege was also rapidly changing. Outsider Anzia Yezierska vividly described her encounter with affluent young people when she won a scholarship to a small-town college:

> What light-hearted laughing youth met my eyes! All the young people I had ever seen were shut up in factories. But here were young girls and young men enjoying life, free from the worry of living. . . . Societies, dances, letters from home, packages of food, midnight spreads and even birthday parties. I never knew that there were people glad enough of life to celebrate the day they were born.

Unbeknownst to Anzia, these students' parents may have looked on them with a similar sense of wonder. The late nineteenth century was an extraordinary period of opportunity. High school and college enrollments boomed, while the stresses of standardized testing and College Boards (first administered on an experimental basis in 1901) still lay in the future. In comparison with their fathers and grandfathers, young Anglo men had an expansive choice of professions with few formal requirements to get in the door. Many entered business or finance with a high school education or less. A study of New Jersey lawyers practicing in 1912 found that 86 percent of those born after 1881 had begun practicing law by age twenty-four and some as early as eighteen. College professors—much in demand with the growth of higher education—had not always gone to college, much less obtained a Ph.D. Careers in fields such as pharmacy, journalism, and advertising were even more accessible.

In this loosely credentialed world the purpose of a high school education was rather vague, and for most Americans it remained an unaffordable luxury. In a pattern typical of other groups, young Italian immigrants in New York tended to go to school until age ten or twelve, after which half the boys and three-quarters of the girls dropped out and went to work. In 1870 about 2 percent of Americans over seventeen years old had completed high school. By 1900 the percentage had risen to only 6.4. Yet this percentage was obviously rising much faster among Americans under twenty-five, and for an elite group of mostly native-born, Anglo youth, high school was becoming a defining experience. In age-graded, coeducational high schools, these students began to identify themselves by class year. With the advent of cheap printing presses they published dozens of student newspapers, distributed them to other schools, and built lively networks of gossip and debate. Male students studied classical subjects that would prepare them for college; they also joined debate clubs and even high school fraternities. In sports, female students were at first recruited to cheer on the boys (and to fundraise for their clubs), but by the turn of the century they began to win, against much resistance, basketball, field hockey, and other teams of their own.

Tensions over competitive sports were part of a larger pattern of gender rivalry. From the 1870s onward girls outnumbered boys at almost all public high schools. This happened in large part because young women received lower pay and fewer job opportunities, and parents could more easily give up girls' income in the teenage years. Many hoped a high school degree would enable their daughters to "marry up," while lessons in typing and math provided an emergency income plan for those who needed to work. Across the country high school commencement became a rite of passage and a striking sign of the opportunities opening up for young women. *Ladies' Home Journal,* the voice of an older generation, argued that the chief task of graduating girls was "to look their prettiest," not engage in "mental calisthenics." But female valedictorians, ignoring such advice, addressed audiences on such questions as "The Negro and His Right to Vote" and "Some Factors of the Labor Problem." Girls swept the honors and prizes so thoroughly that some schools created separate awards for girls and boys to protect the latter from embarrassment. In an 1898 survey 2,000 schoolgirls in Massachusetts said they hoped to teach, become stenographers or bookkeepers, establish businesses, and even become doctors and lawyers. "It was an extraordinary period of awakening," recalled Maritcha Lyons, a black assistant principal in a New York City public school, when young women began "to select their own life plans instead of tacitly accepting those arranged for them."

Leaving both public high schools and private academies, the luckiest girls could choose from a growing number of colleges and universities that admitted women. In the 1860s Vassar became the first women's college to offer a curriculum equivalent to that of men's institutions, rather than a "ladies' seminary" emphasizing domestic arts. Wellesley and Smith followed in 1875,

TABLE 5.1 Percentage of the U.S. population aged 5 to 19 enrolled in school.

	1870	1880	1890	1900
Male, white	56.0	63.5	58.5	53.4
Male, nonwhite	9.6	34.1	31.8	29.4
Female, white	52.7	60.5	57.2	53.9
Female, nonwhite	10.0	33.5	33.9	32.8

The rise of public education ensured a much higher level of basic literacy by the end of this era than ever before. In the wake of emancipation literacy rates among southern blacks made a dramatic leap, but wide racial disparities remained. Census-takers estimated in 1900 that only 4.6 percent of native-born whites were illiterate, but the illiteracy rate was triple that among immigrants (at least for literacy in English) and remained a staggering 44.5 percent among nonwhites.

TABLE 5.2 Degrees conferred by institutions of higher education, per year.

	1870	1880	1890	1900
B.A. or equivalent				
men	7,993	10,441	12,857	22,174
women	1,378	2,485	2,682	5,237
M.A. or second professional	—	879	1,015	1,583
Ph.D. or equivalent	1	54	149	382

By 1900 about 4 percent of the population between the ages of 18 and 21 was attending college or an equivalent institution.

Source for both tables: Carl N. Degler, The Age of the Economic Revolution, *2nd ed. (Glenview, IL, 1977), 169.*

and Bryn Mawr in 1884. Even more important were coeducational colleges and universities, which constituted almost half of the country's degree-granting institutions by 1890. Among state universities only the University of Iowa admitted women before the Civil War, but during Reconstruction the universities of Wisconsin, Kansas, Indiana, Minnesota, Missouri, Michigan, and California followed suit.

The cost of college was, of course, beyond the reach of many families, but even wealthy young women had to overcome obstacles to gain higher education. Many parents feared college would "unsex" their daughters or waste prime courtship years and leave them spinsters. The young Cleo Martínez, from an elite New Mexico family, longed for "a year at one of those fine colleges I saw advertised in my *Home Journal* magazine." She sent back a suitor's engagement ring, but her anxious mother warned, "you will never find another boy like Venceslao." Cleo accepted the proposal and gave up her college dream. Those who made it to college faced further impediments. At Oberlin Mary Church Terrell was discouraged from taking the challenging classical track. She was told that "Greek was hard; that it was unnecessary, if not positively unwomanly, for girls to study that 'old, dead language,' . . . and worst of all it might ruin my chances of getting a husband." Church ignored them, graduated with high marks, and went on to become a leader of the National Association of Colored Women—as well as to marry Robert Terrell, a prominent lawyer unfazed by the intellect of his bride.

The dramatic entry of young women into high schools and colleges prompted a backlash. Medical experts such as Dr. Edmund Clarke warned that too much education would channel young women's energies into their brains instead of their ovaries, leading to infertility, sickly babies, and the "decline of the race." "Identical education of the two sexes," intoned Clarke, "is a crime before God and humanity, that physiology protests against, and that experience weeps over." But experience did not weep. Female college graduates proved themselves healthy and talented, especially when colleges such as Vassar implemented mandatory exercise, naps, curfews, and nutritious diets to reassure nervous parents of their daughters' well-being. Graduates of schools such as Wellesley, Iowa, and Michigan were soon becoming prominent anthropologists, writers, and social reformers. The "coed," depicted in her dorm room studying chemistry or elegantly boating on the college lake, became a prominent role model for American girls.

By the 1890s commentators were describing the arrival of a so-called New Woman, embodied in figures such as the "Vassar Girl" and in Charles Dana Gibson's striking ink-line sketches in leading magazines of his "Gibson Girl." In her purest form the New Woman was a daughter of the Anglo elite, fashionable and rich, who made men swoon at charity balls as she spoke fluently in French about her recent Continental tour. The ideal New Woman also relished a physicality that her grandmother's generation would have frowned on. She enjoyed croquet, archery, tennis, golf, and swimming; perhaps she even tried mountain climbing or the exotic sport of skiing that Scandinavians were introducing in the West. On a more ominous note she subscribed to a new cult of thinness, and she knew—unlike women of her mother's generation—what dress size she wore and the exact weight of her body. At Baylor College for Women in Texas during the 1880s, Gertrude Osterhout was already worrying about these matters in a modern way. Out shopping with classmates in the spring of her freshman year, she agreed to be weighed. She "stepped on the scales as lightly as possible," she reported, "hoping it would balance at one hundred and twenty pounds. But what was my astonishment when the merchant said 'one hundred and forty three.' . . . [I] stepped off with a little more force than I got on with remarking that 'I knew those scales were not right.'" By the 1890s "diet" had taken on new usage as a verb, and doctors had begun to diagnose anorexia nervosa and other eating disorders.

Nothing marked the new physicality of youth more clearly than the bicycle craze, which swept the United States after manufacturers began to sell modern-style bikes in the 1880s. By 1890 U.S. firms were selling ten million bicycles a year; five years later Chicago alone counted 500 organized "wheel clubs." The bicycle foreshadowed the motorcycle and the automobile in giving riders a sense of freedom and personal mobility. Girls' bicycling, in particular, generated considerable controversy. For decades doctors had urgently warned parents that their daughters should never sit astride hobby-horses or seesaws, since this might stimulate them sexually and compromise their innocence. Within a decade bicycles destroyed the taboo. Reformers such as Frances Willard of the Woman's Christian Temperance Union made a point of appearing publicly on their bikes to persuade parents that cycling for girls was healthy and fun.

Not coincidentally, at the same time women began riding bikes and going to college, elite male educators took pains to assert that men were men. "Training for manhood" in school and athletics emerged as a clear response to women's entry into higher education, outdoor pastimes, and the public sphere. There were, of course, other reasons why men's education changed with the times. In a country increasingly driven by commerce, elites expressed hope that centers of higher education would remain sanctuaries from what the novelist Henry James called "the poison plant of the money-passion," a place where ideas could flourish without relentless subjection to the demands of the marketplace. In "The Social Value of the College-Bred" Henry's brother,

Metallurgical/Chemical Lab Crew baseball team, Jones and Laughlin Steel
Company, undated. After the Civil War baseball took off as America's national
sport, and from neighborhood bars to giant corporations businesses of all kinds
sponsored and fielded teams like this one.
Source: Historical Society of Western Pennsylvania, Pittsburgh.

William James, expressed a similar desire for liberal arts graduates to serve as
a "saving remnant," an intellectual class that could think widely and deeply,
in contrast to more narrowly trained recipients of technical and business
degrees. James highlighted the centrality of manhood to this vision when he
described the most important lesson of his college mentor: "Stop your sniveling complaints, and your equally sniveling raptures! Leave off your general
emotional tomfoolery, and get to WORK like men!"

The James brothers were products of Harvard, which became in this era
America's most influential college. Harvard's dynamic president Charles Eliot,
arriving in 1869, revolutionized the curriculum and essentially created what
we know today as the liberal arts. He abolished mandatory chapel, slashed the
number of student regulations, and placed new emphasis on "the pure and
applied sciences, the living European languages, and mathematics" rather
than Latin and Greek. Eliot also created electives, arguing that each individual
needed to develop his own unique talents and strengths. The Harvard system

Vassar Resolutes baseball team, 1870s. Not long after Vassar College opened its doors to offer young women an education equivalent to that of Harvard and Yale, Vassar students made a bid for equality on the baseball diamond as well as in the classroom. Female baseball playing proved too controversial, however; teams such as the Resolutes faded by the end of the 1870s, yielding to other athletic pursuits. Source: Archives and Special Collections, Vassar College Library, Poughkeepsie, New York.

proved wildly popular and spread to many other schools. It did so despite critics' observation's that choice might mean a decline in standards: a 1903 study found that Harvard students studied far less than in the past, and more than half the class of 1898 graduated with only entry-level coursework on their transcripts. "The wisdom of the ages is to be as naught," quipped one Harvard French professor, "compared with the inclination of a sophomore."

Yet to Eliot and his followers such critiques were beside the point. Harvard dedicated itself in this era less to the grasp of knowledge than to defining and strengthening *masculinity*, a word just coming into general use. A Harvard education came to mean the development of manly character and rugged physicality, as much or perhaps more than excellence in the classroom. In their memoirs students remembered a cult of sports dominating campus life. Harvard philosopher Josiah Royce proposed that athletics rather than study provided the best source of character development. Young men took such recommendations seriously: across the nation, flourishing campus sports began to include track, rowing, wrestling, and boxing as well as the wildly popular baseball.

The manly sport par excellence was American football, which spread quickly from the Ivy Leagues (over the vehement but futile objections of President Eliot) to colleges and universities nationwide. Its rules remained alarmingly loose. Yale's 1905 team captain was twenty-seven years old and received for his services free tuition, a vacation in Cuba, and exclusive rights to sell American Tobacco products on campus. Players wore no helmets and little padding. Punching opposing linemen was a popular strategy, and the injunction "three slugs and you're out" went largely unenforced. Charles Eastman, chosen to lead his class squad at Dartmouth on the assumption that he was a fierce Indian warrior from the West, observed wryly that on the football field he had "most of my savage gentleness and native refinement knocked out of me." Intercollegiate competition was much fiercer. In a notorious Harvard-Yale match in 1894 two players' eyes were gouged, another's collarbone was deliberately stomped on and broken, and a fourth player ended up comatose. That same year a Georgetown quarterback died from injuries inflicted on the field. Nationwide, there were reported to be twenty-one deaths during the 1904 season.

Football's supporters gloried in this violence, claiming it cultivated "vitality" and a "manly spirit." They resisted calls for regulation as vigorously as they played the sport, and reform bills presented to various state legislatures failed again and again. William Harper, president of the University of Chicago, defended deaths on the field: "If the world can afford to sacrifice lives for commercial gain," he said, "it can more easily afford to make similar sacrifices on the altar of vigorous and unsullied manhood." Like the era's industrial and financial titans, football players did not so much break the rules as fiercely resist the creation of them. When successful football reformers came along they cited, in fact, economic regulation as a precedent for their work. Purdue University's president took the lead in 1894, organizing the Western Conference (known informally today as the Big Ten) and pointing to the Interstate Commerce Act passed by Congress five years earlier. Like governments, he argued, schools had the right and obligation to set rules and insist on fairness and safety. But football heroes such as Yale's Walter Camp (who went on to become president of the New Haven Clock Company) disagreed. "American business has found in American college football the epitomization of present day business methods," he wrote without apparent irony. He called football "the best school for instilling into the young man those attributes which business desires and demands."

Meanwhile, Austrian bodybuilder Eugen Sandow took America by storm in the 1890s, prompting young men across America to take up weightlifting. Sandow, the son of a Königsberg vegetable peddler, shrewdly hid his origins and presented himself as a product of the middle class, speaking to the American audience most anxious about its self-definition (and most able to pay for admission to Sandow's shows). At least one of Sandow's admirers absorbed the point: a sixteen-year-old named Angelo Siciliano changed his name to Charles Atlas before launching his body-building empire. In the meantime, crowds of well-to-do New Yorkers packed Madison Square Garden to watch six-day bicycle marathons, modeled on earlier working-class footraces. Like their pedestrian predecessors, six-day racers literally tried to get as far as they could in six days without stopping for rest or food. So many severe injuries and even deaths resulted that New York City stepped in to regulate the sport in 1898, just at the moment educators began to set limits on the life-threatening excesses of college football.

As early as the 1850s a few American authors had begun to stress that a rugged physique was a mark of character. Oliver Wendell Holmes, Sr., who ran and rowed, complained in 1858 that "such a set of stiff-jointed, soft-muscled, paste-complexioned youth as we can boast in our Atlantic cities never before sprang from the loins of Anglo-Saxon lineage." By the 1890s his son Oliver, Jr., a Supreme Court justice, was urging American boys "to pray not for comfort but for combat; . . . to love glory more than the temptations of wallowing at ease." The Harvard psychology professor G. Stanley Hall fueled such attitudes with his enormously influential book *Adolescence*, published in 1904. Hall argued that each child retraced various stages of racial development as he grew up. Early childhood corresponded to "primitive" society, when men had played with sticks and rocks; adolescence re-created an era of questing. Differences between the sexes, Hall argued, "ought to be pushed to the very uttermost and everything should be welcomed that makes men more manly and women more womanly." New groups such as the Boy Scouts leaned heavily on Hall's analysis, often seeking explicitly to help boys cultivate and channel "primitive" skills so they could recapitulate early stages of human development and mature to the highest level. The boys most in need of such guidance were Anglos, of course, because they were the most highly evolved. Bernard Berenson, a Jewish Lithuanian immigrant who graduated from Harvard in 1887, satirized this line of thought by dubbing its authors the "Angry Saxons."

Theodore Roosevelt, one of Harvard's most famous graduates and exponents of strong masculinity, summed up the creed in his speech "The Strenuous Life." He equated peace with inaction and denigrated both in comparison with "those virile qualities" that marked "stern men with empires in their brains." He denounced "weaklings" who thought only of commerce, and he told women that if they did not embrace motherhood and domesticity the nation "trembled on the brink of doom." When Roosevelt became a war hero in Cuba in 1898, his brand of masculinity veered into a militarism that earned the disdain of his Harvard mentor, William James. James complained that Roosevelt "swamps everything together in one flood of abstract bellicose emotion" and diagnosed his former student as "still mentally in the *Sturm und Drang* period of early adolescence."

Public opinion, however, ran more with Roosevelt than with James. Masculinity by this point translated into militarism, and the new creed of combative manhood played no small part in justifying the war of 1898 and other imperial undertakings. In this context it became not only elite-based but explicitly racial. As Roosevelt himself put it, a "stronger, manlier power" had to step up and rescue the "wretched" men of Cuba, the Philippines, and other unfit races from themselves. Overseas expansion, one author claimed, would prevent America from deteriorating "toward Chinese immobility and decay." Implicit in such claims was an uneasy awareness that Anglo men no longer had a monopoly on political, economic, and cultural power in the United States. In fact, the new creed of masculinity depended, as in Hall's *Adolescence*, on conscious borrowings from "primitive," working-class, and non-Anglo traditions. The most "civilized" men, as Theodore Roosevelt wrote, needed to combine "barbarian virtues" like physical strength with their own presumed superiority in intellect and culture.

A MODERN YOUTH CULTURE

Elite Americans were beginning to borrow many ideas and practices from the working classes, a sign that cultural conventions were being turned upside down. Before the Civil War America's bourgeoisie had set the cultural tone, and strivers in the working classes were expected to emulate middle-class piety, respectability, and self-cultivation. But by 1900 new ideas and institutions, especially in leisure and mass consumer culture, were undermining older norms. As one critic observed, America had entered the era of the vaudeville theater, the baseball game, the amusement park ride, the dance hall, and the department store display window. All of these appealed "to the individual who wants to be diverted but doesn't want to think." The country was producing "a kind of lunch-counter art," he concluded. "But then art is so vague, and lunch is so real."

The first major innovation was vaudeville, which drew on such working-class traditions as minstrel shows, concert saloons, and variety theater, remaking them for audiences that crossed class and ethnic lines. Vaudeville managers offered something for everyone by featuring a never-ending parade of short acts: banjo players, comedians, jugglers, yodelers, animal trainers, and magicians. Vaudeville began in New York but spread across the country in the 1880s and 1890s. Its long-term impact on the American entertainment industry can hardly be overstated. Stand-up comedy and the variety-show format, both of which vaudeville popularized, would eventually shape radio and television.

Vaudeville also helped give birth to one of America's most popular and lucrative businesses—the movies. After years of experimentation with motion picture photography, inventors introduced large-screen projection in 1896. They quickly found that movies appealed to working-class audiences, tired from a long day's work and eager to stop in for fifteen minutes of light entertainment. Producers obliged these viewers with vaudeville-type skits, risqué scenes, and footage of cockfights and boxing matches. At first vaudeville managers used movies to close their shows, but films proved so wildly popular that separate nickel theaters arose to meet demand. By 1906 hundreds of these had opened in cities from New York to San Francisco, almost always on busy commercial streets in working-class neighborhoods. Film quality was poor, and reformers were horrified by the movies' lack of moral and educational content, not to mention the smooching that went on in dark theaters. But filmmakers were already experimenting with sensational ploys, such as onscreen gunfights, that attracted enthusiastic crowds.

The working class also flocked to beer gardens, boardwalks, and "10–20–30s"—cheap theaters nicknamed for the price range of their seats—

while trolley companies discovered the lure of amusement parks. The most famous of these were Luna Park, Steeplechase, and Dreamland on Coney Island, which New Yorkers could reach for 5¢. Numerous imitators such as Ohio's Cedar Point and Chicago's Riverview sprang up; soon almost every big city in America, as well as many smaller ones, had a trolley park. Drawing on the popularity of the great world's fairs, parks offered "scientific" exhibits such as reenactments of naval battles and replicas of exotic sites. But the most popular attractions were Ferris wheels and fun houses. Some rides lifted women's skirts, while others tossed men and women against one another and invited them to cling. "Will she throw her arms around your neck and yell?" advertised Coney Island's Cannon Coaster. "Well, I guess, yes!" A replica of the canals of Venice, popular with young lovers, prompted the introduction of tunnels of love. "The men like it because it gives them a chance to hug the girls," reported one park employee. "The girls like it because it gives them a chance to get hugged."

Proper middle-class adults avoided amusement parks, and reformers denounced the shocking things that went on there, but all to no avail. In the summer of 1904 four million visitors came to Luna Park alone. By this point city youth were upsetting their elders by patronizing an even bolder institution, the dance hall. "Dance madness" swept America, and syncopated ragtime became the rage after it emerged out of vaudeville. In cities from Seattle to Boston, young men and women flocked to dance halls to practice dance styles that brought a couple's bodies and legs in close contact. By 1905 they were "tough dancing," borrowing styles that originated in San Francisco brothels.

Like the movies, the dance craze marked a great divide between nineteenth- and twentieth-century cultures. The dance hall started off as a working-class institution, but middle-class youths quickly joined in the fun. They bought ragtime sheet music, eagerly followed the latest hits, and went out to clubs to practice the two-step and the bunnyhop. Ragtime also drew directly from black musical traditions and brought them into the cultural mainstream. The process, like acceptance of "tough dancing," was gradual and accompanied by vigorous disapproval from older generations. In part this was because of ragtime's racial imagery and lyrics. Sheet music covers projected a stereotype of fast living and promiscuity. Big hits included "Coontown Ball" and "All Coons Look Alike to Me," which won its author, the black musician Ernest Hogan, considerable criticism. Soon, though, overt racist slurs began to fade, and ragtime lovers popularized "African Reverie" and "African Smile." By 1899 the pianist Scott Joplin was composing complex and lovely hits such as "Maple Leaf Rag," one of 124 piano rags published in that year alone. The American popular music industry was being born in modern form, paving the way for such hybrid inventions as jazz, rock and roll, and hip-hop. All would originate with working-class African-American musicians, all would be deplored by parents, and all would be savored and celebrated by young people across class and racial lines.

In addition to the movies and ragtime, and beginning even earlier, the rise of mass sports also represented a break with old restraints. In parks that had

Stenography and typing class, Bryant High School, Queens, New York, 1906.
Thousands of young women and men trained for clerical positions through classes
at public schools and business colleges. Note, here, that the ratio of female to male
students is roughly two to one.
Source: Museum of the City of New York. The Byron Collection.

been designed four or five decades earlier for strolling and carriage riding, city
governments installed tennis courts, ice-skating rinks, and baseball diamonds.
By 1892 the nation boasted 348 Young Men's Christian Associations (YMCAs),
whose quarter-million members practiced football, calisthenics, swimming,
weightlifting, and bowling. Looking for indoor sports to promote teamwork
and health in the winter months, YMCA leaders invented basketball in 1891
and volleyball four years later. A twenty-four-year-old instructor at Smith
College, Senda Berenson, quickly adapted basketball for women. Newspapers
boosted circulation by filling the avid demand for sports scores, while a
moving-picture recording of an 1897 heavyweight boxing match became one
of the first commercially successful film releases. Americans who were not
riding bicycles, golfing, hiking, or playing team sports seemed to be out root-
ing for their favorites at the racetrack or stadium.

Of all the sports that emerged in post–Civil War America, baseball won the
widest and most enthusiastic following. Labor union picnics featured friendly
baseball competitions; companies sponsored teams for employees; empty lots
in every town and village seemed to sprout after-school stickball games.
Urban streetcar companies found that professional ball stadiums were, like

The Beach at Santa Monica, California, 1890. Saturday at the beach became a
summer rite as trolley companies and railroads offered cheap excursion fares.
The possibility of lake or ocean breezes and a cool dip drew people of all ages;
the short skirts on young ladies' "bathing costumes" had attractions of their own.
Source: Security Pacific National Bank Photo Collection, Los Angeles Public Library.

amusement parks, a lucrative draw. On Saturday afternoons their cars ferried
hordes of young men and boys out to root for the Brooklyn Trolley Dodgers,
Louisville Colonels, and Cleveland Spiders. Those who could not afford the
steep 25¢ ticket to a game could track their team's progress in the papers. For
sons of immigrant Jews, Poles, and Italians, following the home team became
a marker of American identity. (New York's socialist *Jewish Daily Forward* occasionally tried to explain the game to bewildered Russian-born parents, who
found it a mystifying waste of time and physical energy.) A striking number
of African-American and Native American players entered the new professional
leagues, which between the 1870s and the 1890s were not yet segregated. Even
a few women asserted their right to play, though only the pitcher Lizzie
Arlington, daughter of a Pennsylvania coal miner, made it briefly as far as the
minor leagues.

America's vibrant youth culture looked modern because it was consumer-
oriented, national, and in theory accessible to all. It was largely secular—
notwithstanding the YMCA's promotion of "muscular Christianity"—and in
the realm of sports it relied on forms of standardization that echoed those of
the emerging corporate world, from complex team hierarchies to stopwatches

and statistics. Perhaps most of all, youth culture was adventurous and fun. By the 1890s the goal of leisure was less and less to seek refinement and moral elevation and more and more to look for sheer entertainment and physical pleasure. These trends softened some of the cultural boundaries among ethnic groups and between the elite and working class. On a summer Saturday an Italian-born cook, a Jewish tailor, and an Anglo insurance agent might cross paths at the beach or stadium; while few struck up close friendships, all recognized something mutual in their quest for a Red Sox victory or a dip in the ocean. A certain cultural confusion and hybridity resulted. By 1900 the traveling chautauquas, which for decades had provided scientific and cultural programs for middle-class self-improvement, interspersed Chopin etudes and astronomy lectures with jugglers and magic acts borrowed from vaudeville.

It was hard for an old-fashioned American to know which way was up. Men and women in the generation that had fought the Civil War often suggested that the mighty purposes of *their* youth had given way to selfishness and shallow materialism. It was they, in fact, who urged young men to cultivate courage and rugged physicality—even undertake overseas military conquest—to reject commercial values and prove their fitness to rule. Thousands of young men (and women) heeded this call, while young Americans such as Ned Cobb, Charles Eastman, and Anzia Yezierska found higher moral purposes of their own. But at the same time mass consumer culture enticed the rising generation with an array of pleasures. And more and more, Americans gave themselves permission for leisure and fun. The impact of these cultural shifts ranged far beyond the movie theater and dance hall. Makers of mass culture had already learned that "sex sells," and from insinuating ragtime lyrics to Coney Island's tunnel of love, many of the new consumer pleasures were overtly erotic. As Americans refashioned their ideas about their bodies, morality, and respectability, they also renegotiated their beliefs about sex itself.

FOR FURTHER READING

On the orphan trains see Marilyn Irvin Holt's *The Orphan Trains* (Lincoln, NE, 1992) and Linda S. Gordon, *The Great Arizona Orphan Abduction* (Cambridge, MA, 1999). On African Americans, in addition to works listed in earlier chapters, I have used Andrew Ward, *Dark Midnight When I Rise* (New York, 2000) on the Jubilee Singers, and Theodore Rosengarten, *All God's Dangers* (New York, 1974). On Asian immigrants, in addition to works cited earlier, see K. Scott Wong and Suchen Chan, *Claiming America* (Philadelphia, 1998), Charles J. McClain, *In Search of Equality* (Berkeley, CA, 1994), and Sue Fawn Chung, "Ah Cum Kee and Loy Lee Ford: Between Two Worlds," in *Ordinary Women, Extraordinary Lives*, edited by Kriste Lindenmeyer (Wilmington, DE, 2000), pp. 179–196. Suey Hin's story is in Judy Yung, *Unbound Voices* (Berkeley, CA, 1999).

On Mexicans see Arnoldo De León, *The Tejano Community*, cited in Chapter 3, and Martha Menchaca, *The Mexican Outsiders* (Austin, TX, 1995). There is a rich vein of work on young Indians' experiences in boarding schools; see especially David Wallace Adams, *Education for Extinction* (Lawrence, KS, 1995), Michael C. Coleman, *American Indian Children at School, 1850–1930* (Jackson, MS, 1993), and two books by Frederick E. Hoxie, *A Final Promise* (Lincoln, NE, 1984) and *Talking Back to Civilization* (Boston, 2001). I also rely broadly on Hoxie's article "Exploring a Cultural Borderland: Native American Journeys of Discovery in the Early Twentieth Century," *Journal of American*

History 79 (1992): 969–995. For individual reminiscences see *Our Hearts Fell to the Ground*, edited by Colin G. Calloway (Boston, 1996), and Theda Perdue, *Nations Remembered* (Westport, CT, 1980), and on Samuel Blue of the Catawba, James H. Merrell, *The Indians' New World* (Chapel Hill, NC, 1989).

On childhood and education among the professional classes, see Karin Calvert, *Children in the House* (Boston, 1992), Joseph F. Kett, *Rites of Passage* (New York, 1977), Barton Bledstein's *The Culture of Professionalism*, cited earlier, Jane H. Hunter, *How Young Ladies Became Girls* (New Haven, CT, 2002), Barbara Miller Solomon, *In the Company of Educated Women* (New Haven, CT, 1985), Rosalind Rosenberg, *Beyond Separate Spheres* (New Haven, CT, 1982), and on women in the South, Laura F. Edwards, *Scarlett Doesn't Live Here Anymore* (Urbana, IL, 2000). On young women's body images see two books by Joan Jacobs Brumberg, *Fasting Girls* (Cambridge, MA, 1988) and *The Body Project* (New York, 1997), though I use evidence that locates the arrival of dieting and weight-consciousness a bit earlier than Brumberg proposes.

A key source on elite masculinity and education is Kim Townsend's wonderful book *Manhood at Harvard* (New York, 1996). On sports see also John Sayle Watterson, *College Football* (Baltimore, 2000), Elliot Gorn and Warren Goldstein, *A Brief History of American Sports* (New York, 1993), and Stephen Riess's *Sport in Industrial America*, cited in an earlier chapter. I also rely on Michael Attie, "The Gentrification of the Six-Day Bicycle Race," senior history thesis, Vassar College, 1999. On bodybuilding and changing standards of male physicality, see John E. Kasson, *Houdini, Tarzan, and the Perfect Man* (New York, 2001). On political and military ramifications of the "new masculinity," see Kristin L. Hoganson, *Fighting for American Manhood* (New Haven, CT, 1998). General overviews of changing male roles are E. Anthony Rotundo, *American Manhood* (New York, 1993), and the essays in *Meanings for Manhood*, edited by Mark C. Carnes and Clyde Griffen (Chicago, 1990).

Three histories of consumer amusements in this era are Robert W. Snyder, *The Voice of the City* (New York, 1989), John E. Kasson, *Amusing the Million* (New York, 1978), and David Nasaw, *Going Out* (Cambridge, MA, 1993). On the birth of motion pictures see Robert Sklar, *Movie-Made America*, 2nd ed. (New York, 1994), and on dance halls and "charity girls," Kathy Peiss, *Cheap Amusements* (Philadelphia, 1986). An insightful examination of class relations and culture in these decades is Lawrence Levine, *Highbrow/Lowbrow* (Cambridge, MA, 1988). On ragtime see Edward A. Berlin, *Ragtime* (Berkeley, CA, 1980), and David A. Jasen and Gene Jones, *That American Rag* (New York, 2000).

CHAPTER 6

———◈———

Sex

The strongest motive power in the world is the attraction
between the sexes. It even exceeds the desire for gain.
—MRS. E. B. DUFFEY, *WHAT WOMEN SHOULD KNOW*

In the early decades of Queen Victoria's reign (1837–1901), Anglo Americans
so closely followed Britain's cultural lead that society on both sides of the
Atlantic was described as "Victorian." The word conjures up parasols and
bustles, overstuffed parlor furniture, and most of all sexual prudery. According
to legend, Victorian etiquette books advised housekeepers to place covers over
the immodestly exposed legs of their pianos and to keep books by male and
female authors on separate shelves. Sex outside wedlock was supposed to be
shocking, and respectable women too pure to feel any sexual desire. Ideas like
these did hold considerable influence in the 1800s. Unmarried girls and court-
ing couples were usually chaperoned. Many young women learned little
about sex, being told only that doctors brought babies in their medical kits.
Experts warned that too much sexual activity caused mental and physical
weakness, and one infamous advice book instructed married couples to sched-
ule sexual intercourse once every three years, between the hours of 11 A.M. and
noon. The author even made recommendations on what to eat that day for
breakfast.

But today's caricature of Victorian primness would have looked alien to
Americans at the time, especially in the decades after the Civil War. For one
thing, it describes little of the experience of working-class people, including
millions from non-Anglo backgrounds. The tough barrelhouse dance music of
the black South was famously explicit ("squat low, mama, let your daddy see
/ You got somethin' that's worryin' me") but many rural and frontier whites
shared non-Victorian mores. Farming couples in the Ozarks planted spring
crops and then went out before sunrise to make love in the field, which supposedly ensured a good harvest. Arkansas fiddle tunes had names such as

"Take Your Fingers Out of My Pants" and "Grease My Pecker, Sally Ann,"
while a square-dance lyric moved from the suggestive to the specific:

Lead the ace and trump the king,
Let me feel that pretty little thing,
Up and at 'em, everybody dance,
Goose that gal and watch her prance.
Ladies do the shimmy, down goes her britches,
In goes a little thing about six inches.

Though historians as yet know little about the sex lives of working-class
Americans in this era, customs like these hardly suggest a "Victorian" mentality. Even among the Anglo elite, many married couples enjoyed passionate
sexual relations. One respectable lady asked her husband to write her a
naughty letter, "for it makes me want you a lot to read one." The wife of an
army officer teased her husband for having once courted another girl; that
woman, she wrote in a letter, could never have handled "your long Tom!!!"
While they cautioned against excessive lust, most advice books told husbands
they had a conjugal duty to satisfy their wives in bed.

To the extent that it existed at all, sexual Victorianism was clearly on the
wane by the post–Civil War years. By the 1890s even young women from the
elite stepped out on "dates" without chaperones, and the diaries of high school
students record considerable flirting and sex games. Claude Bowers, president
of his class at Indianapolis High School, reported after one party that he had
enjoyed "50 kisses, 3 girls on lap, 25 embraces. . . . Ye Gods!" Married women
also began to challenge Victorian restrictions on their conduct. In the 1880s
a furor erupted in one Iowa town when Methodist ladies appeared in a local
production of Gilbert and Sullivan's *Pirates of Penzance* wearing costumes that
revealed their legs. The minister denounced them the following Sunday with
a sermon drawn from Revelation 19:2: "He hath judged the great whore which
did corrupt the earth with her fornications." The amateur actresses blushed
angrily, and one got up and walked out of church.

While definitions of respectability shifted, a flourishing world of commer-
cialized sex and sexual crime flagrantly contradicted supposed Victorian
norms. Prostitution probably reached an all-time national per capita peak in
the 1870s. New York's vice district was the most notorious, occupying many
blocks along Broadway and offering every imaginable performance and service. But across the country luxurious brothels served elite men in privacy and
comfort, while prostitutes in "cribs" worked in horrific, degraded conditions,
sometimes servicing dozens of partners per night. At least 2,500 prostitutes,
half of them Chinese, worked in San Francisco by 1870. Savannah, Georgia,
had ten top-quality brothels and "quite a number of smaller houses." Officials
counted 517 brothels in Philadelphia. Lumber and mining camps were as
notorious as big cities.

For most prostitutes life held little glamour and much brutality. Virtually
every prostitute in Virginia City, Nevada, dealt with the physical and
emotional pain of the job by abusing alcohol, cocaine, opiates, or all three at
once. Venereal disease was rampant and suicide by morphine so common that

newspapers often just reported that "another unfortunate" had "ended her life by the usual means." A high percentage of prostitutes suffered rapes, beatings, and knife attacks. A study of Chinese prostitutes in California found they were also vulnerable to kidnapping and extortion by Chinese bosses and racially motivated assaults by non-Chinese customers.

What worried respectable Americans most about the sex trade, in addition to the plight of its victims, was the challenge of drawing a clear boundary between themselves and what was politely called the demimonde (a "half-world" of doubtful morality and legality). Red light districts often abutted downtown businesses and working-class residences. Predation at work was a constant danger for wage-earning women. Leonora Barry, an investigator for the Knights of Labor, documented an array of complaints by female workers ranging from demands for sexual favors to outright rape on the factory floor. In one 1888 Minnesota strike female garment workers demanded, as a condition for returning to the job, that male clerks stop "trying to mash us when we go to and from work." One journalist, working undercover at a Chicago department store, was shocked by the dangers she confronted after her shift ended at 10 P.M. "There were always men on the street corners," she reported. "Almost every morning the girls had some story to tell of encounters with men of that class." One night a menacing man stalked her as she made her way home. Terrified, she sprinted the last two blocks to her apartment building and slammed the door just before the man could force his way in.

Sexual exploitation was also a notorious danger for women in domestic service. This was especially true in the South, where as a legacy of slavery many male employers still expected sexual access to black women who worked in their households. Echoing the sentiments of many parents, one African-American woman wrote that "there is no sacrifice I would not make, no hardship I would not undergo rather than allow my daughters to go in service where they would be thrown constantly in contact with Southern white men, for they consider the colored girl their special prey." In northern cities, as well, investigators uncovered a significant pattern: a high percentage of prostitutes turned out to be former domestic workers who had been raped or seduced by employers. (If one was going to be forced into sex on the job, some of these women reasoned, why not earn the high wages of a prostitute rather than the pittance of a maid?) Reformers were as distressed by such discoveries as they were by the uncomfortable fact that some middle-class women contracted syphilis from husbands who visited brothels. Clearly, the lives of prostitutes and respectable married women sometimes intertwined, with both suffering exploitation by the very same men.

Marriage, as Americans of the day were keenly aware, did not always provide women with physical security and sexual respect. Many women wrote sadly in their diaries about acquaintances who were married to alcoholic or abusive men and suffered "hell on earth," often with the specific implication of marital rape. Domestic violence was nothing new, but in the late nineteenth century it became a topic of public alarm as women won legal redress and the problem came out in the open. Newspapers began to report cases of women who secured divorces after extreme sexual abuse. "[He] would force me to submit to him," testified one petitioner, "so that often I could not get out of bed. . . . I would beg him not to do it as I was so very sick. The only answer he gave me was 'you damned bitch, you have no business being a woman.'" One frontier husband told a judge "he would not give two cents and a half for a wife like [his own], who did not give a man all he wanted. . . . It did not seem to hurt whores to be treated in that way and he did not see why it should hurt his wife." In Sacramento a married man with two young children greeted a coworker with this story: "You ought to have been with me last night. I went to Lafferty's stable and got me a buggy and took a ride out aways and met a young cunt, and I took her over the levee and fucked her three times and made her suck my cock." The statement emerged in his trial for rape, of which he was duly convicted.

Much more common than such gross brutality was a set of widespread and stubbornly un-Victorian assumptions about male sexual privilege. After a painful divorce Rheta Dorr moved from Seattle to New York and found that as a divorcée she attracted scores of "game-hunters" who plied her with drinks and told lewd stories to try to get her into bed. Male college students wrote cheerfully to classmates about girls they had managed to "screw." When in the 1880s middle-class women campaigned nationwide to raise the age of consent for girls (which most states set at ten or twelve) numerous male legislators argued, amazingly, against the criminalization of sex with twelve-year-olds. One Nebraska lawmaker dismissed it as "a measure built on sickly sentimentalism." A Texan predicted the new law would allow "working girls" to "blackmail their employers," while a Kentucky legislator, in an even more telling objection, claimed it would put black women "on the same plane as the white female." Writing in the midst of the debate, one medical authority claimed *all* laws against rape were superfluous because no matter how strong her attacker was, no virtuous woman could possibly be raped as long as she was conscious. Such attitudes suggest a certain thinness to many men's veneer of Victorian respectability.

Even the highest circles of society and finance—perhaps especially these—underwent a parade of sex scandals in the post–Civil War decades. One of the most famous involved Congregational minister Henry Ward Beecher of New York, whose love affair with the wife of a parishioner was exposed in 1874. The U.S. senator Roscoe Conkling had a famous liaison with Kate Chase Sprague, the married daughter of Lincoln's secretary of the Treasury. Conkling's Senate colleague from Kentucky, W. C. P. Breckenridge, was convicted of seducing and abandoning an unmarried girl. New Yorkers followed the misdeeds of the financier Jim Fisk, who was shot to death by his mistress's new lover, and the shipping titan Commodore Vanderbilt, whose affairs included simultaneous flings with women's rights advocate Victoria Woodhull and her sister Tennessee Claflin. Philadelphia's elite was shocked by the adultery of streetcar magnate Charles Yerkes, who divorced his wife to marry his ambitious lover. In Denver the U.S. senator and mining millionaire Horace Tabor did the same. If anything made the Gilded Age "gilded," it was a sense that sexual intimacy, the last refuge of noncommercial relations, was being polluted by money and greed. In fact, capitalism exercised its creative and destructive power on sexual relations and family life as much as it did on other aspects of society and culture, and it did so at all levels of society. To some extent, "Victorianism" itself was a response to the seismic shifts in sexual relations that were occurring as part of the century's sweeping economic and social transformations. When people worked for "home protection," they sought to preserve marriage, family, and religious faith from what seemed to be all-consuming material values. Yet in this, as in so many areas of American culture, older norms gradually gave way to the new.

WIVES AND HUSBANDS

During his first term of office, between 1885 and 1889, President Grover Cleveland undertook one overwhelmingly popular act: he got married. His fiancée, Frances Folsom, was the daughter of a deceased colleague, and at the time of their White House wedding she had just turned twenty-two. (Her husband was forty-nine.) Americans went wild for "Frankie," who combined a boyish nickname with sophistication and an elite education that had begun at a new-fangled French kindergarten and ended with graduation from Wells College in upstate New York. Newspapers reported so avidly on the couple's honeymoon that the groom complained about lack of privacy. Cleveland Democrats churned out celebratory books such as *The Bride of the White House*, while even the staunchly Republican *New York Tribune* admitted that "no American wedding has attracted such general and amiable attention." Advertisers quickly borrowed the first lady's face (over the Clevelands' strenuous objections) to sell everything from soap to thread. In the next presidential campaign young women formed Frankie Cleveland clubs to march in Democratic parades.

The Cleveland wedding bestowed a number of political benefits on the groom. It domesticated the Democratic party, which had nominated a striking number of bachelors in the previous three decades, while Republicans had celebrated the moral influence of mothers and wives. It brought liquor back to the White House, since Grover Cleveland's sister Rose, who had served as hostess for her brother, had been a temperance advocate, but Frankie was not. Americans who remembered the lingering death of President James Garfield, and even Abraham Lincoln's assassination in 1865, welcomed the presidential wedding as a joyful counterpoint to those moments of national mourning. But most of all, perhaps, the Cleveland wedding reassured Americans about the intentions of a rising generation of college-educated women. Instead of reform work or a professional career, Frances Cleveland chose domestic life with a portly older husband. In fact, she largely disappeared from public view after the wedding, though the arrival of the couple's first child, nicknamed "Baby Ruth" in the press, sparked another round of feverish publicity and the marketing of a new candy bar.

The Cleveland wedding comforted Americans at a time when they found themselves anxious and uncertain about marriage. After the Civil War, in keeping with other legal reforms, divorce became legal everywhere in the

United States. (Interestingly, on the eve of the war abolitionist Massachusetts had had some of the country's most liberal divorce laws, while secessionist South Carolina had been the only state where no divorce could be obtained for any reason. Divorce reform and emancipation—which removed slaves from the legal "family unit" and the household—thus went hand in hand.) Divorce advocates hoped that the reform would help end bad matches and keep the institution of marriage purer and healthier than in the past. A "good marriage law is prevention," as one sociologist put it, "whereas a good divorce law is cure." The number of divorces skyrocketed in the 1870s and 1880s, and a few states, such as Indiana, became virtual divorce mills. While they deplored this trend, Americans at the same time faced, more than ever before, the uncomfortable fact that marriage was a kind of contract in an era when contracts (and the ability to make and break them) reigned supreme in law. Marriage was, as divorce laws tacitly acknowledged, a legal agreement in which each partner granted the other certain rights and accepted certain responsibilities.

But what exactly were those? Idealists saw marriage as the ultimate expression of the romantic self. Some argued that every individual had a single divinely ordained partner somewhere in the world, and only with that person could his or her soul achieve its fullest development. But for many immigrants and rural folk marriage resulted from more pragmatic concerns. A southern Italian man, working as a railroad boss in New Jersey, remarked to friends that he "could be happily married on my present salary." "I didn't do anything about it," he remembered, "but my friends did, for in about a month's time I had received several photographs of girls of my hometown and other towns adjoining; so that I was not long in selecting one which appealed to me." Soon after her arrival, his wife was contributing to the household income by cooking and washing for two dozen men.

TABLE 6.1 Estimated fertility rates for the white U.S. population, 1850–1910.

Year	Estimated fertility rate
1850	5.24
1860	5.21
1870	4.47
1880	4.24
1890	3.87
1900	3.56
1910	3.42

A long, precipitous decline in the birthrate resulted in the average adult white woman bearing roughly three children by the early twentieth century, down from an average of about seven children a century earlier. Historians still debate how this was accomplished, but it appears that contraceptives were widely used (though little mentioned). The decline was most dramatic for the urban middle classes; their children were not "assets" on the family balance sheet at an early age, as in rural and working-class households, but instead were expensive to raise and educate, with the goal of longer-term prosperity in mind.
Source: Ansley J. Coale and Melvin Zelnik, New Estimates of Fertility and Population in the United States *(Princeton, NJ, 1963).*

Middle-class Americans, uncomfortable with such matter-of-fact calculations, were even more disturbed by millionaire families who shopped their daughters to British aristocrats. How did such practices differ from prostitution, if a young woman's virtue was, in effect, traded for money? A poem in the 10¢ *Munsey's*, published at the height of the titled wedding craze, described a wealthy debutante under the title "Her Shame":

> *No wonder she blushed! For a blush she had need;*
> *'Twas not pride in her triumph that drew it.*
> *She sat there a slave to ambition and greed—*
> *A chattel, for sale, and she knew it.*

Popular writers stoked such views by offering lurid tales of sin and lust in high society, such as Charles Reade's 1871 bestseller *A Terrible Temptation*. Some members of the elite quietly deplored the decline of morals among their own class. Edith Wharton, a daughter of New York's upper crust, structured her story "New Year's Day" around whispered gossip of adultery. A matron in Wharton's *House of Mirth* laments "what society is coming to. Some one said the other day that there was a divorce and a case of appendicitis in every family one knows."

"The Latest Nobleman. 'Girls, girls, don't press his Grace! He can only take one of you, and with him it is purely a matter of business.'" In the 1890s the "Gibson Girl" became a model of female sophistication and beauty. Charles Dana Gibson often depicted his slim-waisted young women golfing or walking outdoors. Here he depicts them in high society, commenting on the phenomenon of "titled matches" between American heiresses and English aristocrats.
Source: Charles Dana Gibson, *Sketches and Cartoons* (New York, 1898).

Advertisement for "The Rambler Bicycle," American Bicycle Company. "Many of the first wheels made in the great Rambler factories, twenty-one years ago," read the accompanying text, "were ridden by boys whose whole families to-day ride." This image reflects the growing popularity of family entertainment, vigorous exercise for all, and domesticity: the husband and father enjoys riding bicycles with his wife and children on the weekend, rather than getting together with other men.
Source: *Harper's Weekly*, 14 April 1900, p. 352.

Even among the middle classes, the role of money in marriage seemed troublesome. Under the law a married woman's body became the property of her husband, to do with as he pleased. But many respectable Americans found this an increasingly distasteful concept, not reflective of what a loving marriage ought to be. The legal standard thus contradicted an intense ideal of romantic love. Husbands' legal obligation to provide necessities for their wives and children also came into question. In one turn-of-the-century case, Wanamaker's Department Store sued the husband of a customer who ran up substantial debts buying toys, shoes, towels, and table linens. The store argued that a husband was legally responsible for his wife's purchase of "necessities . . . in view of her position in life." New York courts reversed themselves twice before making a final ruling against Wanamaker's. The old rule did not apply, they decided, when a woman bought tablecloths and napkins without telling her husband. A wife, in other words, might be supported financially by her husband, but when she shopped she acquired debts as an individual on her own.

With such fundamental issues at stake, almost every major policy debate in the political arena addressed the implications for marriage. Was the

Freedmen's Bureau helping to model proper marital relations for former slaves, Americans asked in the 1870s. Did Union widows' pensions, which ended when the recipients remarried, sustain bereaved women and children, or did they encourage immoral cohabitation? Did the Republican tariff enable wives to stay out of the workplace and elevate home life for their husbands and children, or did it force them to pay more when they went shopping? The Woman's Christian Temperance Union shrewdly chose the name *Home Protection* for its women's suffrage campaign, arguing that wives and mothers needed the temperance ballot to shield their families from the impact of liquor. Home Protection also became the watchword of campaigns to abolish sweatshop wages, raise the age of consent, and eventually to provide state-level "mothers' pensions" to deserving widows and abandoned wives who were struggling to raise children alone.

One of the era's fiercest home protection debates was fought over Mormon plural marriage, a practice that had begun in the 1840s. Politicians and non-Mormons denounced polygamy as a dreadful form of corruption. Diaries and letters by plural wives suggest that, in fact, their experiences, like those of women in monogamous unions, varied greatly. Some first wives resented second wives, and vice versa. Patty Bartlett Sessions, a successful Utah midwife, wrote that she "felt as though her heart would break" when her husband took a second wife, a woman Sessions judged to be self-centered and lazy. But other "sister wives" became close friends, and some felt closer to each other than to their husbands. One wife wrote of another, who had just died, that she had "always loved her." Annie Clark Tanner, a second wife, named her baby Jennie in honor of the first wife, who had been unable to bear a child.

Ignoring such evidence, reformers and Republicans insisted that Mormon women were degraded creatures trapped in "harems" on American soil. Until the Mormon hierarchy officially abolished plural marriage in 1890, the practice was under continuous attack. Missionaries set up a "rescue home" in Salt Lake City to lure plural wives away from their families and offer them training for paid employment. (Very few took up the offer.) In the name of protecting womanhood, Congress even disfranchised Utah women in 1887, after Utah became the second federal territory to give women the vote. The legislative sponsors of this bill swore that Mormon women's votes were helping to sustain polygamy, though they could not explain exactly how.

Even beyond the fight over Mormon practices, plural marriage was a challenge to advocates of home protection. Some abolitionists who went South during Reconstruction found freedmen who, continuing African traditions, practiced Islam and had multiple wives. They suppressed this evidence out of fear that it would look bad to northern whites, and they insisted that all freedmen and freedwomen practice monogamy. Indian agents and missionaries sought to regulate sexual relations among native peoples, none of whom had practiced "marriage" in the Western Christian sense before contact with Europeans, and some of whom carried on traditional forms of polygamy. Under pressure from missionaries and government agents, a Northern Cheyenne named Wooden Leg agreed after much anguish to send away his second wife, who had not yet borne a child. Tormented by the decision, he was relieved to hear a few years later that she had found a loving husband. The government directive shocked older men of the tribe. "Who will be the father to the children?" asked one, outraged at the command to cast part of his family adrift. Wooden Leg, appointed a tribal judge, insisted that each man send away one wife but refused to follow up with careful enforcement. "My heart sympathized with them," he said later. "From time to time somebody would tell me about some man living a part of the time at one place with one wife and a part of the time at another place with another wife. I just listened, said nothing, and did nothing."

While stamping out marriages that did not correspond to Christian norms, crusaders also undertook sweeping campaigns to protect women and children from dangerous or unpleasant information. Here was Victorianism in its most obvious form, driven by fears that commercialism and sexual license were spinning out of control. Pornography proved an especially troubling phenomenon. Union and Confederate soldiers created an avid market for sexually stimulating materials, and after the war's end the efficient networks of mail and trade that stimulated other forms of commerce carried on a lively national trade in pornographic photographs, lithographs, books, and magazines. Wrapped in unmarked brown paper, these publications proved difficult to intercept, and they provoked particular anxiety over information that children and teenagers might obtain without parents' knowledge. Antivice crusader Anthony Comstock, making the case for federal action against pornography, submitted as evidence dozens of requests for pornographic materials sent by students at boarding schools.

Early in the post–Civil War era, Comstock persuaded Congress to ban from the mails all "obscene literature," including information about birth control. (At the time the law passed in 1873, Republicans were reeling from a series of financial scandals; they apparently hoped a vote for sexual purity would bolster their party's reputation.) Most states followed up with similar laws of their own. Undertaking citizen arrests as leader of the New York Society for the Suppression of Vice, Comstock became a controversial figure. Many of the convictions he won were later overturned, and for those who were convicted both U.S. presidents and state governors quietly issued a number of pardons, ruling that Comstock had overstepped the bounds of law. Female reformers in the WCTU and other groups supported Comstock at first, but they broke with him when he began to attack the women's suffrage campaign as a symptom of modern evil.

The results of Comstock's campaigns were ambiguous. There is ample evidence that many Americans continued to manufacture, buy, and use birth control, including diaphragms, condoms, and sponges (most often purchased quietly through the mail). But federal anticontraception provisions remained in effect until the 1930s, and parts of the law lingered three decades more. Comstock's work had a chilling effect on information and public debate, much as the rants of Senator Joseph McCarthy did in a later era. Several writers and editors who challenged Comstock lost their lives to the fight. Ida Craddock, an author of advice books for married women, committed suicide after being hounded by Comstock for several years. Ezra Heywood, whose women's rights tract *Uncivil Rights* sold 60,000 copies, had mixed results in defending his work. In 1877, under the Comstock Law, Heywood was convicted of circulating obscene material but secured a presidential pardon after supporters organized a petition campaign. In a second case concerning ads for a vaginal syringe that Heywood wickedly dubbed "the Comstock Syringe for Preventing Conception," a jury dismissed all charges. But Comstock won the final battle when Heywood was convicted in Massachusetts of circulating obscene literature. He was sentenced to two years of hard labor and emerged from prison in 1892 with his health broken, dying soon afterward. His wife, Angela Heywood, also a women's rights advocate, had to give up her writing career to support and raise their four children alone.

The 1880s and 1890s also brought a wave of censorship campaigns against art and literature, though like Comstock's attacks these met with only partial success. James Herne's 1890 drama *Margaret Fleming*, credited by some as the first realist American play, offended Boston censors with its depiction of a wife who accepts her husband's illegitimate child and begins, onstage, unbuttoning her dress to nurse the baby. A shocked Frank Doubleday, publisher of Theodore Dreiser's *Sister Carrie*, tried to renege on the contract after he read the text of the "indecent" book. Unable to do so legally, Doubleday refused to promote the novel, and the first run, published in 1900, sold less than 500 copies. On the other hand, Mark Twain's *Huckleberry Finn* did not win nationwide attention until a library committee in Concord, Massachusetts, banned it. After the publicity surrounding this act of censorship, the book sold thousands of copies.

In the South the rise of formal segregation was linked closely to fears over interracial sexual contact, which remained as stigmatized among whites as pornography and illegitimacy were for Americans nationwide. In the immediate aftermath of the war, interracial marriage was briefly legalized in many states, but the defeat of Reconstruction brought an end to this openness. As early as 1877 a white Alabama woman, Julia Green, spent two years in prison for the crime of marrying a black man. In subsequent decades many a black man was lynched for simply looking at a white woman in the wrong way, or acting in such a way that whites thought he had. (An unfamiliar black man who knocked on the back door of a farmhouse seeking work or food often risked his life in the process.) In the same years southern states also began to pass myriad laws requiring segregation in everything from railroads to water fountains. Most of these laws separated not just blacks from whites, but white *women* from black *men*. Spaces designed for men only, such as racetracks and saloons, remained largely unsegregated, as did the private homes where thousands of black women, serving as cooks, nursemaids, and housekeepers, worked intimately with white women and children.

Cross-racial courtships and marriages in other regions—for example, between Anglos and Mexican Americans in the Southwest—also became rarer and more stigmatized by the 1890s. Western states actually exceeded the South in passing new laws that forbade the marriage of Anglos to blacks, Asians, and American Indians. As we shall see in Chapter 10, this phenomenon was linked to a large-scale hardening of racial lines as the century drew to a close.

By the time Thomas Dixon published *The Clansman* in 1905, falsely claiming that emancipation and Reconstruction had led to an epidemic of rape by black men, legislators in all regions of the country were working vigorously to "protect" white women from men of "lower races," a cause many white constituents approved and even demanded. Amid a campaign to segregate passenger trains, one New Orleans newspaper declared that any Louisianan "who believes that the white race should be kept pure from African taint will vote against that commingling of the races inevitable in a 'mixed car' and which must have bad results." The editor especially appealed for white men to protect wives and daughters from such a "risk." In all parts of the country, even where segregation was not enforced by law, it was widely argued that black, Chinese, and Mexican men lusted after white women.

Yet amid censorship and racial and sexual discrimination, some Americans carried the Victorian ideal of female modesty in a different, radical direction. Building on beliefs about the purity of womanhood and motherhood, men and women such as Ezra and Angela Heywood used these ideals to question the institution of marriage itself. As talk about sex became more public, reformers were able to speak and write more directly about abuses suffered by wives. Many condemned the assumption that a wife's body belonged to her husband. A popular advice book, Mrs. E. B. Duffey's *Relations Between the Sexes*, urged men to "practice in lawful wedlock the arts of the seducer, rather than the violence of the man who commits rape." The forcible deflowering of a bride on her wedding night, another author wrote, simply constituted "rape and torture." Dr. John Kellogg, in an 1895 health guide for women, addressed husbands as well. "The most heroic battle which many a man can fight," he wrote, "is to protect his wife from his own lustful passions." Warning of the health risks when women were forced to submit to unwanted sex, Kellogg wrote that "every young wife should know that it is her duty as well as her privilege to protect herself. . . . It is no woman's duty to surrender herself soul and body to her husband." Some judges began to agree. While marital rape was not a recognized crime until a century later, it became harder by the 1880s and 1890s for a husband to win divorce on grounds that his wife did not provide him with adequate sexual services. Conversely, it became easier for spouses (overwhelmingly women) to obtain divorce when constant sexual demands impaired their physical and mental health.

Assuming women were less sexual than men, reformers began to call for two sweeping changes in marital relations. The first was "free love," which for most advocates meant wives' freedom to choose when they would engage in sex with their husbands. The closely related movement for "voluntary motherhood" advocated women's right to choose whether and when to bear children. Most reformers expected these choices to be made within marriage, ideally by both partners in a spirit of mutual respect. Defined in this way, voluntary motherhood had become a mainstream cause by the turn of the twentieth century. Doctors, health reformers, and women's rights advocates all condemned marital rape and the dangers of unlimited child-bearing. Women, they argued, risked their lives in pregnancy and were expected to take responsibility for raising the resulting children. Thus, husbands should

not have unilateral power to force wives to submit to intercourse and poten-
tially assume these burdens.

A few radicals went even further in their definitions of free love. The colorful Victoria Woodhull famously announced in an 1871 speech that "I have an
inalienable, constitutional and natural right to love whom I may; to love as
long or as short a period as I can; to change that love every day if I please." In
the novel *Hagar Lyndon*, published in 1893, women's rights advocate Lizzie
Holmes invented a heroine who earned economic independence and then
chose motherhood out of wedlock with the help of a male friend who sympathized with her views. In the novel Hagar endures both the disapproval
of those around her and a change of heart by her friend, who decides that she
and her child need a protector and Hagar ought to marry him. But the heroine
maintains her independence and raises her beloved son by herself. Such ideas
remained scandalous in the late nineteenth century, but they extended the
Victorian ideal of motherhood in directions that presaged the twentieth-
century movement for women's rights. As the radical reformer Moses Harman
phrased it, families would be happiest and most harmonious when women
chose "motherhood in freedom."

BACHELORS AND INDEPENDENT WOMEN

The ideas of radicals such as Lizzie Holmes and Moses Harman reflected a
broader array of changes in the opportunities open to American women. More
than ever before worked, traveled, and lived on their own. Some chose professional or charitable careers and never married at all, while divorced women
also increased in numbers. The independence of such women provided a new
vantage point from which to analyze marriage not as a presumed norm for
all adult women but as a legal and economic relationship that some began to
see as outmoded. Charlotte Perkins Gilman provided a foundation for future
feminist critiques in her 1898 book *Women and Economics*. Drawing on her own
unhappy experience, Gilman argued that the problem with marriage was
wives' economic dependency. Like men, she wrote, women had a wide array
of interests and abilities. The role assigned to married women was "over-sex-
specialized": all wives were expected to keep house and raise children even
though many found (as Gilman had) that they were painfully unsuited for
these tasks. Gilman suggested that isolating children in the home with a miserable mother might be bad for everyone involved, and she proposed cooperative day care centers that would free female energies for other pursuits.

Gilman's ideas were too radical to be widely assimilated in the 1890s, but
one of the ideas she endorsed, day care for the children of working mothers,
reflected a movement that already existed. By 1892, six years before Gilman
published *Women and Economics*, urban reformers had opened 90 day nurseries
in the United States, a number that grew exponentially over the next two
decades. And critiques of marriage were being offered, cloaked in the language of female purity and Christian self-sacrifice. "The purpose of our organization is to educate the girls to that sturdy independence of spirit that can say

no," wrote a Colorado WCTU leader in 1892. She went on to lament that "there are not enough good men to 'go round'" and to argue that "every marriage does not mean a home; . . . it is a mockery to call some of them homes." She told young women it was "better to live alone and unloved a thousand years" than to enter such a marriage, and she suggested an alternative option. "Noble-minded girls" who were working to "support themselves and make their homes with other girls," she wrote, were proving that "homes can be made by women alone."

Though most Americans still presumed that a professional career precluded marriage and motherhood, this WCTU leader was describing a real, growing phenomenon: unmarried women joining together to keep house while each pursued her own work. By 1890 the census found that more than 10 percent of adult wage-earning women in major cities were unmarried and not living with parents or family members (the figure was one-fifth in Chicago, and one-third in St. Paul). About half such women were immigrants, while half were native born. Most lived in boarding houses or joined other independent women to rent lodgings together. Ranging from the elite to those below the poverty line, they included entrepreneurs, clerks, seamstresses, artists, writers, social workers, and factory operatives.

At the same time adult men were escaping the bonds of matrimony in even larger numbers than women. In urban areas by 1890 one-fifth of American men remained unmarried in their thirties and early forties. A substantial percentage of these did not live with parents or kin, a pattern especially marked among blue-collar workers. The reasons so many chose bachelorhood were hotly debated. Many male immigrants came to the United States alone; others, immigrant or not, needed to work for a decade or more to save enough to support a family. But some chose permanent bachelorhood. Three years after the Civil War a writer for *The Nation* was already noting that "the city is the habitat of the single." "By the general diffusion of education and culture, by the new inventions and discoveries of the age, by the increase in commerce," he observed, "the tastes of men and women have become widened, their desires multiplied, new gratifications and pleasures have been supplied to them. . . . The domestic circle does not fill so large a place in life as formerly. . . . Married life has lost in some measure its advantage over single life."

Single men and women not only enjoyed urban amenities ranging from diners to movie theaters; some also built on a Victorian tradition of same-sex friendship and companionship whose meaning was slowly changing. Men and women, both married and single, had long shared homosocial bonds that the culture at large viewed as innocent and praiseworthy. Many such relationships seem to have been erotically charged "romantic friendships" that fulfilled a need for companionship but were not physically sexual in the modern sense of the word. Close female bonds, in particular, were considered appropriate and natural, and parents and husbands thought little of it when girls or adult women held hands, took walks with their arms around each other, or shared a bed when visiting each other's homes. One doctor commented in 1896 that only very recently would anyone have suggested "there could be anything improper in the intimate relations of two women."

But by the time this doctor wrote, medical experts were using the terms *homosexuality* and *lesbianism* to describe what they now saw as unnatural relationships (establishing, in the process, *heterosexuality* as a presumed norm). For both men and women homosexuality was coming to be recognized as an orientation rather than a sexual act that people might engage in without reshaping their identities or seeing themselves as set apart. The transition could be traced at the new women's colleges, where in the 1870s and 1880s students engaged in a practice called "smashing": sending each other love notes and poems, sharing beds, and pursuing all the other rituals of love affairs, including tumultuous break-ups. Girls cheerfully reported the details of their latest "smashes" to parents and professors, and unless it interfered with a student's academic work, the custom was widely accepted as innocent practice for future wives. But by the 1890s and early 1900s statistics showed that almost half of Bryn Mawr, Wellesley, Vassar, and Radcliffe graduates were choosing not to marry after they left school. Instead, they were pursuing advanced degrees and launching careers, often continuing to live with other women, and sometimes forging lifelong female bonds. In light of these developments, "smashing" came to seem considerably more subversive.

Homosexual relationships were not new in the late nineteenth century. The American sculptor Emma Stebbins and the actress Charlotte Cushman, for example, lived openly as lovers before the Civil War (though they did so as expatriates in Rome). In the 1850s Walt Whitman's "Calamus" poems celebrated, among other things, the physical pleasures of male love. Jason Chamberlain and John Chafee, two prospectors who traveled to California in the '49 gold rush, could still be found living there together in the 1890s. Visitors called them the "wedded bachelors." "Which one is the 'ladies man' we could not discover," one caller reported, "each modestly declining the honor." After fifty-four years together, John died in the summer of 1903; three months later Jason spent the day picking apples and then, bereft of his life partner, went into the house and committed suicide.

The recognition of homosexuality emerged in indirect and hidden ways. Many women entered "Boston marriages" that did not necessarily have a sexual dimension, and some saw their relationship with a woman as a second-best substitute for marriage. Mary Woolley and Jeanette Marks, two educators who began their relationship at Wellesley in 1895, lived together for decades afterward, yet Marks insisted in her public writings that only a male-female relationship could be "complete." The New England writer Mary E. Wilkins lived from 1883 onward with a close female companion but then left her to enter a difficult marriage to an alcoholic. The novelist Sarah Orne Jewett, who never married, had a deep romantic friendship with Annie Fields, the widow of leading publisher James T. Fields, but neither woman ever defined herself as a lesbian. Years later, in fact, Jewett seemed perplexed that her young literary protégé, Willa Cather, masked her passion for women by creating male narrators in her novels who in their romantic feelings spoke in certain ways for Cather herself. Cather, twenty-four years younger, lived in a world that viewed homosexuality as a defined orientation; she knew her lesbianism was stigmatized in ways the older Jewett did not seem to understand.

Doctors were not the only ones beginning to see homosexuality as something different from Victorian romantic friendships. In 1892 in Memphis, Tennessee, nineteen-year-old Alice Mitchell slit the throat of her seventeen-year-old lover, Freda Ward, in a murder that shocked the nation, especially since both murderer and victim were from respectable Anglo families. Alice testified that she had begged Freda to marry her and offered to dress as a man so they could escape and live together in St. Louis. Alice had killed Freda after she refused. Judged insane and committed to an asylum, the "girl lover" died of tuberculosis a few years later. The case distressed Americans, in part, because of a marked increase in the number of women who were cross-dressing and living with female lovers, as Alice had intended to do. Cases of this phenomenon were documented all over the country. Even a Tammany ward boss in New York named Murray Hall turned out in 1901 to have been a woman who had lived as a man for a quarter-century. As in this case, women's identities were often discovered only after their deaths, and cross-dressing became a vehicle for same-sex marriage. Murray Hall and "his" wife had been married for many years.

A remarkable memoir published by thirty-year-old Claude Hartland in 1901 offers an even more intimate picture of the emergence of homosexual identity. Hartland, born in 1871 in a southern railroad town, realized at age eleven that he felt desire for men. A few years later a visitor shared a bed with him, as was general practice:

> We had not been in bed five minutes, when he turned toward me and boldly placed his hand upon my sexual organ, which was already erected. . . . He then unfastened my clothing and his own and brought his organs and body in close contact with mine. I was simply wild with passion. All the pent-up desire of years burst forth at that moment. I threw my arms around him, kissed his lips, face, and neck. . . . The intense animal heat and the friction between our organs soon produced a simultaneous ejaculation, which overstepped my wildest dream of sexual pleasure.

Thereafter Hartland experienced both anticipation and anxiety when he shared a bed with other men. Several seemed unapproachable; one gave him a fatherly hug and said, "God bless this boy"; others (including one visiting minister) responded with passion when Hartland caressed them. Several times Hartland sought medical advice, and on the instructions of one doctor he slept with a prostitute, making it through the unpleasant encounter by focusing his thoughts on "a very handsome man." After years of teaching in rural areas, he moved to a big city, probably Baltimore, and later to St. Louis. In the process he discovered to his relief and sadness that "many others were suffering from a disease similar to my own." At the time he wrote his memoir, Hartland had not reconciled himself to his sexual orientation. He viewed it, however, not as a sin but, in a more modern way, as an incurable disease.

It is difficult to estimate how many Americans had such homosexual experiences, much less how they understood them. It is clear, though, that a gay male subculture was flourishing in many cities by the 1880s and 1890s and that it was not invisible or necessarily a source of shame to participants. Statistics also show that unprecedented numbers of both men and women chose not to marry and that substantial numbers lived in long-term, single-sex arrangements, whether sexual or just companionable. Cross-dressing was becoming a familiar practice to many urbanites, while Boston marriages and other female-female relationships were a matter for general comment and analysis.

At the same time, one can trace in the culture a series of related shifts in heterosexual practices. In popular music sentimental songs such as "Sweet Genevieve" and "Molly and I and the Baby" gave way to more flirtatious lyrics, often celebrating brief affairs rather than enduring love. "My Best Girl's a Corker" and "A Hot Time in the Old Town Tonight" fell into this genre; many ragtime songs appropriated a lusty celebration of sex outside wedlock, projecting it onto blacks but popularizing it among Americans of all races and classes. On a humorous note Americans sang "You've Been a Good Old Wagon But You've Done Broke Down," as well as the 1891 smash hit "Ta-ra-ra-boom-de-re," borrowed, like much of the new music and dance, from a red light district, in this case Chicago's. A decade later Americans were singing about a couple who drank beer together and made out "Under the Anheuser Busch." In the same years increasing evidence came to light of premarital sexual play, heavy petting, and explicit talk—an especially striking change

Thomas Eakins, "Thomas Eakins and John Laurie Wallace at the Shore," 1882–1883. Eakins, now considered one of the most talented American artists of his era, believed passionately that artists should work from the human body itself, not from plaster casts. He encouraged students to study anatomy and dissection, and he offended Victorian propriety by encouraging even female students to sketch from live male nudes. As a result he lost his post at the Pennsylvania Academy of Fine Arts in 1887. Eakins and his students, male and female (including his future wife), posed outdoors as models for paintings and photographs.
Source: The Metropolitan Museum of Art, New York, David Hunter McAlpin Fund, 1943. (43.87.23).

among young women. For young men such practices were not so much new as more open and accepted—something your father might have sought out in a brothel but which you might engage in with a girl from a respectable family. Whether you saw the young woman herself as respectable was another question. The double standard that Victorian reformers had lamented by no means died with the old century's mores.

These shifts went along with a larger emphasis on physicality and the body, which encompassed far more than the "discovery" of homosexuality. In this as in many other aspects of the emerging youth culture, middle-class adolescents took their lead from working-class contemporaries. By the 1890s working-class young people spoke of going on a "date": rather than stopping by a young woman's home for a visit, a young man was expected to take her out to a public venue such as a restaurant, theater, or amusement park. There the young man paid for consumer pleasures such as ice cream or carnival rides, and the couple enjoyed themselves without adult supervision. This practice quickly

Elvira Virginia Mugarrieta, known as "Babe Bean." Known to her neighbors in Stockton, California as Jack, Mugarrieta had been living as a man for some years when her identity was discovered in 1897. "Jack," who had liberated herself at age 15 from the convent her mother had chosen for her education, told reporters she disguised herself so she could "travel freely, feel protected, and find work." After much publicity in Stockton, "Jack" disappeared, and enlisted in the Spanish-American War, resurfacing afterward in San Francisco under the name Jack Garland. Garland lived there until his/her death in 1936 at age 66, where he was much admired for providing food and medical care to the destitute. Jack Garland's true identity was discovered after death. Cross-dressing women became a familiar and unsettling phenomenon to Americans after the Civil War.

Source: Sketch from *Stockton Evening Mail*, 9 October 1897; Mugarrieta's story in the San Francisco Lesbian and Gay History Project article, " 'She Even Chewed Tobacco': A Pictorial Narrative of Passing Women in America," in *Hidden from History*, edited by Martin Bauml Duberman, et al. (New York, 1989), pp. 183–194.

affected middle-class courtship. By 1904 even the stodgy *Ladies' Home Journal* was ruling that respectable girls needed to have only one chaperoned home visit, so that parents could meet a young man and assess his character; subsequent dates could be out on the town.

Dating opened a new world of nightlife to young men and women who previously would have courted on their parents' front porches. Like many of the enticements of the new consumer culture, it brought pressures along with pleasures. Young men were expected to spend plenty of money to impress their dates, a process antithetical to the steady saving that prior generations had advised for husbands-in-the-making. For women the pressures were sexual. The "treat" or "date" began as a way for working-class girls to enjoy excursions that their meager salaries did not allow them, since most made far lower wages than did men. But the adventure came with a price: men often expected sexual favors in proportion to the amount spent. This expectation was not, of course, respectable. New York working girls who participated in it won the nickname "charity girls," an ironic play on the fact that they were not quite prostitutes but instead sold themselves for drinks or dance hall admission. Nonetheless, the assumption that young women should deliver sexual favors in exchange for male spending marked a transformation of courtship that eventually affected all manner of dating rituals at all levels of the social scale. In exchange for freedom from parental oversight and the exhilaration of amusement parks, dance halls, and movie theaters, young women assumed a new set of risks.

Dating, like other aspects of youth culture, opened up a host of conflicts between young women and men and their anxious and disapproving parents. A New York reformer reported that many working girls asserted their right as wage earners to come and go as they pleased: "there was no law but their own will." Authoritarian parents did not necessarily win the fight. "If I went out," remarked a young dance hall fan named Maureen Connelly, "and I knew I'd get hit if I came in at twelve . . . I'd stay out till one." To some extent, though, a zest for independence and sexual experimentation emerged even far away from the cities, among young men and women who still trysted in their parents' parlors. Rolf Johnson, a Swedish-born farmhand in rural Nebraska, enjoyed a torrid affair with his neighbor Thilda Danielson. Thilda let Rolf know her feelings directly and invited him over for an afternoon and evening when her family was away. "We played 'love in the dark,'" Rolf reported, "as we lighted no lamp not wishing to be watched from without through the window. When I heard her folks drive into the yard I tried to slip from the house unobserved, as I knew there would be hell to pay if they found us together with no lamps lit." Thilda's father had a "stormy session" with his daughter, calling her a prostitute and warning her that Rolf had no intention of marrying her. Thilda angrily declared her right to love Rolf if she chose. In the end Thilda and her father were both partly right and partly wrong. Rolf did not propose. "I couldn't see it," he wrote. "I am not quite prepared to leave the state of single blessedness for that of double misery." He broke off the relationship and went off to wander and work odd jobs for three years in South Dakota, Colorado, and New Mexico. But when he returned he found that the dire warnings of his girlfriend's father had proven false: instead of suffering a ruined reputation, Thilda had happily married someone else.

Thilda and Rolf lived in a world in which adults told them one thing about premarital sex and a powerful peer culture was beginning to tell them something else. Even in rural Nebraska they enjoyed more freedoms than their parents had had to follow their own inclinations. In some ways they returned to older, pre-Victorian customs. Two centuries earlier, in colonial New England, a third of all brides had been pregnant on their wedding day; in the Victorian era that percentage had dropped, but by 1900 active adolescent sexuality was reemerging. Newly added to the mix was a consumer culture that emphasized flirtation, physicality, and fun. Adults, in the face of these developments, seemed divided on the definition of sex roles and sexuality itself. To the extent Victorians had tried to enforce a single ideal—marriage and parenthood for everyone, with husbands and fathers working for bread and women preserving the purity of the home—that ideal no longer held for large swaths of the population.

As to sex itself, respectable adults were still Victorian enough to give young people little guidance about it, and therein lay some of the power of peers and consumer culture. When WCTU officials ran a nationwide campaign promoting a "white life for two," they hoped it would encourage more equal marriages through the application of a single standard of moral behavior. "The law of purity," the WCTU wrote, should be "equally binding upon men and women." Prospective brides were to tell their husbands, "you must be as pure and true as you require me to be, ere I give you my hand." But the WCTU instructed that the specific meaning of the phrase "a white life" (no sex before or outside of marriage) be explained *only* to boys; girls were not present to hear this information. In the face of such ambivalence and confusion, men and women explored on their own the meanings of sexuality and love. For some that meant creating a family of two women or two men; for others it meant seeking anonymous sexual encounters in the exciting urban underworld. For much larger numbers of young Americans, it meant playing "love in the dark" like Thilda and Rolf or heading out to the amusement park for a ride through the tunnel of love.

FOR FURTHER READING

Two books important throughout this chapter are Karen Lystra, *Searching the Heart* (New York, 1989), a history of romantic love in the nineteenth century, and John D'Emilio and Estelle B. Freedman, *Intimate Matters* (New York, 1988), a history of sexuality. On the emergence of modern public sexuality, see Sharon R. Ullman, *Sex Seen* (Berkeley, CA, 1997).

On prostitution see Benson Tong, *Unsubmissive Women* (Norman, OK, 1994), Joel Best, *Controlling Vice* (Columbus, OH, 1998), Marion S. Goldman, *Gold Diggers and Silver Miners* (Ann Arbor, 1981), and Roger D. McGrath, *Gunfighters, Highwaymen, and Vigilantes* (Berkeley, CA, 1984). On domestic violence see Elizabeth H. Pleck, *Domestic Tyranny* (New York, 1987). Sexual exploitation of domestic servants is documented in the histories of female domestic service cited in Chapter 3. Age-of-consent campaigns are covered in David J. Pivar, *Purity Crusade* (Westport, CT, 1973), and a more nuanced update is provided by Mary E. Odem, *Delinquent Daughters* (Chapel Hill, NE, 1995). On women's moral uplift campaigns in the West see Peggy Pascoe, *Relations of Rescue* (New York, 1990), and on pornography Wayne E. Fuller, *Morality and the Mail in Nineteenth-Century America* (Urbana, IL, 2003). For a brilliant exploration of the Beecher-Tilton affair see Richard Wightman Fox, *Trials of Intimacy* (Chicago, 1999). The quotation about home as haven comes from the title of Christopher Lasch's book *Haven in a Heartless World* (New York, 1977).

On the Cleveland wedding see Rebecca Edwards, "Frances Folsom Cleveland," in *American First Ladies*, 2nd ed., edited by Lewis L. Gould (New York, 2001), pp. 161–169, and on "family values politics" generally, Rebecca Edwards, *Angels in the Machinery* (New York, 1997), and "Domesticity versus Manhood Rights," in *The Democratic Experiment*, edited by Meg Jacobs, William J. Novak, and Julian E. Zelizer (Princeton, NJ, 2003), pp. 175–197. On the pension issue see Megan J. McClintock, "Civil War Pensions and the Reconstruction of Union Families," *Journal of American History* 83 (1996): 456–480, and on polygamy debates, Joan Iverson, *The Antipolygamy Controversy in US Women's Movements, 1880–1925* (New York, 1997), as well as Sarah Barringer Gordon, *The Mormon Question* (Chapel Hill, NC, 2002). On Mormon women's lives I rely also on Lorraine Bellard's study of Patty Bartlett Sessions, "Living Her Faith on the Mormon Frontier," senior history thesis, Vassar College, 1998.

On marriage law see Michael Grossberg, *Governing the Hearth* (Chapel Hill, NC, 1985), Nancy F. Cott, *Public Vows* (Cambridge, MA, 2000), and Amy Dru Stanley, *From Bondage to Contract* (New York, 1998). On judges' changing attitudes toward sex in marriage see Jill Elaine Hasday, "Contest and Consent: A Legal History of Marital Rape," *California Law Review* 88 (Oct. 2000): 1375–1505. On tensions over commerce and domesticity see Ellen Garvey, *The Adman in the Parlor*, Elaine Abelson, *When Ladies Go A-Thieving*, and William Leach, *Land of Desire*, all cited in Chapter 4.

On contraception and sex radicalism, respectively, see Andrea Tone, *Devices and Desires* (New York, 2001), and Joanne E. Passet, *Sex Radicals and the Quest for Women's Equality* (Urbana, IL, 2003). On Angela and Ezra Heywood I am also indebted to Ben Holtzman, " 'Saying Naughty Words and Shocking the Whole World,' " senior history thesis, Vassar College, 2003. On Charlotte Perkins Gilman see Ann J. Lane, *To Herland and Beyond* (New York, 1990). On single life in the cities see Joanne J. Meyerowitz, *Women Adrift* (Chicago, 1988), and Howard P. Chudacoff, *The Age of the Bachelor* (Princeton, NJ, 1999). On romantic friendships and the emergence of homosexuality I draw on Lillian Faderman, *Surpassing the Love of Men* (New York, 1981), George Chauncey, *Gay New York* (New York, 1994), and Leila Rupp, *A Desired Past* (Chicago, 1999), as well as works on early women's colleges, cited earlier. Individual stories of gays and lesbians recounted here appear in Susan Lee Johnson, *Roaring Camp* (New York, 2000), Lisa Duggan, *Sapphic Slashers* (Durham, NC, 2000), and Jonathan Katz, *Love Stories* (Chicago, 2001). On sex in popular music see Nicholas E. Tawa, *The Way to Tin Pan Alley* (New York, 1990), and on the origins of modern dating, Beth L. Bailey, *From Front Porch to Back Seat* (Baltimore, 1988). Rolf and Thilda's story unfolds in Rolf Johnson's diary, published as *Happy as a Big Sunflower*, edited by Richard E. Jensen (Lincohn, NE, 2000).

CHAPTER 7

⸻⸻◦⸻⸻

Science

> Man . . . translated himself into a new universe which had no
> common scale of measurement with the old.
> —HENRY ADAMS, "THE DYNAMO AND THE VIRGIN"

In the summer of 1877, a Union Pacific section foreman and a station agent in Wyoming sent a confidential query to the paleontologist Othniel Marsh. Would the professor, they asked, be interested in some enormous fossils of unknown animals, including a thirty-inch vertebra and a five-foot shoulder blade? If so, how much would he pay? "You are well known as an enthusiastic geologist and a man of means," the men wrote slyly, "both of which we are desirous of finding, especially the latter." Marsh rushed an assistant to the site and received a stunning report. The fossil beds were seven miles long and lay in easy-to-dig sandstone, so close to Union Pacific tracks that workers could load them directly from wheelbarrows onto railcars bound for Marsh's Yale laboratory. Marsh quickly paid his informants and began to dig.

The excavation at Como Bluffs, Wyoming, became one of the most famous in all paleontology. It uncovered the great Jurassic dinosaurs, many of which still carry Marsh's names for them, including *Stegasaurus* with its plated spine, sauropods *Diplodocus* and *Brachiosaurus*, and toothy predator *Allosaurus*. Marsh's lab reconstructed whole skeletons and presented them to eager visitors at museums such as the Smithsonian, where the displays helped revolutionize Americans' understanding of natural history. More than a century earlier the British geologist James Hutton had shocked scientists by proposing that the Earth was more than sixty million years old. That estimate had gained increasing acceptance over the course of the nineteenth century. Charles Darwin's famous theories, first published in 1859 in *The Origin of Species*, depended on Hutton's geological estimates to conceive of evolution as a process taking millions of years; Darwin's ideas, in turn, revolutionized biology.

151

By the 1870s scientists studying fossil oysters and horseshoe crabs spoke confidently of the Triassic and Cambrian eras.

While English scientists conducted almost all the crucial early investigations, in the late nineteenth century Americans began to take the lead. The western United States became the great font of modern paleontology. Its alkaline soils preserved bones beautifully, while eroded buttes and canyons made fossils easy to find and dig. Amid rapid rail construction and settlement, fossil hunts took on aspects of a gold rush. Othniel Marsh and his bitter rival, Edward D. Cope, staked out secret claims and hired spies to report on each other's finds. Their haste to piece together skeletons and claim discoveries left a trail of confusion that lingered for decades. The primate *Notharctus* received seven different names. Skulls got attached to the tails of skeletons or to the wrong bodies altogether. Marsh ridiculed Cope for such mistakes, but he himself invented the now-discredited *Brontosaurus* from the bones of two different species. The legacy of the two men's feud was not unlike that of the era's corporate titans, who left others to clean up the mess from their spectacular and reckless careers. A leading paleontologist of the next generation wrote that he and his colleagues spent "the best years of our lives" sorting out the chaos left by Marsh and Cope.

For the public, unaware of these difficulties, the discovery of the great dinosaurs opened a new window on prehistory and undermined the long-standing assumption that God had created the earth in 4004 BC. Though some clung to the hope that human and dinosaur bones would be found together, dating both to the early biblical era before the Flood, they waited in vain. The fossil lode at Como Bluffs confirmed that dinosaurs had had their own great age. Even more spectacular revelations lay ahead, as astronomers offered evidence for a new understanding of space and time. In 1878 the young Albert Michelson, teaching physics at the U.S. Naval Academy, accurately measured the speed of light and thus proved that there was no "luminiferous ether" between the stars. His work paved the way for a series of breakthroughs in physics that led to Albert Einstein's theory of relativity three decades later. In the meantime, photographers began to offer clear images of the Milky Way, proving it was made up of myriad distant stars. In 1885 observers of the Andromeda nebula witnessed the birth of a star. In the heavens as well as on Earth, scientists were measuring what one naturalist has called "deep time": the true immensity of the geological and astronomical record. As they did, they began to suggest humans' insignificant place in cosmic history.

The late nineteenth century thus brought intellectual as well as economic and social turmoil to the United States. A popular cult of science arose, and the tools of science, from spectroscopes to X-ray machines, offered compelling advancements in knowledge and human welfare. While Americans flocked to museums for explanations of the latest finds in geology and anthropology, industrial laboratories presented them with telephone communication, safer canned foods, and electric light. Science promised progress and delivered on that promise in tangible ways. Medicine, especially, began to hold out the hope of curing diseases that caused incalculable suffering and grief. "There has never been in the history of civilization," declared one observer in 1891, "a period, or a place, or a section of the earth in which science and invention have worked such progress . . . as in these United States in the period since the end of the Civil War."

EVOLUTION

Marsh's discoveries at Como Bluffs by no means brought a simple conquest of science over religion in American thought. Not until 1895 did the National Education Association begin to suggest textbooks based on evolutionary principles, and great battles over the teaching of evolution did not begin for two decades more. In the meantime, biologists and paleontologists reached no consensus on how evolution worked. In one of his greatest achievements, Othniel Marsh traced the fossil record from ancient *Eohippus* to the modern horse, which, he said, proved Darwin's theory of natural selection by random mutation. Marsh, however, was in the minority. Others looked at the same evidence and drew the opposite conclusion: the progression of species was too regularly spaced to be the result of accidental mutations. They argued, in the tradition of the French biologist Jean Baptiste Lamarck, that individual animals developed new traits during their lifetimes and passed them along to offspring. This Lamarckian idea of "acquired traits" dominated evolutionary science for decades. The idea that evolution was driven by random mutations, including painful and fatal ones, seemed utterly cruel. Surely the Creator had developed life by more humane and orderly means.

The struggle between Lamarckian and Darwinian views also translated into a debate over whether human societies and economies evolved, and if so, how. For many, evolution was synonymous with progress. The influential anthropologist Lewis Henry Morgan, writing in the 1870s, proposed that human family structures evolved over time, and he set up a system of classification whose legacy endures in popular thought. Primitive societies, he argued, were "promiscuous"; humanity then rose through "matriarchy" and "patriarchy" to the pinnacle of civilized family life, which not surprisingly turned out to be Victorian-style monogamy. Morgan believed this pattern of progress to be universal. Ethnologists could study the kinship system of any culture and rank it above or below those of other peoples on his scale.

Others looked at the world of commerce and saw a clear application of evolutionary ideas. "The growth of a large business is merely a survival of the fittest," declared John D. Rockefeller in a statement typical of the genre. "This is not an evil tendency of business. It is merely the working out of a law of nature and a law of God." This kind of "social Darwinism" drew on the immensely influential work of the English author Herbert Spencer. It was Spencer, not Darwin, who coined the term *survival of the fittest*. His most prominent American adherents included the steel manufacturer Andrew Carnegie and the Harvard sociologist William Graham Sumner. The latter's view of humanity was especially grim, because he feared that well-intentioned busybodies had interfered for centuries with nature by feeding the hungry and unemployed. Instead, Sumner argued, humans must avoid the interference of "sentimentalists" and allow unfit people to die, or at least not reproduce. Accused of wishing to kill off a large portion of humanity, Sumner denied the charge. But, he added, "as to a great many persons and classes, it would have been better for society, and would have involved no pain to them, if they had never been born."

For other thinkers evolutionary theory had very different implications. One of the most innovative responses to Darwin's theory was the distinctively American philosophy that came to be known as pragmatism. Influenced by the latest scientific ideas as well as by their traumatic experiences in the Civil War, philosophers such as William James and John Dewey began to question whether there was such a thing as universal truth. Instead, they suggested that human ideas operated like genetic mutations: some worked and some did not, and the only way one could judge the difference was through experience and experimentation. All knowledge, James and Dewey proposed, was local, pro-visional, and constantly shifting, just as biological species were constantly adapting and not fixed over time. In the late nineteenth century such ideas were far out of the mainstream. Most natural scientists, as well as legal and social thinkers, still devoted themselves to constructing rigid systems of classification, seeking out truths they assumed to be universal and eternal. In the early twentieth century, though, pragmatist ideas would help undermine this older view and shape new ways of thinking in many fields of knowledge.

In the near term, a much more widespread response to evolutionary theory was to take an optimistic Lamarckian view. If people could acquire strength, wisdom, and moral goodness during their lifetimes and transmit them to their children biologically, then surely every effort at education and uplift would magnify a hundredfold. Reformers spoke of furthering human evolution not by laissez faire economics but by cooperation, especially through collective institutions such as government, schools, and churches. Books such as *The Evolution of Christianity*, in which reform minister Lyman Abbott explored changes in Protestant theology, won broad and enthusiastic readership. Meanwhile, some social scientists challenged the dire views of men such as William Graham Sumner. The sociologist Lester Frank Ward observed that a thorough application of Sumner's views would require humans to dispense with all medicine, government, law, emergency rescue from floods and hur-ricanes, and anything else that might interfere with the "natural" processes of life and death. The lesson to Ward was clear: "if nature progresses through the destruction of the weak, man progresses through the *protection* of the weak."

In other fields, as well, science did not exactly displace religion; instead, faith informed scientific inquiry. Most of the authors who wrote for the American Oriental Society were Protestant missionaries in Asia, whose scholarship emerged from their study of the languages and cultures of people they sought to convert. Experts in the rising fields of Egyptology and Assyriology—the latter focusing on the biblical Babylon, or today's Iraq—sought to confirm the truth of Old Testament stories. Linguists looked for clues to the location of the Tower of Babel, while wealthy patrons funded archaeological excavations in the Near East through American Palestine Exploration Societies. Between 1888 and 1900 the Babylonian Expedition

Fund, based at Philadelphia's University Museum, sent four expeditions to Nippur, south of Baghdad. Both of the Assyriologists who led these expeditions were Protestant ministers, and one edited the national *Sunday School Times*. A participant described their mission as a blend of spiritual and scientific goals. The expedition worked, he wrote, "in the spirit of Christian enlightenment and scientific inquiry to bring forth from its ancestral home, now desolate and forsaken, the heritage of forgotten ages."

Since scientific knowledge was presumed to arise from projects of classification, museums were the era's great institutions of scientific education and study. Institutions such as the Smithsonian displayed not only ranks and ranks of fossils, but stuffed birds and animals, mineral specimens, and pottery and spears in room after room full of glass cases, expecting visitors (including professional scientists as well as the general public) to grasp the essence of each species or culture by examining representative objects. Schools and colleges boasted of the quality of their geological and botanical "cabinets." Some genteel families even transformed their parlors into little museums, cramming into one room all the functions of a science display and an aristocratic drawing room, music room, and art gallery. A collection of seashells might sit side by side with a globe, a specimen case of stuffed songbirds, and a terrarium filled with different types of ferns. To complete the quest for knowledge, plenty of bookshelves or, better yet, a separate library were considered essential even in a modest cottage. Embracing the cult of collection and display, one decorating expert assured readers that "there is hardly likely to be too much in a room."

Similar assumptions underlay the era's deeply influential world's fairs. Starting with Philadelphia's Centennial Exposition in 1876, these fairs introduced millions of Americans to the latest advances in technology and science along with art and artifacts from around the world. The grandest of them all, the Chicago World's Columbian Exposition of 1893, attracted 27.5 million visitors. Its White City displayed the latest wonders of American industry, housed in steel frame structures such as the Palace of Mechanic Arts, the Horticulture Building, and a dozen others. The centerpiece of the Electricity Building was a Tower of Light, featuring an enormous dynamo from General Electric. The Transportation Building displayed the latest rail technology, sponsored by companies such as the Baltimore and Ohio Railroad. Dominating all was the immense Manufactures Building, which had a fifty-foot-wide avenue running through its interior. Here visitors could marvel at the latest innovations in pharmaceuticals, ready-made clothing, clocks, elevators, and thousands of other products. The Remington Company, for example, displayed dozens of its typewriters, adapted to various languages and to specialized tasks such as weather reporting.

In keeping with the mania for classification, human beings from various tribal cultures also went on display in Chicago. The anthropologist Franz Boas of the American Museum of Natural History in New York organized these exhibits, which ranged from North American Penobscot Indians to "little Javanese people." They included some people who were brought to Chicago under false pretenses and held virtually as slaves. The exhibited villagers built

Mary Cassatt, *Young Women Plucking the Fruits of Knowledge and Science*, detail from the center panel of a mural commissioned for the Women's Building at the Chicago World's Columbian Exposition, 1893. Cassatt, a leading American Impressionist painter living in Paris, inverted the Biblical story of Eve and the apple to celebrate women's achievements in science, the arts, and professional life. The original mural has been lost.

Source: This reproduction appeared in *Harpers New Monthly Magazine*, May 1893, p. 837.

samples of their native housing and crafts and performed traditional dances for fairgoers. Guidebooks ranked them, according to Lewis Henry Morgan's theory, from the "savage" to the most "civilized." At the same time, along the fair's midway male visitors lined up to see Syrian-born belly dancer Fahreda Mahzar, billed by the stage name "Little Egypt." Mahzar's "genuine native muscle dance," popularly known as the hootchy-kootchy, afterward became a staple at amusement parks such as Coney Island. This "scientific" display of foreign culture capitulated entirely to the commercial and sexual.

In the burgeoning world of commerce, science and education mingled with for-profit entertainment in a variety of ways. Showmen such as Buffalo Bill laid great stress on the authenticity and instructional value of their offerings. Bill, for example, never called his production a "show," but simply "Buffalo Bill's Wild West." By 1893, when Bill set up shop near the Columbian Exposition in Chicago, his horsemen included Russian Cossacks, Mexicans, Arabs, and Syrians, whom he advertised as an "Ethnological Congress." By 1894 the Barnum and Bailey Circus was also marketed as a "Grand

Laboratory at the Tuskegee Institute, Tuskegee, Alabama, 1902. African Americans as well as women challenged the prevailing assumption that scientific research and discovery were white men's realms, as well as "scientific" claims about the limited intellectual capacity of women and "lower races" of men. Booker T. Washington's showcase for his goal of industrial education, Tuskegee featured by this time a $2-million endowment, a faculty of nearly 200, and an extensive, well-equipped campus.
Source: Library of Congress, Washington, DC.

Ethnological Congress." Promoters suggested that its famous chimpanzees, Chiko and Johanna, belonged on an evolutionary continuum beside "strange and savage tribes" from around the globe. Meanwhile, objects amassed for various world's fairs—from steam engines to pottery and textiles—ended up as the basis for famous museum collections. Artifacts from the Chicago exposition became the foundation for the city's new Field Museum, launched with a million-dollar donation from the department store magnate Marshall Field.

The rage to build distinguished collections led to competition not unlike the dinosaur hunting frenzy unleashed by Marsh and Cope. Edward Thompson, a Harvard professor serving as consul to Mexico in 1901, used a crude mechanical bucket to dredge the sacred well at the ancient Mayan site of Chichen Itza, obtaining (and irreparably damaging) superb gold and jade artifacts that he smuggled illegally to the United States. Even more disturbing were the activities of bone hunters, who robbed American Indian graves and shipped home specimen skeletons of native people killed in conflicts over western land. The Army Medical Museum in Washington amassed hundreds of skulls, including those of Cheyenne people killed in Colorado's Sand Creek massacre and Pawnee killed by Kansas vigilantes. In response many native people began to bury relatives beside their homes in order to watch over the bodies.

TECHNOLOGY AND CORPORATE CAPITALISM

Though American anthropologists won acclaim for studies of native peoples whom they could easily reach by railroad, in other fields the United States remained a scientific backwater. Many of its leading scientists were émigrés trained in Europe, and those born in the United States went abroad to get the best advanced training. As enthusiasm for science swept the country in the early 1870s, a Dartmouth student confirmed the dominance of England. "Ten or fifteen years ago," he reported, "the staple subject here for reading and talk, outside study hours, was English poetry and fiction. Now it is English science. Herbert Spencer, John Stuart Mill, Huxley, Darwin, Tyndall have usurped the place of Tennyson and Browning, and Matthew Arnold and Dickens."

While Europeans led the way in the so-called pure sciences, Americans excelled instead in applied fields such as engineering and materials science, and their efforts tended toward the pragmatic and profitable. Railroads took the lead in this as in many areas of business innovation; they hired metallurgists who designed more powerful and safer steam engines, and chemists developed creosote treatments to extend the life of wooden crossties. Other industries followed suit, and by 1899 almost 150 American corporations had created research laboratories. The steel magnate Andrew Carnegie summed up the benefits when he described the work of a German chemist he employed. "Great secrets did the doctor open up to us," Carnegie wrote. "Mines that had a high reputation were now found to contain ten, fifteen, and even twenty percent less iron than [they] had been credited with. Mines that hitherto had a poor reputation we found to be now yielding superior ore. . . . Nine-tenths of all the uncertainties of pig-iron making were dispelled under the burning sun of chemical knowledge. What fools we had been! But then there was this consolation: we were not as great fools as our competitors, [who] said they could not afford to employ a chemist."

Discoveries in industrial laboratories were proprietary, and corporate scientists and engineers engaged in a constant race for patents. The managers of Bell Telephone, for example, saw that every patent strengthened their control over earlier inventions whose patents had run their seventeen-year course. When competitors could copy an old telephone design but were barred from using a reworked, newly patented receiver, Bell retained the advantage. As one adviser to the company noted, the drive to maintain market dominance pushed Bell to "organize a corps of inventive engineers" and continue filing patent applications. In the emerging electric power industry the rivals Westinghouse and General Electric (GE) followed a similar strategy. When necessary they bought rival patents and squelched them rather than allow new products to compete with their own.

The innovations of Bell and GE engineers were spectacular in a different way than were Marsh's sketch of *Stegasaurus* and the excavations at Chichen Itza and Nippur. Stronger, more flexible steel enabled manufacturers to make better and cheaper typewriters, bicycles, and eventually automobiles. The invention of reinforced concrete allowed architects and engineers to construct such modern marvels as skyscrapers and the Brooklyn Bridge. The largest piece of steel forged in the United States before 1893 was created with pure entertainment in mind: it became the 46-ton axle of the celebrated Ferris wheel at the 1893 world's fair, which lifted 1.5 million riders to vistas far above Chicago. Other innovations reshaped the geographic landscape. Minneapolis flour-milling corporations developed steel rollers to facilitate large-scale milling; thus, they could use spring wheat, previously too hard-kernelled for efficient milling. Great swaths of Minnesota, the Dakotas, and Montana, whose climate permitted the cultivation of only spring wheat, came open to farming.

The post–Civil War surge of innovation sent so many applications and models to the U.S. Patent Office, in fact, that it ran out of space to store them all. Corporations held a large and growing percentage of these patents, but it was not their engineers and chemists who captured the public imagination. Instead, the popular heroes of American technology were independent inventors such as the Scottish immigrant Alexander Graham Bell, who won the race to transmit human voices by wire and introduced the telephone in 1876. A host of other inventors, mostly forgotten today, perpetuated the hope that any clever person could get a patent and strike it rich. Towering above the rest was Thomas Alva Edison, whose New Jersey laboratory produced an astonishing series of new products between the late 1860s and the early twentieth century. Starting off as a humble telegraph worker in the Midwest, Edison moved east at age twenty-one and presented a new telegraph design that enabled operators to send multiple messages at the same time. He went on to produce stock tickers, the phonograph, the incandescent light bulb, improved electric generators, storage batteries, motion picture technology, and even Portland cement. Edison was the consummate entrepreneur, skilled at improving others' ideas and pitching them in the marketplace. He chose to concentrate on electric light, for example, because he knew it would make money, based on his study of the enormously profitable gaslight industry. Edison shrewdly demonstrated his new product by lighting up the headquarters of J. P. Morgan and the adjacent *New York Times* building, ensuring both publicity and investor attention.

In the 1880s Edison became embroiled in a controversy with his corporate challenger, George Westinghouse, who advocated alternating current (AC) rather than Edison's direct current (DC). Their furious public relations battle revealed some of the pitfalls of corporate science, and it tarnished both inventors' reputations. Westinghouse, with the aid of the Croatian-born physicist Nikola Tesla, made false claims about the safety of his AC system, asserting that the electricity entering users' homes would be entirely harmless. Meanwhile, in his effort to discredit AC, Edison electrocuted animals in his laboratory and encouraged New York State to test the electric chair on AC current in 1889, hoping it would not work. The first execution by electric chair was, in fact, terribly botched, but Edison lost the long-term battle. His financial backers saw alternating current as the better bet and wrested control of his company from him. By 1892 Edison's leading enterprise was no longer Edison General Electric but simply General Electric, led by J. P. Morgan. While Americans continued to celebrate Edison as the "Wizard of Menlo Park," for many years the embittered inventor never set foot inside a GE building. In scientific innovation, as in mining and other sectors of the U.S. economy, pioneers were often not the ones who reaped the big rewards.

THE PROMISE OF MEDICINE

With the rapid and dramatic pace of scientific and technological change, America became a nation of scientific enthusiasts. In the 1880s *Popular Science Monthly* and *Science* joined the antebellum journal *Scientific American* as laymen's magazines. By the 1890s curious Americans could attend chautauqua lectures given by a Scottish Darwinist and subscribe to *National Geographic*, whose depiction of foreign cultures blended scientific expertise with photographs of bare-breasted women, studied by generations of schoolchildren in a somewhat different spirit than the editors intended. The mania for science extended in many directions, including popular interest in scientific methods of solving crimes. Anna Katherine Green's *The Leavenworth Case*, considered by many to be the first American detective novel, became a national bestseller in 1878 and spawned dozens of imitations. More urgent was the real crime of Charles Guiteau, who assassinated President James Garfield in 1881. In a landmark trial Guiteau's lawyers argued that he was insane (a judgment historians have upheld). Both the prosecution and defense brought in batteries of specialists, introducing the public to the nascent fields of neurology and psychology. Evidence of Guiteau's insanity did not save him from being hanged, but it persuaded many Americans that science could provide answers to mental illness in an era when asylums merely served as custodians for the insane rather than offering a cure.

At the time Guiteau was hanged, philosopher William James was at work on his revolutionary textbook *The Principles of Psychology*. Psychology had been taught for decades in American colleges and universities, but it had gone by the name of *mental philosophy* and included a broad array of spiritual and philosophical concerns. James laid the foundation for modern experimental psychology, or, as he called it, a "natural science of the mind." James's followers took up this direction so strongly that for two generations they denied the title of psychology to any nonlaboratory, nonexperimental study. James's own views were more complex, but the publication of his *Principles* clearly marked the emergence of American psychology in modern form. Among other things, James suggested that biological processes might trigger emotions rather than the other way around. He also raised questions about the nature of consciousness. He observed that thought flows like a continuous river—a "stream of thought, of consciousness, or of subjective life." This insight influenced modernist thinkers and fiction writers.

In medicine the first striking development of the late nineteenth century was the rise of antisepsis. Understanding for the first time the role of bacteria in postsurgical infection, based on the discoveries of the British surgeon Joseph Lister, American doctors began to use sterilized bandages and tools. Surgeons, their craft boosted by more effective anesthesia, began to work in sterile antiseptic conditions. The results were dramatic: more and more patients survived surgery, and doctors, rather than seeing surgery as a last-ditch defense, began confidently recommending operations ranging from appendectomies to radical mastectomies for breast cancer. By 1900 the surgeons in one leading Philadelphia hospital were performing more operations in a single year than they had ventured in the entire first half of the century. Urban hospitals attracted well-to-do clients by advertising their modern innovations, overturning the older (once accurate) view that a hospital stay was practically a death sentence. By 1903 the new Memorial Hospital in Richmond, Virginia, advertised talented doctors and sterilized linens. "*All germs are destroyed*," its ads assured potential clients, "by the best and most scientific means."

Building on earlier developments in microscopy and chemistry, researchers also applied germ theory to specific ailments. The French researcher Louis Pasteur developed a treatment for rabies and a technique to kill germs in milk, called pasteurization in his honor. Germany's Robert Koch identified the cause of anthrax in 1876 and began research on tuberculosis, work that the German scientist Emil Behring and his Japanese colleague Shibasaburo Kitasato soon refined. A few related discoveries were made in the United States: the researcher Theobold Smith, for example, proved that insects could play a role in disease transmission when he identified ticks as the source of Texas cattle fever. But before 1900, the vast majority of medical discoveries emerged from Britain, Germany, and France.

These advances were greeted with great enthusiasm in the United States. Newspapers trumpeted Pasteur's successful treatment of rabies, a much-feared and fatal disease contracted from animal bites. In 1885 three children from Newark, New Jersey, made headline news for several months after a stray dog bit them. Through a massive campaign led by a New York newspaper, funds were raised to rush the children to Pasteur's clinic in Paris, where he injected an antitoxin and probably saved their lives. Equally celebrated was Robert Koch's 1890 announcement that he had found a cure for the dreaded tuberculosis, a claim that turned out to be premature, as well as 1894 trials of a diphtheria antitoxin. American doctors were soon using the latter, and the *New York Herald* led a high-profile movement to distribute the drug free to at-risk children in urban slums.

The desire for better health was pressing because every nineteenth-century American lived in the shadow of death. Epidemics of cholera had abated by the post–Civil War era, but yellow fever and typhoid continued to wreak periodic devastation, especially in the South. Mary Harris Jones, living in Memphis, lost her husband and all four children to yellow fever in 1867. "All around my house," she recalled, "I could hear weeping and the cries of delirium. . . . I sat alone through nights of grief. No one came to me. No one could. Other houses were as stricken as mine." A decade later in the same city, in a yellow fever outbreak that took 10,000 lives, the future antilynching investigator Ida B. Wells lost both her parents. She received the news while staying with her grandmother in Holly Springs, Mississippi, and immediately boarded a freight train headed to Memphis. Amid disease and quarantine she remembered that "no passenger trains were running or needed. The caboose in which I rode was draped in black for two previous conductors who had fallen victim." By the time Wells reached home her infant brother had also died, and she found two of her younger sisters ill. At the age of sixteen, Wells became sole caretaker for her five surviving siblings.

Among nonepidemic diseases the greatest scourge was tuberculosis, responsible for perhaps one of every five deaths in America. Millions of parents also agonized over the risk of measles, mumps, whooping cough, scarlet fever, diphtheria, and other diseases that struck young children with fatal force. No parent could rest when a child was ill. Typical were the meditations of Laura Hamilton Murray, a young African-American mother living outside Washington, D.C. "Baby sick today, poor little fellow," she wrote of her son Raymond. "I wonder if we will raise him. There is something that I think that

Family of Leonardo and Librada Romero mourning the death of a small child at a funeral in Tucson, Arizona, 21 April 1890.
Source: Arizona Historical Society/Tucson, AHS #64313.

a Christian should not think." Few parents saw all their children reach adulthood, and the number of young children who lost a parent was also high.

Among poor and minority populations, death rates were staggering for both children and adults. American Indians suffered most severely, as the viral and bacteriological assault that had begun in the sixteenth century entered its closing phase. But disease was far more than an Indian problem. In 1900 Atlanta's board of health reported that the death rate among the city's black population was 69 percent higher than that of whites and that almost *half* of black children born in the city died before their first birthday. The toll in urban orphanages was horrifying. Mortality rates at New York's public infant orphanages ranged somewhere between 60 and 75 percent, largely from diarrhea caused by contaminated milk. An alternative hospital for abandoned babies, run by the Catholic Sisters of Charity, won nationwide praise for reducing mortality to 19 percent. The sisters did so largely by providing a friendly atmosphere to new mothers, whom they encouraged to stay and nurse their own babies—and others if they could—through the perilous first months of life.

Yet though disease struck the poor with greatest ferocity, wealth and status offered no guarantees of protection. On a single day in 1884 young Theodore Roosevelt lost both his twenty-two-year-old wife Alice to a postchildbirth kidney ailment and his mother to typhoid fever. First Lady Caroline Harrison died of tuberculosis while living in the White House. "Baby Ruth," the adored

Mrs. Dinsmore's Cough and Croup Balsam. Lithograph trade card, circa 1885. Patent medicine manufacturers, largely unregulated by government in the nineteenth century, held out hope for desperate parents. Many of their products contained alcohol and opiates.
Source: Warshaw Collection of Business Americana, Museum of American History, Smithsonian Institution, Washington, DC.

daughter of President Grover Cleveland and his wife Frances, died of the same illness at age eleven. Her mother was so distraught that she stopped eating, and friends feared she would die. The famous *McGuffey Readers*, which sold more than a million copies a year, included a reading about the death of a four-year-old boy and acknowledged children's fear, upon looking at the record of deaths in the family Bible, that "your own name may soon be there." Almost any parent who visited a lovingly tended Mexican cemetery in the Southwest would have identified with the toys and handcrafted cradles left on tiny graves, along with crosses bearing the words *Bebita Mia* (my baby).

Even access to the best doctors often did not help. One of the nation's first female medical researchers, Dr. Mary Putnam Jacobi, lost her seven-year-old son to diphtheria. Cleofas Jaramillo, an elite young wife in New Mexico, went to Denver's finest hospital to give birth to her first child under the care of a famous obstetrician. But the baby's bladder function was blocked; in attempting to fix the problem the specialist cut a blood vessel, and the five-day-old boy bled to death. Jaramillo came to believe afterward that she should have gone to the old-fashioned *medica* in her community, who cured such problems with traditional remedies. So Jaramillo's second child was born with the help of a Hispanic nurse at a local New Mexico hospital. This time all went well, but at fifteen months the little girl died of cholera infantum (bacterial diarrhea), following eighteen days in which her mother prayed by her crib night and day. The second baby's death, her mother wrote, "tore her out of our hearts." Cleofas's husband died soon afterward of yet another illness, and she was left both widowed and childless.

Such tragedies had plagued humans for thousands of years, and physicians could do little but make patients comfortable and counsel the grief-stricken to accept God's will. But by the 1890s Americans could see that some diseases, such as cholera, were on the wane. At the same time the press hailed advances in antiseptic surgery, and physicians began to use new diagnostic tools such as stethoscopes, thermometers, and blood pressure tests that bolstered patient confidence. In addition, well before antibiotics arrived many improvements were won through better sanitation measures and public education. "The old superstitions which connected unusual sickness with the wrath of offended Deity have faded in the light of science," declared one Michigan medical professor. "The 'mysterious providences' about which we have heard so much are resolving themselves into 'defective drainage,' 'sewage contamination,' [and] 'unwholesome food.'"

New knowledge of such causes of disease led to enthusiastic mass campaigns to improve public health. During the Civil War the work of the U.S. Sanitary Commission had pointed in this direction, and with a sweeping initiative to provide clean water in the 1870s, Massachusetts demonstrated that it could eradicate typhoid fever. Other cities and states began to follow suit. Housekeepers learned to boil milk and water to combat diphtheria and other infant diseases. Urban environmentalists tackled the threat of dirt and waste. Female volunteers and professional nurses undertook the bulk of such work. In New Orleans, for example, male scientists led by Dr. Walter Reed curtailed the city's last yellow fever outbreak in 1905, but the underpinning of their achievement was an 1899 campaign by members of the New Orleans Woman's Drainage and Sewerage League, who did the unglamorous work of collecting taxpayer signatures and funding bonds for a better drainage system.

By 1904 the National Tuberculosis Association had mobilized a nationwide network of volunteers for a tuberculosis (TB) prevention campaign. The first disease-specific effort, it provided the model for an array of later campaigns against diseases such as cancer, diabetes, and AIDS. Since germ theory was still poorly understood, any speck of dirt came to be suspected of harboring disease, and TB educators urged housekeepers to strive for almost surgical cleanliness. The last decade of the century thus marked a shift toward more spare and simple interiors, inspired by a rejection of unhealthy dust on heavy drapes and carpets (as well as all those collections of stuffed birds). Carpets and wooden cabinetry had been the style in bathrooms, but by the 1890s sanitary educators promoted glistening germ-free surfaces and scrubbable tile floors. In children's nurseries and kitchens hardwood floors and fresh paint replaced carpets and brocaded wallpaper. "Scientific hygiene" also influenced personal grooming. Shorter skirts for women were justified as a health measure, since long skirts gathered dirt, and by 1903 *Harper's Weekly* commented on the demise of the male beard in the years since TB had been ruled "not hereditary but infectious." A clean-shaven face, unusual in the nineteenth century, became the middle-class norm.

Public health measures had their ironies and complications, including the circulation of myths such as the idea that germs lingered forever on a sick child's toys. One of the most successful projects of the Woman's Christian Temperance Union (WCTU) was its campaign for Scientific Temperance Instruction, which promoted a long list of dubious "facts." Mandated in every state by 1901, Scientific Temperance probably reached half of all schoolchildren with textbooks directly endorsed by the WCTU. The authors claimed alcohol was a poison whose use, even in small amounts, destroyed the liver, brain, skin, eyes, and bones. Alarming charts and sketches showed the alleged toll on the body of even one glass of wine per day. By the 1890s Scientific Temperance had provoked major controversies in the emerging fields of chemistry, physiology, psychiatry, and clinical medicine. WCTU leaders shrewdly quoted European allies who hinted that American research was not on the cutting edge. Opponents of the program insisted the reverse. "Let us not palm off on innocent minds," wrote one outraged doctor, "pseudo-chemistry and inaccurate physiology." Nonetheless, Scientific Temperance Instruction endured in many schools until after World War I.

Among the saddest unintended consequences of public health campaigns was a new epidemic. In the 1890s polio emerged suddenly as a dreaded childhood disease. Unbeknownst to people at the time, children had traditionally been exposed to polio virus in infancy when they were biologically equipped to combat it. Now, with more hygienic water supplies, the virus reached children at a later age and found them vulnerable. Polio devastated families for a half-century before researchers found an effective vaccine. Even setting aside this tragedy, it must be noted that Americans' enthusiasm for medical advancements outran immediate results. Infant mortality rates did not begin to drop significantly until after 1900. In fact, as new hardships and urban concentration bred disease, the average man born during or after the Civil War could actually expect a lifespan ten years *shorter* than that of a free American man born a century earlier—forty-five to fifty-five years, rather than fifty-five to sixty-five.

At the same time, sweeping advances in science led to arrogance and overconfidence. "If the cause of degradation and ignorance, of poverty, of contagious disease, or of any of the miseries which make a nation wretched, can be pointed out by scientific methods," declared one researcher, "then it is the stern duty of science to step in." But scientists' recommendations were rarely as objective as they hoped. Growing support for "scientific racial hygiene" was a notorious example. As early as 1875 Richard Dugdale's *The Jukes* proposed that crime and alcoholism ran in families, which by the turn of the century was widely interpreted as meaning that heredity caused most social problems. Legislators were already proposing laws that forbade alcoholics to marry. In 1899 a state asylum in Indiana began sterilizing "mental defectives" for the good of society, a practice later upheld by the courts. By the 1920s half the states were experimenting with forced sterilization of those deemed unfit to reproduce.

The treatment of venereal disease showed how racial prejudices informed and could be reinforced by medicine. Many southern whites believed venereal disease was a "Negro problem"; when infected with such diseases, white men (and sometimes women) avoided stigma by seeking treatment from black physicians, who they assumed had expertise in the field. White doctors thus saw relatively few cases of syphilis and gonorrhea, while some African-American doctors built lucrative practices treating them. The fact that cases were largely hidden from the view of whites reinforced myths about who suffered from these diseases. Meanwhile, a notorious case of racialized decision making occurred in San Francisco in 1900, when bubonic plague was discovered in Chinatown. City police and health authorities decided to quarantine the area, but they first went through the neighborhood and urged all non-Chinese to leave. A federal health inspector, working at a bacteriological laboratory in the city, claimed Asians were vulnerable to the plague because they ate too much rice. His antiplague measures, including turning Asian homes and businesses upside down in a mass disinfection campaign, proved not to work. He then proposed forcible experimental inoculations of every Asian person in San Francisco. Attorneys for a coalition of Chinese organizations took the matter to court and were vindicated. It took health authorities four more years to fully eradicate the disease in the city by focusing on the rats that carried the plague to Asians and non-Asians alike.

Medicine was not the only branch of science freighted with prejudice. After 1898, when the Weather Bureau set up operations in U.S.-occupied Cuba, its officers resented competition from local forecasters who were Catholic priests at Havana's Belen Observatory. The priests had developed a series of excellent forecasting techniques over the previous thirty years, but to professionally trained Weather Bureau officials they were amateur "cranks"—and even worse, excitable Hispanics who damaged business confidence by predicting too many hurricanes. To the outrage of Cubans, the bureau banned Belen forecasts from being transmitted over the U.S.-controlled telegraph wires. The result was far more damaging to Americans than to Cubans. In 1900 Belen forecasters accurately described the scope and path of a rising hurricane, which Weather Bureau experts dismissed as a light tropical storm that would head for the Atlantic. The hurricane, the deadliest ever to hit the United States, crossed the Gulf of Mexico and obliterated the city of Galveston, Texas. Survivors buried the uncounted dead—somewhere between 6,000 and 10,000—in huge pyres on the streets of the wrecked downtown. Galveston never regained its position as a leading Gulf port.

PROGRESS OR APOCALYPSE?

Scientists, then, were hardly free of the larger prejudices of their culture, and their inquiries were shaped by the economic, social, and political contexts in which they worked. We can imagine late nineteenth-century American science as located in the middle of a square, pressured on four sides and exercising its own influence in those four directions. On one side were widely held prejudices about race, ethnicity, and gender. On another was the profound power of religious faith, especially Protestant Christianity. On the third side was the voracious economy of corporate capitalism, whose private for-profit laboratories became a key venue in which careers were made and scientific questions asked (or not asked). On the fourth side was government, which affected science through funding provided by the U.S. Geological Survey, agricultural experiment stations, and the new land-grant universities. Connections were already beginning to emerge between these last two sides. After England began to produce steel-hulled naval vessels in the 1870s, the race was on for armor that could resist bombardment. The American inventor August Harvey solved the problem in 1890, and in the next decade Andrew Carnegie's Homestead mill retooled to create nickel-plated "harveyized" steel in open-hearth furnaces. Carnegie's main customer for this steel was the U.S. Navy.

Science thus offered immense hope of progress, but it was also enmeshed in the dangers and problems of the society that produced it, and some observers wondered, in light of this, whose interests science was going to serve. In the emerging genre of science fiction, inspired by European pioneers such as Jules Verne and H. G. Wells, American writers imagined every kind of future luxury and marvel, from time travel to the construction of vast underwater cities. King Camp Gillette, soon to be a famous manufacturer of razors, proposed in one book that future Americans would live in a single metropolis of sixty million people, powered by Niagara Falls, while the rest of the country became a vast parkland. Popular dime novels such as *Edison's Conquest of Mars*, by Garrett Serviss, offered spectacular visions of the triumphs of American ingenuity. The conservative writer Anna Bowman Dodd, predicting the ruin of the world by women's liberation, nonetheless took time to describe the technological marvels she envisioned for 2050 AD, such as an electric pneumatic tube that carried passengers under the Atlantic at 300 miles an hour while they enjoyed saunas and Turkish baths along the way. Edward Bellamy, in his famous and influential *Looking Backward: 2000–1887*, proposed that large corporations would evolve peacefully into a public system of ownership, labor, and distribution.

Yet an equal number of science fiction writers emphasized the dark side of technological progress. Cosmic disasters figured largely in the era's imaginative fiction—speaking, perhaps, to the disturbing links between science and the destruction wrought by the new corporate order. Popular novels featured descriptions of comets and meteors destroying large portions of the planet; in one novel a giant earthquake released poisonous clouds of gas from beneath the earth's crust. In *Caesar's Column*, a science fiction protest novel, the Minnesota Populist Ignatius Donnelly envisioned a future America of cruel aristocrats and "great, dark, writhing masses"—an authoritarian hell on earth.

Bleakest of all, perhaps, was Mark Twain's 1889 book *A Connecticut Yankee in King Arthur's Court*, which was one of the first American novels to feature time travel. Twain's Yankee was Hank Morgan, a superintendent at the Colt firearms factory who found himself accidentally whisked back to sixth-century England. There he became known as The Boss and won almost unlimited power through his shrewd negotiations and technological know-how. Twain used the book to satirize monarchy and organized religion, the cult of Arthurian chivalry, and nineteenth-century Americans' belief in progress and enlightenment. In doing so he managed to offend an array of readers on both sides of the Atlantic. "A book that tries to deface our moral and literary currency by bruising and soiling the image of KING ARTHUR," huffed a British reviewer, "is a very unworthy production of the great humourist's pen." "A tiresome travesty," complained an American writer, who concluded despite obvious evidence to the contrary that Twain was seeking to glorify the United States. More perceptive critics saw that the novel's brilliance lay in its suggestion that industrial technology and militarism were wreaking as much havoc on modern America as Hank Morgan did on King Arthur's England. One reviewer called the book "another and very instructive sort of *Looking Backward*."

If so, *Connecticut Yankee* had a far bleaker ending than Edward Bellamy's utopian tract. In Twain's climactic passage, which a critic has called "one of the most distressing passages in American literature," Hank Morgan kills 25,000 of King Arthur's knights in an apocalyptic battle. Many die in an artificial flood engineered by the vengeful Yankee. Others are burned alive in a great explosion of dynamite. ("As to destruction of life, it was amazing," Morgan comments on this event. "Of course we could not *count* the dead, because they did not exist as individuals, but merely as homogeneous protoplasm, with alloys of iron and buttons.") The rest of the knights, advancing across a field at night, walk into a series of Yankee-designed electric fences. "Our current was so tremendous," Morgan observes, "that it killed before the victim could cry out. . . . One terrible thing about this was the absence of human voices; there were no cheers, no war cries." As the last contingent of knights crosses between the wires, Morgan flips a switch and electrocutes them all. His Gatling gun, an early form of machine gun, mows down the few survivors.

In the same year that *Connecticut Yankee* was published, a catastrophic flood in Johnstown, Pennsylvania, was brought on by the failure of a dam at an elite country club in the nearby hills. (The wealthy Pittsburgh industrialists who owned the property were never held liable.) The same year, 1889, witnessed America's first botched execution by electric chair. Twain's point about the dark uses of science and power seemed even more prescient with the arrival of the twentieth century. Little more than a decade after 1889, wars around the globe were being waged with Gatling guns manufactured in Morgan's hometown of Hartford, Connecticut, as well as barbed wire concentration camps, steel battleships, and dynamite and other new explosives. The gravity of these developments perhaps explains the tone that so unsettled Twain's contemporaries. "I have always preached," Twain remarked later in life. "If the humor came of its own accord and uninvited I have allowed it a place in my sermon, but I was not writing the sermon for the sake of the humor." The final pages of *Connecticut Yankee* were, in fact, a sermon about the ominous bent of modern technology, and the message was grim. Hank Morgan's fatal flaw was not his scientific knowledge, but the fact that he wielded it with serene confidence in his own goodness and wisdom.

FOR FURTHER READING

On the dinosaur hunts see David R. Wallace, *The Bonehunters' Revenge* (Boston, 1999); John McPhee writes about "deep time" in *Annals of the Former World* (New York, 1998). On scientific thought more generally see Paul F. Boller, Jr., "New Men and New Ideas," in H. Wayne Morgan, *The Gilded Age* (Syracuse, NY, 1963), pp. 221–244, Richard Hofstadter, *Social Darwinism in American Thought*, 2nd ed. (New York, 1955), and on pragmatism, Louis Menand, *The Metaphysical Club* (New York, 2001). Two sources that proved immensely useful in shaping this chapter are Peter J. Bowler, *The Eclipse of Darwinism* (Baltimore, 1983), and Steven Conn, *Museums and American Cultural Life* (Chicago, 1988).

On parlor collections see Katherine C. Grier, "The Decline of the Memory Palace," in Jessica H. Foy and Thomas J. Schlereth, *American Home Life, 1880–1930* (Knoxville, TN, 1992), pp. 49–74. On grave-robbing in the West see David H. Thomas's *Skull Wars* (New York, 2000), and on anthropology in the Near East, Bruce Kuklick's fascinating study, *Puritans in Babylon* (Princeton, NJ, 1996). Thomas R. Trautmann, *Lewis Henry Morgan and the Invention of Kinship* (Berkeley, CA, 1987), is helpful on this leading anthropologist. On the world's fairs see Norman Bolotin and Christine Laing, *The World's Columbian Exposition* (Urbana, IL, 2002), Robert W. Rydell, *All the World's a Fair* (Chicago, 1984), and Alan Trachtenberg, *Incorporating America* (New York, 1982); on the "ethnologies" marketed by Buffalo Bill and Barnum and Bailey see Janet M. Davis, *The Circus Age*, cited in Chapter 4.

On technology and business see Nathan Rosenberg's thorough article, "The Commercial Exploitation of Science by American Industry," in *The Uneasy Alliance*, edited by Kim B. Clark, Robert H. Hayes, and Christopher Lorenz (Boston, MA, 1985), pp. 19–51, and on corporate laboratories, David F. Noble, *America By Design* (New York, 1977). Two excellent introductions to famous inventors are Theresa M. Collins and Lisa Gitelman, *Thomas Edison and Modern America* (Boston, 2002), and on the battle between Edison and Westinghouse, Jill Jonnes, *Empires of Light* (New York, 2003).

On mental illness see Charles E. Rosenberg's *The Trial of the Assassin Guiteau* (Chicago, 1968), Sarah C. Sitton, *Life at the Texas State Lunatic Asylum, 1857–1997*

(College Station, TX, 1999), and Gerald N. Grob, *The State and the Mentally Ill* (Chapel Hill, NC, 1966). On medicine more broadly see W. F. Bynum, *Science and the Practice of Medicine in the Nineteenth Century* (Cambridge, 1994), and Paul Starr, *The Social Transformation of American Medicine* (New York, 1982); on hospitals I have drawn on Charles E. Rosenberg, *The Care of Strangers* (New York, 1987). For a lively history of anti-TB campaigns see Nancy Tomes, *The Gospel of Germs* (Cambridge, MA, 1998). On popular reception of medical advancements see also two articles by Bert Hansen, "America's First Medical Breakthrough," *American Historical Review* 103 (1998): 373–418, and "New Images of a New Medicine," *Bulletin of the History of Medicine* 73.4 (1999): 629–678.

On demographics see Michael Haines, "Life Expectancy," in *The Oxford Companion to United States History* (New York, 2001), pp. 444–447. Scientific temperance education is treated in Jonathan Zimmerman, *Distilling Democracy* (Lawrence, KS, 1999). On racial prejudice in medicine see Donald K. Pickens, *Eugenics and the Progressives* (Nashville, TN, 1968), as well as Leon F. Litwack's *Trouble in Mind* and Charles J. McClain's *In Search of Equality* both cited earlier. On the Galveston disaster see Erik Larson, *Isaac's Storm* (New York, 1999). For a detailed look at the emerging military-industrial complex see B. Franklin Cooling, *Gray Steel and Blue Water Navy* (Hamden, CT, 1979), on Johnstown, David G. McCullough, *The Johnstown Flood* (New York, 1968), and on science fiction Dolores Hayden, *The Grand Domestic Revolution* (Cambridge, MA, 1981). For helpful guides to *Connecticut Yankee* see the books on Twain by Justin Kaplan and Bryant Morey French, cited in the introduction. The quotation about the "distressing passages" at the novel's end, from Henry Nash Smith, is in Kaplan's *Mark Twain and His World*, p. 144.

CHAPTER 8

Faith

The great task of modern times [is] to solve, on the basis of
justice and righteousness, the problems presented by the contrasts and evils of the present organization of society.
—RABBI EMIL G. HIRSCH, CHICAGO

In September 1893 an unprecedented meeting took place on the grounds of
the Columbian Exposition in Chicago. The World's Parliament of Religions
attempted to bring representatives from every "great faith" into conversation
with one another. In attendance were not only delegates from many Protestant
denominations, Roman Catholics, and Jews, but also Muslims, Hindus,
Confucians, Jainists, Zoroastrians, and Buddhists from around the globe.
Scholars lectured on comparative world religions, while reformers touched on
such topics as "Human Brotherhood" and "The Role of Spiritual Matters in
Human Progress." One organizer declared in the closing session that "what
men deemed impossible, God has finally wrought. The religions of the world
. . . have conferred together on the vital questions of life and immortality in a
frank and friendly spirit, and now they part in peace, with many warm expressions of mutual affection and respect."

The World's Parliament was not the first interfaith conversation in the
United States, much less in the world. The rise of ecumenical groups such as
the Sunday school movement and the Young Men's Christian Association
(YMCA) had already strengthened ties among different Protestant denominations, as had cooperative efforts in foreign missions. Some liberal Protestants,
Catholics, and Jews were already working together in the cause of social
reform. More radically, followers of Theosophy had been trying for a decade
to reconcile Christian and Buddhist principles into a universal faith. They had
presented this program to several Asian Buddhist leaders who were, themselves, responding to the threat of Christian missions with tentative efforts at
cooperation. Anagarika Dharmapala of Ceylon, a prominent delegate to the

World's Parliament in Chicago, was a friend of the elite Bostonian Henry Olcott, who some years earlier had moved to Ceylon (now Sri Lanka) to study Buddhism and promote Theosophy.

Such delegates came to Chicago, in part, to offer pointed critiques of Western imperialism. A number of Hindu and Buddhist speakers described Christian missionaries as arrogant and bigoted. Pung Kwang Yu, a Chinese representative, denounced the entanglement of foreign missions with Western economic and political designs. Jesus, he observed sharply, had not advised his followers to league themselves with "the foreign masters that were exercising supreme political control over his own country at the time." Even Asians who accepted Christianity warned against chauvinism. "We do not want the Christianity of England nor the Christianity of America," declared the Japanese Protestant Nobuta Kishimoto. "We want the Christianity of Japan." An Armenian Protestant, Herant Kiretchijian, likewise identified himself with "the Orient" and informed Westerners that "you have unwittingly called together a council of your creditors. . . . We have given you science, philosophy, theology, music and poetry, and have made history for you at tremendous expense. . . . With that rich capital you have amassed a stupendous fortune, so that your assets hide away from your eyes your liabilities."

These sophisticated messages shocked many Americans who had come to the World's Parliament to meet and convert the heathen. "The people expected pagans. And pagans, they thought, were ignorant and impotent of mind," wrote one Methodist. "The Parliament was a stunning revelation." Protestants found to their dismay, in fact, that others had come to Chicago to convert *them*. One delegate, a former U.S. diplomat named Mohammed Webb who had converted to Islam in Turkey, created a stir by announcing the foundation of a Muslim mission in New York City. The Hindu Swami Vivekananda undertook a national lecture tour after the Parliament ended, and his followers created the American Vedanta Society. After hearing a speech by the charismatic Anagarika Dharmapala, a journalist reported that "one trembled to know that such a figure stood at the head of the movement to consolidate all the disciples of Buddha and 'spread the light of Asia' throughout the civilized world."

Christians, in the meantime, negotiated painful differences among themselves. One Protestant speaker dismissed Catholicism as an "ethnic faith" and its rites as mere superstition. Catholic spokesmen fired back, deploring Protestant laxity and "the shame and mischief of the divorce evil." Conflict surfaced within religious groups as well as among them: Jewish women were outraged when rabbis excluded them from the speaker's platform, and in response they organized a separate Jewish Women's Congress that led to the foundation of the National Council of Jewish Women. At the same time, the Parliament's very existence provoked angry responses from conservatives of all faiths. Sultan Abdul Hamid II refused to allow anyone from the Ottoman Empire to participate, and Islam was thus poorly represented. So was the Church of England, after the archbishop of Canterbury condemned the idea of meeting with non-Christians in a spirit of mutual inquiry. The Presbyterian Church of the USA declined to participate, while one Protestant missionary wrote from Hong Kong to accuse conference organizers of planning "treason against Christ." A U.S. Catholic bishop who attended the Parliament endured fierce criticism for allegedly violating the principle of *communicatio in sacris*, which forbade Catholics from participating in any non-Catholic service.

At the same time, ironically, the Parliament planners overlooked some of the most creative religious movements emerging in the United States. The vibrant African-American Protestant denominations were grossly underrepresented. No delegates spoke from the Mormon church, the Holiness movement, or the growing ranks of Christian Scientists. The Native American peyote faith, taking hold in Indian Territory during the early 1890s, might have been of great interest to scholars of comparative religion, since it blended the use of peyote spirit medicine with hymn singing, prayers to Jesus, and use of eagle feathers. Similarly, the Ghost Dance religion of native peoples greatly interested anthropologists such as James Mooney. Originating with a Paiute shaman, the Ghost Dance was a pan-Indian movement that strove to bring back bison and drive invaders from the land. Though peaceful, its rituals were so frightening and little understood by non-Indians that a tense stand-off between Ghost Dancers and a U.S. cavalry unit at Wounded Knee, just three years before the Parliament, had ended in the massacre of more than 200 Sioux men, women, and children. The Parliament leaders, reflecting prevailing prejudice, found Indian beliefs and practices too alien for inclusion.

Despite its limitations and failings, though, the Parliament of Religions did strengthen a tentative global interfaith dialogue. Well before Americans grasped all the implications of their nation's rising political and economic power, they were debating pluralism, cultural differences, and foreign relations in the arena of religious faith. In doing so they raised fundamental issues that would haunt future American society and politics. Anglo-American Protestants still largely presumed that the United States was a Christian nation and that Christians (especially Protestants) led and spoke for the best interests of their country and even the world. But their provincialism provoked spirited challenges both at home and abroad. Both Mormonism and the dynamic black denominations had arisen to complicate Protestantism. Movements ranging from Theosophy to Christian Science took Christian belief in radical new directions. And the rise of a working class drawn from many continents was changing America's religious landscape. New immigrants included not only hundreds of thousands of Catholics, Greek Orthodox Christians, and eastern European Jews, but also many Asians who were opening Buddhist and Taoist temples in Chinatowns from San Francisco to New York. All these faith were, in turn, being molded and modernized in America.

Thus, the late nineteenth century was an era of immense creativity in American spiritual life. The forces of economic and social change pushed in two broad directions: some people turned toward ecumenical liberalism of the sort pioneered at Chicago, while others, reacting against this trend, turned to evangelical groups and movements, many of which rejected modernity and its implications. It was as if the various institutions of traditional religion sat atop a giant ice floe that was being melted and reshaped by the heat of change. Cracks opened where there had been none before; pieces of ice floated off in new directions. Eventually some of these would drift together into two loose clusters, one fundamentalist and one liberal. The era's intellectual upheavals carried many Americans far beyond the bounds of their childhood faiths. Some, following the tradition of antebellum Transcendentalists such as Ralph Waldo Emerson, began to see God more in the world around them than in a distant heaven, giving birth to modern environmentalism. In all these movements, Americans sought to overcome materialism and social and economic conflict by strengthening the spiritual dimensions of their lives.

GLOBAL MISSIONS

As the protests of Asian delegates in Chicago showed, Protestant foreign missionaries were reaching new heights of ambition in the 1890s. The steamships that facilitated immigration and tourism also carried U.S. missionaries abroad in record numbers, with more than 5,000 serving by the turn of the century. Missionaries could now reach remote sites with relative case, bring extensive supplies, and return regularly to the United States for fundraising tours. They enjoyed vigorous support from the largest grassroots American movement of the era, the Protestant missionary societies, whose combined membership in 1900 totaled more than one million.

Though foreign mission work had decidedly mixed results for "heathens," it offered bracing challenges for Americans who dedicated their energies to it, drawing especially on young people's idealism and desire for adventure and self-testing. Men and women at headquarters prided themselves on efficiency and good communication, publishing magazines such as *The Heathen Woman's Friend* and organizing national fundraising drives and study programs. Missionaries themselves often discovered their calling in emotional revival meetings. Many were swept up in the Student Volunteer Movement, an offshoot of the Young Men's Christian Association (YMCA) that recruited earnest, idealistic college graduates for the mission field, hoping to achieve "the evangelization of the world in this generation." George Campbell and Jennie Wortman, two students at an Illinois college, separately reached the conclusion that they should go into mission work before they met and married. "Oh, how I want to *do* something," Jennie wrote in her diary. With the mission board pressing George to find a wife, the two arranged to meet, conduct a quick courtship, and marry—a not uncommon strategy for women to find their way into overseas service.

A decade later more women went into foreign missions by themselves, as part of a bold expansion of female authority. By 1903 more than 60 percent of foreign Protestant missionaries were women, a number that did not include many missionary wives who assisted unpaid in their husbands' work. Women argued that they were indispensable to the mission project, since uplifting "degraded" women and modeling Christian family life were central goals of the Protestant enterprise. Sarah Goodrich, who went to China as a single female missionary, explained her choice as one of selfless faith: "Sometimes I feel as if a woman could comprehend the Christ, this utter sacrifice of self, as no man can." "Among uncivilized people woman is a slave, nude, filthy, her

TABLE 8.1 Largest religious denominations in the United States, 1895.

Denomination	Estimated number of communicants
Roman Catholic	7,988,322
Methodist Episcopal	2,629,985
Southern Baptist	1,448,570
Methodist Episcopal, South	1,379,928
Colored Baptist	1,343,530
Northern Baptist	985,752
Disciples of Christ	923,663
Presbyterian, North	902,757
Protestant Episcopal	616,843
Congregational	600,000
African Methodist Episcopal	594,776
Lutheran Synodical Conference	479,221

H. K. Carroll, who compiled these statistics, reflected contemporary prejudices when he lumped together as "pagan" all Buddhists, Theosophists, followers of the Ethical Culture movement, and communal utopian societies. He did count, however, 182 Chinese temples and religious organizations.
Source: H. K. Carroll, The Religious Forces of the United States (New York, 1898).

life by a degree above the brute," declared the president of the Congregational Woman's Board of Missions. "Only a woman can teach her purity, delicacy, and the divine art of home-making."

Despite such condescension, many missionaries reacted to the cultures they encountered with a mixture of fascination and respect. Many came to understand the havoc wrought by Western imperialism and commercial interests, and some became openly critical of European and U.S. designs. Those who expected to encounter "barbarism" often came to appreciate the worldviews of people they served. Others shifted in the opposite direction, finding that a custom such as Chinese footbinding turned them into vigorous critics of the societies they hoped to alter. Jean Kenyon Mackenzie, who served as a Presbyterian missionary in West Africa, began her service expressing great sensitivity to African customs, but after a year in the field she wrote home, "Polygamy is terrible. I had too open a mind about it when I came to Africa— and now I have so many sad thoughts of it." Mackenzie came to believe that she had a special mission to comfort African women who suffered "superstition and blame" because they could not bear children. Wielding scientific explanations as well as a Gospel message, Mackenzie wrote, "I am coming to be a kind of doctor to the hearts of childless women."

As Mackenzie's account suggested, foreign missionaries found that medicine and education were among the most enticing offerings they carried with them. Earlier in the century Protestants had emphasized straightforward preaching in foreign lands, without much attempt to shape customs or cultures. Now they recognized that science was a selling point as well as a tool of self-defense, useful to those who were enduring political and economic upheaval. Missionaries thus shaped and fostered modernization, especially by bringing medical training and support for women's rights and female education. Ida Scudder, born in South India, was a granddaughter of American missionaries and daughter of a missionary doctor. She grew up expecting to move to the United States and marry, but local men began asking her to serve as a midwife since her father, as a man, was not permitted to fulfill this role. Ida was untrained in medicine and refused, but her conscience was seared after three women died in childbirth. Ida headed back to the United States for a medical degree from Cornell and then returned to India, where she worked as a traveling doctor for half a century in rural areas around Vellore. Among other achievements, she helped found a hospital, a nursing school, and a women's medical college.

Other missionaries advanced far more dubious projects, sometimes by accident and sometimes by intent. Violence against Protestant missionaries in China provided the chief justification for Western military intervention around the turn of the century, which forced an open door to business interests. By that time the Presbyterian missionary Horace Allen had been a key player in Asian politics for decades. One of the first Protestants to begin work in Korea, Allen had become by the mid-1880s the United States' key diplomat there. Lending his influence to a promodernization faction, Allen also helped Secretary of State James Blaine and the Wall Street firm of Morton Bliss obtain large tracts of Korean real estate and access to fabulously rich gold mines. Allen ended up quite wealthy himself, while his business and diplomatic maneuvers helped leave Korea weak. When the peninsula fell under Japanese control Allen protested bitterly, but partly due to Allen's own actions, Japan's power over Korea was by then a fait accompli.

Home missions, undertaken within the boundaries of the United States, could also have troubling consequences. From Reconstruction onward Christian reform groups such as the Indian Rights Association played major roles in developing federal Indian policy, working to convert native peoples and "kill the Indian to save the man." Women's mission groups throughout the West raised money to convert American Indians, Chinese immigrants, and even Mormons. Such efforts were viewed suspiciously by those being proselytized, but missionaries were not always unwelcome. San Francisco's Presbyterian Mission Home, run by the energetic Donaldina Cameron, became popular with Chinese prostitutes who arranged to escape from brothels and meet Chinese-American husbands-to-be inside the mission's sheltering space, away from employers who sought to hold them in virtual slavery. Cameron, who supervised the home for almost forty years, argued that this validated her work, and she strove to win conversions among those who asked for her aid. At the same time she defended Chinese Americans against what she saw as racist stereotypes in the larger culture. She studied Chinese literature and history, often wore traditional Asian clothing, and worked side by side with Chinese-American "native helpers" such as Ah Tsun Wing and Tien Fu Wu, converts who, like the missionaries, negotiated between the expectations of different worlds.

African Americans found themselves in a very different position than their Anglo Protestant counterparts. Participating in the extraordinary growth of black religious institutions after emancipation, members of the Baptist, African Methodist Episcopal (AME), and other churches focused much of their attention on pressing problems near at hand. Church members helped their communities by providing adult education, aid to the unemployed, and care for children, orphans, and the elderly. Black churches also became vehicles for temperance, racial justice campaigns, and other expressions of African-American identity, so much so that a noted sociologist once described them as "a nation within a nation." Black women carved out key roles in the churches, using Christian respectability as a bridge between themselves and white women interested in reform. As churches became expressions of race pride, they also served as vehicles for drawing a line between the respectable and the unchurched. Mindful of white stereotypes, some black ministers condemned not only gambling and fast living but loud talk, bright clothes, and Sunday baseball games.

Overseas, white Protestant denominations increasingly refused to sponsor black missionaries, even in Africa. At the same time, European colonial governments on that continent discouraged almost all educational projects on the grounds that they might cause unrest, and thus Africa, unlike Asia, saw the creation of very few Christian schools founded by Western donors. In 1899 AME missionaries from the United States were stymied when they undertook an outreach campaign in what is today South Africa. A leader of the project, Bishop Henry McNeal Turner of Georgia, advocated education and collective action for racial justice. His lectures on "The Unity of the Race" frightened British and Boer authorities. AME representatives were denied permits to travel in rural areas and for decades afterward had to offer financial and legal aid from afar.

Foreign missions, then, had the capacity to carry Protestants far beyond their provincial worldview, but at the same time missionary work could reflect and even magnify existing prejudices. Given their cosmopolitan experience it is not surprising that some missionaries offered vocal and enthusiastic support for the World's Parliament of Religions. One minister in southern India, writing to endorse the plan, reported that he and local Brahmins were "continually comparing Christianity with Hinduism" and "having conferences with the representatives of Islam." Criticized by Asian delegates, some Christian missionaries at the Parliament freely acknowledged the shortcomings of European and American policy makers and expressed hope that Christianity might provide colonized peoples with tools to defend their rights. Yet Christian missionaries retained a persistent tone of chauvinism, and those who brought home news of their exploits often reinforced the condescension of American audiences. One speaker at the Parliament, having returned from a trip around the world, attacked Islamic "superstition and bigotry" and dismissed Asia as a "stagnant pool of heathenism." In the worst cases, such as that of Horace Allen in Korea, Protestant missionaries facilitated bold grabs for imperial power and enjoyed the fruits of that power themselves.

ROOTS OF FUNDAMENTALISM AND LIBERALISM

In Harold Frederic's wonderful novel *The Damnation of Theron Ware*, published in 1896, a young Methodist minister named Theron Ware finds himself posted in the imaginary town of Octavius, New York. Reverend Ware is supremely confident in his beliefs, but he has not reckoned on the forces of modernity and pluralism. Theron first meets a Catholic priest who studies anthropology and speaks casually of "this Christ-myth of ours." Then he encounters a doctor who keeps up with the latest scientific research and endorses Darwin's theory of evolution. Last Theron is swept away by the beautiful Celia Madden, a wealthy Catholic girl whose father came to the United States many decades ago as a starving Irish immigrant. Celia is a leisured, free-thinking music lover with the ambition to do what she pleases. Hearing Celia sing and play Chopin, Theron is smitten. He contemplates adultery while becoming ever more cruel and patronizing toward his devoted wife. At the end of the novel, Theron receives an intellectual and spiritual come-uppance. The author leaves him in limbo—no longer satisfied by the old ways, but woefully unsuited to the new.

Through the character of Theron Ware, Harold Frederic explored the forces that were eroding mainstream Protestantism in the last decades of the nineteenth century: materialism, science, and the increasing presence of Catholicism and other competing faiths. But Frederic suggested that new ideas held their power because Protestantism was rotting from the inside. The elders in Theron's church are mean and narrow-minded. They forbid the minister's wife to wear flowers in her bonnet, and they force Theron to pay the parsonage gas bill from his skimpy salary. Meanwhile, two of the elders are profiting from high-interest loans they made to the church. When the congregation hires a professional evangelist for a fundraising campaign, she corrupts Theron far more thoroughly than the priest, the doctor, and Celia do. She tells him he must manipulate people to get what he wants, and her successful revival suggests that her strategy works. Protestantism, in this light, was becoming another venue for marketing and commercial empire building. "You simply *can't* get along," the evangelist tells Theron, "without some of the wisdom of the serpent."

At the time *Theron Ware* appeared, Protestants faced an array of profound challenges. Old denominational barriers were weakening, and conflicting attitudes toward modernity were pushing Protestants down divergent paths. By 1900 the rough outlines of two emerging camps were already discernable. Fundamentalists, though they did not yet go by that name, denounced modern secularism and defended the literal truth of the Bible, while adopting new technologies and marketing techniques that helped them build Gospel empires. Liberal Protestants, on the other hand, made common cause with one another and occasionally with Jews and Catholics in the work of the Social Gospel, a movement to address what the theologian Walter Rauschenbusch would call the era's "social crisis." They challenged Americans to leave their comfortable Sunday pews and take their faith into the world, fighting the poverty, degradation, and despair that industrialization had wrought.

The United States in these years was evangelized as well as evangelizing. That fact was dramatically illustrated one May afternoon in 1880 when eight Englishmen and Englishwomen marched off a steamship in New York and re-enacted Columbus's discovery of America. To the bewilderment of onlookers, they hoisted a "Blood and Fire" flag and, on behalf of the Salvation Army, claimed the United States in the name of God. It was the first wave of an invasion launched by William and Evangeline Booth, founders of the Salvation Army in England. The army's first American efforts met ridicule (especially when a banner informed New Yorkers by mistake that the army would "Attract the Kingdom of the Devil" rather than "Attack" it). But within a decade, Salvation Army street ministers and rescue workers had become a familiar sight across the United States.

The Salvation Army focused on action—saving souls for Christ. Its founders were not so much theological innovators as brilliant publicists who adopted modern advertising and mass marketing to serve their cause. "ATTRACT ATTENTION," advised William Booth, an early proponent of the idea that there is no such thing as bad publicity. "If the people are in danger of the damnation of Hell, and asleep in the danger, awaken them," he wrote. Salvationists alerted bystanders through music, bell-ringing, pageants, dramatic readings, and personal testimony. Many were drawn from the working class or had once been "down and out," and they took their movement to people they thought needed it most. Salvation Army bands played and preached on the streets and at parks where people gathered to relax. Most of all, they invaded slums and skid rows to offer food and shelter to the destitute. Advancing no systemic critique of poverty and avoiding most political issues (though they did denounce lynching in 1895), Salvation Army leaders offered, instead, "heart religion" and direct material aid.

Paralleling developments in England, the Salvation Army's American branch evolved into a sophisticated social welfare agency with conversion as its core goal. In 1891 it opened the New York Lighthouse, a shelter for men in Greenwich Village. Those who needed a bed could stay for 7¢ a night, and the penniless could sweep or chop wood to cover the fee. Unlike most charitable agencies, the Salvation Army made no judgments about a person's past or whether he or she "deserved" aid, a strategy crucial to its success. At the height of the severe depression of the 1890s the New York branch housed as many as 3,000 homeless men per night, as well as providing day care for working mothers and a "rescue home" for women who wanted to stop working as prostitutes. Aggressive evangelical campaigns could be dangerous, and workers who preached in rough neighborhoods were frequently beaten up and sometimes even killed. Like foreign mission work, though, the Salvation Army held out great spiritual rewards.

The Salvation Army succeeded in part because of its savvy tactics and in part because it captured the emerging priorities of a diverse array of Protestants. Its founders emphasized emotional passion and individual salvation, hallmarks of emerging fundamentalism, but like proponents of the Social Gospel, they advanced a public mission. The army was unusual in bridging both camps, which may explain why it has endured so long. Doctrinally, the

Mormon town of Manti City, with temple on the horizon, circa 1900. One of the
first temples built in Utah, Manti dominated the local desert landscape when it was
completed in 1888. This picture was probably posed to suggest the temple's effect
on native peoples and travelers who viewed it from a distance.

Booths and their followers emerged from Holiness, a cross-Atlantic spiritual
revival movement. Holiness thinkers stressed the ability of the Holy Spirit to
fill a person with direct, ecstatic power. Army followers spread that gospel in
an atmosphere of warmth and festivity. When the movement arrived in
Kingston, North Carolina, one local woman dismissed it at first as "a minstrel
or comic show," but she changed her mind, reporting that "I never saw such
a happy set of people before and I soon became convinced that they were a
very different set of Christians."

Holiness, a radical outgrowth of Methodism, attracted people from many
racial and economic backgrounds by encouraging believers to celebrate a personal experience of Christ's power and dedicate their lives to God's service.
Holiness teachings broke down barriers of all kinds. In Arkansas the widow of
one charismatic Holiness preacher was asked to speak before 500 men at a
penitentiary. Terrified, she felt a spiritual "loosening" that helped her testify
to God's love, launching her on her own preaching career. By the turn of the
century Holiness had produced cross-racial congregations in all parts of the
country, during a decade when racial lines were hardening. Outside Houston,
Charles Fox Parham preached Holiness ideas and faith healing in his new
Apostolic Faith Movement. One of his disciples, a former slave from Louisiana

Salvation Army, "Cathedral of the Open Air." Christians could envision crowded urban squares as well as rural landscapes as sacred spaces for the faithful. The Salvation Army excelled in urban missions.
Source: *War Cry*, 7 October 1893, Salvation Army Archives, Alexandria, Virginia.

named William Seymour, took this gospel to Los Angeles, where he shared the gifts of faith healing and speaking in tongues. Parham and Seymour's followers created a faith soon known as Pentecostalism. Intensely personal and emotional, it would exert a profound influence on twentieth-century Protestantism.

Even more influential was the preaching of Dwight Moody, the era's most famous evangelist. Born in 1837, Moody drew his faith not from a traditional denomination but from service to the ecumenical YMCA. By the end of the Civil War, Moody had given up work as a shoe salesman to build a street church in Chicago. He soon embarked on international preaching tours, and after winning mass conversions in England and Scotland in 1873, he came home a celebrity. Appealing to audiences through his rugged physique and friendly, colloquial style, Moody departed sharply from "perfectionism," the optimistic belief that Christians could bring about the millennium through good works. Moody instead argued that the world was preordained by God to fall further and further into sin and wretchedness. When humanity had reached the nadir, Christ would come to resurrect the righteous and consign sinners to hell. "I look upon this world as a wrecked vessel," Moody declared. "God has given me a lifeboat and said to me, 'Moody, save all you can.'" This pessimistic view was a starting point for the slow revival of expectations over the course of the twentieth century that the world would end with Armageddon and the Rapture. Such a theology suggested that humanitarian and reform projects were a useless distraction from the business of filling the lifeboat. In contrast to the Salvation Army, Moody told Christians to look beyond this world to the next. Yet Moody was a transitional figure who did not call himself a fundamentalist—as his successors would by the 1920s—and he refrained from attacking those who held different theological views.

Other Protestants were less willing than Moody to consign the world to doom, especially since earlier nineteenth-century movements had left a legacy of energetic activism. Proponents of the Social Gospel urged Christians to respond directly to the evils of industrialization, as they had to slavery and other national sins. Charles Sheldon's novel *In His Steps*, which originated the phrase "What would Jesus do?" perhaps captured the essence of the Social Gospel more fully than any other text. Sheldon's story, published in 1896, was set in Raymond, a fictional midwestern railroad hub that looked suspiciously like the author's own Topeka. At the start of the book, a visiting tramp enters the First Church of Raymond and asks the congregation about their faith. "Somehow I get puzzled," he says,

> when I see so many Christians living in luxury and singing "Jesus, I my cross have taken, all to leave and follow Thee," and remember how my wife died in a tenement in New York City, gasping for air and asking God to take the little girl too. Of course I don't expect you people can prevent every one from dying of starvation, lack of proper nourishment and tenement air, but what does follow-ing Jesus mean? . . . It seems to me there's an awful lot of trouble in the world that somehow wouldn't exist if all the people who sing such songs went and lived them out.

Moved by the tramp's speech and subsequent death, the minister of First Church invites members of his congregation to join him in a pledge: for a year they will ask themselves before taking any action, "what would Jesus do?" The results revolutionize the congregation and the city of Raymond. A number of church members quit their ethically compromising jobs. A department store

magnate begins paying higher wages to his employees, and a railroad superintendent submits evidence of his company's illegal activities to the Interstate
Commerce Commission. Professors at the local college take part in a temperance campaign, even though they hate the rough-and-tumble world of politics.
A young heiress and her brother endow a local newspaper, whose editor finds
that in order to stick to principles rather than money, he must operate the
Raymond Daily News as a nonprofit venture. The minister himself finds that
following Jesus requires him to practice more "self-denial and suffering." He
gives up his comfortable position at First Church and moves to the slums to
work with the poor. Intentionally or not, the author of *In His Steps* also gave
up his profits: Charles Sheldon filed his copyright claim incorrectly and thus
got no proceeds from his enormously popular book. He wrote later that he
was glad of this, since it increased the circulation of his ideas.

Social Gospel leaders included many Congregationalists, such as Sheldon
and his colleague Washington Gladden, an outspoken supporter of labor
unions who advocated government activism to regulate corporate enterprise,
improve working conditions, and reduce poverty. Congregationalists were, on
the whole, far ahead of Presbyterians, Methodists, and Baptists in the Social
Gospel cause. But one Congregationalist minister left the denomination's
ranks to develop a more radical program. W. D. P. Bliss, born in Istanbul to
missionary parents, advocated not only political and labor reforms but also
collective ownership of key industries. Bliss became attracted to the Church
of England, which he saw as a church of national and theological breadth as
well as the point of origin for English Christian Socialism, a movement he
much admired. Bliss converted in 1885 to the Episcopalian Church, known in
the United States for wealth and social exclusivity rather than reform zeal. But
Episcopalians in America, like their Anglican counterparts, were being transformed by industrialization into a church with a strong social calling. Bliss
became a leader in the movement, founding a variety of Christian Socialist
organizations and magazines. "The teachings of Jesus Christ," he declared,
"lead directly to some specific form or forms of Socialism."

Though few would have acknowledged the connection, Social Gospelers
sought many of the same goals as did Holiness and Pentecostal Christians.
Both turned in different ways to the history of the early Christian church and
sought to bring its principles and practices into the modern world. But they
sought this goal by different paths, and some, such as Bliss, combined their
social concerns with a renewed emphasis on high-church ritual. Harold
Frederic captured this angle neatly in *The Damnation of Theron Ware* when
he depicted Theron peeking into a Catholic Mass for the first time in his life
and being swept away by the smell of incense, the sight of a priest in rich
vestments, and the echoes of a haunting Latin chant. Anglican and Roman
Catholic traditions offered a sense of mystery and wonder. Though the actual
extent of Protestant conversion to Catholicism is unclear, medieval saints such
as Francis of Assisi and Joan of Arc began to enjoy cult status in literature
and art. Such medievalism drew deeply on the era's wellspring of spiritual
need: the search for a profound and authentic faith in a world ruled by material values.

In emphasizing Christians' work in the world, some Catholics met Social Gospel Protestants on middle ground. One of the most prominent was Father John Ryan, a Minnesota farmer's son who became a leading figure at the St. Paul Seminary and in 1906 wrote the influential progressive text *A Living Wage*. Ryan drew on Catholic doctrine as well as other sources to argue that every breadwinner should earn enough money to provide basic shelter, food, and security for his family. Such arguments were part of a broader struggle to claim a place for Catholics in modernizing America, in which they played an increasingly visible role. The number of Catholics in the United States doubled between 1870 and 1900; by the latter year they constituted 20 percent of the population. Even the most prejudiced Protestants could not fail to note the significance of Catholicism, while the Vatican could no longer overlook the power and size of its church in the United States.

American Catholics were made up of a diverse mix of peoples, including eastern Europeans, Italians, French Canadians, and Mexicans as well as the more established Irish and Germans who dominated the church hierarchy. Lay Catholicism was often strong in areas where church infrastructure was weak. Though most Mexicans in the Southwest lived far from the nearest priest (who, when he visited, often spoke no Spanish) they carefully tended family altars, celebrated holy days, and each December mounted elaborate productions of the Spanish drama *Los Pastores* (the shepherds), a Christmas story that spoke to the circumstances of their daily lives. Similarly, immigrants from southern Italy brought with them the rituals and beliefs surrounding a beloved image of the Virgin Mary, the Madonna del Carmine. In Italian Harlem each July, the *festa* of the Madonna brought Italians together to give thanks and petition for healing. More Americanized Catholics were embarrassed by the public procession to the church, which included barefoot penitents with bloodied faces and women who crawled on hands and knees and in some cases expressed their devotion to Mary by dragging their tongues along the stones of the church floor as they approached the altar.

From the 1880s onward the American Catholic church was riven by conflict between traditionalists and so-called Americanists who sought to raise the church's stature in the United States through projects of assimilation. The Vatican did little to help Americanists and much to undercut them. In 1870 the First Vatican Council announced the doctrine of papal infallibility, a bulwark against lay dissent as well as science and secularism. In 1896, when Father John Zahm tried to reconcile Darwinian science and Catholic faith in a popular series of lectures under the title *Evolution and Dogma*, he met intense criticism and censorship from the Vatican, as did the American Sulpician priests Francis Gigot and John Hogan when they proposed that modern scientific ideas be included in Catholic seminary education. The Vatican's crowning statement of orthodoxy was Leo XIII's *Testem Benevolentiae* in 1899, which warned against "theological Americanism," or excessive accommodation to the forces of modernity, secularism, and religious relativism. "There are some among you," Leo warned, "who conceive of and desire a church in America different from that which is in the rest of the world." This the Vatican could not tolerate.

Leo XIII handed one clear victory to Catholic liberals. In his 1894 statement *Rerum Novarum*, an encyclical on the relations of capital and labor, he critiqued industrial capitalism and issued a clarification on Catholic membership in labor unions, an issue hotly disputed among U.S. bishops. *Rerum Novarum* gave Catholics the pope's explicit permission to join worker brotherhoods such as the Knights of Labor. And though he condemned socialism and ruled private property to be "in accordance with the law of nature," Pope Leo also criticized industrialization, arguing that "working men have been surrendered, isolated and helpless, to the hardheartedness of employers and the greed of unchecked competition." He noted the vast disparity between the new superrich and "the utter poverty of the masses" and described some wage earners as under "a yoke little better than that of slavery." *Rerum Novarum* thus opened avenues for American Catholic theologians and reformers such as John Ryan to speak out on questions of economic justice.

In the meantime one of the greatest areas of conflict between Protestants and Catholics, as well as among Catholics themselves, was the issue of schooling. Catholic conservatives feared rapid Americanization, believing it would lead immigrants and their children (like Celia Madden in *The Damnation of Theron Ware*) into the temptations of secularism. They argued for separate Catholic schools where students could be taught in immigrant languages rather than English, because "language saves faith." In Wisconsin an 1889 law requiring all school instruction to be in English precipitated a furor among German speakers, including Lutherans and especially Catholics who had 40,000 children in the state's parochial schools. Catholic liberals, while distressed by Protestant prejudice, believed, in contrast, that the solution lay in English-language schooling that would integrate Catholic immigrants into the mainstream. The Vatican tolerated a brief effort by Archbishop John Ireland of St. Paul, a leading Americanist, to operate joint public-Catholic schools in two Minnesota districts, but such experiments were rare. Most of the energy of priests and lay leaders went toward parochial education, based on the mandate of the First Vatican Council that Catholics around the world should help to create and maintain local Catholic schools.

American Jews faced a number of problems similar to those of their Catholic counterparts. Like Irish and German Catholics who had emigrated in large numbers before the Civil War, German Jews had prospered in America for a generation. In the late nineteenth century both assimilated groups watched with dismay as waves of newcomers altered the face of their religions. Most eastern European Jews, like Italian and eastern European Catholics, arrived poor and clung to the bottom rungs of the economic ladder. Their poverty and alien customs seemed to heighten Protestant prejudices against all Catholics and Jews, and they swamped existing structures of worship and social services. Though many immigrant Jews attended services only a few times each year, makeshift arrangements had to be made for open-air services on the High Holy Days, which were attended in New York by as many as 164,000 people.

Newly arrived Jews also presented a theological challenge for German Jews who were comfortably established in the United States. Before the 1880s

American Judaism was led by figures such as Rabbi I. M. Wise of Cincinnati, who hoped, like Catholic Americanists, to adapt his faith to a climate of relative religious freedom in the United States. Wise helped establish what is known today as Reform Judaism, but he gave it the name *American Judaism*. He instituted such reforms as seating men and women together in synagogue, providing religious education for girls as well as boys, having music sung by mixed choirs, and even using organ music. By 1880 Wise had created a nationwide Union of American Hebrew Congregations and a seminary, Cincinnati's Hebrew Union College. Yet the use of the term *union* masked a number of debates and disagreements among those who considered themselves Reform, American, or modern Jews. Should American Jews keep kosher, or was that a superstitious form of "kitchen Judaism," as Wise once called it? How much Hebrew and Talmudic education should boys receive—and how about girls? To what extent should American Jews think of themselves as a separate nation or people? In assimilating, were they losing their identity and faith?

Eastern Europeans complicated these questions by bringing a very different kind of Judaism to the United States. While some were secular in outlook, many others arrived with a heightened sense of tradition in light of the brutal anti-Semitism from which they had fled. The first great influx from Russia occurred in 1882, after the assassination of Czar Alexander, when government officials and the press blamed Russia's Jews as a convenient scapegoat and touched off rounds of violence. Another even deadlier wave of pogroms began in 1903. During both decades synagogues and Jewish homes were set on fire, women raped, Jews beaten to death and burned alive in their homes, and small children thrown out of windows. Harsh laws followed, expelling Jews from towns and cities and restricting their employments and access to education. Chaim Khisin, studying in Moscow in 1882, recalled that "until these *pogroms* began I myself had thrust aside my Jewish origins. I considered myself a devoted son of Russia. I lived and breathed a Russian life. . . . But whether I wish it or not, I am a Jew." One Jewish veteran of the Russian Army, decorated for his heroism on the battlefield, was stunned to find himself expelled from Moscow. He decided he had "only one exit, to seek my fortune in America."

By the mid-1880s the increasing diversity of American Jews was already precipitating conflicts. The Hungarian Rabbi Alexander Kohut, arriving in the United States at the invitation of traditionalists, declared that American Reform Judaism had gone too far from the "Mosaic-rabbinical tradition. . . . It is suicide; and suicide is not reform." (He delivered this condemnation in German.) Reform Jews responded vigorously, calling a conference in Pittsburgh to formulate a clear statement of their views. They shared two goals with the traditionalists: they considered Judaism "the central religious truth for the human race," and they sought to combat indifference and secularism among the American Jewish masses. But taking a historical perspective, they argued that most biblical laws had stemmed from the "primitive ideas" of ancient times, and they argued that modern Judaism should be rooted in progressive ideals and Enlightenment rationalism. The Pittsburgh Platform called for women's religious equality and mission work among the poor. It also declared that American Jews "consider ourselves no longer a nation, but a religious community." This controversial statement, which distanced Reform Judaism from Zionism and the quest for a Jewish state in Palestine, stood afterward for fifty years.

The Pittsburgh Platform was a strong rallying point for progressives, but it hardly created unity among Jews, especially with the steady increase of new arrivals from eastern Europe. While there had been only about twenty Orthodox synagogues in the United States in 1880, by 1910 there were nearly 2,000. By that date these Orthodox congregations constituted 90 percent of all American synagogues and served more than two million people. Yiddish-speaking communities sprang up in the large cities of the Northeast—especially New York—and built rich traditions of worship, literature, theater, street life, and political activism. Many of the new immigrants joined *landsmanshaftn*, clubs made up of people from a particular village for the purpose of maintaining home ties and sending aid in time of crisis.

But at the same time, traditional Jews confronted some of the same problems as did Reform leaders. Religious practice was compromised by the conditions of American life, especially in a commercial metropolis such as New York. Poverty-stricken immigrants suffered dislocation and long hours of work, often on Saturday, the Jewish Sabbath. The majority of children received little religious or Hebrew teaching. Jews were, in their own ways, susceptible to the same forces that worked on Theron Ware: the promise of material plenty and religious relativism in a pluralist society. Like Protestants and Catholics, they struggled in various ways to blend old and new. Jewish women, for example, traditionally excluded from religious leadership and learning, took on prominent roles in American Judaism through nationwide women's organizations and local sisterhoods connected to synagogues. Ray Frank of Oregon, an inspiring speaker, represented the tensions between tradition and modernity when she went on the lecture circuit urging women to help men uphold Jewish tradition.

Through projects to revitalize and adapt Judaism in the United States, a range of traditions developed between the poles of Orthodoxy and Reform. Rabbi Solomon Schechter, who arrived in 1902 to become leader of the Jewish Theological Seminary in New York, tried to challenge Reform principles while at the same time speaking of "Catholic Israel," the unity of all Jews. Schechter succeeded no better than his predecessor, Isaac Wise, in bringing all American Jews under one spiritual umbrella. Instead, the term *Conservative Judaism* came into use to describe his particular blend of tradition and modernity. Eventually, Jewish synagogues in the United States fell roughly into the categories Orthodox, Conservative, and Reform, but all differed markedly from European tradition. In the most prominent Orthodox synagogues of Boston and New York, men and women worshipped (separately) in quiet surroundings, according to prevailing American tastes rather than eastern European custom. They vied to hire the most talented cantors, and they sat beneath spectacular chandeliers on velvet cushions, as proud of these material manifestations of faith as were prosperous urban Protestants and Catholics, sitting in their grand urban churches and cathedrals.

The adaptability and creativity of religious faith was illustrated even more dramatically by religious liberals and by those who did not fit clearly on any continuum between the traditional and modern. Orthodox Jews pointed in horror to Felix Adler's Society for Ethical Culture, which carried Reform Judaism past its furthest limits and remade it into an essentially secular form of moral inquiry. Movements such as Theosophy and Christian Science also carried Americans into new spiritual territory. Experimental colonies abounded, from the Shiloh Movement in Durham, Maine, to the *bruderhof* colonies of Hutterites, who emigrated from the Ukraine to South Dakota in 1874. The Koreshan Unity Movement, followers of a Union veteran and medical doctor who in 1869 experienced a celestial vision of himself as a messiah, established itself in Chicago, San Francisco, and other cities. In 1895 Elizabeth Cady Stanton and a group of feminist theologians published *The Woman's Bible*, challenging the idea that the Bible called for women's subordination. (The project was so controversial that it cost Stanton her position as head of the National American Woman Suffrage Association, where a rising generation of young leaders wanted to appear more mainstream.)

Meanwhile, in Belton, Texas, a devout Methodist housewife named Martha McWhirter founded a sort of Protestant convent. Grieving over the deaths of two children, McWhirter attended a passionate revival meeting in 1869 and afterward heard the voice of God urging her to bring women together. She and other Belton women (including at least five who had suffered domestic violence) declared themselves celibate, left their husbands, and created the Sanctified Sisters. They supported themselves with a cooperative hotel and farm, rotating tasks and organizing their work so efficiently that no one labored more than five hours a day. The Sanctified Sisters moved to Washington, D.C., in 1898, renamed themselves the Woman's Commonwealth, and flourished well into the twentieth century. The extraordinary diversity and energy of experiments such as these showed the extent of the challenges that traditional religion faced; they also suggested that Americans responded to modernity not only with secularism and skepticism, but also with new and creative forms of religious practice.

NATURE AND FAITH

In 1902 the Dakota Sioux author Zitkala-Sa published a bold declaration to the Christian world that she remained unconverted. "When the spirit swells my breast," she wrote in *Atlantic Monthly*, "I love to roam leisurely among the green hills; or sometimes, sitting on the brink of the murmuring Missouri, I marvel at the great blue overhead. . . . Drifting clouds and tinkling waters, together with the warmth of a genial summer day, bespeak with eloquence the loving Mystery about us." The shape of a prominent rock along the riverbank reminded her of the "subtle knowledge of the native folk which enable[s] them to recognize a kinship to any and all parts of this vast universe." Visited by missionaries and converts among her own people, Zitkala-Sa rejected their beliefs. "A wee child toddling in a wonder world," she wrote, "I prefer to their dogma my excursions into the natural gardens where the voice of the Great Spirit is heard in the twittering of birds, the rippling of mighty waters, and the sweet breathing of flowers. If this is Paganism, then at present, at least, I am a Pagan."

For centuries American Indians like Zitkala-Sa had listened politely to Christian missionaries and then gone off to continue their own religious practices, but before 1902 none had explained his or her rejection of Christianity to a nationwide audience in the pages of *Atlantic Monthly*. Zitkala-Sa was meeting Christians on a spiritual middle ground. In the same year she published "Why I Am a Pagan," the Anglo author Mary Austin was putting the finishing touches on a series of meditations called *Land of Little Rain*, destined to become famous for its melding of Christian and native traditions in a tribute to the southwestern desert and its peoples. Austin, who had moved to a ranch in the Owens Valley of Southern California with her husband in 1892, had grown up a devout Methodist in rural Illinois. Pressed by her grandfather to learn large parts of the Bible by heart, she had experienced spiritual revelations as a young child but found herself dissatisfied with the limits of Christianity. In the desert Austin undertook a religious quest, studying Paiute and Shoshone beliefs and prophecies. Among her main characters in *Land of Little Rain* were Seyavi, a Paiute basket weaver, and Winnenap, a Shoshone healer, both based on neighbors who taught Austin that God could be found in reverence for the land.

Americans had good reason to discover such reverence at the turn of the twentieth century. Like Mary Austin, who grieved over the sale and development of beautiful grasslands near her ranch, Americans had witnessed an immense push to clear old growth forests, drain swamps and deltas, and mine and farm the earth. The landscapes left in the wake of these enterprises were ugly: burned-over clearcuts, arid fields stripped of topsoil, hillsides littered with oil derricks, and noxious piles of mine tailings. Those very landscapes helped bring forth an ethos of respect for the untouched places that remained, and from that impulse emerged a loosely organized but popular movement of nature worship, often blended with Christianity and other traditional faiths but sometimes supplanting them. At the same time, railroads and resort hotels made it easier for affluent Americans to visit remote locations and contemplate awe-inspiring vistas. In most parts of the United States by 1900, "wilderness" could be enjoyed without fear of wolf attacks or Indian raids. The old contrast between the dangerous backwoods and the safety of human settlements was being reversed, and the wildest spots on the continent were becoming places of refuge from the ills of a human-dominated continent. Nature, as *Outlook* magazine observed in 1903, was coming to be seen as "the playground of the soul."

Love of nature thus became an increasingly important component of Americans' spiritual life, and it took many forms. Magazines such as *Outing* (launched in 1885) and *Outdoor Life* (1897) not only dispensed practical travel advice but also celebrated the spiritual awe and sense of peace that nature could impart. Many Protestants relaxed old prohibitions on Sunday recreation, arguing that fresh air and exercise were appropriate for the Lord's Day.

"The Puritan Sabbath has been definitely renounced," wrote a minister in 1900, endorsing Sunday afternoon golf. The landscape architect Frederick Law Olmsted designed not only urban parks but walkways and landscapes at sites such as Yosemite and Niagara Falls, seeking to minimize the impact of growing hordes of visitors. Yosemite, he wrote, represented "the union of the deepest sublimity with the deepest beauty." He advocated public ownership of such sites so that they could bring rejuvenation to all.

Such impulses were most closely associated with the grand vistas of the West. Congress set aside Yosemite for the state of California in 1864, specifying that it be preserved for "public use, resort, and recreation." Yellowstone became the first national park in the world in 1872, followed by Yosemite, which returned to federal ownership in 1890; Sequoia in the same year; Mt. Rainier in 1899; Crater Lake in 1902; and South Dakota's Wind Cave in 1903. (The first national park east of Mississippi River did not appear until 1916, with the creation of Acadia in Maine). In an article titled "The Wilderness," a writer in *Overland Monthly* extolled the benefits of escaping to such locales. "You think of the civilization you have left behind. Seen through the eyes of the wilderness, how stupid and insane it all seems. The mad eagerness of money-seeking men, the sham pleasures of conventional society, the insistence upon the importance of being in earnest over trifles, pall on you when you think of them. Your blood clarifies; your brain becomes active. You get a new view of life."

Winslow Homer, *An Adirondack Lake*, 1870. Homer painted many tranquil scenes in the Adirondacks, capturing the appeal of wilderness in an increasingly urban, industrialized, fast-paced society.
Source: Henry Gallery, University of Washington, Seattle, Horace C. Henry Collection, 26.71.

For the era's greatest advocate of wilderness preservation, John Muir, nature worship served as a replacement for Christian faith. Born in Scotland and raised in Wisconsin, Muir suffered brutal beatings and overwork at the hands of a harsh Presbyterian father. Like Mary Austin, he learned to recite large portions of the Bible by heart, though in Muir's case he recalled learning his verses through "sore flesh." From an early age Muir found solace in the natural world. Handy with tools, he presented some of his inventions at the Wisconsin State Fair when he was twenty-two; an impressed onlooker encouraged him to attend college. At the state university in Madison he fell in love with botany and came to question his father's austere doctrines. Fleeing to Canada to escape the Union draft during the Civil War, Muir experienced a spiritual revelation when he found two rare orchids growing beside a stream. "I never before saw a plant so full of life; so perfectly spiritual, it seemed pure enough for the throne of its Creator," Muir wrote. "I felt as if I were in the presence of superior beings who loved me and beckoned me to come. I sat down beside them and wept for joy."

Muir carried this feeling on a long trek from Kentucky to Florida in 1867, the journal of which was published after his death a half-century later. Inside the front cover of his notebook the author signed himself "John Muir, Earthplanet, Universe." In Kentucky he recorded an encounter with a blacksmith who criticized Muir for roaming the country looking at flowers instead of doing a man's work. Well prepared by his youthful training, Muir offered a Biblical response. "Do you not remember," he asked, "that Christ told his

Frank Jay Hayes. Old Faithful Geyser, Yellowstone National Park, 1880s. Yellowstone and other national parks served a growing tourist industry. Visitors like these could contemplate sublime landscapes while also enjoying the comforts of modern hotels built by the railroad companies.
Source: The Frances Lehman Loeb Art Center, Vassar College, Poughkeepsie, New York.

disciples to 'consider the lilies how they grow,' and compared their beauty with Solomon in all his glory? Now whose advice am I to take, yours or Christ's?" The blacksmith "acknowledged that he had never thought of blossoms that way before." "From the dust of the earth," Muir wrote, "from the common elementary fund, the Creator has made *Homo sapiens*. From the same material he has made every other creature, however noxious and insignificant to us. They are earth-born companions and our fellow mortals. . . . This star, our own good earth, made many a successful journey around the heavens ere man was made, and whole kingdoms of creatures enjoyed existence and returned to dust ere man appeared to claim them."

In the 1870s Muir began publishing his nature writings in leading magazines, and he headed to California for what became a world famous residence at Yosemite. Rambling through the valley, he proved to be an astute scientific observer who solved the mystery of Yosemite's glacial origins at a time when professional experts offered other explanations. But Muir became more famous for spiritual explorations than for scientific ones. He repeatedly argued that plants, animals, and the universe had purposes distinct from those of humans, and awe-inspiring in their own right. In one article he described how he climbed an immense evergreen in the Yuma Valley during a wild thunderstorm to see how it felt to be a tree in the wind. "It never occurred to me until this storm-day," he reported, "that trees are travelers, in the ordinary sense. They make many journeys, not very extensive ones, it is true; but our own little comes and goes are only little more than tree-wavings—many of them not so much."

Muir shared his love of great trees and natural wonders with many influential contemporaries, and it led him from writing into political activism. In 1892 Muir and Robert Johnson, his editor at *Century* magazine, founded an "association for preserving California's monuments and natural wonders." That association, the Sierra Club, became Muir's great life work, despite his confessed fear that he had "no genius for managing societies." The club lobbied for preservation of old-growth forests and wilderness sites, and after 1901 it sponsored outings in the backcountry led by Muir himself. By this point its members were making common cause with nature lovers across the United States. The Appalachian Mountain Club had been sponsoring hikes and nature studies for two decades and in 1893 had persuaded the New York legislature to designate part of the Adirondacks "forever wild." To protect wildlife, especially birds, northeasterners had also founded several state chapters of the Audubon Society. Between 1901 and 1905—just when Zitkala-Sa and Mary Austin published their writings—the Audubon Society became a nationwide organization.

Environmental conservation was not wholly a spiritual affair, and some of its earliest successes stemmed from economic concerns. In 1891, for example, Congress gave the president power to set aside federal forests to protect watersheds and topsoil, and both Benjamin Harrison and Grover Cleveland set aside millions of acres. Enforcement arrived in 1897, when the secretary of the Interior was given the right to regulate use of such lands. President Theodore Roosevelt, who expanded this initiative into the U.S. Forest Service in 1905, had in some ways a more pragmatic vision of conservation than did men such as Muir, advocating "wise use" rather than pristine preservation. But Roosevelt in his own way shared Muir's spiritual values. That was evident in 1903 when Muir welcomed the president on a tour of the Sierras. Recalling the massive sequoias that surrounded him as he camped with Muir, Roosevelt wrote that "the majestic trunks, beautiful in color and in symmetry, rose round us like the pillars of a mightier cathedral than was ever conceived by any human architect."

While sublime monuments such as Yosemite won preservation, less spectacular environments as yet did not. Gene Stratton Porter, who grew up in Indiana, lost her mother at age eleven and found the same kind of spiritual solace in the vast Limberlost Swamp, near her childhood home, as Muir at Yosemite. Stratton Porter became famous for a series of novels mythologizing the Limberlost, beginning with *The Song of the Cardinal* in 1903. But her Indiana swamp, unlike western geysers and sequoia groves, did not meet contemporary definitions of sublimity. Before Stratton Porter's books appeared, much of the Limberlost had already been drained and converted to farmland, and only recently have wetland projects recreated a small portion of what was destroyed.

Thus, the post–Civil War era witnessed continued landscape destruction while seeds of spiritual renewal also began slowly emerging from the drained, mined, and burned-over soil. Writers such as John Muir, Mary Austin, Zitkala-Sa, and Gene Stratton Porter paved the way for a new environmentalist faith, seeing in nature not cause for terror or conquest but holy opportunities for contemplation and renewal. They created, in effect, a new and popular American religion, one whose place of worship was not in a church or synagogue but in nature itself, in "cathedrals," as Roosevelt put it, greater than those of any human architect. By the 1930s one could look back and trace a spiritual revolution that had taken place between the end of the Civil War and the first decade of the twentieth century. In *A Sand County Almanac* the naturalist Aldo Leopold told that history backward, marking it along the rings of a giant oak tree that had been struck by lightning on his Wisconsin farm. As Leopold himself was keenly aware, that farm lay next door to the county in which John Muir had grown up and developed his philosophy of the brotherhood of all living things. Sawing, with his neighbor, through the outer rings of the dead trunk of his tree, Leopold recalled recent struggles against waste and conquest. Then he sawed deeper, back into the rings of an earlier era.

We cut 1906, when the first state forester took office, and fires burned 17,000 acres in these sand counties. . . . We cut 1892, another year of fires; 1891, a low in the grouse cycle. . . . It was likewise in 1890 that the largest pine rafts in history slipped down the Wisconsin River in full view of my oak, to build an empire of red barns for the cows of the prairie states. . . .

Now our saw bites the 1870s, the decade of Wisconsin's carousal in wheat. . . . In 1873 one Chicago firm received and marketed 25,000 prairie chickens. The Chicago trade collectively bought 600,000 at $3.25 per dozen. In 1872 the last wild Wisconsin turkey was killed, two counties to the southwest. . . . In 1871, within a fifty-mile triangle spreading northwestward from my oak, 136 million pigeons are estimated to have nested, and some may have nested in it, for it was then a thrifty sapling 20 feet tall. Pigeon hunters by scores plied their trade with net and gun, club and salt lick, and trainloads of prospective pigeon pie moved south-ward and eastward toward the cities. It was the last big nesting in Wisconsin, and nearly the last in any state.

The same year brought other evidence of the march of empire: the Peshtigo Fire, which cleared a couple of counties of trees and soil. . . . In 1870 a market gunner boasted in the *American Sportsman* of killing 6,000 ducks in one season.

Cutting to the heart of his old oak, Leopold calculated that it had emerged from its acorn in the same year when John Muir had first conceived the idea of a wilderness refuge. In 1865, the year that had brought emancipation and peace to millions of Americans, Muir had asked his brother to sell him a piece of land to create a wildflower sanctuary. "His brother declined to part with the land," Leopold reported, "but he could not suppress the idea." Muir would have approved of Leopold's conclusion: "1865 still stands in Wisconsin history as the birth-year of mercy for things natural, wild and free."

FOR FURTHER READING

On the World's Parliament of Religions, in addition to the original report of the organizers, see Richard H. Seager, *The World's Parliament of Religions* (Bloomington, IN, 1995). On encounters between Europe and Asia see Stephen R. Prothero, *The White Buddhist* (Bloomington, IN, 1996), and Amiya Sen, *Swami Vivekananda* (New York, 2000). On Protestant missions, both domestic and foreign, the best recent scholarship focuses on women; see Patricia Hill, *The World Their Household* (Ann Arbor, MI, 1985), Jane Hunter, *The Gospel of Gentility* (New Haven, CT, 1984), Maina Chawla Singh, *Gender, Religion, and "Heathen Lands"* (New York, 2000), and Peggy Pascoe, *Relations of Rescue*, cited in Chapter 6. See also the essays in *Black Americans and the Missionary Movement in Africa*, edited by Sylvia M. Jacobs (Westport, CT, 1982), as well as George M. Frederickson's *Black Liberation* (New York, 1995). On women's roles in African-American churches see Evelyn Brooks Higginbotham, *Righteous Discontent* (Cambridge, MA, 1993). The quotation about "a nation within a nation," from sociologist E. Franklin Frazier, is on page 11 of this book.

On Protestantism generally and the emerging split between liberals and fundamentalists, I have relied heavily throughout this chapter on George M. Marsden, *Fundamentalism and American Culture* (New York, 1980). On the Salvation Army see Diane H. Winston, *Red Hot and Righteous* (Cambridge, MA, 1999), and on liberal Protestantism, Robert T. Handy, *The Social Gospel in America, 1870–1920* (New York, 1966), and Henry F. May, *Protestant Churches and Industrial America* (New York, 1949). On medievalism as a response to modernity see T. J. Jackson Lears, *No Place of Grace* (Chicago, 1981).

On Catholicism I rely on Patrick W. Carey, *The Roman Catholics in America* (Westport, CT, 1996), and on specific Catholic communities, Arnoldo De León, *The Tejano Community*, cited in Chapter 3, and Robert Anthony Orsi, *The Madonna of 115th Street* (New Haven, CT, 1985). On parochial school controversies in politics see Richard E. Jensen, *The Winning of the Midwest* (Chicago, 1971). On Father Ryan I am grateful to Robert Prasch, Department of Economics, Middlebury College, for "Father John Ryan and *A Living Wage*," manuscript in author's possession. On Judaism I rely largely on Jonathan D. Sarna, *American Judaism* (New Haven, CT, 2004); see also Hasia Diner, *A New Promised Land* (New York, 2003), and Gerald Sorin, *Tradition Transformed* (Baltimore, 1997). On events in Russia see Stephen M. Berk, *Year of Crisis, Year of Hope* (Westport, CT, 1985), and on the origins of the National Council of Jewish Women, Faith Rogow, *Gone to Another Meeting* (Tuscaloosa, AL, 1993). For background on various experimental communities, see Donald E. Pitzer, ed., *America's Communal Utopias* (Chapel Hill, NC, 1997), as well as Wendy E. Chmielewski, "Heaven on Earth: The Woman's Commonwealth, 1867–1983," in *Women in Spiritual and Communitarian Societies in the United States*, edited by Wendy E. Chmielewski et al. (Syracuse, NY, 1993), pp. 52–67.

On American Indians, in addition to works cited in other chapters, two starting points are Omer C. Stewart, *Peyote Religion* (Norman, OK, 1987), and for native influences on Mary Austin, Mark T. Hoyer's *Dancing Ghosts* (Reno, NV, 1998). On religion and the outdoors see Clifford Putney, *Muscular Christianity* (Cambridge, MA, 2001). On Olmsted see Anne Whiston Spirn, "Constructing Nature," in *Uncommon Ground*, edited by William Cronon (New York, 1996), pp. 91–112. Also very influential to this section of the chapter is Cronon's provocative essay "The Trouble with Nature: On Getting Back to the Wrong Wilderness," in the same volume, pp. 69–90. For an innovative look at the "trouble with nature" in national parks, see Mark David Spence, *Dispossessing the Wilderness* (New York, 1999). My thanks go also to the Vassar graduate Emily Avery-Miller for her research and our conversations in History 367. Stephen Fox, *The American Conservation Movement* (Madison, WI, 1981), is my key source on Muir and the early Sierra Club in addition to Muir's own writings. I am also grateful to the historian Adam Rome for his observations on the Christian roots of Muir's thought. On conservation generally, a good starting point is Ted Steinberg's environmental history of the United States, *Down to Earth* (New York, 2002). "Good Oak" appears in Aldo Leopold's *A Sand County Almanac* (New York, 1949), pp. 6–17.

PART III

THE FIRES

A t the age of 24 José Martí, born in Havana in 1853, had already joined the movement for Cuban independence from Spanish rule and been convicted of treason by Spanish authorities. He had served part of a six-year sentence at hard labor, had the sentence commuted to exile, and lived by turns in Spain, Mexico, and Guatemala. Not long afterward he moved to the United States, where he lived for more than a decade and wrote articles for a number of North American and Latin American newspapers. In the late 1880s and early 1890s, convinced that peaceful methods would never succeed against Spain, Martí helped plan and lead the Cuban Revolution.

In the meantime, Martí reported for Argentina's *La Nación* on the funeral of four anarchists who were hanged in Chicago in 1886 after allegedly throwing a bomb in Haymarket Square. Martí argued that the U.S. anarchists had been wrong to advocate violent revolution in a democracy, but he was fascinated by the power of their rhetoric. He compared them to volcanoes erupting from a vast underground reservoir of molten rock—that is, the working class in the new economy. The United States, he observed, "is terrified by the increased organization among the lower classes. . . . Therefore the Republic decided, by tacit agreement resembling complicity, to use a crime born of its own transgressions as much as of the fanaticism of the criminals in order to strike terror by holding them up as an example."

The anarchists, Martí wrote, "come from hell; what language must they speak but the language of hell?" He was less worried about their influence than he was about what he saw happening more broadly in the United States. Earlier in the nineteenth century, he argued, European immigrants had found in America

> a republican form of government [that] enabled the recent arrival to earn his bread and lay aside a portion of his earnings for his old age, and in his own house. But then came the corrupting war and the habit of authority and domination which is its bitter aftereffect. Then came the credit that stimulated the creation of colossal fortunes and the disorderly foreign influx. . . . The Republic changed from a wonderfully desirable village to a monarchy in disguise.

The United States, Martí concluded, "because of its unconscionable cult of wealth, and lacking any of the shackles of tradition, . . . has fallen into monarchical inequality, injustice, and violence."

Martí, like many Latin Americans, had long hoped the United States would serve as a model republic and defend the rights of other American nations to resist European aggression. During the years he lived in the United States, Martí did come to see parallels between it and Latin America, but they were not such flattering ones. Noting that Anglo Americans thought of their country as more rational, civilized, and orderly than its southern neighbors, he saw instead "the crude, uneven, and decadent character of the United States, and the continuous existence there of all the violence, discord, immorality and disorder [that North Americans] blamed upon the peoples of Spanish America." By the early 1890s Martí warned that the United States, rather than being a friendly ally, was more likely to develop its own imperial ambitions. Martí died on a Cuban beach in 1895, as he and his allies launched a rebellion against Spain. In the years that followed, his words proved accurate. The United States "helped" Cuba win independence and then asserted its own control over the island's military, government, and economy.

U.S. intervention in Cuba was in many ways an extension of the conflict Martí had observed in Chicago. Post–Civil War America was a tremendously violent place, and by the 1890s the domestic conflicts generated by rapid transformation spilled over into other parts of the world. American policy makers sought overseas markets for U.S. products in order to ensure domestic stability and deflect the prospect of "socialistic" solutions within the United States. Chapter 9 of *New Spirits* examines various wars of incorporation that raged within the boundaries of the United States over the lands of the West and the control of labor. Workers of all classes and trades, as well as the landscape itself and the people who had lived on it for centuries, were integrated into a hierarchical corporate and political order, managed from urban centers of financial power. Chapter 10 describes a series of creative nonviolent responses that arose in the face of these conflicts, from the settlement movement to the People's Party. Chapter 11 explores how, in the wake of a massive depression in the 1890s, such projects were postponed or transformed, paving the way for long-term changes in the twentieth century but also defeating the most radical options and setting narrower limits on Americans' reform vision.

Sharply conservative reactions to the depression included a hardening of class and racial lines, and they ended with the consolidation of new conservative powers both in Washington, D.C., and in corporate boardrooms. Those powers are the subject of Chapter 11, and they included the building of an overseas commercial and military empire in response to upheaval at home. The 1890s were a critical turning point, in part, because U.S. political leaders responded to domestic upheaval with imperial ventures overseas. Their justifications for America's new military exploits ran along racial lines, and here the continuities between domestic and foreign policies were also strong. Having rejected the civil rights legacy of Reconstruction, shunted American Indians onto reservations, and passed an Exclusion Act barring Chinese workers from the United States, Americans had laid the groundwork for offering second-class citizenship to Cubans and Filipinos. José Martí was right: the United States had become something different from what it once had been, and different from what most Americans still believed it to be. The fires of incorporation, both at home and abroad, left future generations a legacy of material progress and hope, but also violence and confusion.

CHAPTER 9

—⟫●⟪—

A State of War

If the club of the policeman, knocking out the brains of the rioter, will answer, then well and good; but if it does not promptly meet the exigency, then [use] bullets and bayonets. ... Napoleon was right when he said that the way to deal with a mob was to exterminate it.

—THE INDEPENDENT, NEW YORK

[The propertied classes] everywhere and always fall back upon the use of *force*. ... In the midst of such a struggle, to talk of peace and peaceful methods ... is blasphemous and exasperating to the last degree.

—THE ALARM, CHICAGO

For Europe's most powerful nations, the 1870s and 1880s were an era of high imperialism. Britain crowned Queen Victoria empress of India. France laid claim to Indochina. Germany, Belgium, and Italy joined them in carving up coastal China into spheres of influence, and the Great Powers divided eleven million square miles of Africa into colonial territories. The United States took a different path in these decades. It had already claimed an empire in the West, contiguous to existing states; while Europeans sought colonies overseas, Americans waged ferocious battles for control and development of what the nation had already claimed. The two-million-square-mile West yielded most of the raw materials European powers sought abroad: gold, silver, copper, coal, oil, old-growth timber, and diverse lands that could support cattle, sheep, grain, and semitropical crops.

In 1893 the historian Frederick Jackson Turner famously described the American frontier as a zone of "free land," but, in fact, the process of wresting it from people who already lived there was bloody, complicated, and costly. Subjugation of western tribes brought little peace in its wake, since conquering

Anglos then clashed with Mexicans, Chinese immigrants, and one another. Among the most famous of dozens of violent incidents was the California farmers' war against the Southern Pacific Railroad, which Karl Marx followed with interest in the London papers and which became the basis for Frank Norris's novel *The Octopus*. The conflict centered on Mussel Slough, a patch of land thirty miles south of Fresno where homesteaders and the Southern Pacific held conflicting claims. In 1880 a judge who was a close friend of the railroad's leading shareholders ruled in favor of the road. When the Southern Pacific sent an armed posse to evict farmers, the resulting gun battle left seven dead. Daring train robbers later carried out a three-year crime spree against the Southern Pacific, during which many farmers cheered for the outlaws.

In the meantime, western mining and railroad workers organized thousands of strikes and shutdowns and even acts of sabotage. Corporate managers fought back by calling in armed detectives, state militias, and the U.S. Army. Conflict was especially violent in the mining industry. In 1892 six men died in clashes at Idaho's Coeur d'Alene mines, whose owners ultimately destroyed the local affiliate of the Western Federation of Miners (WFM). A few years later Idaho's ex-governor was assassinated in a revenge killing orchestrated by leaders of the WFM. In Colorado conflict between owners and miners was so bloody and constant that historians have dubbed it the Thirty Years' War. At one point vigilante businessmen in Cripple Creek forced the sheriff and other town officials sympathetic to workers to resign at gunpoint. As late as 1914 at Ludlow, Colorado, state militia and local deputies killed thirty-nine people in a camp of striking coal miners. Among the dead were two miners' wives and eleven children, whose tents were set on fire by the attack.

As violent as the West became, labor conflict was equally fierce in many other parts of the country. Pennsylvania miners waged the same kinds of fights against employers as their compatriots in Colorado and Idaho, including several assassinations carried out in the 1870s by a secret cadre of Irish-born workers known as the Molly Maguires. Whether labor protests were peaceful or not, Eastern employers struck back with the same repressive measures as they did in the West, often escalating strikes into full-scale war. The Great Railroad Strike of 1877, centered in Pittsburgh and other eastern cities, resulted in ten times more deaths than the shootout at Mussel Slough in the so-called Wild West. The new economy also brought violence to the South. In Appalachia the famous Hatfield-McCoy feud resulted partly from the rising value of Hatfield land, as railroads and coal companies undertook large-scale operations. The folktales surrounding "Railroad Bill," a famous black train robber in Alabama, had much in common with those attached to Jesse James's gang and the California bandits who attacked the trains of the Southern Pacific. Bill won admiration from both whites and blacks who were suffering hard times in the depression of the 1890s and who resented the wealth and power railroads represented. Long after Bill was shot dead by an Alabama sheriff, blues songs celebrated him (inaccurately, it appears) as a man who stole from the rich and gave to the hungry.

So vicious and continuous were the battles of these decades that we might call them "wars of incorporation," a second Civil War that persisted into the twentieth century. Incorporation was a geographic process, consolidating networks of commerce and control across the continent; it was also a hierarchical process that took power from many and consolidated it in the hands of a few. Labor fought its most important and spectacular battles against large emerging corporations, from railroads and mining companies to manufacturing firms such as Carnegie Steel, McCormick Reaper, and Pullman Palace Car. And, as we shall see in Chapters 10 and 11, the hierarchical institutions of incorporated America also had negative implications in politics. About the best that can be said for the violent processes of incorporation is that they produced results that were more democratic—by some measures, at least—than similar conflicts in other parts of the world. The Australian Outback ended up even more dominated by big landholders than did the American West. In the conquest of the Argentine pampas, which took place in the same years as the U.S. wars of incorporation, native peoples were hunted to extinction like the wild ostriches, while Argentina's dictator handed over enormous tracts of land to his cronies. Considering the unspeakable atrocities that occurred in the African Congo under the sponsorship of Belgium's King Leopold, the wars of incorporation in the United States look relatively mild. Yet what happened in Europe and America (for example, the arrival of bicycles and automobiles with rubber tires) was inextricably bound to what happened in the cruelest corners of the Congo and Peru (rubber harvesting). Confronted with violence and dislocation on a global scale, many came to agree with commentator Washington Gladden: the new economy brought with it a "state of war."

INCORPORATION IN THE WEST

The most famous of America's violent struggles in the post–Civil War years was not new: it was the final stage in a three-century-long conquest that dispossessed American Indians of their land. At first glance, the task seemed pathetically easy. By 1865 consolidation of the continent seemed inevitable to most observers; an army that had just defeated the Confederacy could surely subdue small bands of nomads with primitive weapons, even if the latter had intimate knowledge of their home terrain. By 1870 the federal government had created reservations for almost every surviving Indian nation, and President U.S. Grant proclaimed a "Peace Policy" focused on education and assimilation rather than military campaigns. But conquest looked far from inevitable to Indians themselves. "All the land south of the Arkansas belongs to the Kiowas and Comanches, and I don't want to give away any of it," the Kiowa chief Satanta informed treaty commissioners in 1869 in a speech that brought shouts of support from men standing behind him. The Comanche chief Ten Bears voiced the same sentiment, explaining that his people had no interest in Anglo customs. "I want to live and die as I was brought up," he declared. "I love the open prairie." What followed were a series of conflicts that one historian has ironically dubbed "the Wars of the Peace Policy."

In these wars the U.S. Army bore responsibility for a long string of atrocities. Men such as General Philip Sheridan, sent west after the Civil War, ruthlessly punished Indians who left reservations or attacked outsiders invading their lands. In January 1870, after a series of murders and revenge killings by white ranchers and Blackfeet warriors in Montana, Sheridan ordered a strike on the camp of a resisting chief. With the band's warriors away hunting, U.S. troops opened fire and set lodges ablaze in a surprise dawn attack beside the Marias River. Bear Head, a young boy at the time, heard the screams of women and children as burning lodge covers collapsed around them (a scene eerily similar to the militia attack on miners at Ludlow, Colorado, forty-four years later, though the casualties at the Marias massacre were far higher). "I sat before the ruin of my lodge and felt sick," Bear Head remembered. "I wished that the seizers had killed me, too. . . . I could not pull up the lodge-skin and look under it. I could not bear to see my mother." At least 173 people died. They turned out to be members of a friendly band whom the army had attacked by mistake.

In many other acts of violence, though, U.S. troops were last on the scene. Unlike the Canadian West, where the Royal Mounted Police served as respected go-betweens and law enforcers, the American West was notably weak in federal authority. Disputes and revenge killings between Indians and local traders, ranchers, and farmers triggered escalating cycles of violence, with federal agents playing confused or secondary roles. Before the 1872 Modoc War on the Oregon-California border, the Modoc believed they had reached an agreement with U.S. negotiators on their future. But officials in Washington changed the terms, refusing to situate the tribe near their ancestral lands. One faction of Modoc, led by a chief named Kientpoos or "Captain Jack," resisted the move and stuck to the terms of the treaty they had signed. U.S. troops, accompanied by local armed whites, went in to relocate them by force. They were shocked to find themselves beaten back. Captain Jack and his followers fled to nearby lava beds, where they hid out for months, eluding capture and killing many men sent after them. The U.S. Army defeated the rebels only with the help of other Modoc—including, ironically, some of the men who had killed white settlers and persuaded the reluctant Captain Jack to launch a surprise attack on a U.S. peace commission. These Modoc were pardoned, while Jack and three others, none of whom had at first advocated violence against negotiators or civilians, were convicted and hanged.

Whether they won or lost a battle, the U.S. Army's role in the Indian wars was almost always controversial. Bungled campaigns such as the Modoc War aroused the wrath of westerners at army incompetence, while incidents such as the slaughter on the Marias River provoked eastern outrage. The latter atrocity, in fact, persuaded Congress to reject a measure that would have transferred the Bureau of Indian Affairs back from the Interior Department (where it had been since 1849) to the War Department. Reformers in the Northeast clashed with western politicians who saw the "Indian problem" as their own affair. Congress and a succession of presidents fought over what policy to follow, and in the meantime local agents and missionaries pursued their own conflicting agendas. The Kiowa chief Satank pointedly observed that he was tired of hearing contradictory explanations and pledges. "We do not break treaties," he said of his people. "We make but few contracts, and them we remember well. The whites make so many they are liable to forget them. The white chief seems not to be able to govern his braves." The young Chief Joseph of the Nez Percé voiced similar frustration. "I cannot understand why so many chiefs are allowed to talk so many different ways, and promise so many different things," he wrote. "It makes my heart sick when I remember all the good words and all the broken promises."

The first source of dispute was often, as in the Modoc War, the question of what was being given up. Some chiefs hoped to keep peace by sharing their territories with encroaching settlers; few believed they were consenting to be removed from ancestral homes. A few managed to stay: the Crow, for example, who allied with the United States out of hatred for their traditional Sioux and Cheyenne enemies, retained a portion of their lands for their reservation. The Crow cooperated with federal officials, Chief Plenty Coups said later, "not because we loved the white man who was already crowding other tribes into our country, . . . but because we plainly saw that this course was the only one which might save our beautiful country for us." Yet many other tribes were carted off to arid wastelands far from home. The Wichita, Osage, Cheyenne, Arapaho, Kiowa, and Comanche, all of whom lived on coveted lands, were deposited in Indian Territory (now Oklahoma), just as the Cherokee of Georgia had been during the 1830s "Trail of Tears."

Most of the era's Indian wars occurred *after* such removals, as peoples who had reluctantly moved to reservations found themselves subject to new forms of oppression. Appalling corruption among agents in the field exacerbated federal stinginess. Pensions, blankets, medical supplies, and rations never materialized or were skimmed off by unscrupulous agents while the intended recipients froze and starved. When the Ponca, a settled farming people in Nebraska, were shipped to Indian Territory, more than a third of the nation died of exhaustion, starvation, and contaminated water. "They took our reapers, mowers, hay rakes, spades, ploughs, bedsteads, stoves, cupboards, everything we had on our farms," remembered Chief Standing Bear. "After we reached the new land, all my horses died. The water was very bad." Standing Bear led repeated escape attempts, in one case taking the body of his son back to his homeland for secret burial.

Similar conditions led to the last major Indian war, fought by the Mimbre and Chiricahua Apache in the 1880s. Despite promises to the contrary, these Apache were forced onto a consolidated reservation at San Carlos, along Arizona's Gila River, in brutally hot country rife with malaria. "There was nothing but cactus, heat, rattlesnakes, rocks, and insects," one man remembered. "No game; no edible plants. Many, many of our people died." After a two-year struggle to live under these conditions or negotiate a move, the Apache revolted. Mimbre leader Victorio led the first fight, eventually crossing into Mexico, where he and seventy-seven warriors were killed in a battle with Mexican soldiers in 1880. A year later Chiricahua leaders Juh and Geronimo also abandoned San Carlos and engaged in a rebellion that lasted six years. When Geronimo finally surrendered, the federal decision to imprison 300 Apache at Fort Marion, Florida, seemed an exercise in randomness as capricious as the hanging of the Modoc Captain Jack. The prisoners

"Libby, McNeill & Libby's Cooked Corned Beef. 'Heap Good, circa 1880.'" This lithograph trade card reflects popular views of "primitive" Indians, but shows that for the average corned-beef customer, Indians were now more a source of disdain than a threatening frontier presence.
Source: The Warshaw Collection of Business Americana, Smithsonian Institution, Washington, DC.

included not only Geronimo but also several scouts who had fought with U.S. forces *against* him as well as a number of men who had never left the reservation at all.

Many Americans were distressed by these events. A San Francisco newspaper judged the government "murderous," calling the country's entire Indian policy "a miserable one and a failure." President Rutherford B. Hayes bluntly stated in a message to Congress that "many, if not most, of our Indian wars have had their origins in broken promises and acts of injustice on our part." Helen Hunt Jackson's *A Century of Dishonor*, which was published in 1881 and remains one of the most damning accounts of U.S. Indian policy ever written, won widespread praise, and its author hoped it would serve as another *Uncle Tom's Cabin* to sear the national conscience. But the abolition of slavery had been synonymous with progress and uplift, while few Americans—even Jackson herself—could imagine letting "primitives" live in their traditional ways. As Theodore Roosevelt put it crudely in his book *The Winning of the West*, "The Indians never had any real title to the soil. . . . This great continent could not have been kept as nothing but a game preserve for squalid savages." The federal courts ruled in *Standing Bear v. Crook* that the U.S. government could not treat Indians as permanent noncitizens, but they did not set a clear limit or deadline on this "temporary" status. (In addition to this lawsuit, the Ponca chief, helped by sympathetic journalists and ministers in Nebraska, undertook a lecture tour, and the public outcry that followed won his people the right to return to their lands.)

Cohoe, *War Dance at Fort Marion*, circa 1875–77. A Cheyenne taken as a prisoner of war, Cohoe was held for several years at Fort Marion, Florida. In this sketch from one of several notebooks left by Fort Marion prisoners, Cohoe records a dance performed for tourists. The detail with which Cohoe renders the tourists' clothing and accessories suggests that the prisoners observed the visitors at least as carefully as tourists watched them.
Source: From *A Cheyenne Sketchbook* (Norman, OK, 1964), p. 83. University of Oklahoma Press.

By the 1880s the "Wars of the Peace Policy" had launched a new attempt to replace armed conflict with Indian assimilation and citizenship. The crux of the plan was to divide reservations into individual parcels for families to farm, a goal set forth in the Dawes Severalty Act of 1887. Ownership of private property, the bill's sponsors believed, would motivate Indians to follow Anglo ways, and they demanded acceptance of this system as a precondition for granting voting and citizenship rights. In many ways the Dawes Act unintentionally finished the job that violent removal had begun. Under the allotment system Indian peoples lost enormous swaths of their remaining lands to intruders. A few agricultural peoples who, like the Ponca, kept or regained part of their traditional lands, fared decently under the system, and some large nations such as the Navajo and Cherokee held on to significant resources. But most tribes entered a nether region between citizenship and dependency. Catastrophic losses of land continued until federal policy underwent sweeping revisions in the New Deal of the 1930s, by which point incalculable damage had been done. Allotment also divided tribes. When the Choctaw nation in Indian Territory was given a choice of adopting or rejecting the new land system, the election created a rift. "There was bitter feeling on both sides and even some killing," remembered one council member. A similar decision split the Hopi pueblo of Oraibi. The winning assimilationists forced 400 traditionalists to leave the village and go into exile, taking only what they could carry. The refugees formed the new town of Hotevilla.

Despite severe hardship, many Indians found ways to resist. Indeed, within a decade of Geronimo's surrender, young men and women such as Dr. Charles Eastman and Zitkala-Sa were exploring new avenues for cultural survival, while Indian leaders mounted legal challenges over land and human rights. Sacred dances and feasts continued secretly, while grandparents passed down legends in the traditional tongues. Well aware that census-takers thought they all looked alike, people on the Lakota reservation in South Dakota filed by the census table multiple times to raise their official count and thus their rations. On the second and third time through the line they quietly registered their contempt by submitting names that translated into obscenities such as "Shit Head." In Indian Territory, the Creek writer Alexander Posey used the same kind of biting satire to critique federal policy, referring to Theodore Roosevelt as "President Rooster Feather" and the local Indian agent, a Mr. Shoenfelt, as "Sho-am-fat."

On some reservations Indians who accepted Anglo ways found themselves ostracized. Laura Pedrick, one of the first full-blooded Indians appointed a field matron among her own people, exposed the performance of secret dances and feasts to reservation authorities. She found herself under immediate pressure as Kiowa, Comanche, and Apache on the reservation told authorities they found Pedrick "objectionable." Other native leaders skillfully blended old and new. Local agents considered William Wash of the White River Ute to be "pro-white"; when the tribe debated the land allotment system he accepted it, prospering afterward as a rancher and farmer. Yet Walsh used his power to advocate on behalf of all Ute, and he shared much of his prosperity with less fortunate neighbors, building community ties in the fashion of a traditional chief.

In the face of overwhelming forces of dislocation and dispossession, much was gained by a strategy such as Walsh's. But much was also lost. Speaking to an interviewer in the early twentieth century, an elderly Hidatsa named Buffalo Bird Woman traced the changes she had experienced through the story of her own family. "My little son grew up in the white man's school. He can read books, and he owns cattle and has a farm. He is kind to me. We no longer live in an earth lodge, but in a house with chimneys; and my son's wife cooks by a stove. But for me, I cannot forget our old ways. Often in summer I rise at daybreak and steal out to the cornfields, and as I hoe the corn I sing to it, as we did when I was young. . . . Sometimes at evening I sit, looking out on the big Missouri. . . . In the river's roar I hear the yells of warriors, the laughter of little children as of old. It is but an old woman's dream."

In the decades when the United States quelled the last armed Indian resistance, wars of incorporation were also waged over Mexican-American ranches and farms in the Southwest. At issue were property titles in the Mexican cession, lands the United States had seized in 1848 after the Mexican-American War. The lives of Mexicans living in remote parts of Texas, New Mexico, and

Arizona had been largely undisturbed for decades afterward, and these rural outposts—as well as small cities such as Tucson and Santa Fe—remained overwhelmingly Latino. But after the Civil War Anglo ranchers and developers began moving in to stake their claims. As in the Indian wars, many took the law into their own hands, using violence and intimidation to get what they wanted. Faustino Morales, a cowboy employed on a giant Texas ranch, described the process there. "There were many small ranches belonging to Mexicans, but then the Americans came in and drove the Mexicans out. . . . After that they fenced the ranches."

Some Mexicans fought back, especially in New Mexico and south Texas, where their communities were strong. Men such as Juan Patrón and Juan Gonzalez, a county clerk and deputy sheriff in New Mexico's Pecos Valley, tried to protect their neighbors during waves of violent land seizures, in this case instigated in the 1870s by invading Texans. The resulting Lincoln County War temporarily stalled the newcomers. The New Mexico Territorial Governor Edmund G. Ross, sympathetic to his state's Mexican residents, wrote to one cattle company in indignation. "I understand very well," he wrote, "and so do you, what a cowboy or cattle herder with a brace of pistols at his belt and a Winchester in his hands, means when he 'asks' a sheepherder to leave a given range. It means instant compliance or very unpleasant consequences to the herder and his flock." Ross denounced the company for setting "these men and your cattle upon a quarter of the public domain that has been occupied exclusively by these Mexican sheep herders for a generation or more." But officials more friendly to Anglo interests soon replaced men like Ross.

When intimidation did not work, property rights could be manipulated. With taxes overdue on one coveted Mexican ranch in Hidalgo County, Texas, during the depression of the 1870s, the sheriff sold all 3,000 acres to an associate for $15. More often, powerful business interests hired teams of lawyers to contest Mexican land titles, most of which were communally held, poorly documented, and decades or even centuries old. In New Mexico leaders of the notorious Santa Fe Ring got immensely rich through such litigation. Powerful lawyers played both sides of the fence, working for corporate investors but also offering to defend Mexican land titles in exchange for taking a portion of the estate as their fee. By these methods, as well as armed occupation of several parts of the territory, the Santa Fe attorney Thomas Catron came to possess nearly two million acres of land.

Because property claims in the Mexican cession were so tangled, Congress set up a federal Court of Private Land Claims in 1891 to sort them out. The results were dramatic: the court recognized almost no Mexican *ejidos*, or traditional communal properties, returning only 5 percent of the thirty-five million disputed acres to Mexicans living there. The court awarded most of the other acres to another kind of collective owner: corporations, who consolidated their landholdings and undertook ranching, lumbering, and mining on a grand scale. Some of the court's rulings precipitated more violence, such as protracted battles on the Maxwell Land Grant in northern New Mexico and southern Colorado. This tract was occupied by villages of Mexican farmers who held their land by informal recognition from large landholders. The grant had also attracted Anglos such as Richard and Marian Russell, a Union veteran and his wife, who staked a claim in a Colorado valley where they built a ranch, dug a small lake, planted an orchard, and raised six children. When Lucien and Luz Maxwell, brothers who owned the "two million acres more or less" of the Maxwell Grant, sold out to a consortium of European investors, a lengthy and violent conflict ensued. As early as 1875 a Methodist minister who opposed corporate takeover was found dead in a canyon near Cimarron, New Mexico. The conflict escalated after 1882, when the Supreme Court ruled that the grant belonged to the consortium. Investors proceeded to "clear the grant"; they wanted it empty to begin a vast cattle ranching operation of their own.

The consortium's agents employed a divide-and-conquer policy, brokering deals with individual residents and isolating those who tried to hold out. Pressured by the agents, county sheriffs all over the grant undertook eviction procedures against farmers who remained. They met stiff resistance. In Raton, New Mexico, armed men defended the property of the outspoken editor O. P. McMains. Along the Vermejo River the farmer Jacinto Santistevan and his sons led their neighbors in a decade of stubborn refusal to leave. Farther south, along the Poñil, the killing of the rancher Julio Martínez by two Anglo deputies triggered a wave of shootouts. But ultimately, across the grant, the consortium prevailed. One of the last episodes of protest took place on Main Street in Stonewall, Colorado, where farmers and ranchers barricaded corporate agents inside the local hotel. In the shootout that followed, the homesteader Richard Russell watched as two of his neighbors, "Frenchy" Giradet and Rafael Valerio, were gunned down. Russell himself was shot in the left side and lay in the line of fire for several hours. He died five days later at home, and though his wife pursued her legal right to hold on to the family's land, the courts ruled against her. In 1895 she, too, was forced to leave.

On the Maxwell Grant some Anglo and Mexican-American farmers worked together to resist eviction, but nationwide such cross-racial cooperation was more often the exception than the rule. Americans had always been divided along ethnic and racial lines, and the upheavals of incorporation intensified long-standing hatreds and precipitated new ones, not only among Anglos, Indians, and Mexicans but even more against immigrants from China. Some Chinese had entered California as early as the Gold Rush in 1849, but starting in the 1870s employers pinned their hopes on a much larger supply of cheap Asian labor, and the immigrants spread beyond the Pacific coast. In several parts of the South planters sought (unsuccessfully) to replace militant freedmen with Chinese workers. In an infamous 1870 incident the shoe manufacturer Calvin Sampson shipped seventy-five Chinese workers into Massachusetts to replace French-Canadians and Irish who were out on strike. His maneuver forced the strikers back to work with a 10 percent pay cut, fomenting bitter resentment against the Chinese. Around the same time the owner of a large steam laundry in South Belleville, New Jersey, recruited Chinese men to replace Irish-American women. In almost every case the goal was to cut wages, though the long-term results were mixed. As soon as they could, many Chinese quit low-paid jobs and set up small businesses of their own.

Thus, the Chinese, like blacks in the South, confounded the stereotype that they were pliant and obedient employees. During anti-Asian violence in San Francisco, Chinese business leaders wrote to the mayor warning that if attacks continued they had "neither the power nor disposition to restrain our country-men from defending themselves to the last extremity and selling their lives as dearly as possible." Having endured a winter of avalanches and subzero temperatures in the Sierra Nevada, 5,000 Chinese construction workers on the Central Pacific Railroad struck in the spring of 1867. They asked for wages of $45 a month (the company offered $31) and showed keen awareness of the national campaign for an eight-hour workday. "Eight hours a day good for white men," they declared, "all the same good for Chinamen." Bosses cut off food to the camps and wired New York about the possibility of import-ing 10,000 blacks as replacements. The strikers held out a week before they surrendered.

Despite such evidence that they shared common goals with the Chinese, some leaders of the American labor movement devoted more energy to anti-Chinese agitation than they did to more constructive goals. The most notori-ous was Dennis Kearney, the head of San Francisco's Workingmen's Party, who denounced Chinese immigrants as "almond-eyed lepers" and promoted the slogan "The Chinese must GO!" During one boycott of businesses in San Francisco that employed Chinese, a group of Chinese workers at one of the boycotted firms went on strike for higher wages. Instead of seeing them as potential allies, the Anglo workers announced they were exempting that employer from the boycott, on the grounds that if the Chinese disliked him, he must be OK. Kearney stirred up a public that was already deeply anti-Asian. Chinese faced hostility not only because they worked for low wages but because they were not white, not from Europe, and for the most part not Christians. Magazines and newspapers depicted Chinese women as diseased prostitutes and Chinese men as scheming cheats, opium addicts, and potential rapists. A typical article in the *New York Tribune* denounced Chinese immi-grants as "utter heathens, treacherous, sensual, cowardly and cruel."

In the West hatred of the Chinese fueled brutal violence. Mobs in San Francisco went on a three-day rampage in July 1877, burning and looting Chinatown and beating up residents. Eight years later in Rock Springs, Wyoming, vigilantes burned to death twenty-eight Chinese men in one of dozens of incidents in which Chinese were lynched or driven out of mining camps and towns across the West. One of the first activities of the Knights of Labor in Wichita, Kansas, was to organize a boycott of Chinese laundries. African-American women who resented competition had already forced Chinese laundrymen out of Galveston, Texas. Even in the absence of large-scale violence, Chinese faced steady harassment. In his old age one immigrant remembered the boundaries of his world as a youngster in San Francisco: if you ventured outside the few square blocks of Chinatown, "the white kids would throw stones at you." "We kept indoors after dark for fear of being shot in the back," recalled another man. "Children spit upon us as we passed by and called us rats." Chinese-American workers had to negotiate between two worlds. Family and friends at home in China might think a man was happily collecting riches in "Gold Mountain," while he actually found himself living as a pariah, sometimes in fear of his life. Maintaining their pride, some immigrants told relatives in China that they were "clothing entrepreneurs" in order to hide the fact that they worked in sweaty laundries.

Deep hostility toward the Chinese expressed itself in two federal laws of pathbreaking significance. The first, the 1875 Page Act, subjected all female Chinese immigrants to interrogation and exclusion as potential prostitutes. Rigid enforcement denied entry to almost all Chinese women, even wives seeking to join their husbands. Since the early Chinese population in the United States, like that of many other immigrant groups, was overwhelmingly male, the Page Act kept the gender ratio skewed. It thus had the opposite of its intended effect, perpetuating prostitution while also helping sustain hostile stereotypes about Asians' supposed inability to sustain proper family life. As late as 1900, less than 5 percent of all Chinese in the United States were women. Though a few worked as cooks and seamstresses, most were indeed prostitutes: in a community of single men and others with families thousands of miles away, they aptly fulfilled the Chinese name for their work, *baak haak chai*, or "hundred-men's wife."

In the meantime, the Chinese Exclusion Act of 1882 barred all poor Chinese laborers from entry into the United States. In an era of unrestricted immigration, this was an unprecedented measure to bar newcomers of a single nationality. It was extremely popular with voters, but never as effective as supporters claimed. Though immigration became more difficult, Chinese men found ways to get in and out of the country—and powerful business interests helped see to it that they did. Indeed, both the Chinese and U.S. governments estimated after the act's passage that nine out of ten Chinese men in America had entered illegally. Some disguised themselves as Mexicans and crossed through the desert from Mexico, a dangerous journey that regularly claimed lives. Others arrived as stowaways on cargo ships or, in the Pacific Northwest, on local ferries from Canada. Many others, known as "paper sons," established false identities based on fictitious relationships with Chinese who were already in America and permitted to bring their children. Border officials kept extensive records and interrogated newcomers, but their screening procedures proved ineffectual. Prospective immigrants memorized long lists of "facts" about their alleged hometowns, families, and neighbors. Their "memory books" eventually ran to 200 or 300 pages, keeping paper sons a few steps ahead of the voluminous records in U.S. immigration files.

The Chinese thus became the nation's first illegal immigrants. As Congress tried to ratchet up enforcement, the issue remained a focus of public anger for three decades, especially in the West, while the Exclusion Act also remained a sore point in U.S.-Chinese relations until its repeal in 1943, when the two nations allied during World War II. As early as 1877 the Chinese government set up a permanent consulate in San Francisco, and its representatives protested that Chinese should have the right to enter the United States on the same basis as everyone else. Chinese-Americans also protested their treatment. "The Chinese must stay," asserted journalist Yan Phon Lee, contradicting Dennis Kearney's rallying cry. He noted that "it was by the application of

Chinese 'cheap labor' to the building of railroads, the reclamation of swamp-lands, to mining, fruit culture, and manufacturing, that an immense vista of employment was opened up for Caucasians, and that millions now are enabled to live in comfort and luxury. Besides," he added, "are you sure that Chinese laborers would not ask more if they dared, or take more if they could get it?" While defending themselves from racism, Chinese spokesmen sometimes revealed prejudices of their own. Lai Chun-Chuen, a San Francisco merchant, bridled at being classed with "Indians and Negroes"—especially the former, whom he described as barbarians living naked in caves.

The Page and Chinese Exclusion Acts had a profound long-term impact on immigration policy. As the first laws barring entry to people of a specific race or nationality, they served as models for twentieth-century immigration quotas. Follow-up legislation brought additional harbingers of things to come, requiring Chinese immigrants to register with the government and carry identification cards. Chinese-Americans put up vigorous legal challenges to these and other discriminatory laws. In the decade after 1882 they filed more than 7,000 habeas corpus petitions in northern California courts, and these suits helped shape definitions of U.S. citizenship. By the early twentieth century the Supreme Court had confirmed that anyone born in the United States was a citizen, and judges had struck down a range of discriminatory laws. But the courts also granted the federal government broad leeway to naturalize or deport immigrants on whatever basis it saw fit. Congress made increasing use of these powers, excluding polygamists in 1891, anarchists in 1903, and four years later, people suffering from tuberculosis, epilepsy, or physical disabilities. By 1921 this had evolved into a stringent quota system for immigrants from all parts of the world. Enforcement was, in the meantime, handed over to a Bureau of Immigration (later the Immigration and Naturalization Service), and those subject to deportation were denied access to the courts, even if they had evidence that they were U.S. citizens. "If the Commissioners [of Immigration]," remarked one federal judge, "wished to order an alien drawn, quartered, and chucked overboard they could do so without interference."

In every major case that denied due process to aliens, the plaintiffs were Asian-born. Occasionally they were Japanese (as in the 1892 case *Nishimura Ekiu v. US*), but most often they were Chinese. It was thus hostility to Asians that fueled the rise of a Bureau of Immigration with unprecedented powers, and the definitions of legal and illegal immigrants have remained highly racialized ever since. As economic growth brought millions of Europeans into the harbors of New York, Philadelphia, and Boston and thousands of Mexicans across the unmarked and unguarded border into El Norte, anti-Asian prejudice laid the foundations for later policies that would shut those doors.

LABOR, RACE, AND VIOLENCE

All the wars of incorporation were race wars in at least some of their dimensions. In the West they pitted Anglos against American Indians and Mexican *ejidos*, in the South struggles between landowners and laborers often boiled down to Anglo versus black, and across the country hostility toward the Chinese fueled violence and exclusion. The upheavals of the post–Civil War years also intensified a range of other racial and ethnic hatreds. One Massachusetts writer described French-Canadian workers as "the Chinese of the Eastern States." The leader of a Pennsylvania steelworkers' union complained in 1883 about Italians, Hungarians, Bohemians, and Poles who were imported during strikes, and whom he also compared to the Chinese. He declared himself "disgusted" by their degraded living conditions and willingness to work for low pay. Others voiced similar sentiments, conveniently forgetting their own immigrant pasts. One Irish-American woman told a visitor angrily that there ought to be a law "to keep all them I-talians from comin' in and takin' the bread out of the mouths of honest people."

Such attitudes sprang in part from lived reality. Many of the new immigrants *did* work for lower pay and lived as cheaply as they could, saving to return home or send money back to families in poorer parts of the world. Employers exploited the divisions within a working class that hailed from five continents. Hawaiian sugar planters, for example, carefully maintained a one-half Chinese and one-half Japanese workforce, and when they suspected the two halves were beginning to cooperate, they imported Portuguese. Employers brought in Italians to break a strike in the New York construction trades in 1874, and Italians arrived in Pennsylvania coalfields that same year as employers sought to cut local wages. Three were murdered in the ensuing conflict. A Vermont quarry owner, when Irish-American workers demanded union recognition and an eight-hour day, wrote to a steamship company and asked for 300 Swedes. Fifteen years later steamboat operators on the Mississippi also tried to recruit Swedes, in this case to replace blacks (though the new workers quit in disgust, having many other employment options). Discrimination did not always start at the top, but with white unions. "I was on the Southern Pacific Railway in 1884," recalled one black rail worker, "when 295 colored fireman and an equal number of brakemen were dis-

SECTARIAN BITTERNESS.

Thomas Nast, "Sectarian Bitterness," detail from a political cartoon satirizing conflicts over school funding. In this cartoon schoolyard fight Nast captures an array of prevailing stereotypes against Jews and Irish (the central figures) and blacks and Chinese (on the right).
Source: *Harper's Weekly*, 26 February 1870.

charged. . . . I could name five more roads where colored men have been relieved by the request of the white brotherhoods."

In the face of such deep hostilities, however, labor activism did occasionally cross ethnic and racial lines, especially at the local level. The U.S. labor movement was loose and decentralized, and most strikes began at the grassroots rather than with a decision by union leaders. Such "wildcat strikes" were most often prompted by a wage cut or another sudden injustice. At Montana's Gregory Consolidated mine in January 1887, company officials announced that they were closing down and workers would not receive pay for their previous two months' employment. After a hasty meeting miners seized the town and took four company men as hostages. They then wired A. J. Seligman's New York banking firm, which held a large interest in the mine, and warned that they would not surrender until back pay arrived. They got their money right away. (Astutely, they had chosen as one of their hostages Jesse Seligman, the banker's son).

Americans in the late nineteenth century witnessed an enormous number of such spontaneous local protests, as many as 1,500 in a single year. The first

Police during the 1903 Chicago City Railway strike. In hundreds of late nineteenth- and early twentieth-century conflicts between labor and capital, urban police played a decisive antilabor role.
Source: Photograph by a *Chicago Daily News* photographer. Chicago Historical Society.

nationwide upheaval was even more explosive, centering on that transformative enterprise, the railroad. The Great Railroad Strike jolted the nation for two weeks in July 1877. It began when managers of the four largest railroads met and agreed to slash wages, on top of a series of cuts already made over the previous three years. When the Baltimore & Ohio announced reductions of 10 percent, workers in West Virginia simply walked off the job, followed by railmen all over the East Coast and as far away as St. Louis and Chicago. Within days the walkout effectively shut down the transportation system. Ironworkers, dockworkers, and thousands of others gathered in the streets to join the revolt. In an indication of the breadth of anger against the roads, those arrested for joining a militant crowd in Buffalo included masons, blacksmiths, clerks, merchants, and even a stove manufacturer.

As railroad officials pressured state governors to send in the militia, Republican President Rutherford B. Hayes declared the strike an "insurrection" and called up U.S. troops. The arrival of armed units with instructions to get the trains running, no matter what, transformed the peaceful walkout into a bloody fight. After a militia unit fired into a crowd in Baltimore, killing eleven, the mob went wild. In Chicago crowds of strikers clashed with police near the McCormick Reaper Works and the Burlington & Quincy roundhouse, where they destroyed two locomotives. The *Chicago Times* demanded in response that hand grenades be used against the "unwashed mob." Referring to the ruthless Union General Philip H. Sheridan, who was busy fighting Indians in the West, one Massachusetts man remarked to his neighbor, "I wish Sheridan was at Pittsburgh."

Sheridan's counterparts did go to Chicago. The 9th and 22nd U.S. Infantry regiments, two cavalry companies, and an artillery unit were called from the South Dakota Indian wars to patrol Chicago's streets. The struggle was equally dramatic in Pittsburgh, hub of the much-hated Pennsylvania Railroad. Knowing that most local residents sympathized with the strikers, the railroad's president called up militia units from other parts of the state. "My troops," he declared, "will see that the trains pass." Met by an angry mob, the militia killed twenty people with random rifle fire. Infuriated workers then looted and set fire to the Pennsylvania railyard, leaving behind the charred hulks of freight cars and engines. By the time federal troops suppressed the strike in Pittsburgh, forty-five people were dead.

The 1877 strike exposed a widening chasm between affluent Americans and those who identified with the working classes. Many of the former—and most of the press—considered the strike itself illegitimate. No matter how much strikers disciplined their ranks and how many deaths were caused by militia rifles, protesters were depicted as disruptive and violent thugs. Thus, for organized labor, spectacular strikes brought visibility and mass solidarity, but they also provoked an intense backlash. After 1877 prosperous Americans became increasingly panicked by labor militancy. Denying that conditions in the United States warranted such protests, they blamed strikes on "foreign-born agitators," in an ironic variant on the hostility many workers themselves showed toward newer immigrants such as the Chinese. Small wonder that labor leader Terence Powderly struggled desperately to *prevent* strikes.

Powderly led the most visionary and successful labor organization of the era, the Knights of Labor. Its growth depended in part on a successful 1885 strike against Jay Gould's Southwestern Railroad, begun at the grassroots by workers who had not yet joined the union. The Knights took on most of the labor issues of the day: the deskilling of crafts that robbed workers of power on the job, employers' refusal to recognize unions or submit to arbitration, and the growing movement for an eight-hour workday. The Knights sought to bring under their umbrella skilled and unskilled workers of all races and backgrounds, whether rural or urban, male or female, immigrant or native-born. (There was one crucial and predicable exception to the Knights' inclusiveness: they denounced the Chinese and refused to accept them even when they applied to join.) " 'Each for himself' is the bosses' plea," proclaimed a sign carried by Knights members in a Detroit parade; "Union for all will make you free." Or as a Boston man explained, the Knights' strength came from "the fact that the whole life of the community is drawn into it, that people of all kinds are together, . . . and that they all get directly the sense of each others' needs."

The Knights were most visible in the growing cities of the Northeast and Midwest. St. Louis and Cleveland workers founded one hundred assemblies each, and twice that number were established in Brooklyn. Philadelphia, where garment cutters had first founded the order in 1869, boasted almost 300 locals among workers ranging from carpet weavers to beer wagon drivers. The order was well represented in other parts of the country as well. Knights in Omaha, Nebraska, organized grocery clerks, mattress makers, and musicians. The Arkansas Knights boasted locals in 48 different counties, including coal miners, cotton mill workers, and farmhands. At one point a strike by Knights telegraphers in the ex-Confederacy halted communications among Atlanta, Montgomery, Charleston, Jacksonville, and Wilmington. In Pensacola, Florida, lumbermen and stevedores joined the Knights in 1886, followed by laundry-women and housekeepers. The Knights boasted all-black, all-German, all-Jewish, and all-Italian locals; some women formed their own separate assemblies, while others joined clubs along with men. In San Miguel County, New Mexico, the Knights organizer Juan José Herrera and his brothers Pablo and Nicanor organized secret midnight raids, calling themselves Las Gorras Blancas, or "White Hats," cutting barbed-wire fences and burning railroad bridges to protest Anglo intrusion. Clearly, in parts of the West, the rise of the Knights was a direct extension of the wars of incorporation. "There is a wide difference between New Mexico's 'law' and 'justice,' " the Gorras Blancas declared in their 1890 manifesto (signed "1,500 Strong and Growing Daily"). "Justice is God's law, and that we must have at all hazards."

Law and politics eventually defeated the Knights after other tactics did not, as events illustrated in the town of Rutland, Vermont. Rutland's marble quarries employed large numbers of Irish and French-Canadian immigrant workers. Under the banner of the United Labor Party in 1886, such workers and their allies in the Knights swept a full slate of candidates into office. But well-connected quarry owners immediately pressured the state legislature to divide Rutland into three separate jurisdictions. They then unseated a newly elected judge and fifteen justices of the peace on grounds that they had no jurisdiction in the newly created districts; they also demanded that each local official post an expensive $1,000 bond. As a historian of the incident writes, "it was as if [the Knights] had sat down to dinner only to discover that the main course had just been removed." The new town of Proctor (named after the leading quarry owner) became staunchly Republican; West Rutland, saddled with debts by the reorganization, fell back in the hands of old-line Democrats. Only in the third district, the now much smaller town of Rutland, did the Knights of Labor continue to hold sway.

At the time of the Rutland election the Knights, with nationwide membership peaking at 750,000, were suffering from the repercussions from an infamous episode of violence that shaped the course of American labor relations. The Chicago reaper manufacturer Cyrus McCormick was determined to end union activity at his plant. In February 1886 he instituted a lockout and replaced all remaining union workers with nonunion ones. For months afterward angry ex-employees picketed the so-called Black Road beside McCormick's plant, taunting those who had taken their jobs. In a May 3 clash policemen fired into the crowd, killing two and wounding more. The leaders of Chicago's militant anarchist movement, one of whom had been addressing a meeting of the Lumber Shovers' Union only a few blocks from the site of the shootings, called for a protest rally the following day in Chicago's Haymarket Square. On May 4, as the teamster and labor leader Samuel Fielden addressed a sparse crowd, police closed in with clubs to break off the meeting. Someone (to this day, no one knows who) threw a bomb that killed a policemen. The panicked police opened fire, killing one of their own and wounding many others. Seven more officers died of their wounds.

Amid public hysteria blame for the bomb was quickly pinned on leaders of Chicago's fiery anarchists. The historian who has researched Haymarket most thoroughly believes an anarchist may well have thrown the bomb—but it was not any of the eight men who stood trial. Among the eight was Albert Parsons, a charismatic anarchist who had grown up in Texas and fought in a Confederate regiment at age fourteen. As active Republicans during Reconstruction, Parsons and his wife, Lucy, had been harassed because of their politics and their interracial marriage (Lucy was of mixed Mexican and African-American descent) and had moved to Chicago, where they joined the anarchist cause. Knowing police wanted him for questioning, Parsons fled into hiding in Wisconsin, but on the first day of the Haymarket trial he created a sensation by walking into the courtroom and asking to be tried along with the defendants. "As in former times," Parsons declared in a public statement, "a privileged class never surrendered its tyranny, neither can it be expected that the capitalists of this age will give up their rulership without being forced to do it. . . . There remains but one resource—FORCE! Our forefathers have not only told us that against despots force is justifiable, because it is the only means, but they themselves have set the immortal example." Parsons's associate Louis Lingg, a twenty-two-year-old immigrant carpenter, put it more bluntly in his final statement. "I do not recognize your law, jumbled together as it is by the nobodies of bygone centuries, and I do not recognize the decision of the court," Lingg said. "I am the enemy of the 'order' of today, and

I repeat that, with all my powers, so long as breath remains in me, I shall combat it."

In the small number of lives lost, the violence at Haymarket paled in comparison to that of many other clashes of incorporation, but its influence on public opinion was profound. A jury convicted all eight defendants of conspiracy and sentenced four to death. Despite a nationwide petition campaign, Parsons and three others were hanged, while Lingg killed himself in his cell to resist execution by the state. Across the nation the labor movement divided over how to respond. The Knights of Labor leader Terence Powderly distanced himself from the defendants, declaring that he would rather see the hanging of "seven times seven" innocent men than show any sympathy for anarchism. Powderly even viciously slandered Parsons's wife as a "woman of bad reputation." After Haymarket, in fact, Powderly became increasingly obsessed with purging the Knights of dissenters. Divided, demoralized, and discredited, the Knights lost two-thirds of their members within a year. Meanwhile, some Americans were shocked at the unfair convictions, clearly based on what the defendants had said rather than anything they had done, and the anarchists became known as the "Haymarket martyrs." The journalist Henry Demarest Lloyd feared the results portended "government by police," a massive erosion of the rights of free speech and fair trial. The novelist William Dean Howells called the executions "civic murder," an "atrocious piece of frenzy and cruelty, for which we must stand ashamed forever before history."

But Lloyd and Howells were in the distinct minority among the country's prosperous and intellectual classes. Both faced intense criticism and social ostracism because of their stand, as public sentiment turned against the entire labor movement. In what has been called the nation's first "Red Scare," Chicago police helped feed the hysteria. Captain Michael Schaack and Inspector John Bonfield, in particular, used Haymarket as a career-making opportunity. They and other police arrested hundreds of Chicagoans, mostly without warrants, and alternately beat and bribed many to extract confessions. For weeks they issued almost daily warnings of imminent danger, suggesting they were uncovering an immense nationwide anarchist conspiracy. Newspapers reprinted these reports under banner headlines. "[Captain Schaack] saw more anarchists than vast hell could hold," one commentator wrote later. "Bombs, dynamite, daggers, guns, and pistols danced ever across his excited vision." One of Schaack's own superior officers admitted later that the captain "wanted bombs to be found here, there, all around, everywhere" and sought to "keep himself prominent before the public." Nonetheless, the damage was done. Editors denounced all labor leaders as the "scum and offal of Europe," "long-haired, wild-eyed, bad-smelling, atheistic, reckless foreign wretches" and "a danger that threatens the destruction of our national edifice." "As we cannot shut them up by love," E. L. Godkin wrote in *The Nation*, "we must do it by fear." In the wake of Haymarket many Americans concluded that the whole movement for worker rights and an eight-hour workday was a vast, violent, antidemocratic conspiracy.

Employers used the opportunity provided by Haymarket to marginalize and roll back the labor movement. Before the end of the year, 100,000 workers had been locked out and replaced, suffering the same fate as Cyrus McCormick's unionized workers in Chicago. Strikes across the country were crushed, including protests by packinghouse workers in Chicago and laundry workers in Troy, New York. The following year, striking under the banner of the Knights of Labor, African-American sugarcane cutters in Thibadaux, Louisiana, were mown down by field artillery and a Gatling gun wielded by state militia and local sheriffs' posses. These defeats further divided a labor movement whose more conservative leaders were already so fixated on distancing themselves from radicalism that they rejected May Day—the labor holiday recognized in all other industrialized countries—and invented a separate Labor Day in September. (Already, the year before Haymarket, Chicago union leaders had banned any red flags or socialist symbols from their Labor Day parade.) Haymarket intensified the predicament that the labor editor John Swinton had described three years earlier: "We have openly arrayed against us," he wrote, "the powers of the world, most of the intelligence, all the wealth, and even law itself."

Economic incorporation, then, brought violence not just to the Reconstruction South and the western frontier but to the entire nation. The upheavals of the Indian wars, the displacement of Mexican *ejidos*, anti-Chinese violence, and the suppression of strikes were connected phenomena that to some extent took place all at the same time. The single year of 1877, for example, witnessed not only the Great Railroad Strike but the Combahee rice workers' strike in South Carolina (discussed in Chapter 1); in the same year the National Guard was created to respond to domestic unrest, partly because the understaffed army was fully occupied fighting Indians in a series of battles including that year's Wolf Mountain in Montana and Clearwater in Idaho. In the very same year anti-Chinese demagogues were inciting riots in San Francisco, while Jesse James was still at large somewhere in Missouri (or perhaps Nebraska) and the Santa Fe ring was wrapping up the first phase of its consolidation of property in New Mexico.

In most of these conflicts public opinion, as reflected in both popular culture and the mainstream press, projected violence onto the victims (who were, themselves, not always inclined toward peaceable self-defense). Not only did Anglos widely accept stereotypes of bloody-minded Indians, cruel Mexicans, and treacherous Chinese immigrants, similar stereotypes applied to labor activists. A New York newspaper called the Haymarket defendants "foreign savages . . . as much apart from the rest of the people of this country as the Apaches of the plains." John Hay, later secretary of state under William McKinley and Theodore Roosevelt, anonymously published a novel in 1884 on the same theme. The hero of Hay's *The Breadwinners* was a cavalry officer who fought in the Black Hills against the Sioux and then came east to suppress the Great Railroad Strike in Chicago. The former army captain Charles King wrote three similar bestsellers in which officers with combat experience against the Apaches helped defeat "savage" strikers in Chicago and Colorado.

The western artist Frederic Remington was one of the most extreme proponents of this view. Writing and illustrating for *Harper's*, he justified violent repression of labor protests by depicting workingmen as savages. Remington, in fact, expressed more admiration for Indian warriors than for strikers, though in his increasingly racist rants he did not differentiate ethnic or racial groups with a great deal of clarity. At one point he referred to the Sioux War as a "jihad" against the United States, and in private correspondence he expressed deep hatred toward all non-Anglos. "Jews, Injuns, Chinamen, Italians, Huns,—the rubbish of the earth I hate," Remington wrote. "I've got some Winchesters and when the massacring begins, I can get my share of 'em, and what's more, I will." Though few Americans expressed views as crude as Remington's, many shared them in part. Across the country middle-class Anglos looked down on Indians, Mexicans, African Americans, and strikers for similar reasons: all were supposedly dirty, violent, and unwilling to accommodate themselves to the "natural" order of the new economy. Men who did some of the country's hardest and most dangerous physical labor were, ironically, stereotyped as not wanting to work.

Such judgments were changing and unstable; the categories of "colored" and "working class" were not the same, and sometimes popular commentary pitted one against the other instead of blending them together. In 1879, when thousands of blacks migrated out of the South into Kansas to seek a better life, many observers compared these earnest "Exodusters" favorably with strikers in the Northeast. An Anglo in the Southwest might characterize a pious Mexican housekeeper, with her flower garden and well-scrubbed children, as a "Spanish woman"; her husband, brothers, and sons, resisting Anglo encroachment on their grazing lands or striking with a mineworkers' union, were more likely to be classed as "greasers" or "Indians." Hard-working people received praise from antilabor conservatives when they "knew their place," but in episodes of protest and conflict the same people became "indolent, bigoted, cheating, dirty, cowardly."

In this reading of the world, up was down and down was up. Geographic consolidation and new systems of corporate capital and labor relations, which in fact were causing immense disruption and dislocation, were seen as agents of order and civilization. Gold-seekers who encroached on Indian lands were, if Indians retaliated, innocent victims. Militia units that fired into unarmed crowds were preservers of the peace. This explains why the term *riot* became mysteriously affixed to various confrontations such the "Haymarket riot" (which was not one) and a long series of "race riots" in the South, which, in fact, were carefully planned military attacks. In a "riot" the exact source of violence became fuzzy and could be shifted about. Despite considerable evidence to the contrary, comfortable Americans needed to believe that order was prevailing, that the sources of violence were meeting defeat, and that the new system in which they lived was promoting domestic tranquility.

Above all, Americans needed to believe that incorporation was a form of progress. Politicians and editors often expressed this view, and it also circulated through paintings and sketches such as Remington's as well as in popular novels. Starting in the 1860s an avid public bought thousands of dime westerns that told the tales of "savage redskins, vicious greasers, or heathen Chinee" who met their defeat at the hands of manly Anglo heroes. Books such as *Diamond Dick's Decoy Duck* and *Out with the Apache Kid* typically featured the rescue of a white maiden from the clutches of a dark-skinned captor (though working girls relished dozens of stories in which frontier heroines defended themselves). Some dime novels celebrated real incorporators such as Buffalo Bill Cody, who had started his career as a bison hunter feeding railroad construction crews. By the time of his death, various episodes in his life and mythology had been featured in more than 1,700 dime novels.

Buffalo Bill himself was one of the most successful salesmen for incorporation. His Wild West made a huge splash at the Chicago World's Fair and toured Europe as well as the United States before immense crowds. As the show began, small herds of bison thundered into the arena pursued by skilled Sioux and Pawnee riders (whom Bill, to his credit, treated as respected employees). Bill claimed to display more buffalo in his arena than remained wild "on the whole American continent," a claim that was, sadly, off by only a few hundred or so. The climax of the Wild West was a re-creation of the famous killing of George Armstrong Custer by Sioux and Cheyenne warriors at Little Big Horn, one of the few battles incorporators had lost. Americans dwelled almost obsessively on this incident after its occurrence in 1876; by depicting the tragedy and heroism of "Custer's Last Stand," they reassured themselves that the Indian wars had been a necessary fight against a ruthless and savage foe and that civilization had triumphed in the end.

Buffalo Bill suggested such a lesson when he strode into the arena to re-enact his killing of a Cheyenne warrior in a sequence called "First Scalp for Custer." These scenes became such a popular part of the Wild West that the Anheuser-Busch brewing company, seeking a promotional angle for Budweiser beer, commissioned a lithograph of Custer's last stand on the twentieth anniversary of the battle. (Borrowing from a book on South Africa, it depicted Custer's attackers carrying Zulu shields.) Reprinted many times, the lithograph hung for decades in saloons across the United States. Neither Buffalo Bill nor Anheuser Busch had much interest in the complexity of the events they depicted—but they were hardly alone. The very first reports of Custer's death had been filed by a man who falsely claimed to have been at the battle and built a lucrative career out of his "eyewitness" account. Buffalo Bill carried on the tradition when he brought on tour with him the real scalp of the Cheyenne warrior Yellow Hand, without explaining that he had orchestrated the encounter in anticipation of selling the story. (Nor did Bill ponder, apparently, the irony of taking a scalp on behalf of civilization.)

Significantly, by the 1890s Buffalo Bill's Wild West began to draw connections between conflicts in the West and those emerging overseas. After an international coalition, including 5,000 U.S. troops, suppressed the Boxer Rebellion in China in 1899, the Wild West introduced "Buffalo Bill's New and Greatest Military Spectacle: The Rescue at Pekin[g]." (The Sioux and Cheyenne employees of the Wild West donned pigtails to play the Chinese.) The popular narratives of incorporation, like incorporation itself, were already assuming international dimensions. Mythologizers like Buffalo Bill found large and enthusiastic audiences for their message that violent conquest was inevitable, and that it brought political, economic, and cultural progress to all the races of humanity. Among peoples subject to such conquest, responses were as varied on other continents as they were in North America. But to many observers overseas, as well as in the United States, the presumed triumph of civilization was a matter of serious doubt.

FOR FURTHER READING

My analysis in this chapter draws first of all on Richard Maxwell Brown's essay "Violence," in the *Oxford History of the American West* (cited in Chapter 2; pp. 803–834). In *The Incorporation of America*, Alan Trachtenberg also uses the term *incorporation* in both geographic and hierarchical senses to describe consolidations of power. In analyzing the international dimensions of such conflicts, Walter LaFeber's *The American Search for Opportunity, 1865–1913* (New York, 1993) has been immensely helpful here as well as in Chapter 11. For international comparisons see Walter T. K. Nugent, "Comparing Wests and Frontiers," also in the *Oxford History of the American West*, pp. 393–425. On conflict in the South see Altina Waller, *Feud* (Chapel Hill, NC, 1988), Gordon McKinney, "Industrialization and Violence in Appalachia in the 1890s," in *An Appalachian Symposium*, edited by Joel W. Williamson (Boone, NC, 1977), pp. 131–44, and Burgin Mathews, "Looking for Railroad Bill," *Southern Cultures*, Fall 2003, 66–88.

Patricia Nelson Limerick, "Haunted America," in her collection of essays *Something in the Soil* (New York, 2000), pp. 33–73, is quite possibly the most eloquent forty pages ever written about the so-called western Indian wars; I borrow from her analysis here. For Plains Indian viewpoints see Colin G. Calloway, ed., *Our Hearts Fell to the Ground* (Boston, 1996). "Wars of the Peace Policy" is the title of Chapter 6 in Robert M. Utley's *The Indian Frontier of the American West, 1846–1890* (Albuquerque, NM, 1984). On assimilation policy see Frederick E. Hoxie, *A Final Promise*, cited in Chapter 5. Material on Native Americans here is also drawn from the articles by Thomas Biolsi, Lisa A. Emmerich, and David Rich Lewis in *American Nations*, edited by Frederick E. Hoxie, Peter C. Mancall, and James H. Merrell (New York, 2001). On Posey see Betty Booth Donohue, "Alexander Posey," in *Native American Writers of the United States*, edited by Kenneth M. Roemer (Detroit, MI, 1997), pp. 233–241.

For conflicts over the Mexican cession I depend on six books: Howard R. Lamar, *The Far Southwest, 1846–1912* (New Haven, CT, 1966), Robert J. Rosenbaum, *Mexicano Resistance in the Southwest* (Austin, TX, 1981), David Montejano, *Anglos and Mexicans in the Making of Texas, 1836–1986* (Austin, TX, 1987), Richard White, *'It's Your Misfortune and None of My Own'*, and Richard G. de Castillo, *La Familia*, both cited earlier, and most of all, María E. Montoya's study of conflict on the Maxwell Grant, *Translating Property* (Berkeley, CA, 2002). See also Sarah Deutsch, *No Separate Refuge* (New York, 1987). On conflict over the arrival of new immigrants see works on immigration cited in Chapter 2, as well as Gwendolyn Mink, *Old Labor and New Immigrants in American Political Development* (Ithaca, NY, 1986). On anti-Chinese agitation and violence see in addition James W. Loewen, *The Mississippi Chinese* (Cambridge, MA, 1971), Robert G. Lee, *Orientals* (Philadelphia, 1999), John Kuo Wei Tchen, *New York Before Chinatown* (Baltimore, MD, 1999), and Patricia Nelson Limerick, "Disorientation and Reorientation in the American West," in her book *Something in the Soil*, cited above, pp. 186–213. On Chinese exclusion see Erika Lee, *At America's Gates* (Chapel Hill, NC, 2003), the essays in Sucheng Chan, ed., *Entry Denied* (Philadelphia, 1991), and Charles J. McClain, *In Search of Equality*, cited in Chapter 5.

On labor organizing and labor conflicts, in addition to works cited in Chapter 3, see John Higham's *Strangers in the Land* (New Brunswick, NJ, 1955) and Leon Fink's *In Search of the Working Class* (Urbana, IL, 1994), and Robert M. Fogelson, *America's Armories* (Cambridge, MA, 1989). On the Knights of Labor see Melton McLaurin, *The Knights of Labor in the South* (Westport, CT, 1978), Jonathan Garlock, *Guide to the Local Assemblies of the Knights of Labor* (Westport, CT, 1982), and Rosenbaum, *Mexicano*

Resistance, cited above. On the Southwest see also Juan Gómez-Quiñones, *The Roots of Chicano Politics, 1600–1940* (Albuquerque, NM, 1994). For the great 1877 strike see Robert V. Bruce, *1877* (Chicago, 1959), David O. Stowell, *Streets, Railroads, and the Great Strike of 1877* (Chicago, 1999), and David Roediger, "Not Only the Ruling Classes to Overcome, But Also the So-Called Mob," *Journal of Social History* (Winter 1985): 213–39. The best general source on Haymarket is Paul Avrich, *The Haymarket Tragedy* (Princeton, NJ, 1984); see also Carl S. Smith, *Urban Disorder and the Shape of Belief* (Chicago, 1995).

On the popular mythology of the frontier see two massive studies by Richard Slotkin, *Fatal Environment* (New York, 1985) and *Gunfighter Nation* (New York, 1992), as well as Joy S. Kasson, *Buffalo Bill's Wild West* (New York, 2000), and Janet M. Davis, *The Circus Age*, cited in Chapter 4.

CHAPTER 10

Cooperative Dreams

> I am for development and progress along social and spiritual lines, rather than those of commerce, nationalism, or material efficiency.
>
> —DR. CHARLES EASTMAN (OHIYESA), SANTEE SIOUX

In 1885 a former surveyor from Chester, Pennsylvania, set out to build a spectacular city on the Pacific coast of Mexico. While touring there, Alfred Kimsey Owen had glimpsed paradise north of Mazatlán at a site called Topolobampo Bay. He published a book, *Integral Cooperation*, to describe his proposed project. Pacific City would guarantee each shareholder a home and job. Its internal economy would work on the principle of cooperative exchange, and colonists could choose to build private homes or live in cooperative hotels that would feature restaurants, libraries, and day care centers. Twenty-five-acre parks would be scattered through the city, and eventually streetcars would carry residents from place to place. Homes and businesses would have electric light and the latest sanitary plumbing. Public schools would educate each citizen free to the age of twenty, after which he or she would work eight hours a day, six days a week, for thirty years and then retire to enjoy the balmy climate. Pacific City would have no taxes, no rents, no prostitution, no saloons, and very little crime. With such encouragements to family life, Owen believed few residents would be single for long. To avoid religious conflicts he planned to allow no churches, but he said individual residents could preach whatever they chose. Pacific City would be modern, scientific, and harmonious in every detail.

Unfortunately, the future of Pacific City depended on Owen's related plan to build a railroad from Topolobampo to the U.S.-Mexican border, where he hoped his rail connections would create a "Great Southern" stretching all the way from his colony to Norfolk, Virginia. The dream of such a road was the chief reason that Mexican President Porfirio Díaz permitted Owen to try his cooperative experiment. But building across the Mexican Sierras would have been a spectacular feat, and Owen, in the end, had neither the money nor the engineers to pull it off. Other problems beset Topolobampo in the meantime. Having read *Integral Cooperation*, dozens of enthusiastic colonists arrived before Owen was ready for them; few had useful skills, and many wrangled over the harsh conditions they found at the site. The utopian author Marie Howland created a scandal by bathing nude in the ocean and conducting an affair with a businessman from Enterprise, Kansas, who had emigrated with his family. Owen himself proved short-tempered and autocratic under stress. About 200 colonists managed to set up houses and schools, dig irrigation canals, start farms, and sustain themselves for a decade, but Pacific City never materialized. In fact, it was the Mexican government, after the revolution of the 1910s, that eventually achieved two of Owen's goals. In the 1930s it national-ized the old Topolobampo property (which had fallen into the hands of a wealthy U.S. sugar planter) and gave it back to local farmers as *ejidos*, village allotments that were communally held. Thus, Topolobampo became a co-operative farming community for Mexicans. In 1961 the Mexican government also undertook one of the great engineering feats of the twentieth century and completed a railroad over the Sierras.

Owen's Pacific City experiment was one among dozens of utopian schemes and communities created by Americans in the post–Civil War decades, an era marked by the watchword *cooperation*. After emancipation freedmen and freed-women across the South created economic cooperatives to work the land. Two decades later Jews arriving from Russia created agricultural colonies in seventeen states, ranging from Arkansas to New Jersey. A leader at an Anglo socialist colony in Tennessee proudly told a reporter that "in our new cooperative kitchen the people can be fed at a cost of eighty cents to one dollar a week, a great saving upon the individualistic plan of single homes." There were a host of projects like Topolobampo all over the United States: the single-tax Fairhope Colony in Alabama, the Longley Communities in Missouri, the Kaweah Cooperative Commonwealth in California, and the Niksur Cooperative Colony in Minnesota, for example. The list was particu-larly long in Washington Territory, where the Puget Sound Cooperative Colony evolved into the city of Port Angeles and, despite its short life, was followed by such ventures as the Glennis Cooperative Colony and an anarch-ist community called Home.

Millions of Americans who did not move to utopian colonies also partook of a spirit of hopeful cooperation. Urban women's groups formed shopping cooperatives and cooperative exchanges to sell female handicrafts. There were cooperative boardinghouses and kindergartens and farmers' cooperative stores. Workers and farmers paid dues to cooperative insurance ventures such as the Farmers' Mutual Benefit Association. Across the country Americans founded alliances, unions, commonwealths, sisterhoods, and brotherhoods. Such projects took many troubling forms. Leading industrialists, for example, spoke directly of the benefits of cooperation when they created corporate pools and trusts. Even members of the Ku Klux Klan saw themselves as a cooperative brotherhood banding together to protect white supremacy, just as vigilante lynchers in the West claimed to represent the collective voice of their communities. In racial terms, one American's utopia could be another's nightmare. To its founders Washington's Puget Sound Cooperative Colony was an experiment in harmony, but to Chinese workers it was just another hostile Anglo venture, one that emerged out of a spate of anti-Chinese protests in Seattle.

Utopia, then, was in the eye of the beholder. Which, for example, was the truest cooperative experiment in Chicago: Was it the company town of Pullman, founded as a supposed worker paradise by the autocratic manufacturer George Pullman? Or was it the beautiful suburb of Riverside, designed by Frederick Law Olmsted as a place where prosperous families could escape urban noise and crime? Or was it Eugene Debs's Social Democracy of America, a union-led cooperative launched in Chicago a quarter-century later? Cooperation could serve purposes of exclusion and social control, it could also bridge class and racial divides, or it could accomplish a little of both. Various impulses competed with each other as Americans sought to reorder their lives and pursue authenticity and harmony in a tumultuous era.

Many of the more radical experiments in collective living were inspired by books such as *The Cooperative Commonwealth*, published in 1885 by the Danish immigrant Laurence Gronlund, who argued that socialism would arrive in America through gradual change rather than the violence predicted by Karl Marx. Evolution, rather than revolution, reflected Americans' optimism, their trust in democracy, their religious faith, and their hope of scientific progress. But the cooperative dreams of the post–Civil War years were shaken to their foundations by an earthshaking crisis in the 1890s. Confronted by a massive economic depression and unprecedented social and political upheaval, many Americans wondered how to move their democracy forward, or whether progress was possible at all. Yet out of the crisis emerged new public leaders, and their ideas and institutions helped usher in an unprecedented era of reform. While many cooperative dreams died in the 1890s, new spirits also arose to carry forward Americans' hopes for peace and progress.

THE OTHER HALF

Over the course of the nineteenth century, prosperous Americans took advantage of new opportunities to set themselves apart, especially in their homes. In the decades before the Civil War, as cities grew, middle-class and professional families had begun withdrawing into distinct residential neighborhoods. That process accelerated in the postwar years, aided by commuter railroads and other transportation links that fueled the growth of suburbs. As early as the 1870s, a key marker of economic and social success was to move to a place such as Riverside. Sited on a major rail line eleven miles from downtown Chicago, it was far enough away that the annual cost of commuting—equivalent to $1,500 or more today—excluded all but professionals and well-to-do businessmen and their families. Olmsted envisioned Riverside as a place of "healthfulness and permanent rural beauty." Arguing that "the essential qualification of a suburb is domesticity," he provided playgrounds and safe spaces for children as well as meandering parkways along the Des Plains River to encourage leisurely drives. Almost half of Riverside's land was set aside for parks. A more exclusive expression of the desire for shelter and security was the town of Tuxedo Park in Orange County, New York (two of whose founders introduced a new type of men's formal wear without tails that took the name *tuxedo*). Developed by the heir to a tobacco fortune and built by a crew of 1,800 Italian and Slovak immigrants, Tuxedo Park featured a clubhouse, hotel, commuter rail station, and three fishing lakes as well as homes and shops. It also seems to have been America's first gated community. Following the tradition of aristocratic estates, a stone wall surrounded the resort, and visitors entered through a staffed gatehouse.

Along with the exclusive suburb came the country club, a well-recognized elite institution in all regions of the United States by the 1890s. Featuring beautifully landscaped grounds in semirural settings, country clubs offered members the pleasures of boating, swimming, fox hunting, clay-pigeon shooting, tennis, and the increasingly popular golf. In Philadelphia polo was the craze. The Elkridge Fox-Hunting Club outside Baltimore was noted for its fine chef. In addition to a physical play space, country clubs offered the assurance that fellow members were the "right sort," protecting women and children, especially, when they went out for pleasure or exercise. Henry James, who waxed rhapsodic over country clubs on his 1905 visit to the United States, noted their centrality to elite domestic life. He wrote that in the country club—as opposed to the traditional gentlemen's club—one saw "everything staked [on] the active Family as a final social fact." Within the enclave of the club, an elite family could withdraw from the public eye.

One did not have to move to the suburbs to see many forms of such segregation in American life. Visitors to a port city such as New York or Baltimore could wander through large slum districts where poverty was the norm. Even in an inland city such as Detroit, cross-class ethnic neighborhoods faded, and rich and poor increasingly went the rounds of daily life without encountering each other. Public celebrations as well as residential space diverged. By the 1880s citizens in the factory town of Worcester, Massachusetts, held an array of distinct Fourth of July gatherings. Working-class Irishmen gathered for firecrackers, music, and drinking at a picnic sponsored by an Irish fraternal order. Swedish workers marched from church to their own picnic grounds for ice cream and games, while French-Canadians gathered in family enclaves for "pique-niques," as did Welsh, Finns, Armenians, and Jews. In the evening many of these working-class groups mingled at a nearby lake and amusement park, but native-born Protestants retreated for the holiday to private clubs and summer resorts away from town.

Segregation was equally obvious in hundreds of other factory and mining towns, where wage workers and immigrants were nearly synonymous categories. In Clifton, Arizona, Anglo copper mine managers built their homes and country club in North Clifton, while Mexican residents were shunted into polluted districts along the narrow canyon of Chase Creek. In Los Angeles, the burgeoning numbers of Mexican-American residents were increasingly segregated into separate *barrios*, creating by 1900 the foundations of East Los Angeles. New amenities available to wealthy urbanites set the standard for what poor city folk and rural people keenly knew they lacked: indoor running water, bathroom fixtures, sidewalks, streetlights, gas, electricity, and telephones.

Though obvious everywhere, residential segregation was informal rather than legal and never sanctioned by federal courts. It nonetheless separated the prosperous from the poor, contributing to the ease with which many of the former ignored the plight of the latter. In the 1880s and 1890s important movements arose to ensure, in effect, that prosperous Americans who lived above Henry George's "wedge" remained aware of the plight of those below. Journalists ventured into tenements and slums to report with pen and camera on what they saw. The most famous was Jacob Riis, a Danish working-class immigrant who became a police reporter for the *New York Tribune* and was inspired by the invention of flash photography in 1887. Persuading photographer friends to help him experiment with the new equipment, Riis published the results in his sensational 1890 book *How the Other Half Lives*. He charged that "the half that was on top cared little for the struggles, and less for the fate of those who were underneath, so long as it was able to hold them there and keep its own seat."

Riis took middle-class readers on a tour through a New York City few of them had seen: the streets of "Jewtown" and "The Bend," interiors of stifling tenements and sweatshops, cellars where immigrant workers slept for 5¢ a night, and heating grates where homeless children slept huddled together against the cold. Riis blamed "wealthy absentee landlords," and being pessimistic about the prospects of government action, he suggested instead that private investors come forward to buy and improve notorious slums. "Upper half" readers of *How the Other Half Lives* were invited to feel a complex blend of compassion, revulsion, and fear. The tenements, as Riis wrote in a typical passage,

> are the hot-beds of the epidemics that carry death to rich and poor alike; the nurseries of pauperism and crime that fill our jails and police courts; that throw off a scum of forty thousand human wrecks to the island asylums and workhouses year by year; that turned out in the last eight years a round half-million beggars to prey upon our charities; that maintain a standing army of ten thousand tramps with all that that implies; above all, that touch the family life with deadly moral contagion.

Riis attracted the attention of prominent reformers such as Theodore Roosevelt while stimulating a much broader debate over urban poverty.

Riis was not the pioneer of this form of journalism, though he made it vivid through photography. Among his notable predecessors was Helen Campbell, also a writer for the *New York Tribune*, who in the 1880s published exposés such as *Studies in the Slums* and *Prisoners of Poverty*. Campbell considered herself a socialist and an instructor in "survival economics" who brought the latest findings in sanitation, diet, nutrition, health care, and budgeting to the poor. As an investigator she conducted interviews and published detailed statistics on women's wages, working hours, and the effects of layoffs and

Children on the playground at the Webster School, Chicago, 1902. Across the
United States settlement workers and other civic activists worked to beautify city
neighborhoods, improve health practices and combat disease, and build schools,
day care centers, and safe spaces for children to play.
Source: This photograph was taken by a *Chicago Daily News* photographer. Chicago Historical Society.

injuries. Far more sweeping than Riis in her vision, Campbell advocated equal
pay for women, labor organizing, government abolition of sweatshops, the
appointment of factory inspectors, and more educational opportunities for the
next generation.

At the same time that investigative journalism flourished, an influential
group of young reformers proposed that middle-class people not just read
about the slums but connect themselves directly to the poor by living among
them. The settlement movement began in London in the mid-1880s, but
idealistic Americans soon brought the idea across the Atlantic. The first U.S.
settlement began in 1886 on New York's Lower East Side, founded by a group
of young men influenced by Felix Adler's Society of Ethical Culture. It was
followed a year later by a coalition of Smith graduates led by the Wellesley
instructor Vida Scudder, whose College Settlement Association drew interested members from northeastern women's colleges and beyond. The movement grew rapidly. In 1891 there were six settlements in the United States;
by 1905 there were 200, and five years later, 200 more.

As the movement arose it brought together trained professionals from the
new social sciences, advocates of the Social Gospel, and an array of other
reformers. Most of all it brought together energetic, educated young people.
Almost all settlement founders and participants were young, and four-fifths

Virginia Day Nursery, East Fifth Street, New York City, 1906. Founded in 1879, the nursery cared for the children of working mothers on the Lower East Side. It is still in operation today.
Source: Museum of the City of New York, The Byron Collection.

were recent college graduates. The most famous was Jane Addams, who founded Chicago's Hull House in 1889 at the age of 29. A graduate of Rockford Female Seminary in Illinois, Addams experienced a crisis when she left school that she later came to understand as systemic rather than personal. Addams quoted a young woman from a wealthy family who met her on a European tour: " 'I am simply smothered and sickened with advantages. It is like eating a sweet dessert the first thing in the morning.' This then, was the difficulty," Addams wrote, "the assumption that the sheltered, educated girl has nothing to do with the bitter poverty and the social maladjustment which is all about her, and which, after all, cannot be concealed, for it breaks through poetry and literature in a burning tide which overwhelms her; it peers at her in the form of heavy-laden market women and underpaid street laborers, gibing her with a sense of her uselessness."

Addams suffered special griefs, having lost her mother when she was a young child and her father only six weeks after she graduated from college. But she shared her passionate need for a life of moral purpose with many other young women who held college degrees and as yet had no clear sense of what profession they might follow. (Belle Kearney, from a wealthy Mississippi family, felt similarly paralyzed after she left an Ohio boarding school. "If my life had to be spent on the plantation," she wondered, "what was the use of reading, of trying to cultivate my mind, when it would have the effect of making me more miserable?" Kearney added that "In those days I died ten thousand deaths. I died to God and to humanity. . . . A deadness settled upon my soul . . . for ten dreary agonizing years." She eventually built a public career as an advocate of temperance and women's suffrage.) Addams borrowed the phrase "the snare of preparation" from the much-admired Russian writer and pacifist Leo Tolstoy. That snare, she wrote, was the education "we spread before the feet of young people, hopelessly entangling them in a curious inactivity at the very period of life when they are longing to construct the world anew and to conform it to their own ideals."

Despite Addams's grief over the death of her father, his will provided her with the opportunity she craved by leaving her independently wealthy. After years of travel and indecision, she returned from Europe, moved to Chicago with several close friends, and purchased a run-down mansion in one of the city's poorest immigrant districts, formerly the property of Charles J. Hull. Like many other settlement workers, those at Hull House sought, at first, to provide "uplift" to the poor through concerts, art exhibits, and classes in literature and history. With humor and self-deprecation, Addams later described these early efforts as naïve. The early programs of many settlement houses, in fact, fit the satirical description of the novelist Sinclair Lewis, who later claimed they had offered to the downtrodden lectures on "trout fishing, exploring Tibet, pacifism, sea shell collecting, the eating of bran, and the geography of Charlemagne's Empire."

But culture was not always alien to poor immigrants: settlement founders connected to many who were delighted to study history, gain access to a piano, or gather for readings of poetry from their home country. A fruit vendor from Athens beamed when he found a picture of the Acropolis at Hull House. He told Addams that he had talked to thousands of Chicagoans and never yet found one interested in the glory of classical Greece. At the same time, wise settlement workers such as Addams learned much from their new neighbors about the urgent problems of urban poverty. Within a few years Hull House, like many other settlements, was building safe play spaces for children and tackling the urban crises in housing, medical care, and garbage collection. A mere five years after Hull House opened Addams was already serving as a citywide mediator in tense Chicago strikes and lobbying for the appointment of Illinois factory inspectors. The first such appointee, Florence Kelley, was herself a Hull House resident whose socialist views influenced Addams's outlook on labor and poverty. Still another Hull House luminary, Julia Lathrop, served on the State Board of Charities and helped design the nation's first juvenile court system.

Similar campaigns went on around the country. Boston settlements, for example, played a leading role in reducing the use of child labor and advocating public ownership of urban utilities. For its day, the settlement movement was remarkably diverse. Jamie Porter Barrett, an African-American graduate of the Hampton Institute, remained in Hampton and formed the Locust Street Settlement to provide work and child-care training for troubled young women. The White Rose Mission, founded by the African-American reformer Victoria Earle Matthews, helped blacks arriving in New York City from the South. Lillian Wald, the founder of the Henry Street Nurses' Settlement in New York, was a Jew who won the support of the city's leading Jewish charities. Her team of 175 nurses, including 25 African-American women, pioneered in healing the sick and teaching hygiene in the tenements. Settlement houses thus offered an array of public roles and professional careers for women. A reporter observed in the early 1900s that "twenty years ago . . . a young woman who was restless and yearned to sacrifice herself, would have become a missionary or married a drinking man in order to save him. Today she studies medicine or goes into settlement work." Even more important, settlement houses laid the groundwork for an array of twentieth-century public welfare projects.

At the same time settlements arose, another movement began to address some of the same economic and political ills, but it emerged from a very different sector of society. The Farmers' Alliance had been founded in Texas during the depression of the 1870s, but only in the mid- to late 1880s, with cotton, corn, and wheat prices plunging to new lows and drought devastating the West, did it supplant the Grange and other farmers' groups in mobilizing rural people. Like these older groups, the alliance brought farm families together for picnics, debates, and educational lectures. But it took self-help in bolder directions as its leaders, like other innovators of the day, hailed the benefits of cooperation. Texas alliance members formed cooperative stores, inviting members to pool their money to obtain bulk discounts from manufacturers. Alliance wheat farmers in South Dakota ran a similar enterprise and also experimented with offering crop insurance and establishing direct links to British milling companies to eliminate middlemen and get a better price. Alliance leaders in North Carolina set up their own tobacco warehouse as an alternative to the American Tobacco Company's control of crop auctions. In the deep South cotton belt alliance leaders organized a coordinated response after makers of jute, a wrapping for cotton bales, used their monopoly power to raise prices by 60 percent. The Farmers' Alliance persuaded millions of farmers to substitute cotton bagging, and in Georgia and South Carolina this forced the "jute trust" to lower prices.

Cooperative organizing also pushed the alliance into electoral politics, since much of its agenda rested on government action. A looser money supply and federal regulation of railroads—demands held over from the Greenback movement of the 1870s, and still unfulfilled—topped the wish list. In addition, some alliance leaders endorsed a subtreasury plan, modeled on the national banking system, that would allow farmers to store crops in government-run warehouses so that they, rather than middlemen and futures traders, could benefit from seasonal price swings. Southern Farmers' Alliance members tried to work through the Democratic party until 1892, when they became disillusioned with the Democrats' conspicuous lack of action. In the meantime, Alliance farmers nationwide began to hope for partnership with the Knights of Labor, which was also turning its energies to politics. As early as 1888 Farmers' Alliance and Knights of Labor leaders in Kansas, Texas, and

Arkansas cooperated in Union Labor campaigns. A gathering in St. Louis in February 1892 to create a new national party featured representatives from an array of groups. They included the various Farmers' Alliances; sympathetic middle-class reformers in the West who organized themselves as the Citizens' Alliance and the Women's Alliance; the Knights of Labor and a number of other unions; proponents of Henry George's single tax on land and of Edward Bellamy's Nationalist utopian ideas; and the economically progressive wing of the Prohibition Party, led by Frances Willard herself. It was one of the era's most diverse and radical gatherings.

The new People's Party (soon known as Populists) held a second convention to draft a platform and nominate national candidates. Their platform, adopted at Omaha, Nebraska, on July 4, 1892, called for federal expansion of the money supply, public ownership of railroad and telegraph networks, and a progressive income tax levied on the very rich. Among other proposals were laws enforcing the eight-hour workday and the establishment of public savings banks at the nation's post offices, where people could safely and conveniently deposit small sums. The People's delegates offered a scathing assessment of the state of the union in their preamble:

> We meet in the midst of a nation brought to the verge of moral, political and material ruin. . . . The newspapers are largely subsidized or muzzled; public opinion silenced; business prostrated; our homes covered with mortgages; labor impoverished; and the land concentrating in the hands of capitalists. The urban workmen are denied the right of organization for self-protection; imported pauperized labor beats down their wages. . . . The fruits of the toil of millions are boldly stolen to build up colossal fortunes for a few, unprecedented in the history of mankind; and the possessors of these, in turn, despise the republic and endanger liberty. From the same prolific womb of governmental injustice we breed two great classes—tramps and millionaires.

In blaming "governmental injustice," Populists recognized the active role of state and federal policies that over the prior three decades had favored corporations over small business, investors over producers, and the Northeast over the West and South. Populists declared themselves not so much in favor of more government as of a different kind of government, one that served "'the plain people,' . . . to the end that oppression, injustice, and poverty shall eventually cease in the land."

With similar state platforms the People's Party won considerable power in the West in the early 1890s, from Nebraska and Kansas through the Rocky Mountain states to Oregon and Washington. Nationwide their presidential ticket won a million votes in 1892, even though southern opponents engaged in fraud and acts of terror to keep power in Democratic hands. Few southern alliance members were racial egalitarians, but they did court black voters, denounce disfranchisement attempts, and cooperate with a separate Colored Farmers' Alliance that had organized its own cooperative experiments, such as a Norfolk, Virginia, cotton exchange. Democrats deeply feared an alliance of poor southerners that crossed racial lines, and while the People's Party never fully embodied this dream, it came closer to doing so than any other movement after Reconstruction's end.

Democrats, in response, refused to accept their opponents' legitimacy and justified any tactic to crush them. One Georgia Democrat, who assisted in an 1894 "recount" that turned a Populist victory into defeat, said later, "We had to do it! Those damned Populists would have ruined the Country." Where they could not win by such means, Democrats removed opponents forcibly from office in ways that harkened back to the overthrow of Reconstruction. Instigators described an 1898 coup in Wilmington, North Carolina, where Republicans and Populists had forged an effective coalition, as a "race riot." But, in fact, it was a carefully planned attack by Democrats, who had maintained a vigilante presence throughout the preceding political campaign. (One observer wrote that it was "an awesome sight to drive through town in the dark and see synods of armed men standing at each corner.") The "race riot," carried out with a Gatling gun, resulted in not only the deaths of two dozen African Americans but the resignation at gunpoint of local Populist and Republican officials.

The People's Party faced a number of other daunting challenges. Backed by relatively poor voters, it suffered from a chronic lack of cash. The mainstream press, centered in New York and Boston, ridiculed its leaders as hayseeds and wild-eyed fanatics, echoing the media hysteria over strikes and other protests by the working class. In addition, the U.S. winner-take-all political system and its complex set of checks and balances hampered the Populist cause. Kansas Populists won control of the lower house of the legislature in 1890, but since the Republican-dominated upper house did not face reelection until 1892, the result was deadlock and lost momentum. Colorado's Populist governor faced a hostile legislature backed by powerful mining corporations, which along with railroads spent liberally to defeat the new party. In states such as Iowa savvy Democrats picked up aspects of the Populist agenda and prevented the new party from developing. In other states "fusion" arrangements with another party (usually Democrats in the West and Republicans in the South) watered down the new party's program and led to bitter infighting and disillusionment. Thus, the People's Party fell prey to some of the very conditions it arose to combat: the poverty of farmers, rifts within the American working class, the power of elite interests, and the entrenchment of Republicans and Democrats. Most of all, a national economic cataclysm spelled doom for the party as an institution, if not for some of its most enduring ideas.

THE THIRD EARTHQUAKE

Between 1890 and 1892 the success of the People's Party showed how seriously the rural economy had deteriorated in the South and West. Unluckily for Populists and for the nation as a whole, the situation got much worse. Even as Populists met in Omaha, railroad investment was slowing down. Early in 1893 the Philadelphia & Reading went bankrupt, and many businessmen began to feel uneasy. Then, on May 5, 1893, the storm broke: Philadelphia's National Cordage Company went under, taking with it two Chicago banks and three brokerages heavily invested in its stock. As in previous economic panics during the era before federal deposit insurance, people who held savings in private banks risked losing every dime. Desperate financiers in the heartland began calling in their deposits from New York's national banks; by July 25 those banks partially "suspended," turning away depositors who wanted to withdraw funds. Those who rushed to the bank and found they had lost everything began frantically hoarding cash. Manufacturers laid off workers. Railroads lost shipping revenue and began to go under. By the end of the summer, the country had slid into a deep depression that lasted until decade's end.

To a country that had endured the hard times and Great Railroad Strike of the 1870s, followed by the Haymarket conflict in 1886, the depression of the 1890s was devastating—a "third earthquake," as one historian has called it, or perhaps a fourth if one counts the shattering experience of the Civil War. Once again it appeared that the nation was headed not toward lasting peace but into distress and turmoil. While J. P. Morgan and the Cleveland administration struggled to shore up the gold standard, unemployment in major cities rose to 20 or 25 percent. The resulting misery was starkly obvious to settlement workers such as Jane Addams, who nearly bankrupted herself keeping Hull House open to provide emergency aid. Walter Rauschenbusch, serving as a street minister in New York City's Hell's Kitchen during these years, wrote that "one could hear human virtues cracking and crumbling all around." Urban police, finding themselves utterly overwhelmed, ended their long-standing practice of allowing homeless people to take shelter on station floors. Year-round, but especially during the terrible winters between 1893 and 1897, urban newspapers published a steady stream of reported deaths from starvation, freezing, and suicide.

The impact was as severe in small towns and the countryside as it was in the great cities. "Never in my life of forty-five years of responsible activity," wrote one Ohio congressman, "have I seen a time when in spite of the hardest labor, strictest temperance, plainest frugality, and closest economy, the 'average farmer' has grown so poorer." Camps of wanderers sprang up along railroad sidings. Tramps became a familiar sight at farmhouse doors, begging for work or food. In Wisconsin business failures and bankruptcies triggered suicides and mental breakdowns. "Jan. 3, 1894," read a typical entry at the state insane asylum. "Town of Melrose. Norwegian. Age 27. Single. Farmer. Poor. . . . Deranged on the subject of finances. Disposed to injure others." A Nebraska banker wrote in January 1895 that it made him "heartsick to look at this once prosperous country. The suffering is terrible. . . . We have several families who for a month past have had nothing to eat but flour and water and they are very thankful to get that. Scores of women and children have to stay in their sod shanties bare-footed for the want of something to cover their feet. All this was brought on these people through no fault of theirs. They are hard working, industrious people."

The United States had, of course, suffered depressions before and would do so again. But by some measures the crisis of the 1890s was larger even than the Great Depression of the 1930s, and it was accompanied by determined, collective protests that shocked the nation's elite. In 1892, the year before the depression hit with full force, Americans had already witnessed showdowns in the steel mills of Pennsylvania and the mines of Idaho, along with a general strike in New Orleans and smaller ones in such diverse locations as Buffalo, New York, and Tracy, Tennessee. The first full year of the depression, 1894, brought two more large-scale labor conflicts. In April 125,000 Pennsylvania coal miners walked off their jobs (the United Mine Workers' official membership rolls counted 20,000). The strike spread to mines in Illinois, West Virginia, Ohio, and elsewhere. Two months later the American Railway Union (ARU) announced that its members would no longer carry Pullman cars, in sympathy with workers at Pullman's Illinois plant who had walked out after wage cuts of 25 to 40 percent. (There had been no corresponding cut in their rents for company-owned housing, nor in shareholders' dividends). Eugene Debs had purposely built the ARU as a broad-based, industrywide union, having witnessed past defeats when brakemen, switchmen, and engineers tried to negotiate separately. The strategy worked brilliantly. On June 26 ARU workers all over the Midwest began shunting Pullman cars to the sidings. By the following day traffic on twenty railroads had slowed to a near halt, and at passenger stations as far apart as Delaware and California, Pullman cars ceased to run.

While the Pullman boycott paralyzed parts of the country for a month, Americans were also astonished witnesses to a novel form of protest: the first march on Washington, undertaken by legions of unemployed men in an appeal for federal aid. The founders of this project called it the Commonweal of Christ, but the press dubbed it Coxey's Army after its leading spokesman, the Ohio businessman Jacob Coxey. Coxey proposed an immense public works project to prevent starvation. Hundreds of thousands of Americans needed jobs and bread, he observed; at the same time, the nation's dirt roads were in terrible condition for wagons, bicycles, and automobiles. Coxey proposed that the federal government hire unemployed men to build good roads.

Only 122 men accompanied Coxey as he left Massillon, Ohio, on Easter Sunday morning in 1894, but the number swelled to more than 400 by the time they arrived on the outskirts of the District of Columbia at the end of April. In addition, throughout spring and summer new "armies" organized across the West, with thousands setting out from Los Angeles, San Francisco, Portland, Tacoma, and many inland points. Crossing into the Midwest and Pennsylvania, each group picked up followers. Their appointed "generals" worked hard to keep the marchers organized and prevent theft of property, and along the route these efforts paid off. Having reviewed the California army led by Charles T. Kelley, a manager of the Rock Island Railroad described them as "intelligent determined men. . . . Their leader is a man of brains and character and great determination. He is a religious man, too." The manager added that "it is a terrible thing, and it made me sad to find that there were sixteen hundred respectable, well-meaning men reduced to such desperate straits in this country."

The Commonweal of Christ prompted a tremendous outpouring of compassion. Chapters of the Woman's Christian Temperance Union organized lunch stations to feed marchers along the route. People in dozens of cities and towns held mass meetings of welcome, and churches opened their sanctuaries and basements as sleeping quarters. In Omaha, where the People's Party had taken its stand, Mayor George Bemis and the prominent merchant Emil Brandeis joined a crowd of 40,000 who greeted Kelley's marchers and helped raise money and gather supplies. The Populist governor of Kansas issued a statement of support. "I am in sympathy with these men," declared the sheriff of Council Bluffs, Iowa. "They are creatures of circumstances." But more ominously, the cities of Detroit and Cleveland offered a cold shoulder. And as the armies traveled down rural roads and suburban streets, some citizens sat on their front porches cradling shotguns.

In the major protests of the early 1890s, as well as in the march of Coxey's Army, labor leaders tried to make sure their followers were orderly and law abiding. Officials of the ARU stressed again and again that participants must use "no threats" and "let liquor of all kinds alone." Aware that violence might precipitate military intervention, most participants obeyed, but as the leaders of Coxey's Army discovered, damage to property was harder to avoid. Hungry men walking across the continent got weary, and unemployed marchers "borrowed" at least fifty trains in various parts of the country, including some during the weeks when the Pullman boycott had already brought chaos on the railroads. Having walked all the way from San Francisco, Kelley's Army decided to speed things up in Council Bluffs. They flooded aboard an eastbound train that sympathetic local women were decorating with American flags. "Pop, you are our prisoner," a jobless railroadman cheerfully informed the engineer as he took over the cab. In Montana Hogan's Army fired up the Northern Pacific's most powerful locomotive, attached it to empty coal cars to carry their men, loaded up three tons of food and supplies donated by Bozeman supporters, and ordered rail officials to clear the tracks. Furious, the railroad managers complied, but they also telegraphed Washington. Hogan made it 300 miles east to Forsyth, where a superintendent spiked the switches and U.S. troops, under instructions from the attorney general, intercepted and captured the train.

The wild ride of Hogan's Army highlighted two factors that ultimately defeated the protests of the 1890s. First, many Americans were terrified by such bold challenges to the established order. Newspapers and magazines played a major role in feeding and shaping public opinion, especially in the East. "This is no time to arbitrate," declared the *Christian Advocate*. "The battle of law and order must be fought to the end. . . . Despotism would settle this matter better than we can." The *Chicago Tribune* covered ARU activities under screeching headlines such as "Law Is Trampled On—Riotous Emissaries of Dictator Debs." "Chicago at the Mercy of the Incendiary's Torch," echoed the *Washington Post*. The spectacle of unemployed men organizing themselves into so-called armies and commandeering trains—which they obviously knew how to run—struck further terror into timid hearts. During Hogan's ride, when police deputies panicked and fired into a Billings crowd, headlines in the *New York Times* screamed "Blood Flows from Coxeyism" and "Battle Between Law and Anarchy." Many Americans remained firm in their conviction that striking and marching were per se illegitimate tactics; disrupting rail traffic and demanding government aid went beyond the pale.

The ultimate arbitrator of events was not conservative public opinion itself, but the government power wielded on its behalf. In almost every major protest, it was the arrival of armed troops that touched off violence. The Pullman conflict proved especially bloody, despite the open sympathy of the Illinois chief executive with workers' plight. While the Republican governors of Pennsylvania and Idaho called in state militia to Homestead and Coeur d'Alene, Illinois governor John Peter Altgeld chose not to do so in response to the ARU boycott. He observed that it was a peaceful stopping of trains and ruled that Illinois did not need any help from outside. Over his outraged protests, the U.S. attorney general sent federal troops to Illinois anyway. ARU leaders such as George Howard, a Union Army veteran, found themselves facing ranks of rifles. In a replay of the great uprising of 1877, the arrival of troops severed crowds from labor leaders' control. Mobs joined in looting and rioting, with at least fifty-three killed in violence that, like the strike, radiated outward from Chicago to other locales. Angry crowds overturned trains, burned engines, and attacked rail stations and roundhouses, destroying millions of dollars worth of equipment. Much of it, ironically, did not exactly belong to the roads, which had been bankrupted in the depression and were being run "in receivership" under the supervision of courts and creditors.

It is not quite right to call these conflicts showdowns between labor and capital. Though labor relations were obviously at stake, it was government intervention on the side of capital that, as in the days of Reconstruction, decided the outcome. Thus, Pullman, Homestead, and the march of Coxey's Army can be described as three-way struggles in which government proved to be the critical corner of the triangle. (At Homestead government even helped generate the dispute itself: the plant produced specialized steel for U.S. Navy vessels, and the Amalgamated Steelworkers Union hoped Washington would demand arbitration. The calculations of Andrew Carnegie and his deputies, who expected the state of Pennsylvania to intervene on their side, proved more accurate.) U.S. troops halted both the Pullman strike and Coxey's armies after courts granted injunctions ordering each protest to cease. In Washington officials prepared for Coxey's arrival by mobilizing the Secret Service and troops from surrounding states. With wild rumors circulating that Coxey's men intended to attack the Treasury, though they were armed only with white flags, department officials stockpiled weapons and ordered clerks to prepare for defense. After his parade into town, Coxey tried to stand on the Capitol steps and read an appeal for government aid. Police beat back the marchers, and Coxey was, to his shock, arrested, tried, and sentenced to twenty days in jail for the crime of trespassing on the Capitol grass.

The impulse for law and order in the mid–1890s accompanied a hardening of racial and religious antagonisms. Americans had viewed many of the other conflicts of incorporation through a racialized lens, and not surprisingly they responded to economic cataclysm by, among other things, stigmatizing and attacking non-Anglos. This trend manifested itself in a variety of ways, some subtle and some obvious. During the 1890s Jews began to be systematically excluded from elite colleges, resorts, and social institutions—even from New York's Union League Club, which Jews had helped establish during

Reconstruction. The American Protective Association (APA), peaking at perhaps half a million members in 1894, campaigned against immigration and circulated fraudulent "proof" that the pope was instigating the murder of non-Catholics. The APA advised Protestants to boycott Catholic businesses and fire Catholic workers. Their agitation provoked at least three riots, partly because some APA members were, ironically, immigrant Orangemen who had brought hatreds with them from northern Ireland. Many Scandinavian and English immigrants also joined the APA's call to shut the door against new arrivals.

Meanwhile, in sports, the League of American Wheelmen excluded African Americans in 1894. Chicago's Young Men's Christian Association (YMCA), one of a handful that was racially integrated, held out until 1900 before it segregated—the same year the South's last black congressman, George H. White of North Carolina, left office, and the ex-Confederacy's congressional delegation turned all-white for the next six decades. Meanwhile, 1898 was the last year any black player appeared in major- or minor-league baseball until Jackie Robinson joined the Brooklyn Dodgers in 1947. Separate Negro leagues began to arise in the face of exclusion. The same was true among women's literary and social clubs. The newly formed General Federation of Women's Clubs barred black clubs from joining, despite protests from the National Federation of Afro-American Women. Advocates of women's suffrage sailed with the prevailing tide. In a particularly nasty episode Susan B. Anthony asked her elderly colleague Frederick Douglass, a long-time champion of women's rights, not to attend an 1894 suffrage convention in Atlanta because his presence might alienate Anglo women in the South. Douglass stayed home. Southern suffragists, in the meantime, argued that Anglo women's votes would be "a means to the end of securing white supremacy."

In central Texas, as the turn of the century loomed, school segregation began extending to Mexican Americans as well as blacks, and a few districts in the South even forced Italian students into nonwhite schools. One group of Anglo Texans undertook a legal campaign to disfranchise all Mexican immigrants, though federal courts rejected their case in 1897. In New Mexico Territory, still predominantly Latino, the 1890s brought a transformation in attitudes toward the long-standing practice of bilingual schooling. By the early twentieth century Anglos fought to conduct public schools on an English-only basis, and Congress rejected New Mexico statehood in 1902 on the grounds that too many of its residents were "alien" in language and custom.

Many racial animosities spilled over into violence. In the deep South Jews were not only targets of social discrimination, as in the North, but had their farms and businesses attacked and burned. In the coal fields of western Pennsylvania two dozen unarmed Polish and Hungarian miners were gunned down by police in one of many incidents stemming from suppression of strikes. (The United Mine Workers were by this point, wisely, bringing recent immigrants into the union fold.) Chinese farm workers were beaten and driven out of California fields and orchards. Violence intensified most of all against blacks. During the 1890s lynchings occurred in almost every state outside New England, and the number of lynchings during the decade exceeded

1,500. Most of the victims were black men, but they included Mexican and Italian men and even some women.

While increasing in number, lynchings also became a public blood sport, with large crowds of white men and women gathering to watch for hours as victims were tortured and burned alive. Though such rituals of terror were most frequent in the former Confederacy, they also occurred in the West and Midwest. Newspapers advertised the places and times in advance, and photographers rushed to the scene to sell souvenir pictures. Two of the most notorious examples were the lynchings of Henry Smith in Paris, Texas, in 1893 and of Sam Hose in Newman, Georgia, in 1899. Both men were accused of the rape and murder of Anglos, but the charges later proved false. Investigators found that Hose, for instance, had been involved in a dispute with his employer. At the time, however, newspapers asserted that "the usual crime" had been committed, with the alleged rape victims cloistered from interviews. Smith, Hose, and others were slowly burned and cut to death over many hours before large crowds, with railroads running excursion trains for those who wanted to watch. Afterward some onlookers hacked off fingers and toes to keep as mementos.

Why did such a confluence of race hatreds take place in the 1890s? Or, to put it another way, why did Americans respond to economic crisis and social upheaval in such deeply racialized ways? As we have seen, they had long been conditioned to do so, and with a new century approaching it was clear that Anglos no longer securely dominated any part of the country, at least in numerical terms. An influx of Mexicans, Asians, and southern and eastern Europeans was remaking the national landscape; nervousness about their presence was openly expressed in calls for "Anglo-Saxon" rule. In the case of blacks, Anglos also responded with fear and anger to the coming of age of the first freeborn generation, who in the late 1880s and 1890s were reaching adulthood. Some writers noted that this generation had never been whipped by masters or known the submission of enslavement. Anglos' loss of secure control was obvious here as in many other areas of society and culture. Lynching victims were often described as "strange Negroes"—itinerant laborers in transit, men unknown in the community and thus suspect and vulnerable. But in a much broader sense, by the 1890s all young African Americans were "strange" to whites, and those with education, property, and ambition were the strangest of all. Three young men lynched in Memphis in 1891, for example, had committed the crime of opening a grocery store across the street from a white competitor. (Their murder launched their friend Ida B. Wells on a distinguished but lonely career as an antilynching investigator.)

Most of all, it was politics that helped shape a broad climate of racial violence and hostility. The earlier depression of the 1870s had also provoked a sharp conservative turn, but at that time federal and state governments had been engaged in the bold and optimistic projects of Reconstruction. In the 1890s no such revolution was in progress, and the country moved not from radical reform toward greater conservatism, as it had in the 1870s, but into deep reaction, accompanied by the rise of what one scholar calls "radical racism." Through politics, that racism became firmly embedded in law. The last effort to preserve a piece of Reconstruction was an 1890 bill, sponsored by the Massachusetts senator Henry Cabot Lodge, that would have sent U.S. marshals to supervise the polls in any congressional district where one hundred citizens petitioned for aid. The Lodge bill, which would have blunted the power of intimidation and fraud, passed the House but was defeated in the Senate by a single vote. In the wake of this and related developments, southern Democrats became increasingly bold. Along with engaging in open fraud and terror in the 1890s, they chose "white supremacy" as the banner under which to unite white voters and defeat Populism.

Wherever they won power, they then passed disfranchisement and ballot laws that further secured their position. These culminated in new state constitutions in the South that entrenched white supremacy for decades to come. In much of the South, black voters were shut out of politics for decades afterward. Voting among poor Anglos also declined, a result intended to disfranchise Populists. The percentage of Anglos voting dropped 34 percent in Mississippi, 46 percent in Louisiana, and 48 percent in Virginia as poll taxes,

UNITED WE STAND, DIVIDED WE—FIGHT ONE ANOTHER.

"United we stand, divided we—fight one another." A People's Party cartoon envisioning cooperative political action by American farmers and working men. Those coming to the ballot box include a former Northern Republican and former Southern Democrat who have joined the Farmers' Alliance; a Colored Allianceman; and members of the Knights of Labor, the American Federation of Labor, and the Brotherhood of Locomotive Engineers.
Source: *Kansas Commoner*, 14 January 1892.

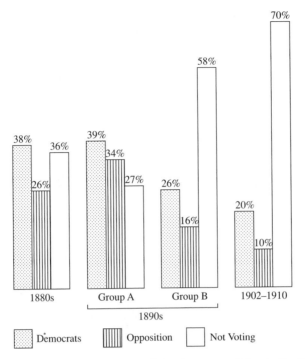

The impact of disfranchisement. Party politics was competitive in the South during the 1880s, and it remained so in the 1890s wherever suffrage restrictions had not been passed (in the states of Group A, consisting of Alabama, Louisiana, North Carolina, Texas, and Virginia). In the states of Group B (Arkansas, Florida, Georgia, Mississippi, South Carolina, and Tennessee), poll taxes, grandfather clauses, and other restrictive measures were already in place by 1894. Group A followed suit over the next decade. The results were dramatic. Not only were the vast majority of black southerners disfranchised, but many poor whites were excluded as well; with the Democratic party fully ascendant, apathy and nonvoting set in even among those still eligible to go to the polls.

Source: From J. Morgan Kousser, *The Shaping of Southern Politics: Suffrage Restriction and the Establishment of the One-Party South, 1880–1910* (New Haven, CT, 1974), p. 225.

registration laws, and ultimately new state constitutions went into effect. It was "horrible," wrote one observer in the Appalachian districts of Virginia, "to see the marks of humiliation and despair that were stamped on the faces of honest but poor white men who had been refused registration and who had been robbed of their citizenship. . . . We saw them as they came from the presence of the registrars with bowed heads and agonized faces." The South was transformed from a democracy into what one historian calls a "broad-based oligarchy." In Washington, meanwhile, the South regained its pre–Civil War advantage of being able to count large swaths of its population toward its representation in congressional and presidential elections, but allowing only a fraction of them to vote. On top of the Senate's bias toward rural representation (with two senators per state no matter how many people lived there), this gave the South's voting elite an extremely disproportionate share of power.

Disfranchisement was not just a southern matter. Anglos in other parts of the country acquiesced because they shared many of the key tenets of southern conservatism. Influential commentators such as E. L. Godkin of *The Nation*, who had shaped public opinion since Reconstruction days, heartily agreed with the Virginia politician Carter Glass that "nothing can be more dangerous to our republican institutions than to see hordes of ignorant and worthless men marching to the polls." Though they pointed to different men, nonsoutherners' definitions of "dangerous" were also grounded in class and race. Westerners were fighting their own bitter war to control Asians and Mexicans. Everywhere Anglo elites denounced the "lower races," from Irish to Italians to Russian Jews, for their alleged tendencies toward ignorance, corruption, or political radicalism. The pressures and struggles of the 1890s, from strikes to Populism, brought such prejudices to the fore. To use an agricultural metaphor, the seeds of radical racism had existed all along but did not always have a chance to sprout until events in the 1890s soaked them well. Institutionally, lawmakers, judges, and voters then set up a virtual irrigation system that nurtured racism's poisonous plants for decades to come.

The emerging radical racism of the 1890s and 1900s also carried a strong component of sexual conservatism. White supremacists spoke over and over of protecting the "purity of white womanhood." Long past the time when they had driven black voters from the polls, demagogues such as Mississippi's James Vardaman dwelled obsessively on the virtue of young Anglo women, sending a message almost as much to their own daughters as to blacks. In a statement typical of the genre, the Arkansas Democrat Jeff Davis declared that "I would rather tear, screaming from her mother's arms, my little daughter and bury her alive than to see her arm in arm with the best nigger on earth." Likewise, an interviewer who spoke with Thomas Dixon, the author of *The Clansman* and other best sellers, reported that Dixon intended his books "to create a feeling of abhorrence in white people, especially white women against colored men. Mr. Dixon said that his desire was to prevent the mixing of white and Negro blood."

Dixon and his allies both exploited and helped orchestrate a shift in culture. As early as 1888 one critic noted that literature was becoming "not only Southern in type, but distinctly Confederate in sympathy." Popular novelists such as Mrs. E. D. E. N. Southworth described the Old South as an idyllic place, where plantation families dwelled in beauty and chivalry and contented slaves frolicked in the quarters. By 1900 professional scholars were joining writers such as Southworth and Dixon in rewriting history. Slavery was depicted as benign or even beneficial to slaves, and Reconstruction as an orgy of rape and arson instigated by northern carpetbaggers, ending with the supposed "rape epidemic" that justified the lynching of black men. Antislavery was dismissed as a movement of hysterical women and ministers that had dragged sober men into an unnecessary war. Both black and white southerners who challenged such views—including the novelist George W. Cable, the congressman George H. White of North Carolina, the antilynching advocate Ida B. Wells, the historian John Spencer Bassett, and the Emory College professor Andrew Sledd—found it impossible to stay in the South. All became exiles in New

England or the Midwest. A degree of intellectual chill touched even these regions: the University of Wisconsin economist Richard Ely, for example, faced pressure to resign after he wrote sympathetically about socialism.

Mark Twain was well aware of these trends in 1901, when a Texas lynching prompted him to write his powerful essay "The United States of Lyncherdom." Twain began by reprinting a telegraph news report. "The Negro was taken to a tree and swung in the air," it said. "Wood and fodder were piled beneath his body and a hot fire was made. Then it was suggested that the man ought not to die too quickly, and he was let down to the ground while a party went to Dexter, about two miles distant, to procure coal oil. This was thrown on the flames and the work completed." Noting that 203 lynchings had been reported in the previous year, Twain asked his readers to

> read that telegram again and yet again, and picture the scene in their minds. . . . Then multiply it by 115, add 88; place the 203 in a row, allowing 600 feet of space for each human torch, so that there may be viewing room around it for 5,000 Christian American men, women, and children, youths and maidens; make it night, for grim effect; have the show in a gradually rising plain and let the course of the stakes be uphill; the eye can take in the whole line of twenty-four miles of blood-and-flesh bonfires unbroken, whereas if it occupied level ground the ends of the line would bend down and be hidden from view by the curvature of the earth. All being ready now, and the darkness opaque, the stillness impressive— for there should be no sound but the soft moaning of the night wind and the muffled sobbing of the sacrifices—let all the far stretch of kerosened pyres be touched off simultaneously and the glare and the shrieks and the agonies burst heavenward to the Throne.

"O kind missionary!" Twain concluded. "O compassionate missionary, leave China! Come home and convert these Christians!"

If anyone had the moral and intellectual authority to force Americans to confront such hard truths, it was Twain, the most famous and beloved writer in the country, a man who found himself a celebrity as far away as Cape Town and Calcutta. But Twain never published "The United States of Lyncherdom." He and his publisher worried that it would damage his reputation and sales in the South. "I shouldn't have even half a friend left down there," Twain wrote privately, "after it issued from the press." He set aside the essay, which was found in his papers after his death, and turned his attention to a little parody of Sherlock Holmes.

What changed in the 1890s, then, was both the shape of the political left and the nature of the constraints and challenges it faced. It was a measure of the insularity of prosperous Americans that many of them remembered the decade as "The Gay Nineties," full of fun and good cheer, while the other half spent the desperate years between 1893 and 1899 struggling to find work and food. Ensconced in suburban homes and country clubs, elites could view violence and misery as something distant from their own lives. Lecturing in the towns and cities of eastern Pennsylvania, the Nebraska Populist Cecilia O'Neill found this attitude everywhere. When she described the plight of farmers and the unemployed, she met "heartless indifference." Warned of "the dangers imminent from the unrest of the people," her listeners airily replied,

" 'O, that is only around the mines, the Army and our Militia will keep order there.' No one," O'Neill added, "can make the fortunate and comfortable comprehend that humanity around the mines is of the same nature as his own."

Such attitudes translated in 1894 to stunning Republican victories. Across the north and west Democrats and Populists were swept out of state offices and congressional seats. Two years later William McKinley confirmed the Republicans' lock on national power with his presidential victory. This reaction to the depression was so powerful that it eliminated the intense party competition that had raged since Reconstruction: after 1896 Republicans controlled the White House and both houses of Congress for sixteen years. Theirs was a very different party than that of their predecessors during Reconstruction, and it also lumbered forward in a transformed political climate. Though Theodore Roosevelt and Progressive Republicans would soon bring reform ideas into the party, Republicans on the whole had lost their innovative edge and become the party of capitalism and law-and-order repression of protests and strikes.

Amid hardship and political backlash, few of Americans' cooperative dreams survived the 1890s in unaltered form. Instead, the theme was regrouping and retrenchment. "Oh I have been through the partisan battle," remarked a weary Susan B. Anthony, whose suffrage movement got caught during the decade in the battle between western Republicans and Populists. After the Prohibition Party fragmented and declined, Frances Willard sadly dismissed parties as "of no more value than so many tin cans." With the progressive Illinois governor John Altgeld replaced by a conservative Republican, Hull House reformer Florence Kelley lost her post as a factory inspector to a pro-business successor. Numerous cooperative colonies and experiments failed in the economic crisis, and new ones focused on the cause of sheer survival. The Salvation Army created unemployment colonies in California, Colorado, and Ohio, as did the founders of New York's Straight Edge Industrial Settlement. One Maine activist proposed abandoning reform at the national level and moving as many radicals as possible to a single western state, which he hoped to convert into a cooperative commonwealth. The plan, briefly supported by Eugene Debs and others, brought a series of socialist and anarchist colonies to Washington, but it did not ultimately succeed.

Other reformers suggested withdrawing from the United States altogether. The Populist Henry Demarest Lloyd toured New Zealand, which had given women the vote and instituted a host of labor reforms; he returned on lecture tours to describe New Zealand's charms to disillusioned Americans. Among African Americans interest in overseas colonization reached an unprecedented peak. The African Methodist Episcopal bishop Henry McNeal Turner proposed establishing an African state whose "glory and influence will tell upon the destinies of the race from pole to pole." The International Migration Society carried several shiploads of migrants to Liberia, while several thousand more left the Gulf states and emigrated to a Mexican colony founded by the black Texas businessman William Ellis.

But emigration schemes proved far less important and popular than other strategies for cooperation and self-defense. During the 1890s African

Americans created a striking number of organizations for race pride and defense of human rights. Among them were the Afro-American League, formed in 1890 in Chicago, and the National Association of Colored Women, created in 1895 from the merger of several women's groups. A year later the American Negro Academy gathered intellectuals from across the nation for a convention in Chicago, which became an annual event, and Atlanta University began hosting an annual Conference on Negro Problems. Between 1900 and 1906 black leaders in a number of southern cities launched popular boycotts against segregation on streetcars in a campaign that presaged the later strategies of the civil rights movement. The streetcar boycotts showed—like interest in emigration projects—that ordinary blacks in places such as Houston, Memphis, Pensacola, and Mobile held on to a strong collective dream of equal treatment under the law. Unfortunately, conditions were not ripe for sympathetic white southerners, northerners, or the national press to offer a supportive response.

Nonetheless, in the summer of 1905, W. E. B. DuBois and other race leaders gathered near Niagara Falls to draft a statement of principles. Young and well-educated, the Niagara signers represented the new generation of leaders who were setting out to challenge Booker T. Washington's strategy of compromise and conciliation. They argued, instead, for the defense of voting rights, good schools, decent work and pay, and healthy housing and streets. They reminded Americans of the meaning of the Thirteenth, Fourteenth, and Fifteenth Amendments—"articles of freedom" that Reconstruction had enshrined in the Constitution—and insisted that they be enforced. The Niagara signers also strongly denounced racism in the churches and public opinion. Follow-up meetings in 1906 and 1907 helped lay the foundations for the twentieth-century civil rights movement, and most immediately for creation of the NAACP (National Association for the Advancement of Colored People) in 1909.

In the very same years Mexican men in Arizona developed the Alianza Hispano-America, a mutual aid society that spread rapidly across the Southwest and become a vehicle for labor advocacy. The Texas equivalent was La Unión Occidental Mexicano, and Mexican-American women matched this with their own Sociedad Benificencia. Meanwhile, a coalition of American-born Chinese founded the Native Sons of the Golden State (later renamed the Chinese American Citizens' Alliance). The group's founders came from a generation of merchants' sons, often criticized by their Chinese-born elders for lacking seriousness and respect for tradition. But the Native Sons gained grudging admiration when they defended themselves from the virulently anti-Chinese Native Sons of the Golden West, who brought suit claiming that the term *native sons* was proprietary to their Anglo group. The Chinese, to their great satisfaction, won the right to keep their name.

The crisis of the 1890s also brought new proposals and institutions to address the problems of the poor. With reformers such as Jacob Riis and Jane Addams winning public interest, the obvious plight of the unemployed during the depression—and the obvious bias of courts against labor—began to provoke regret and reconsideration. Attorney General Richard Olney, for example, much-hated in 1894 for his central role in suppressing the Pullman and Coxey protests, found to his dismay that he had been duped by the machinations of railroad executives. A commission investigating the Pullman conflict discovered that 3,600 of the U.S. marshals whom Olney had authorized in Chicago had been hand-picked, armed, paid, and supervised by the railroads themselves. Olney also discovered that the railroads had deliberately attached Pullman passenger cars to U.S. mail trains in order to hinder those trains and provoke federal intervention. Confronted with these facts, Olney began to lean toward arbitration, seeing the need for government to take a more even-handed role in struggles between capital and labor.

In a broader sense, the massive depression began slowly to undermine affluent Americans' assumption that poverty and unemployment resulted from personal moral failings. Even earlier, amid the depression of the 1870s, the Massachusetts Bureau of Statistics and Labor had begun trying to measure the extent of "involuntary idleness." They had begun to use the term *unemployed* to describe those who wanted work and could not find it, rather than those who did not want to work. The noun *unemployment* made its debut in 1887 in one of the bureau's reports. By the 1890s, with Coxey's Army on the march, it became increasingly clear that economic forces, not personal laziness, drove joblessness. The New York Charity Organization Society, which had once warned that soup kitchens would damage the morals of the poor, changed its views. In 1898 it undertook a joint scientific study with social scientists from Columbia University and concluded that unemployment, illness, and disabling accidents were the overwhelming causes of poverty. One New York charity leader declared that such troubles were "as much beyond [workers'] power to avert as if they had been natural calamities of fire, flood, or storm." "Personal depravity," wrote another reformer, "is as foreign to any sound theory of the hardships of our modern poor as witchcraft or demonic possession."

Though it provoked a sharp conservative response, the crisis of the 1890s also suggested that the nation's problems were far outstripping the ability of private charities and churches to address them. Government, some onlookers decided, needed to exercise its powers in new directions. Democrats, as we have seen in earlier chapters, had long mistrusted centralized authority and identified themselves as the smaller-government party. But they had also represented the working class (with the conspicuous exception of blacks), and economic concerns as well as electoral pressures from the Populists now nudged Democrats to consider government welfare measures. With William Jennings Bryan's 1896 presidential bid, Democrats began to argue for stronger government regulation of business and for a progressive income tax. This led the party gradually in the direction of Franklin D. Roosevelt's New Deal, which in the 1930s would introduce Social Security, federal aid to farmers, and a variety of jobs programs for the unemployed.

At the same time, almost all the major leaders and institutions of early twentieth-century progressive reform had taken their place on the public stage by 1905. They ranged from Jane Addams at Hull House, to John Muir of the Sierra Club, to Carrie Nation and the Anti-Saloon League, which initiated a new high-profile antiliquor campaign that eventually carried the prohibition movement to national victory. Investigative journalism was carried forward by the powerful documentary photographs of Lewis Hine, taken for a National Child Labor Committee that sought to keep children in school and out of the workplace. After witnessing the impact of the depression, Jane Addams's colleague Florence Kelley launched the national Consumers' League, which organized female shoppers to choose products made by workers who earned fair wages in decent working conditions. The Women's Trade Union League began to experiment with similar cooperative ventures that brought together women from the elite and the working class.

Having expanded their public roles over the previous four decades, women claimed a prominent place in much of the work that emerged during and after the 1890s. Women's literary and study clubs, which had flourished over the past two decades, began to turn their attention to education and civic reform. Joining settlement activists, professional nurses and social workers, and advocates of the Social Gospel, club women argued that they had a role to play in "municipal housekeeping," since forces outside the home were threatening their families' health and safety. "Very early," wrote an officer of the General Federation of Women's Clubs in 1906, "club women became unwilling to discuss Dante and Browning over the teacups in some lady's drawing room . . . while unsightly heaps of rubbish flanked the paths over which they had passed in their journey thither." They resolved, she wrote, to devote themselves to "civic usefulness." Conditions in the growing cities merited particular attention, but reformers in rural areas also undertook campaigns to improve education, housing, hygiene, and health care. Across the South chapters of the WCTU and other groups worked across racial lines for prohibition and public health. By the early twentieth century such efforts would bear fruit in an array of interracial conversations and cooperative projects.

City governments, especially in the Midwest, underwent a new wave of innovation as dramatic as that which had followed the Civil War. Rebuilding after a horrific hurricane in 1900, Galveston, Texas, introduced the commissioner system of city government, copied soon afterward from Oakland to Buffalo. Samuel "Golden Rule" Jones of Toledo, Ohio, proved to be one of the nation's most inspiring mayors between 1897 and 1904. An industrialist who had prospered in the oil well business, Jones believed in treating workers as he would his kin. He established an eight-hour workday and a minimum wage for city workers, as he had in his company's plants, and he gained broad support for construction of better parks and schools. Mayor Tom Johnson of Cleveland offered similar social welfare programs beginning in 1901, while during the depression years the Detroit mayor Hazen Pingree had already won nationwide praise by opening vacant lots for community gardens. Dubbed Pingree's Potato Patches, the gardens fed thousands of grateful residents and were copied as far away as the Netherlands.

In the meantime, the ARU leader Eugene Debs, arrested for failure to heed the Pullman injunction, refused bail on principle and spent several weeks in the rat-infested Cook County Jail. His cell there overlooked the courtyard where the Haymarket anarchists had been hanged. Debs emerged from the experience as a socialist, and the new party he led became the first home-grown, English-language movement for socialist democracy in the United States. At once more narrow in its base and more radical than the People's Party, it nonetheless included practical municipal gas-and-water socialists such as Detroit's Pingree and Milwaukee's Victor Berger. While socialism grew in the heartland amid economic distress, the arrival of radical Russian Jews and "Red Finns" invigorated the ranks of the political left. Abraham Cahan's socialist *Jewish Daily Forward*, founded in the 1890s, soon had the largest circulation of any Yiddish newspaper in the world. As a presidential candidate Eugene Debs went on to win 6 percent of the popular vote in 1912.

At the state level Wisconsin's Republican governor "Fighting Bob" LaFollette carried forward such progressive reforms as higher corporate taxes and tougher railroad regulation. In 1900 Maryland became the first state to make employers compensate employees injured on the job, and western states such as Utah and Oregon were at the forefront in setting minimum wages and maximum working hours. Oregon also introduced the initiative and refer-endum, measures Populists had advocated for more democratic decision making. State and local reforms were accompanied by federal initiatives such as antitrust and environmental conservation measures, marking the first great peak of progressive reform around 1906. In the ten years that followed rural voters in the states that had given birth to Populism elected many of the con-gressmen who championed federal deposit insurance for investors, the Federal Trade Commission, the Federal Reserve, and the progressive income tax. Ultimately, it was the South and West, more than the urban Northeast, that provided powerful support for the New Deal.

The achievement of nationwide women's suffrage was a convoluted pro-cess. While the need for economic reforms was glaring after the crisis of the 1890s, the suffrage movement was so closely associated with Populism that it became discredited after the party's defeat. With Populist support Colorado women won full voting rights in 1893, and Idaho women in 1896. But after that suffragists endured a decade in the doldrums, winning no further victories during the first decade of the twentieth century. Reflecting a new atmosphere of gender conservatism, the author Helen Kendrick Johnson claimed that female voters in Colorado, having won the vote, had supported "socialism and anarchy"; suffrage should be confined to men only for the "defense of national honor." Johnson was not wrong in connecting suffrage with progressive politi-cal movements. After 1910, when the Progressive Party emerged in the West, suffragists again made alliances with a radical third party that brought victory in Washington, California, and Arizona. With women across the West already voting, and with no ex-Confederate state except Tennessee endorsing the measure, women finally won the vote nationwide through a constitutional amendment passed in 1920.

In the long run, then, even though the Populist Party and other cooperative dreams of the 1890s foundered, many of their ideas endured, though they did so in an altered political climate. Evolution away from capitalism had been at the core of utopian projects and books such as Owen's *Integral Cooperation* and Gronlund's *The Cooperative Commonwealth*. The slow transformation of that vision set crucial precedents for the future. Had Americans, for instance, nationalized their telegraph system during the late nineteenth century, a measure seriously debated by Congress at several junctures, that single reform would have had important implications for future generations. Accustomed to a public communication network, later Americans might have been more inclined to insist on public ownership of telephone lines, radio and television stations, cable bandwidths, cellphone frequencies, and Internet connections. As one looks down such paths not taken, the scenery fades into the mists of uncertainty. To take just one example, a Populist proposal that *did* win later adoption, the federal income tax, was originally designed to tax only a small percent of Americans, the very richest, and use the proceeds to help level the playing field for all. Over nine decades the program has mutated into something very different indeed.

In a similar way, the ideas advanced by utopian colonists, settlement workers, Populists, and many other reformers and dreamers changed shape during the critical decade of economic depression. They established a lasting legacy in American politics, a deep well into which future progressives could dip their buckets. But the crisis of the 1890s sharply altered the direction in which cooperative dreams sailed off into the twentieth-century future. America's immediate collective response to depression and crisis was grounded in experiences of harsh conflict and privation. In her novel *A Lost Lady*, Willa Cather later wrote that the 1890s brought to the forefront "a generation of shrewd young men, trained to petty economies by hard times. . . . The space, the color, the princely carelessness of the pioneer they would destroy and cut up into profitable bits, as the match factory splinters the primeval forest." More than the frontier West was at stake. The 1890s also brought a consolidation of new powers by U.S. presidents and corporate leaders that shaped the future of the nation and the world.

FOR FURTHER READING

Ray Reynolds tells the story of Topolobampo in *Catspaw Utopia*, 2nd ed. (San Bernardino, CA, 1996). A wonderful source on such projects generally is Donald E. Pitzer, ed., *America's Communal Utopias*, cited in Chapter 8; for another case study see W. Fitzhugh Brundage, *A Socialist Utopia in the New South* (Urbana, IL, 1996). On suburbanization see Stuart Blumin, *The Emergence of the Middle Class* (Cambridge, 1989) and Kenneth T. Jackson, *Crabgrass Frontier* (New York, 1985); on urban segregation see Olivier Zunz, *The Changing Face of Inequality* (Chicago, 1982), and Roy Rosenzweig, *"Eight Hours for What We Will"* (Cambridge, 1983). I have also relied on Nora E. Schlesinger, "Riverside, Illinois: Frederick Law Olmsted's Bourgeois Utopia," research paper, American Culture 250, Vassar College, fall 2003.

On settlement houses see Allen Davis, *Spearheads for Reform* (New York, 1967), and Victoria Bissell Brown's introduction to her edition of Jane Addams's *Twenty Years at Hull-House* (Boston, 1999). On Addams see Louise W. Knight, *Citizen* (Chicago, 2005). On Hull House see also Kathryn Kish Sklar, *Florence Kelley and the Nation's Work* (New Haven, CT, 1995). The best short overview of Populism is Robert McMath, *American Populism* (New York, 1993); see also the first two chapters of Michael Kazin, *The Populist Persuasion* (New York, 1995), as well as John D. Hicks, *The Populist Revolt* (Minneapolis, 1931), and Lawrence Goodwyn, *Democratic Promise* (New York, 1976). Also helpful here was Barbara Fields, "Ideology and Race in American History," cited in Chapter 1, and Stephen Kantrowitz, *Ben Tillman and the Reconstruction of White Supremacy* (Chapel Hill, NC, 2000).

In *Protestant Churches and Industrial America*, cited in Chapter 8, Henry F. May uses the metaphor of "three earthquakes" that I borrow here. Also see Charles Hoffman, *The Depression of the Nineties* (Westport, CT, 1970), Kenneth L. Kusmer, *Down and Out, On the Road* (New York, 2002), H. Roger Grant, *Self-Help in the Depression of the 1890s* (Ames, IA, 1983), and Michael Lesy's nightmarish and disturbing *Wisconsin Death Trip* (New York, 1973). On Pullman see David Ray Papke, *The Pullman Case* (Lawrence, KS, 1999), and the essays in *The Pullman Strike and the Crisis of the 1890s*, edited by Richard Schneirov, Shelton Stromquist, and Nick Salvatore (Urbana, IL, 1999). The best account of the Commonweal of Christ is Carlos A. Schwantes, *Coxey's Army* (Moscow, ID, 1994).

For a broad analysis of the rise of "radical racism," see Joel Williamson, *The Crucible of Race* (New York, 1984). On various forms of heightened racial and ethnic segregation and animosity see also three works previously cited: John Higham, *Strangers in the Land*, Steven A. Riess, *Sport in Industrial America*, and Gerald Sorin, *Tradition Transformed*. In addition I have drawn on Rosalyn Terborg-Penn, *African American Women in the Struggle for the Vote, 1850–1920* (Bloomington, IN, 1998), and Marjorie Spruill Wheeler, "Race, Reform, and Reaction at the Turn of the Century," in *Votes for Women*, edited by Jean H. Baker (New York, 2002), pp. 102–117. On Mexican Americans throughout this chapter, see four books on the Southwest that were cited earlier: Linda Gordon's *The Great Arizona Orphan Abduction*, Matt S. Meier and Feliciana Ribera's *Mexican Americans/American Mexicans*; Arnoldo De León, *The Tejano Community, 1836–1900*, and David Montejano, *Anglos and Mexicans in the Making of Texas*. Also helpful on New Mexico is Erlinda Gonzales-Berry, "Which Language Will Our Children Speak?" in *The Contested Homeland*, edited by, Erlinda Gonzales-Berry and David Maciel (Albuquerque, 2000), pp. 169–189.

On lynching see James Allen's powerful book *Without Sanctuary* (Santa Fe, NM, 2000), W. Fitzhugh Brundage, *Lynching in the New South* (Urbana, IL, 1993), and for both lynchings and the broader pattern of political and racial conflict in the South, Edward L. Ayers, *The Promise of the New South*, cited in Chapter 1. A statistical summary is the NAACP's *Thirty Years of Lynching in the United States, 1889–1918* (originally 1919; reprinted New York, 1969). On Ida B. Wells's investigations see Patricia Schechter, *Ida B. Wells-Barnett and American Reform* (Chapel Hill, NC, 2001), as well as the introduction by Jacqueline Jones Royster in her edition of Wells's *Southern Horrors and Other Writings* (Boston, 1997).

For overviews of politics in the 1890s, see R. Hal Williams, *Years of Decision* (New York, 1978), and Samuel T. McSeveney, *The Politics of Depression* (New York, 1972). On western Populism and the structures of the political system see Peter H. Argersinger's two books, *Structure, Process and Party* (Armonk, NY, 1992), and *The Limits of Agrarian Radicalism* (Lawrence, KS, 1995), as well as Jeffrey Ostler, *Prairie Populism* (Lawrence, KS, 1993). On legacies of Populism see, in addition to McMath's *American Populism*, Elizabeth Sanders's impressive *Roots of Reform* (Chicago, 1999). On disfranchisement in the South, see J. Morgan Kousser, *The Shaping of Southern Politics* (New Haven, CT, 1974); the quote on the rise of southern "oligarchy," from Walter Dean Burnham, appears on p. 224. On southern sympathies in literature and the chilling of the intellectual climate, see Nina Silber, *The Romance of Reunion* (Chapel Hill, NC, 1993), Ayers's *Promise of the New South*, above, and David W. Blight's *Race and Reunion*, cited in Chapter 1. On the case of Richard Ely, see Mary O. Furner, *Advocacy and Objectivity* (Lexington, KY, 1975).

For shifting responses to poverty amid the crisis of the 1890s, see Alexander Keyssar, *Out of Work* (Cambridge, 1986), Walter I. Trattner, *From Poor Law to Welfare State*, cited in Chapter 1, Daniel T. Rogers, *Atlantic Crossings*, cited in Chapter 2, and Anne Firor

Scott, *Natural Allies* (Urbana, IL, 1991), and Glenda Elizabeth Gilmore, *Gender and Jim Crow* (Chapel Hill, NC, 1996). On the rise of socialism, see Howard S. Quint, *The Forging of American Socialism* (Columbia, SC, 1953); on black nationalism and pan-Africanism, Edwin S. Redkey, *Black Exodus* (New Haven, CT, 1969); and on the Niagara movement, John Hope Franklin's *From Slavery to Freedom*, cited in Chapter 1. On the origins of the Chinese American Citizens' Alliance see Sue Fawn Chung's article in *Claiming America*, cited in Chapter 5, and on boycotts see August Meier and Elliott Rudwick, "The Boycott Movement Against Jim Crow Streetcars in the South, 1900–1906," *Journal of American History* 55 (1969): 756–775. Willa Cather's comment on the depression's impact is in *A Lost Lady* (New York, 1923), p. 90. For emphasis on positive long-term outcomes of the crisis of the 1890s, see Steven J. Diner, *A Very Different Age* (New York, 1998), and Michael McGerr, *A Fierce Discontent* (New York, 2003).

CHAPTER 11

Executive Powers

> Modernity, with its pockets full of money and its conscience
> full of virtue, its heart really full of tenderness, has seated itself
> there under pretext of guarding the shrine.
> —HENRY JAMES, *THE AMERICAN SCENE*

It is hard to pinpoint an exact date when the United States took over the Hawai'ian Islands. Protestant missionaries arrived in 1820, and over the decades that followed they converted the island's royal family. New laws in the 1840s, advocated by the missionaries, opened land for market purchase and resulted in rapid takeover by American-born landowners, at the same time that American whaling ships made Honolulu a key port and brought an influx of foreigners and trade. By the 1850s and 1860s Hawai'i's legal code had been thoroughly transformed, and high-quality sugarcane was replacing whales as the most lucrative natural resource. Anglo cane planters imported thousands of laborers from China, Japan, and Portugal, who soon made up a majority of Hawai'i's population. Rapid growth of the sugar industry created, in turn, momentum for U.S. political annexation. In 1887 militant Anglos forced King David Kalakaua to accept a constitution that brought "American-style democracy" to the islands. (Eligible voters included all Anglos, no Asians, and only some native Hawai'ians.) A coup by U.S.-born locals in 1893 against Kalakaua's successor, Queen Liliuokalani, when she tried to replace the 1887 constitution with a royal charter of her own, paved the way for Hawai'i to become a territory of the United States.

The conquest of Hawai'i illustrated in microcosm almost all the major themes of U.S. history in these years. Epidemic diseases—smallpox, typhoid, leprosy, syphilis—reduced the islands' native population from perhaps a half-million to 30,000, making resistance as difficult for Hawai'ians as it had been for native peoples on the North American continent. The land reforms of the 1840s offered lessons that the authors of Reconstruction should have heeded:

missionaries hoped it would turn the peasantry into landowners, but instead 85 percent of the islands' land fell to outsiders, most of whom were elite men from the United States. No one wanted an Asian majority on the islands, but the interests of powerful sugar planters brought them anyway. The result was racial hysteria and violence against Chinese and Japanese cane workers. They, in turn, struck repeatedly for better wages and working conditions despite planters' attempts to keep the labor force racially divided. Many planters actually opposed U.S. political annexation for many years, fearing that enforcement of the Chinese Exclusion Act would undercut their source of cheap labor.

But regardless of whether they wanted to be, sugar planters had become deeply enmeshed in American politics. In the coveted U.S. market they competed with Louisiana cane growers and western sugar-beet farmers, whom Republicans protected with a high tariff. After an 1875 treaty placed Hawai'ian sugar inside the tariff barrier, the islands' sugar exports to the United States grew twenty-fold in two decades. When the treaty came up for renewal in 1887, U.S. negotiators demanded exclusive naval rights to Pearl Harbor, and after some debate they received it. But in 1890, notwithstanding this concession, Congress lifted all tariffs on sugar in response to intense lobbying from beet growers and instead began paying a direct subsidy of 2¢ a pound to producers inside the United States. The result in Hawai'i was catastrophic. Sugar prices plummeted. Some smaller-scale planters went bankrupt, precipitating, in part, the final drive for annexation so that Hawai'i could claim a secure place in the U.S. economy.

Annexation was thus a culmination of events stretching back many decades, although the machinations of annexationists show that it was hardly inevitable as late as 1890. On the model that Republican Secretary of State William Seward had promoted back in the 1860s, the United States let "the flag follow trade" (and follow missions). Officials repeatedly denied that they sought to conquer Hawai'i. U.S. diplomats who pulled strings in island politics often did so without help from Washington, or even against direct orders. But by the 1870s U.S. warships began to materialize offshore when business interests were at stake. After 1891 the U.S. consul-general in the islands, the Republican appointee John L. Stevens, issued regular denunciations of the native monarchy and flouted diplomatic protocol by joining a secret Annexation Club that conspired to overthrow the queen. During the subsequent coup he called in U.S. marines armed with Gatling guns, who stationed themselves near the royal palace to "watch" as the queen surrendered control. (The queen had ten Gatling guns herself and without direct U.S. intervention might well have fought to keep her throne.) Stevens recognized the new government before it had even secured control of Honolulu.

The coup leaders, of course, hoped the United States would immediately annex the islands, but that did not happen for five more years. In the intervening period, uncertain whether their political and economic system would even survive the crisis of the mid-1890s, policy makers in Washington undertook a massive quest for new foreign markets in which to sell U.S. products. This initiative helped lead to war in 1898 and the acquisition of not only Hawai'i but also the Philippines, both way stations for American ships steaming to and from the markets of Asia. At the same time, in coastal China, the Caribbean, and Central America U.S. policy makers made bold grabs for direct control of overseas territories. Isolationists and anti-imperialists in the United States hotly contested this process, but after massive Republican victories in 1894 and 1896, critics of imperialism were relegated to the political sidelines.

In effect, Republicans chose to export America's economic and social troubles in order to achieve stability at home. In doing so they exported many of the fires that had burned in the United States in the era of incorporation, and notwithstanding strenuous claims to the contrary, they helped bring revolution and upheaval, not stability, to Latin American, Caribbean, and Pacific shores. Turmoil in those regions, like Hawai'ian resistance to conquest, justified in turn a long series of U.S. military occupations to protect business interests and missionary lives. As one historian bluntly puts it, "U.S. leaders without the intelligence, courage, or moral values to use the domestic market to develop a just and humane society [found that] Latin America and Asia offered promising opportunities to extract the wealth needed to sustain domestic material accumulation and well-being."

Two critical configurations of power emerged clearly between 1896 and 1906. First was the growing dominance of the presidency in relation to Congress, so closely linked to the nation's rising power on the world stage that some historians describe William McKinley and Theodore Roosevelt as creators of an "imperial presidency." McKinley—often wrongly depicted as a reluctant warrior—helped launch the process, but after 1901 Roosevelt made even more sweeping claims to power. In many ways Roosevelt shared the worldview of Liberal Republicans such as E. L. Godkin of *The Nation*, who fiercely attacked "socialistic" ideas but also wanted stronger forms of government administration and regulation—as long as government lay in the hands of experts and the elite.

Roosevelt, who came from a wealthy and privileged family, also called for men of his class to reclaim political power from immigrants and men of "lesser breeding," and he saw his own career as an embodiment of that ideal. As president he pioneered overseas police actions and executive agreements, circumventing the constitutional rules that gave Congress authority over war making and required presidents to seek the Senate's consent for foreign treaties. In the domestic arena Roosevelt's expansion of presidential authority brought him head-to-head with another set of chief executives who were wielding unprecedented power: leaders of multinational corporations. Through intervention in a 1902 coal strike and through vigorous Justice Department actions, Roosevelt's administration made some of the first federal attempts to block corporate monopolies and force CEOs to negotiate with workers. The imperial presidency, the multinational corporation, and the struggle between them left Americans a double legacy of consolidated power.

IMPERIAL CLAIMS

From the depression of the 1870s onward, intellectuals and policy makers in the United States, fearful of the rising tide of strikes and political protests, worried that the country would adopt "socialistic" measures to resolve this unrest. The brief success of the People's Party, which advocated just such measures, heightened their anxiety. The alternative, imperialists believed, was to secure overseas markets for American products, ensuring jobs and prosperity to ease domestic distress. The result was what some historians call "social imperialism," focused not on building a European-style administrative empire but on creating favorable conditions of trade. But what benefited the United States often proved detrimental to its commercial partners—especially in Latin America and Asia—and the United States frequently wound up creating "favorable conditions" at gunpoint through military intervention.

Social imperialism stemmed directly from William Seward's vision of "the flag following trade," and it was underway as early as 1879, when the United States and Germany muscled into the South Pacific kingdom of Samoa to claim rival harbors and coaling stations. By 1890 a Republican-controlled Congress was appropriating massive funds for steel battleships to match those of Britain and Germany. The Vermont senator Justin Morrill, arguing for aggressive trade policies and "enlargement of our Lilliputian Navy," noted that Russia, Germany, France, and Britain were already competing for economic supremacy. "To lag behind when all the world is on the move," he stated, "is to accept the fate of the decrepit and dull-pated bison who lingers on the prairie in the rear of the ongoing herd."

On the domestic front commentators worried in the 1890s that workers were tending toward socialism or even revolution. Apocalyptic forecasts abounded, with one newspaper predicting that "fire and sword will devastate the country." The political thinker Brooks Adams, in his influential 1896 book *The Law of Civilization and Decay*, wrote that "the time has now come" when surplus American products "must be sold abroad," especially in the immense markets of Asia. Otherwise the United States "would be devoured by the gangrene which attacks every stagnant society and from which no patient recovers." Senator Henry Cabot Lodge of Massachusetts argued that "we must have new markets . . . unless we would be visited by declines in wages and by great industrial disturbances, of which signs have not been lacking." Such observers agreed with Populists on the economic basis of the nation's woes, but they had a radically different view of what government should do in response.

The elections of 1894 and 1896 brought to national power Republicans (and some Democrats, especially in the South) who were committed to solving domestic conflict by opening overseas markets. To implement this vision American policy makers had to readjust their view of the country's role in the world. Many decades earlier President James Monroe, in the Monroe Doctrine, had told Britain and Spain that the United States would come to the aid of any fellow republic in the Western Hemisphere that was threatened by European powers. The crisis of the 1890s culminated in 1904 with Theodore Roosevelt's Corollary to the Monroe Doctrine, which was, in fact, an entirely different doctrine. Roosevelt asserted that the United States had an exclusive right to intervene in other New World countries as it saw fit. He and his predecessor,

McKinley, gave even more careful attention to the Pacific basin, believing favorable trade with China and other Asian markets was the key to prosperity in the United States.

The war that brought the United States to power on the imperial stage, however, and swept away the last vestige of Spain's New World empire started not in Washington, but with Cuban rebels such as José Martí. They conducted their revolution at a time when Cuba's sugar economy was suffering through the same crisis that hit the U.S. mainland. Cubans' fight for independence was widely popular in the United States. Men smoked Cuba Libre cigars, and editors sympathized with the plight of a people who, like the thirteen colonies of North America had in 1776, sought freedom from European monarchy. Newspaper magnates such as William Randolph Hearst used front-page headlines to trumpet Spanish atrocities. (They did not need to exaggerate much: rounding up Cubans into concentration camps and conducting a war of extermination, Spanish commanders unintentionally deepened resistance and spread the revolt across the island.) When the U.S. battleship *Maine* sank in Havana harbor, apparently due to a boiler explosion, Spain was instantly blamed, and McKinley faced a surge of support for American troops to assist in making Cuba free.

Congress, through a law called the Teller Amendment, reassured Cubans that this was, in fact, their country's goal. It declared that the Cuban people "are, and of right ought to be, free and independent," and that the United States "disclaims any disposition or intention to exercise sovereignty, jurisdiction, or control over said island except for the pacification thereof." The resolution, one senator stated, ensured "the absolute and unqualified independence of the Cubans." But the actions of the McKinley administration suggest that its objectives were quite distinct from those of Congress and much of the American public. The *Maine* had been sitting in Havana harbor because administration officials (as well as jubilant Cubans) perceived that Spanish control was already collapsing. "Cuban independence is absolutely impossible," wrote McKinley's minister to Spain. State Department officials, taking for granted that U.S. control of Cuba was their objective, debated how to avoid fighting "both the Spaniards and the Cubans." They explored the option of buying the island, since "some way must be found by which Spain can part with Cuba . . . with certainty of American control."

At the same time, the McKinley administration focused considerable attention on Spanish holdings in the Pacific. In Asia both American and European interests were facing sudden and aggressive competition from Japan, which had handily won a short war against China at mid-decade. "Japan has leaped, almost at one bound, to a place among the great nations of the earth," wrote the secretary of the navy. With China weakened by the war, Germany had moved swiftly to seize a portion of Shandong province for a port and development of railroads. Britain, France, Russia, and Belgium then fought for their own pieces of the pie. Their combined invasions along the coast provoked an uprising of militant Chinese societies known in the West as "Boxers," who eventually won the backing of the dowager empress Cixi. In 1898 these patriotic groups began attacking Germans in Shandong, seeking to drive out the invaders. To American and European officials, much-coveted access to Asian markets seemed imperiled.

Thus, before the United States declared war against Spain in April 1898, the McKinley administration prepared carefully in the Pacific as well as the Caribbean. U.S. military forces actually launched attacks on the Wake Islands, the Philippine Islands, and Guam—all Spanish holdings in the Pacific—during April and May, well before they joined the Cuban revolutionary front in late June. With Spanish control already weakened by years of rebellion, the fighting in Cuba lasted only a few months. Spain formally withdrew its claims to Cuba, Puerto Rico, and an array of Pacific possessions before the end of the year. But the resulting pact differed sharply from the goals Congress had set forth in the Teller Amendment. The United States took Puerto Rico and the Philippines as "protectorates," and although negotiators acknowledged Cuban independence, they excluded Cubans themselves from diplomatic negotiations with Spain. Two years later the Platt Amendment officially amended U.S. intentions. Congress and the president now asserted the right to intervene in Cuba whenever the United States deemed necessary, set limits on its government budget, established a permanent naval base at Guantánamo Bay, and banned treaties between Cuba and any other power. Cuba, as one U.S. general wrote to Roosevelt after the amendment passed, had "little or no independence left."

In the war of 1898 the United States acquired, for the first time, territories with no apparent prospect of future statehood, though many Cubans and Puerto Ricans had hoped for U.S. statehood as a second-best outcome. Instead, the McKinley and later the Roosevelt administrations justified continued "protectorate" status on the grounds that the islands needed economic "stability." The United States could not leave Cuba, they argued, unless American business interests were fully secure. In the wake of the war, given exactly this opening, U.S. sugar interests tightened their hold over the plantation economies of Cuba and extended their reach in Puerto Rico and the Dominican Republic. By the early twentieth century these Caribbean islands produced 1.6 million tons of sugar a year, with Hawai'ian and soon Philippine sugar added to this total. (Per capita consumption of sugar on the American mainland, not coincidentally, rose to 75 pounds a year in 1910, more than double what it had been on the eve of the Civil War.) In the Pacific imperialists spoke of the need to hold the Philippines in order to secure access to Chinese markets. The islands were "our only safeguard for our trade interests in the East."

In explaining their policies to the American people, the architects of social imperialism appealed to the same racial thinking so evident in domestic affairs. In both the Philippines and Cuba the indigenous revolutionary movements that had challenged Spanish rule were overwhelmingly made up of non-Anglos. Local elites in both Cuba and the Philippines, threatened by popular uprisings, encouraged North Americans in the belief that the rebels were incompetent to govern and that race war would result if the United States did not remain in control. But officials in Washington needed little encouragement to frame policy in racial terms. "My own belief," Roosevelt wrote privately of the Filipinos, "is that there are not 100 men among them who comprehend what Anglo-Saxon self-government even means." "God has not been pre-paring the English-speaking and Teutonic peoples for a thousand years for nothing," declared the influential senator Albert Beveridge of Indiana. "No! He has made us the master organizers of the world to establish system where chaos reigns. . . . He has made us adept in government that we may admin-ister government among savage and senile peoples."

Filipinos presented something of a complication to such views. Inhabitants of the islands were racially and linguistically diverse, indisputably Asian if one consulted a map, but including both Spanish-speaking Catholics and ethnic groups such as so-called Negritos, whom Americans saw as black. Many U.S. soldiers dismissed all Filipinos as "gu-gus" and "niggers" and compared the islands to the American South. To make things even more com-plex, the Indian wars of the West served as the most convenient analogy for the war that ensued in the Philippines after Spain withdrew and the United States set itself to subdue the islands. Since Americans denied a voice in government to the Indian at home, asked Beveridge, "how dare you grant it to the Malay abroad? . . . There are people in the world who do not understand any form of government . . . [and] must be governed." If the United States was "morally bound to abandon the Philippines," declared Theodore Roosevelt, it was "also morally bound to abandon Arizona to the Apaches."

Such connections were more than just rhetorical. Most military leaders in the Philippine war came directly from the Indian wars of the West (a few having detoured for riot control in Chicago). Even more important, the legal treatment of American Indians set the stage for annexing "dependent peoples." The relevant legal framework had developed over several decades. In 1871 the Supreme Court had ruled that Congress no longer had to nego-tiate treaties with Indian peoples but instead could enact legislation without their consent. In 1885 the Court gave the federal government jurisdiction over crimes on Indian reservations. American Indians belonged to a new category, "nationals," or "persons owing allegiance to the United States but without those privileges which go only with citizenship." The Court drew on exactly these precedents for its arguments in the *Insular Cases*, a series of rulings issued between 1901 and 1910 that relegated Filipinos and Puerto Ricans to the same category. Like American Indians, they were "nationals" without citizen-ship rights. As in the Standing Bear decision, the justices suggested that such a status could not be indefinite, but they did not set any deadlines on its use.

The anti-imperialist movement, meanwhile, suffered internal divisions. Most of the leading anti-imperialist spokesmen and spokeswomen came from the Anglo elite; their arguments ranged from humanitarian and democratic to openly racist, and since the latter struck a powerful chord, many rivaled the imperialists in championing Anglo-Saxon superiority. In *The Nation* E.L. Godkin warned of the perils of admitting "alien, inferior, and mongrel races to our nationality." Congressman Champ Clark of Missouri, speaking of Filipinos, declared that "no matter whether they are fit to govern themselves or not, they are not fit to govern us." Senator Ben Tillman of South Carolina drew explicit comparisons to white supremacy at home. Being from a state, he said, "with 750,000 colored population and only 500,000 whites, I realize what you [imperialists] are doing, while you don't; and I would save this country from the injection into it of another race question which can only breed bloodshed." Though there was considerable anti-imperialist sentiment among working-class immigrants and African Americans, arguments such as Godkin's and Tillman's hardly fostered alliances. Anti-imperialists in the Catholic press, along with prominent black editors such as John Mitchell of the *Richmond Planet*, had little in common with the elite Boston-based Anti-Imperialist League, much less with demagogues such as Clark and Tillman. Thus, anti-imperialists made up a disjointed, fragmentary opposition.

In the wake of the popular Cuban campaign, the McKinley administration moved swiftly to protect U.S. access to the Asian markets so central to its new exploits in the Pacific. When Boxer revolutionaries in China reached Beijing, the United States sent a contingent to join Russian, British, French, German, and Japanese troops, who marched together on the capital. In August 1900 the combined expeditionary force took Beijing, engaging afterward in brutal acts of rape, looting, and indiscriminate murder. (German and Japanese soldiers were especially rapacious, but their allies made no efforts to stop them, and some joined in.) The Beijing expedition marked a crucial turning point in American foreign policy. For the first time since the American Revolution U.S. troops joined those of other nations in a multinational force, and they fought side by side with the regiments of European imperial powers.

Having participated in a rank campaign of conquest, the United States got its share of the spoils: 7 percent of a $333 million indemnity that China was forced to pay for its rebels' resistance. ("Poor China!" exclaimed Sarah Conger, the wife of the U.S. minister in Beijing. "Why cannot foreigners let her alone with her own? China has been wronged, and in her desperation she has striven as best she could to stop the inroads." The United States, in fact, later had second thoughts and returned the indemnity.) The United States and Britain enforced China's "open door" to foreign trade. As in Cuba and the Philippines, this entailed sharp restrictions on China's political and economic autonomy. Unlike Cuba and the Philippines, though, China fell under the sway of many competing powers rather than just one. Germany, France, Belgium, Russia, Japan, and the United States all pursued railroad contracts and access to Chinese markets. The "open door" became a blueprint for America's twentieth-century pursuit of trade relationships in Africa and the Middle East.

Just as in China, where imperial incursions provoked violent local responses, upheavals arose in many parts of the world as the Western powers—including, now, the United States—made aggressive demands for empire and trade. Some of these struggles ran along lines of race and class similar to those in the United States; others were struggles for national independence. Thus, while U.S. policy makers claimed to bring stability to such turbulent parts of the world, in fact they helped precipitate the reverse. The decision to support or repress rebellion in a given place, from Hawai'i to the Philippines to Cuba, depended on what policy makers perceived American interests to be. In Panama, for example, U.S. warships intervened in 1901 to stop a popular uprising against Colombia, which had long claimed Panama as part of its

U.S. occupation of the Philippines brought a spate of reports about the islands in *National Geographic*. The images and language used in these articles suggest some of the ways in which scientific racism helped justify military conquest and political dependency. Depictions of bare-chested women, an important marker of "primitivism" for Westerners, had only recently begun to appear in the magazine. "Adult Negrito woman, showing relative size," *National Geographic* readers learned in the text accompanying this photograph. "The Negritos are physical and mental weaklings, and are rapidly disappearing. . . . There are about 30,000 of them left." (I am grateful to Vassar student Anna Kichorowsky, who located this image in her research.)
Source: *National Geographic*, May 1903, p. 209.

territory. But in late 1903, when the Roosevelt administration felt ready to press a broader claim, the United States sent naval vessels to block Colombia from ending the Panama uprising, essentially backing a coup and violating a long-standing treaty. In exchange for abetting the Panamanian revolution, the United States demanded from the country's new government "titular sovereignty" over a strip of land on which it planned to build a canal, the long-yearned-for shortcut to Pacific trade.

It was the Philippines that offered the fiercest resistance to U.S. conquest and the greatest challenge to Americans' belief in their country's good intentions. Following a brief opening campaign in 1898 to take control of the islands after Spanish withdrawal, U.S. forces found themselves bogged down in a frustrating guerrilla conflict. Some began to take seriously the Filipinos' widespread armed opposition to their supposed liberation by the United States. Referring to Emilio Aguinaldo, the veteran leader of resistance to Spain who now led the nationalist forces, General Arthur McArthur wrote, "When I

"Ground Over Which the Montana Troops Advanced on Caloocan. Dead American Soldier in the Foreground." Caloocan was the first major battle of the opening stage of the Philippine War, in 1898. Modern standards of documentary photography had not yet emerged, and like his counterparts in the U.S. Civil War, this photographer may have repositioned the soldier's body to achieve the effect he desired.
Source: From Marrion Wilcox, *Harper's History of the War in the Philippines* (New York, 1900), p. 126.

first started in against these rebels, I believed that Aguinaldo's troops represented only a faction. I did not like to believe that the whole population of Luzon . . . was opposed to us and our offers of aid and good government. But after having come this far, after having occupied several towns and cities in succession, . . . I have been reluctantly compelled to believe that the Filipino masses are loyal to Aguinaldo and the government which he heads." A sergeant in the 1st Nebraska Regiment put it more bluntly. "I am not afraid, and am always ready to do my duty, but I would like someone to tell me what we are fighting for." "I deprecate this war," wrote an officer of the 13th Minnesota, "because it seems to me that we are doing something that is contrary to our principles in the past." Both Filipino and American critics of the war found it keenly ironic when a U.S. commander in Manila seized copies of the U.S. Declaration of Independence that had been translated into Spanish, calling it "an incendiary document."

Many African-American soldiers found their loyalties especially conflicted. "The future of the Filipino, I fear," wrote a private in the 24th Infantry, "is that of the Negro in the South. Matters are almost to that condition in Manila now. No one (white) has any scruples respecting the rights of a Filipino. He is kicked and cuffed at will and he dare not remonstrate." Another wrote that he had privately interviewed a number of Manila residents, who spoke more freely to him than to whites. "I must confess they have a just grievance. All of this never would have occurred if the army of occupation would have treated them as people." Yet fighting for their lives side by side with fellow Americans as proud volunteers, other black soldiers rejected any identification with the enemy. One described the slaughter of Filipinos in battle as "awful," but added simply, "it was fight or die with us." Thinking back later on his war service, another black veteran wrote, "I was filled with the spirit of adventure and also possessed a reasonable share of bigotry. It never occurred to my simple mind that there could be anything wrong, morally or otherwise, with any of our government's undertaking."

The guerrilla war proved long and bloody. Most Filipino nationalists fought with bolo knives against U.S. troops armed with the latest Springfield and Norwegian-made Krag-Jorgensen rifles. With the fight hopelessly one-sided, the nationalists sought the advantage of stealth on home terrain and the shelter and aid of civilians. Americans found the bodies of fellow soldiers beaten to death or mutilated. Filipino women and children enlisted as spies or actively aided the fight, escalating American troops' hostility toward the civilian population. Some U.S. commanders resorted to executing captured prisoners or refusing to take prisoners at all, and for interrogations they ordered the soon-infamous "water cure," forcing prisoners to drink water until their stomachs were distended and then punching, kicking, or jumping on them. Eventually, in some districts U.S. soldiers forced residents into concentration camps and treated the countryside as a free-fire zone, burning villages, destroying crops, and shooting anything that moved.

Even this did not fully defeat the rebel movement. At Balangiga on the island of Samar in September 1901, Filipino nationalists smuggled arms into a local church, hiding them inside a number of small coffins that, they told guards from the 9th Infantry, Company C, held the bodies of children who had died of cholera. (It was a measure of the war's devastating effects that the delivery of such coffins seemed routine.) The "women" who brought the coffins turned out to be men in disguise, and in a surprise dawn attack they killed 59 U.S. soldiers and wounded 23. Only six members of the company escaped unharmed.

News of the massacre jolted Americans, who thought that resistance had faded and that U.S. occupation was winning Filipinos' support. Denouncing the attack as "treacherous savagery," editors across the country likened Balangiga to Custer's defeat at Little Big Horn and called for retaliation. They did not wait long. Major General Adna Chaffee, the commander of U.S. forces in the Philippines, held a press conference to explain that Company C's officers had been guilty of "soft mollycoddling of treacherous natives." He sent in Brigadier General Jake Smith, a ruthless veteran of the Indian wars, to avenge the American dead. Smith ordered the immediate execution of any Filipino male in the area who was over age ten. "I want no prisoners," he instructed. "I wish you to kill and burn, the more you kill and burn the better it will please me. . . . The interior of Samar must be made a howling wilderness." These written orders emerged later as evidence when one of Smith's subordinates faced court-martial for murder and argued—successfully—that he had just been following orders.

The result was a campaign of arson and slaughter that capped three years of increasingly bitter conflict. Investigating journalists soon discovered that a year earlier Smith had ordered the execution of prisoners and held other captured Filipinos in makeshift cages for weeks at a time, boasting to reporters of the resulting death rate. In a sensational trial Smith was court-martialed and found guilty (the first court-martial of a general in U.S. history), but he retained the loyalty of many soldiers, who believed rightly that he was taking the fall for his own superiors. One Massachusetts volunteer wrote home that harsh measures were routine throughout the islands; he himself, he declared, had helped systematically execute 1,300 prisoners in Batangas, on Luzon, and had witnessed the hanging of the priest who had administered last rites to all those killed. In the meantime, returning General Fred Funston told Americans that excessive leniency was prolonging the war. He held anti-imperialists responsible for U.S. casualties and proposed that "the whole lot of them" be "hung for treason."

In the wake of Smith's scorched-earth tactics, fighting diminished, and on July 4, 1902, President Roosevelt declared the Philippines conquered. (He did so, ironically, ten years to the day after the People's Party had met in Omaha to propose a radically different government agenda to address America's economic woes.) Thousands of troops came home, and though sporadic conflict continued on some islands for years afterward, the United States to a large extent settled into the business of administering its overseas "protectorate." The toll was high: more than 5,000 American soldiers were dead, and so were at least 200,000 Filipinos, many of whom were displaced civilians (particularly children) killed by malnutrition and disease. Americans also sustained a serious blow to their national self-image, especially during 1902, when Smith's trial and several others that followed brought daily revelations of torture and brutality. Distressing to even the most ardent imperialists, high casualties and the excesses of the "water cure" steered policy makers away from military campaigns for territorial acquisition and reconfirmed instead the benefits of pursuing commercial advantage without colonial rule.

Yet to a great extent Americans' national optimism and sense of righteous mission survived the ferocity of the Philippine war intact. "The American public eats its breakfast and reads in its newspapers of our doings in the Philippines," anguished the anti-imperialist *New York World*, remarking on how little soul-searching Smith's trial provoked. "[It] takes another sip of its coffee and remarks, 'how very unpleasant!' . . . Where is that vast national outburst of astounded horror which an old-fashioned American would have predicted at reading such news? Is it lost somewhere in the 8,000 miles that divide us from these abominations?" President Roosevelt sent General Smith quietly into retirement, arguing that he had faced "well-nigh intolerable provocation" from savage foes. "I heartily approve of the employment of the

sternest measures necessary," Roosevelt wrote, while also skillfully disas-
sociating himself from torture and military crimes. The president went on to
crush his Democratic opponent in 1904, and his subsequent assertions of power
in Panama, the Dominican Republic, and elsewhere seemed to enhance rather
than dim his popularity.

McKinley's and Roosevelt's foreign exploits, though, depended to a large
extent on disjunctions between policy makers' public statements and their private calculations. Presidents who were ambitious for land and trade were not,
in themselves, something new. In the 1840s James K. Polk had become perhaps
the most successful imperialist in all U.S. history when he waged a popular
war against Mexico and took a third of it by force. But Polk had made his
objectives clear to voters, who elected him on a platform of annexation and by
implication war. The new imperial presidency rested on a somewhat different
relationship between Americans and their chief executive. Increasingly,
McKinley and his successors expanded their powers by circumventing
Congress and undercutting the Senate's constitutional role in foreign policy,
which one imperialist dubbed "the constitutional lion in the path" blocking
full presidential control.

There had been moves in this direction during the Civil War and in 1879,
when the Hayes administration had negotiated an agreement with Samoa
without bothering to ask for Senate approval. But it was Roosevelt who most
expanded presidential authority, partly because anti-imperialists in Congress
succeeded in blocking (or nearly blocking) some of his early initiatives, and
Roosevelt refused to recognize their right to do so. In 1905, after the Senate
defeated a pact that would have put the United States in charge of customs
revenues in the Dominican Republic, Roosevelt went ahead on his own to
sign an "executive agreement" with the compliant Dominican government.
(Roosevelt had already sent troops to protect U.S. sugar and shipping interests.) The president followed this up with further executive agreements in
Latin America and Asia, setting a precedent for enormous presidential authority in foreign policy. Already, during the wars of 1898, one English newspaper
had observed that the U.S. presidency was becoming "neither more nor less
than elective monarchy, limited as to duration, and regulated as to finance, but
otherwise nearly unfettered." His remark echoed José Martí's insight that the
United States was becoming a "monarchy in disguise." For foreign observers
fear of America's rising military and economic power went hand in hand with
the recognition that power was becoming more centralized in the White
House, and the U.S. political system was becoming less democratic.

McKinley and Roosevelt pioneered a number of modern tools of executive
power used by a succession of presidents in the decades since. Both were skillful managers of information and public opinion. They staged press conferences at locations ranging from the front porch of McKinley's family home in
Canton, Ohio, to wilderness settings where Roosevelt spoke of his support for
conservation. Both kept tight control of news from overseas in order to accent
positive reports. In elections they experimented with an array of modern techniques, from McKinley's expensive, sophisticated, and multilingual marketing campaigns to Roosevelt's forceful stump-speaking tours, which ironically

followed the precedent set by his archrival, the Democrat William Jennings Bryan. But the imperial presidents were successful innovators, in part, because they operated in a different climate than did their predecessors. The electorate had been considerably restricted, the Republicans had secured dominance in Washington, Democrats held the South, and the political reaction of the 1890s had popularized a new conservative agenda.

Americans' support for this agenda and for a strong presidency at home and abroad resulted from a shadow of disorder that had international as well as domestic dimensions. Violent anarchists, in particular, provoked enormous public fear. Anarchist assassins succeeded in killing the French President Carnot in 1894, a year when Americans were worrying about the Pullman boycott and the march of Coxey's Army. There followed the assassinations of Spain's prime minister in 1897, the empress of Austria the following year, King Umberto I of Italy in 1900 (an assassination planned in Paterson, New Jersey), the king of Serbia in 1903, and two more Russian ministers in 1904 and 1905. In 1901, amid this string of European assassinations and several more botched attempts, an anarchist in the United States shot and killed President William McKinley. For those who believed European conditions might be emerging in the United States, McKinley's death offered grievous confirmation. It also marked the third assassination of a U.S. president since 1865, and though anarchists had had nothing to do with Lincoln or Garfield's deaths, public alarm and anger ran high. In retrospect, violent anarchists were a tiny and politically isolated cadre, but at the time many frightened Americans equated anarchists with all labor unions, all radical European immigrants, and the entire political left. Even before McKinley's assassination, and even more afterward, they accepted harsh measures to deal with the threat.

While projecting a tougher and more aggressive image on the global stage, McKinley's successor proved willing to use his presidential powers at home for innovative ends. The Roosevelt administration launched key federal initiatives for environmental and consumer protection, creating the Food and Drug Administration in 1906, for example, to oversee food and medicine safety. Roosevelt even undertook efforts to reign in the power of corporations. During a 1902 Pennsylvania coal strike he refused to follow his White House predecessors in sending troops to crush the protest. Instead, he insisted that mine owners hear the union's grievances, and when they refused to take arbitration seriously, he threatened to seize the mines and run them under federal authority. The owners hastily agreed to talk, and Roosevelt brokered a compromise. Two years later his Justice Department went to court to block an attempted merger of two giant railroads by J. P. Morgan and James J. Hill. In the resulting *Northern Securities* case, the Supreme Court upheld the government's right to prevent the merger under the Sherman Antitrust Act. The administration's crowning achievement was the 1906 Hepburn Act, which strengthened the Interstate Commerce Commission by giving it the right to set railroad rates, subject to court review.

While Roosevelt helped usher in the first wave of twentieth-century progressivism at home, other Americans were offsetting imperialism by joining international campaigns for human rights, continuing the work begun by

Clara Barton in support of the Red Cross and the Geneva Convention. Mark Twain lent his stature to the cause of anti-imperialism, criticizing both the United States and the European powers for their conquests; his pamphlet "King Leopold's Soliloquy" was a devastating indictment of atrocities in Belgian Central Africa. The Ottoman massacre of thousands of Armenians in the mid-1890s had already provoked a humanitarian mobilization in the United States. Industrialists such as John D. Rockefeller, Sr., helped fund a National Armenian Relief Committee. The American Red Cross sent teams to help refugees, marking the organization's first work outside the United States. Congress's 1896 resolution condemning Sultan Abdul Hamid II for the murder of 100,000 Armenians marked the first U.S. resolution on international human rights. Four years later it was the farmers of Kansas, organized by People's Party leaders, who sent the first shipments of donated grain to India during a horrific famine, and a terrible pogrom against Russian Jews in Kishinev in 1903 provoked a series of public meetings in American cities to condemn czarist policies. "The most important fact in this new century," Charlotte Perkins Gilman wrote that year, "is the rapid kindling of the social consciousness." She hoped in the wake of the Armenian massacre that "America, with the blended blood of all peoples in her veins," would lead the civilized world in demanding "international law to restrain, prohibit, [and] punish; best of all, to prevent."

Thus, there were signs, even amid the grim reports of U.S. atrocities in the Philippines, that Americans had the capacity to translate their democratic heritage into what Jane Addams called "an international patriotism." In a series of lectures given at the peak of U.S. imperialism, around the turn of the century, Addams sought to articulate what that might mean. "For good or ill we suddenly find ourselves bound to an international situation," she told a Chicago audience. "Do we mean to democratize the situation? Are we going to trust our democracy?" She added, "some of us were beginning to hope that we were getting away from the ideals set by the Civil War, that we had made all the presidents we could from men who had distinguished themselves in that war, and were coming to seek another type of man. That we were ready to accept the peace ideal, to be proud of our title as a peace nation. . . . Then came the Spanish war, with its gilt and lace and tinsel, and again the moral issues are confused with exhibitions of brutality." "Unless the present situation extends our nationalism into internationalism," she warned, "unless it has thrust forward our patriotism into humanitarianism, we cannot meet it."

Future reformers, intellectuals, and policy makers would answer Addams's call in a variety of ways. But American history books would also go on to describe the Philippine conquest as "benevolent" and the defeat of Aguinaldo's forces as a brief addendum to Americans' glorious liberation of Cuba. As the twentieth century unfolded Americans largely forgot that the Philippine war had happened at all. When the United States granted Philippine independence in the wake of World War II, the turn-of-the-century war receded even further in American national memory. It was only in 1968, after U.S. troops perpetrated the My Lai massacre in Vietnam, that journalists went looking for elderly veterans who remembered the earlier conflict. Most expressed few regrets. They argued that harsher tactics should have been used earlier and even more ruthlessly in the Philippines; troops in Vietnam should beware, they said, of the treachery and cruelty of "Asiatics." "My personal opinion is that they were horrid little people," wrote one veteran, "and while time has mellowed my opinion, I can never forgive them for their treatment of some of my buddies." Only a few looked back with doubt. One interviewee who had served on Samar, avenging the Balangiga massacre, remembered his platoon advancing through tall grass to make a stealth attack on a village of fishermen. "We opened fire and killed all but one," he recalled. "They were unarmed." There had been, this old soldier remarked, "earlier My Lais." Veterans of an even earlier generation, who had witnessed General Sheridan's burning of a Blackfeet village on the Marias River back in 1870, or any number of other massacres that marked incorporation inside the United States, could have said the same.

GLOBAL LEVIATHANS

By the early twentieth century the United States was providing overseas missionaries and businessmen with military protection and aids to trade and travel, such as the $720 million Panama Canal that U.S. engineers would complete in 1914. Control over Puerto Rico, Cuba, and the Dominican Republic secured access to the mouth of the canal, while the navy's Great White Fleet sailed the world to protect Americans and their property abroad. In domestic policy, also, despite Roosevelt's modest antitrust and prolabor initiatives, Republicans continued in the main to cater to corporate interests. They maintained protective tariffs and the gold standard, considerably benefiting manufacturers and investors. Equally critical were the role of state governments and the U.S. Supreme Court. In a bid to attract business, New Jersey and Delaware invited controversial "trusts" to transfer headquarters to their states, giving them unprecedented freedom to consolidate power in one giant corporation. The Supreme Court upheld the states' rights to do so, and though the justices did set certain limits on monopoly power, they struck down a number of state and federal laws designed to protect workers and mitigate extremes of wealth.

The Court had already showed conservative leanings in *Wabash v. Illinois* (1886) and the *Minnesota Rate* case (1890), which struck down regulatory laws of the 1870s and set complicated limits on the ability of state legislatures to set shipping rates and counter the power of monopolies. In the Minnesota case the Court began to define property as not just land, buildings, and other possessions but as the "exchange value" of anything; regulation of rates was thus a theft of private property. In response to this weakening of state-level power, Congress had passed the 1887 Interstate Commerce Act, creating an Interstate Commerce Commission for business oversight, and followed this three years later with the Sherman Antitrust Act, a distressingly vague law that tried to prohibit combinations "in restraint of trade." But in *United States vs. E. C. Knight* (1895), the Court ruled that the Sherman Act gave the federal government no authority over manufacturing, even if the sugar refinery in question belonged to the American Sugar Refining Company, which controlled 98 percent of the national market.

The same year, 1895, brought other pivotal decisions, as the Court came under the sway of the dogmatic Justice Stephen Field and his allies. In a case stemming from the Pullman affair, *In re Debs*, the justices upheld the use of injunctions to halt strikes. Ironically, they based their opinion on the Sherman Antitrust Act, arguing that a boycott by a labor union, unlike a sugar refiner's bid for monopoly power, was an act "in restraint of trade." In *Pollock v. Farmers' Loan and Trust*, meanwhile, the Court struck down a federal income tax that Congress had passed in 1894. The Court argued that unless a constitutional amendment were enacted, such a tax must be apportioned on a state-by-state basis (a requirement that proved unworkable, leading eventually to passage of the Sixteenth Amendment for a federal income tax in 1913). The justices followed up these rulings with two more in 1897 that shaped the relationship between government and the economy. In *Smyth v. Ames* they declared that state regulators could set rates only according to guidelines written by the Court itself; in *ICC v. Cincinnati, New Orleans, and Texas Pacific Railroad* they declared that the federal Interstate Commerce Commission had no power to set rates at all. As in the years of Reconstruction, a conservative Supreme Court effectively gutted the most progressive federal legislation that reformers had managed to obtain.

The justices did mitigate these decisions with some that recognized new government regulatory powers. In the 1899 case of *Addystone Pipe* and several related decisions, they ruled that price-fixing among corporations was illegal and upheld government sanctions against it. They also responded favorably to the Roosevelt administration's antitrust work and followed this up in Swift and Company (1905) by reconsidering the ruling in *E. C. Knight*, acknowledging to some extent that corporations engaged in interstate commerce fell under federal authority. By 1911 the justices would shift even further in this direction, upholding the U.S. government's right to break up a massive monopoly such as Standard Oil. Yet in cases relating to the states' "police powers" to protect the health, safety, and welfare of citizens, the Supreme Court proved hostile to the most important reforms sought by labor advocates, a stance it maintained until the 1930s. The justices defined "police powers" by old-fashioned moral principles: laws to regulate or prohibit liquor met approval, as did bans on prostitution and gambling. In cases such as *Holden v. Hardy* (1898) they also allowed states to regulate working conditions and hours in certain dangerous industries, such as mining, and to end child labor. But they refused to let the states or Congress set minimum wages, and in most industries they struck down laws limiting working hours. The crowning case in this area was *Lochner v. New York* (1905), which overturned a New York law setting a sixteen-hour workday for bakers. Workers, the Court argued in essence, had the contractual right to labor as many hours as they chose. If they did not want to work more than sixteen hours a day, they should look for a different employer.

The Court's juggernaut between 1890 and 1905—especially in cases related to unions, working hours, and wages—rivaled in significance its critical role in the collapse of Reconstruction. *In re Debs* had an especially devastating long-term effect on the labor movement, paralleling in some ways the impact that *U.S. v. Cruikshank* and related cases had had on black voting rights. One historian estimates that between 1880 and 1930 state and federal courts issued more than 4,000 injunctions to stop strikes, almost always at the request of employers. By upholding this tactic (until Congress finally made the practice illegal in 1932) the Supreme Court tipped the odds in labor conflicts heavily in favor of employers, even before state militias or the U.S. Army intervened. It is hardly surprising that after the 1890s, trade unions such as the American Federation of Labor chose narrower and more limited goals.

The justices did not believe they were rolling out a red carpet for unrestrained corporate power, even though their decisions had that effect. Instead, the aging judges on the court (Stephen Field, the oldest, had been born in 1816) reacted to another set of imperatives, similar to those felt by the era's natural scientists. Over the span of their lifetimes the American judiciary had overturned English common law and systematized legal thought, creating elaborate theoretical categories. The justices of the 1890s believed such categories were scientific, universal, and immutable; their chief task as judges was not to balance competing interests but to make expert rulings about the category into which a particular case fell. Judges, in other words, shared with many other professionals a serene confidence in the scientific basis of their enterprise. Believing themselves experts who were uncovering natural and universal laws, they prided themselves on dismissing the real-world impact of their decisions. It was this approach to law, which we might call high legal formalism, that reached its apex between 1894 and 1905 in some of the cases noted above.

Formalists were influenced by their conviction that the United States was a Christian nation, and that Christianity meant the defense of private property and public order, especially from labor unions that in their view interfered with the freedoms of individual citizens. The Court's thinking was also rooted in anachronistic assumptions about government, labor, and capital. The primary reference point for tyranny remained European-style monarchy, and on economic questions the justices associated this with the power to tax. In decisions such as *Pollock* they thus saw themselves as guardians of both private property and the health of the republic, menaced by an over-reaching Congress. Meanwhile, in seeking to keep the playing field "level," they assumed businessmen and laborers contracted as equals in the marketplace and that government intervention on the side of labor would oppress business. The aging justices conceived of business as primarily the small-scale enterprise that had dominated the American economic landscape during their youth.

In this as in many other matters they were behind the times, and nothing showed this more clearly than their acquiescence on the issue of corporate personhood. As late as the early 1900s the Court clung to an old definition of the corporation, assuming state governments were setting limits on what such entities could do. This had once been correct: as late as 1888 all states continued to set certain boundaries on corporate activity. But then New Jersey, seeking to attract enterprise, passed a revolutionary law inviting trusts, which had emerged in the 1880s and were finding themselves beset by legal challenges, to form "holding companies" under extremely lenient terms. The vast American Sugar Refining Company, with operations stretching from Cuba and Louisiana to California and Hawai'i, was among the first to take advantage of New Jersey's offer. Henry O. Havemeyer, a leader of the sugar trust in the 1880s, summed up the result of becoming a New Jersey holding company. "From being illegal as we were," he observed, "we are now legal as we are."

The result was a mass migration of corporations to New Jersey and later Delaware, after it relaxed regulations even further in 1899. By 1904 all seven of the largest trusts, with a combined capitalization of $2.5 billion, operated under New Jersey charters. By 1905 the Supreme Court had essentially accepted New Jersey's definition of the corporation. In *Hale v. Henkel* it extended to corporations the Fourth Amendment right against self-incrimination, as if a corporation had a "self." In doing so the Court shifted from a definition of a corporation as a special entity, created by the state for public purposes, to the modern idea that it was the functional equivalent of an individual citizen (albeit one that existed in many places at once and could, in theory, live forever).

By the time Theodore Roosevelt and his successors bestirred themselves to limit the powers of these new leviathans and the Supreme Court began accepting their right to do so, corporate power had already undergone a dramatic concentration. New Jersey's and Delaware's laws, combined with the depression of the 1890s, enabled the largest trusts and holding companies to press their advantage against smaller competitors, many of which failed in the economic crisis. The depression also convinced businessmen in some sectors that they must merge to prevent price wars. Between 1895 and 1904, with a sharp peak at the depression's end in 1899, hundreds of American firms took this path, usually moving their headquarters to New Jersey or Delaware in the process. Almost 2,000 companies vanished, joining consolidated holding companies such as American Locomotive, DuPont, Eastman Kodak, International Harvester, International Paper, National Asphalt, Otis Elevator, U.S. Box Board and Paper, and U.S. Gypsum, each of which controlled more than 70 percent of its product's national market share by the turn of the century. Laurence Gronlund had foreseen this development in *The Cooperative Commonwealth*. "These gentlemen," he wrote of the nation's leading executives, "have already found that while Competition is a very excellent weapon against their weaker rivals, Combination pays far better in relation to their peers. It is evident that it is combination they mainly rely on for their future aggrandizement."

Not all consolidations achieved such dominance, and not all businessmen found the strategy successful. But taken as a whole, the wave of mergers transformed the economy further in the direction of large-scale multinational enterprise. In the 1890s many of these consolidated companies also won trademark protection through the courts, so that Ivory became synonymous with soap, Wrigley's with gum, and Gillette with razors. It is not an accident that these names remain famous today. The most successful corporations became "first movers," taking a position of overwhelming dominance from which they could use their power (much as Republicans and southern Democrats were doing in politics) to shut out newcomers and rivals.

The result was an American economy even further integrated and financially centralized. A single national market in short-term credit linked the West Coast with the East by 1900. J. P. Morgan assumed control of the bankrupt Southern Railway (formerly thirty different companies), which gave his investors access to coal, iron, cotton, tobacco, lumber, sulphur, turpentine, and Florida fruit. The 1890s also saw a substantial movement of textile mills from New England to the low-wage South, starting with three Massachusetts firms that moved in 1895. At the behest of John D. Rockefeller, Sr., Henry Flagler opened a series of southern luxury resorts. "By 1896," writes one historian, "palace cars from Bar Harbor and Newport could roll unimpeded through the poverty-littered Carolinas and all the way to Miami and its Royal Palm Hotel."

The most successful corporations emerged from the depression with increased multinational reach. Companies ranging from Borden to International Silver acquired factories in Canada. American Tobacco enlarged its empire, entering the twentieth century with plants in Germany, Japan, and Australia. Behemoths such as United Fruit and U.S. Rubber regularly made purchasing and marketing decisions that impacted two or three continents. By 1897 U.S. direct investment overseas totaled $635 million, and in the next decade it rose to more than a billion and a half. By 1900 New York's most powerful financiers had fully intertwined their fortunes with those of the great industrialists, creating unprecedented centers of power. National City Bank, the predecessor of today's Citigroup, counted among its directors not only John D. Rockefeller, Jr., and his brother William but also Henry Clay Frick of Carnegie Steel; Cleveland Dodge from the Phelps Dodge Corporation, one of the nation's largest mining concerns; the reaper magnate Cyrus McCormick; the railcar manufacturer George Pullman; and the financier J. P. Morgan. National City Bank could by the first decade of the twentieth century exchange any currency into another in twenty-four hours and deliver it virtually anywhere in the world.

The bank knew what it was doing in choosing J. P. Morgan for its board. It was Morgan who had knocked Thomas Edison's name off Edison General Electric and taken it over in 1892. It was Morgan who had bailed out the gold standard and the Cleveland administration and who in 1901 engineered the triumphant merger that created U.S. Steel, the first company in America with a billion-dollar valuation. Morgan's famous "Trio," consisting of himself and two close associates, provided links to investors and banks in Britain, France, Belgium, and Germany. The Trio, by this date, customarily swapped 15-percent shares in their U.S. and Mexican ventures for equivalent interests in Asian and African investments organized by their European partners. Thus, association with the "House of Morgan" offered the most influential businessmen access to fabulous sums of investment capital and financial networks that stretched around the globe.

No one exemplified the new configuration of executive power better than Andrew Carnegie, who officially became the world's richest man when

Morgan bought out his company. Carnegie Steel had thrived during the depression of the 1890s, largely through government contracts for the naval fleet that helped make America a world power. Back in 1886, when Carnegie had first been approached about the possibility of such contracts, he had lectured Grover Cleveland's secretary of the navy on the dangers of a military build-up, stating flatly that he was "opposed to every dollar spent by our Republic upon instruments of any kind for destructive purposes." Carnegie pointed out that Britain and Germany were unlikely to attack the United States, and he suggested that a naval arms race would increase rather than reduce the possibility of war. But on Christmas Eve, 1886, Carnegie announced that a new open-hearth mill at Homestead would be built to roll out armor plates of the size the navy needed. "There may be millions for us in armor," he wrote privately.

The prices Carnegie then charged the U.S. government for steel became the focus of repeated congressional investigations. Four former employees, embittered among other things by the defeat of the Amalgamated Steelworkers at Homestead, came forward in 1893 with persuasive evidence that the company had masked flaws and weakness in its armor. Carnegie was fined 10 percent on his current contracts, though officials to some extent hushed up the damage. Four years later Congress investigated allegations of over-charging. Carnegie, it turned out, was making profits of perhaps 30 percent or more on his U.S. government contracts while selling similar steel to the Russian navy for a much lower price. "We are in the hands of this great steel combine," fumed Colorado Senator Henry Teller. "The Republicans seem to have set their hearts upon giving to these people practically whatever they ask." Despite evidence that competing bids from smaller firms such as Midvale Steel were more cost-effective, Republicans handed the vast majority of contracts to the two big firms, Carnegie and Bethlehem. The independent-minded Carnegie then had the temerity to challenge the very policies that had made him rich. Amid national debate over annexation of the Philippines, he offered to buy the islands outright from the United States for $20 million in order to give Filipinos their freedom. (The government declined.)

No incident was more telling than the moment in early 1897 when Grover Cleveland's secretary of the navy, Hilary Herbert, got fed up with the false information he was receiving from U.S. steel suppliers and boarded a ship to confer with European manufacturers. Herbert wanted to know what French and British steelmakers were actually charging their governments for naval steel, and he wanted to hear the answers directly from them. He made his trip top secret, but Carnegie, who had negotiated price-fixing agreements with Krups, Vickers, Schneider, and other European steelmakers as well as with Bethlehem Steel, had agents in the administration who tipped him off. Unbeknownst to Secretary Herbert, the ship that carried him to Europe also carried an employee of Carnegie Steel who disembarked immediately and rushed to reaffirm the steelmakers' pact and warn them of Herbert's visit. The secretary of the navy got only vague answers on his tour and came home with little useful information. In the meantime, he and the French minister of marine commiserated with each other in Paris. Both governments, they felt sure, were at the mercy of steelmakers who were fixing prices and charging exorbitant rates, but neither man could prove it.

The late 1890s, then, seemed at first glance to mark the dawn of an era of fierce nationalism and unprecedented military escalation, in which the United States vied with European powers to amass battleships and claim overseas prizes, with each government eyeing the others suspiciously over the turrets. The U.S. government (as this story goes) had been weak in the Gilded Age but was emerging in the late 1890s as an invigorated global power, with Theodore Roosevelt equally aggressive in his policies abroad and his attack on trusts at home. There is some truth to this interpretation, as any Cuban or Filipino could attest. The significance of the imperial presidency, in particular, can hardly be overstated, and only seven years after Roosevelt won the presidency in 1904, federal courts would order the break-up of Standard Oil to demolish its monopoly power.

Secretary Herbert's journey, however, offers a glimpse into a different reality. During the Civil War and its aftermath the U.S. government had exercised immense powers and engaged in a series of bold experiments. But that war, along with the wars of incorporation that followed, had launched an economic revolution that left the authority of even the American president and the German kaiser humbled by that of Carnegie and others in his secret pool. Carnegie frequently argued that he had, setting aside his anti-imperialist principles, placed his enterprise at the service of his country. (He also went on to create the Carnegie Endowment for International Peace and fund construction of the Peace Palace in the Netherlands, home of today's World Court—while his company simultaneously forged the steel for dozens of warships.) To whatever extent Carnegie did or did not serve his nation's interests, the reverse was clearly true: through its rising military expenditures, the U.S. government served the interests of Mr. Carnegie.

FOR FURTHER READING

An excellent short account of the U.S. conquest of Hawai'i is Scott B. Cook, "Islands of Manifest Destiny," in his book *Colonial Encounters in the Age of High Imperialism* (New York, 1996). See also Sylvester K. Stevens, *American Expansion in Hawaii, 1842–1898* (Harrisburg, PA, 1945), Merze Tate, *The United States and the Hawaiian Kingdom* (New Haven, CT, 1965), Gary Y. Okihiro, *Cane Fires* (Philadelphia, 1991), and Sally Engle Merry, *Colonizing Hawai'i* (Princeton, NJ, 2000).

My key sources on U.S. foreign relations throughout this chapter are Walter LaFeber, *The New Empire* (Ithaca, NY, 1963), and also his book *The American Search for Opportunity*, cited in Chapter 1; Louis A. Pérez, *The War of 1898* (Chapel Hill, NC, 1998); Thomas J. McCormick, *China Market* (Chicago, 1967); Dennis Merrill and Thomas G. Paterson, *Major Problems in American Foreign Relations to 1920*, 5th ed. (Boston, 2000); and Thomas Schoonover, *Uncle Sam's War of 1898 and the Origins of Globalization* (Lexington, KY, 2003). The quote about U.S. policy makers' lack of vision and moral values is from Schoonover, p. 29. Very helpful in placing foreign relations in cultural context is Matthew Frye Jacobson, *Barbarian Virtues* (New York, 2000). On the economic and cultural dimensions of expansion, see also Emily S. Rosenberg, *Spreading the American Dream* (New York, 1982), and for an environmental angle on U.S. consumption of tropical crops, Richard P. Tucker, *Insatiable Appetite* (Berkeley, CA, 2000).

Links between western frontier expansion and overseas imperialism are brilliantly analyzed in Walter L. Williams, "United States Indian Policy and the Debate over Philippine Annexation," *Journal of American History* 66 (1980): 810–831. On the perhaps under-recognized influence of Brooks Adams see William A. Williams, "Brooks Adams and American Expansion," *New England Quarterly* 25 (1952): 217–32. For alternative views of American imperialism see, for example, Ernest May's influential *Imperial Democracy* (New York, 1961), Kevin Phillips, *William McKinley* (New York, 2003), and James A. Field, Jr.'s provocative article, "American Imperialism: The Worst Chapter in Almost Any Book," *American Historical Review* 83 (1978): 644–668. On Jose Martí see the introduction by Deborah Shnookal and Mirta Muñiz in *The Jose Martí Reader* (Melbourne, Australia, 1999).

For the economic results of the 1898 wars in the Caribbean, see César J. Ayala, *American Sugar Kingdom* (Chapel Hill, NC, 1999). On the conflict in the Philippines I have drawn primarily on Stuart Creighton Miller, *"Benevolent Assimilation"* (Haven, 1982), and on black soldiers in the Philippines, Willard B. Gate, *"Smoked Yankees" and the Struggle for Empire* (Fayetteville, AR, 1987). On Americans' response to the massacre of Armenians, see Peter Balakian, *The Burning Tigris* (New York, 2003), and on Populist shipments of grain to India, Mike Davis, *Late Victorian Holocausts* (London, 2001).

My treatment of the U.S. Supreme Court draws primarily from Morton J. Horowitz, *The Transformation of American Law, 1870–1960* (New York, 1992), Owen M. Fiss, *The Troubled Beginnings of the Modern State, 1888–1910* (New York, 1993), and William E. Forbath, *Law and the Shaping of the American Labor Movement* (Cambridge, MA, 1991). On the importance of Christian faith, see Linda Przybyszewski, "Judicial Conservatism and Protestant Faith: The Case of Justice David J. Brewer," *Journal of American History* 91 (2004): 471–96. An overview of laissez-faire constitutional thought is Michael Les Benedict, "Laissez-Faire and Liberty," *Law and History Review* 3 (1985): 293–331. I also rely here once again on Richard F. Bensel, *The Political Economy of American Industrialization*, cited in Chapter 1, as well as on the following: Lawrence M. Friedman, *A History of American Law* (New York, 1985), Charles W. McCurdy, "The *Knight* Sugar Decision of 1895 and the Modernization of American Corporate Law, 1869–1903," *Business History Review* 53 (1979): 304–342, and Papke, *The Pullman Case*, cited in Chapter 10.

On the consolidation of power by multinational corporations see Naomi R. Lamoreaux, *The Great Merger Movement in American Business, 1895–1904* (Cambridge, 1985), and Walter Licht, *Industrializing America* and Mira Wilkins, *The Emergence of Multinational Enterprise*, both cited in Chapter 2. On credit markets see John A. James, "The Evolution of the National Money Market, 1888–1911," and "The Development of the National Money Market, 1893–1911," which appear respectively in *Journal of Economic History* 36 (1976): 271–275 and 878–897. On trademarks see Susan Strasser, *Satisfaction Guaranteed* (New York, 1989). The quotation on palace cars rolling through the Carolinas is from C. Vann Woodward, *Origins of the New South, 1877–1913* (Baton Rouge, LA, 1951), p. 297. The phrase "first movers" is drawn from Alfred D. Chandler's *Scale and Scope* (Cambridge, MA, 1990). On Mexico I return here to John M. Hart, *Empire and Revolution*, cited in Chapter 2. On Carnegie see Joseph Frazier Wall, *Andrew Carnegie*, and B. Franklin Cooling, *Gray Steel and Blue Water Navy*, both cited in previous chapters.

Epilogue: The Partridges and the Hippopotamus

For America, if eligible at all to downfall and ruin, is eligible
within herself, not without.
—WALT WHITMAN, *DEMOCRATIC VISTAS*

During the hopeful years after the Civil War, Walt Whitman's essay "Democratic Vistas" described his hopes for the triumph of American democracy. A visitor to the St. Louis World's Fair of 1904, three and a half decades later, would have found considerable evidence of the fulfillment of Whitman's dream. Marking the centennial of the Louisiana Purchase, which in 1803 had transformed the United States into a continental power, the St. Louis exposition was the largest ever held in the world. So vast were its grounds and exhibits that medical experts urged patients with weak nerves not to attend. (Coincidentally or not, the novelist Kate Chopin died of heart failure after a day of touring the fair.) The initial capitalization was $15 million, exactly the amount Thomas Jefferson had persuaded Congress to pay for the whole purchase itself, and enthusiastic commentators spoke of the fair as a "coronation." "If all man's other works were by some unspeakable catastrophe, blotted out," declared the chair of the exposition board, "the records here established by the assembled nations would offer all necessary standards for the rebuilding of our entire civilization."

If technology was the measure of progress, the fair offered plenty of it. With officials counting almost twenty million visitors, St. Louis streetcars carried up to 120,000 passengers per hour to and from the site, while a double-track electric trolley whisked visitors around the fair itself. On evening strolls along the exposition's pathways visitors could bask in the soft glow of thousands of incandescent lights. Technological marvels displayed at the fair ranged from the new wireless radio to designs for future airships. A large exhibit heralded the "Era of the Automobile." A somewhat less glamorous one hailed the "Age of Concrete." An entire building was devoted to fossil fuels, and visitors could marvel at a 3,000-horsepower gasoline engine and a locomotive weighing 100 tons. (On the Pike, equivalent to Chicago's Midway, St. Louis wisely reused Chicago's famous Ferris wheel, whose enormous popularity had helped pull the 1893 exposition out of debt.) The fair had "deep, far reaching, ethical, and educative import," wrote one observer, who described what he had seen as "a succession of mental shocks."

Those who needed a rest could enjoy the full range of urban amusements in St. Louis, famous for its ragtime scene. In clubs near the exposition visitors could hear the great Scott Joplin perform his "Maple Leaf Rag" and "The Entertainer," the latter composed in honor of the fair itself. Baseball fans could go out for a Cardinals or Browns game, while movie palaces offered both newsreels and dramatic thrillers such as *The Great Train Robbery*, a full eleven minutes long. St. Louis also had its proud new skyscrapers, including an 1892 Louis Sullivan masterpiece, the Wainwright Building. The vibrant features of the American city that had so fascinated Whitman in his day were coming into full flower, their petals unmistakably flecked with commercial gold.

If social progress was the measure of democracy, then the fair offered much evidence of that as well. An exhibit on U.S. settlement houses featured model playgrounds, reports on public health campaigns, and innovations in hygiene and medicine. The Model Street showcased designs for public fountains and septic systems. The fair's Department of Physical Culture demonstrated exercises for pleasure and health. Government agencies proudly advertised their roles in improving citizens' lives. Germany's exhibit explained its new workingmen's insurance program, which would influence a similar U.S. program created four years later. The Smithsonian Institution showcased its recently built children's room. The U.S. Life-Saving Service gave daily demonstrations on a special lake, while elsewhere visitors could visit displays on Yellowstone Park and the indigenous fauna of the United States. The overall design of the fair's "Forest City" showed, in fact, more than a glimmer of environmental consciousness. Situated in a hundred-acre woodland park, it featured naturalistic landscaping and soothing cascades.

There were other signs that would have pleased Walt Whitman. Thirty years earlier all eyes had looked to London and Paris, but the United States now showed unmistakably that it was asserting its own authentic culture. Educated European visitors probably knew the names of American writers such as William Dean Howells and Stephen Crane—certainly Mark Twain— as well as artists such as Winslow Homer, Thomas Eakins, James McNeill Whistler, and Mary Cassatt. Any English or Scottish tourist knew about the evangelist Dwight Moody, while the name Othniel Marsh was familiar to devotees of Darwinian science. The fame of such figures both contributed to and resulted from a shifting flow of information. Back when Whitman had excoriated his countrymen for their lack of cultural patriotism, far more Americans had subscribed to British journals and newspapers than the other way around. But by the 1890s American monthlies such as *Harper's* and

ury began to outsell British monthlies—not only at home, but in England,
One American editor noted that "a few British magazines and reviews
tinue to be imported into the United States, but they are very few indeed."
Yes, the 1,100-plus acres of the Forest City held irrefutable proof that the
ited States was becoming an economic, political, and cultural world power.
rks of militarism and empire were much in evidence, with the United States
iming pride of place. Along with models of the battleship USS *Missouri*
d thirty other vessels, the U.S. Navy posted an immense map charting the
ations of all its ships around the globe. The centerpiece of the entire fair,
dely discussed and almost universally attended by visitors, was the so-
lled Philippine Reservation, an unabashed imperial display that cost more
an $1 million. It centered on a plaza showing an elite Filipino home, govern-
ent offices, and a reproduction of Manila's museum of commerce. At a
eplica school missionary teachers led classes in singing "My Country 'Tis of
hee," while in the plaza uniformed Filipino policemen and scouts (more than
00 of them, making up nearly half the reservation's population) conducted
drills. Surrounding the plaza were ethnological villages displaying thirty-eight
3agobo "savages" and other representatives of Filipino tribes. The exhibit was
considered so crucial as a public justification for U.S. occupation of the islands
that President Roosevelt himself issued detailed instructions on how to clothe
the tribal peoples on display. If they seemed too primitive, officials worried,
anti-imperialists might argue they were unfit to be Americans; if they seemed
too civilized, that might fuel sympathy for Philippine independence.

Looking around the fair one found markers of the violence of incorporation
at home as well as overseas. The Apache leader Geronimo and the Nez Percé
Chief Joseph were "among the noted Indians on exhibition." To greet visitors
at the entrance to the Pike, Frederic Remington sculpted "Cowboys Shooting
Up a Western Town," which one guidebook described as a "frolicsome" scene.
Meanwhile, Chinese visitors were fingerprinted and forced to wear numbered
tags as long as they remained in the United States, reassuring the American
public that they would not remain after the fair was over. Japan, fresh from
its stunning victory in the Russo-Japanese War, received more respectful
treatment on the basis of its obvious military might. The anthropologist
W. J. McGee, who directed the fair's ethnological displays, explained that the
Japanese were progressing because of their "complexity of blood," equivalent
to that of Anglo-Saxons.

Few systems of racial categorization were ever presented with any more
confident assurance than McGee's, which turned the entire fair into an
elaborate hierarchy of racial types designed to contrast "the barbarous and
semi-barbarous peoples of the world" with the "full-blown enlightenment of
America." McGee believed the keys to Anglo-Saxon superiority were larger
cranial size and greater manual dexterity, as well as "sensitiveness to tempera-
ture, delicacy of touch and taste, [and] acuteness of vision and hearing." Even
more obvious racial condescension emerged when a group of white St. Louis
schoolteachers invited Filipino scouts to stroll with them through exposition
grounds. The scouts were taunted with shouts of "nigger," beaten up by members of the fair's police force, and attacked by a group of marines who shot

revolvers in the air and shouted "Let's clean the gu-gus off the earth!" A lynching was narrowly averted.

Such incidents suggested that Americans had not achieved all they claimed in the areas of civilization and progress. Much at the fair would have thrilled Walt Whitman, but much else would have grieved him deeply, and in retrospect it is hard to avoid the conclusion that Americans understood little about the world that their institutions and desires now played a key role in shaping. To some extent, in the most generous possible reading of Americans' national mentality in 1904, they had fallen victim to a naïve misunderstanding of themselves. The philosopher William James captured this attitude and its consequences in a public letter denouncing the Philippine war. "Among the charming 'Fables' which the New York *World* printed many years ago," James wrote, "was one about a hippopotamus, which, walking one day in the forest, . . . scared a hen-partridge from her nest of new-hatched fledglings. Touched with compassion, the kind-hearted animal exclaimed: 'You poor, forsaken babes! Let me be a mother to you.' So she sat down upon the nest of little partridges."

James proposed that the United States bore a strong resemblance to the kind hippopotamus. "Unquestionably the great heart of our people means well by the islanders," he wrote. "But what worse enemy to a situation of need can there be than dim, foggy, abstract good will, backed by energetic officiousness, and unillumined by any accurate perception?" He could have extended the point from the Philippines to the Caribbean, Central America, and China. As one historian has put it, America came onto the global stage with "a desperately parochial understanding" of the world outside its borders. It did so in part because geographic expansion on the North American continent— ending with the wars of incorporation—had already been romanticized. The public mythology surrounding conflicts within the borders of the United States provided a powerful intellectual template for the "schooling" and uplift of Cubans and Filipinos.

It would be wrong, however, to see the innocence of the hippopotamus as a personal failing on the part of individual Americans. Rather, the structures that now linked the United States to the rest of the world actively obstructed a clear view. The St. Louis World's Fair, which claimed to represent the objective truth about the world when in fact its exhibits were sponsored by corporations and powerful empires (as well as a deeply misguided anthropologist) was a prime example in itself. But larger and more subtle processes were at work. Americans were experiencing the world first and foremost as consumers. The very genius of corporate capitalism was to obscure the distant origins of rubber, sugar, and beef and to whisk them to consumers as if by magic. To an unprecedented degree, Americans could enjoy the fruits of the global marketplace without guilt or thought. Just as state legislatures and courts had extended "limited liability" to investors and executives sued for acts committed by their corporations, manufacturers and advertisers offered a kind of psychic limited liability to consumers.

New political structures, like commercial ones, often obscured rather than clarified Americans' views of the world. In 1898 Americans had fought a war to free Cuba and found, in retrospect, they had conquered an overseas territory in the Pacific, a circumstance that was explained, like the failure of Reconstruction, by reference to the racial incapacity of the liberated people. The most powerful of all imperialist spokesmen, Theodore Roosevelt, had at the time of the St. Louis fair just been elected with an astonishing 57 percent of the popular vote, the highest any president had won since the 1820s. He had watched McKinley's campaign manager, Mark Hanna, market McKinley "as if he were a patent medicine," and Roosevelt in turn skillfully marketed himself as an embodiment of masculine vigor, law and order, and Anglo supremacy who also spoke eloquently of the wonders of nature and the benefits of fair play.

Roosevelt's bellicose assertions of "Anglo-Saxon manhood" are all too easy to caricature. Though racial assumptions played an important role—probably *the* most important role—in Americans' misapprehensions about their place in the world, it would be wrong to dwell on only the hate that fueled lynchings and the slaughter of Filipino civilians. Other forms of racialized thinking were more complex. A key example was the Protestant foreign missionary movement, which by 1904 was publishing *Via Christi*, a sophisticated set of textbooks through which Americans could study the histories and cultures of people around the globe. *Via Christi* was one of the most accurate sources of information an ordinary American could obtain about foreign peoples at the start of the twentieth century, but it was read by Christians seeking to alter those cultures and convert them to a different faith.

An Orientalist fad, evident at the St. Louis fair, captured many of the contradictions in Americans' racialized thinking. The Englishman Edward Fitzgerald's loose translation of the *Rubáiyát* of Omar Khayyám, a twelfth-century Persian poem, came into vogue on both sides of the Atlantic in the 1890s. Americans rushed to put "Turkish corners" in their parlors, and as early as 1885 Gilbert and Sullivan's parody *The Mikado* started a rage for Japanese lanterns and kimonos. In the 1890s American artists had begun studying eighteenth-century Japanese prints and reflecting their influence in bold prints and posters. The Japanese newspaper artist Beisen Kubota had visited the Chicago World's Fair, where he shaped the work of the young American artist John Sloan.

Perhaps the culminating moment of Orientalism was the publication of "Madame Butterfly," an 1898 short story by John Luther Long that the playwright David Belasco borrowed two years later. "Madame Butterfly" reflected American racial condescension while at the same time critiquing it. The popular play centered on Cho-Cho-San (Butterfly), a Japanese woman who believes her lover, a U.S. Navy lieutenant, will return for her and their child. The lieutenant returns, but with his blonde American bride. He has no intention of marrying Butterfly and has written a revealing letter to a fellow officer about "that little Jap girl." "You won't believe it," he remarks, "but for two weeks after I sailed I was dotty in love with her." Cho-Cho-San wants to become an American but also to retain her honor. Finding that her lover's betrayal prevents this, she commits suicide, placing in her baby's hand just before her death a little American flag. The play's critique of imperialism is complicated by the lieutenant's attempts to buy off Cho-Cho-San with "lots of money," as well as the presence of his new wife Kate, who helps prompt Butterfly's suicide by telling her she will take away the child and raise him in an Anglo family. "Let us think first of the child," she tells Butterfly. "For his own good . . . let me take him home to my country." Butterfly responds, "He not know then—me—his mother?" Kate responds, "It's hard, very hard, I know; but would it not be better?" The playwright clearly assumed audiences would agree.

In some ways "Madame Butterfly" is the story of three women, Cho-Cho-San, Kate, and Butterfly's wise maidservant, Suzuki, who tries to warn her mistress of the lieutenant's faithlessness. It is thus a critique of men's exploitation of women and perhaps of elite women's self-delusions as well as of racial prejudice. Yet onstage in the United States Cho-Cho-San was always played by Anglo actresses, raising troubling questions of class as well as racial condescension. Blanche Bates, the most famous actress in the role, claimed she learned her Japanese mannerisms from family servants in San Francisco and from a personal maid, Suki, whom she employed in New York. Suki had a *real* tragic story: her fiancé in Japan, on the eve of boarding a steamship to join her in America, was murdered. To complicate things further, Belasco forced his heroine to speak broken English ("tha's mak' me mos' bes' happy female woman in Japan—mebby in that whole worl'—w'at you thing?"), verging on the exaggerated dialect that Anglo audiences of the time found cute and funny when attributed to blacks.

For turn-of-the-century audiences Butterfly's story had many meanings. She was an exotic, sexualized figure, and in light of U.S. marriage laws many Anglos surely rejected her aspirations to marry a white man. Yet her strong sense of honor highlighted the values of a feudalistic past in the days before money had meant everything, and her suicide was surely intended as a critique of Western imperial designs. Thus, racial condescension went hand in hand with admiration and desire, as non-Asians described (or invented) a version of Japanese culture useful to themselves. In sum, at the turn of the century, Americans did not have to take other nations and peoples very seriously in their own right. Those nations now had to take the United States very seriously indeed.

Americans were afflicted by plenty of raw hate and hypocrisy, but even more by confusion. The many calls to extend "Anglo-Saxon civilization" around the globe vied with the vision of Walt Whitman and his heirs that the United States, as a crossroads of people from all continents, would be defined by its heterogeneity. The humorist Peter Finley Dunne, who created the Irish-American character Mr. Dooley, addressed the problem when he had Mr. Dooley comment to a friend on race-based justifications for the war of 1898. Dooley, he averred, was a proud "Anglo-Saxon" name:

> They're a lot iv Anglo-Saxons in this country, Hinnissy. There must be as many as two in Boston. . . . Me ol' friend Domingo will march at the head of the Eyetalian Anglo-Saxons when th' time comes. There ar-re twenty thousan' Rooshian Jews in th' Sivinth Ward . . . [and] when th' sons iv Sweden, and th' Circle Francaize, an' th' Polacky Binivolent Society, an' th' Benny Brith, an' th'

Afro-Americans an' th' other Anglo-Saxons begin f'r to raise their Anglo-Saxon battle cry, it'll be all done with th' eight or nine people in the wurruld that has th' misfortune iv not bein' brought up Anglo-Saxon.

Dunne captured with humor a fundamental contradiction between what the United States had become and what most of its elite leaders understood it to be.

The summer of 1904 waned into fall. Workers at the St. Louis fairgrounds disassembled the Ferris wheel and the giant dynamos and tore down the buildings and grand façades. Fair managers totalled up their expenses and profits and filed their official reports. Tourists, entrepreneurs, and the diverse people who had gathered went home (or in the case of some native peoples who had been put on display, struggled to raise funds to get home and ended up as wanderers). But America's new wealth, military power, and economic reach—revealed through the fair as if through a fun-house mirror—endured.

On the morning after the fair closed, as the eastern sky lightened with dawn, thousands of Cuban, Puerto Rican, Filipino, and southern sugarcane workers headed out to the fields at harvest time; in Louisiana, scattered Italians and Portuguese trudged out among the black work crews. In Hawai'i, Chinese and Japanese women went out to labor beside the men, stripping dried leaves from the stalks as their husbands cut and loaded cane. Japanese women sang *hole hole bushi*, songs to match the rhythms of their work:

Worse than the birds crying
Or the temple bell tolling
Is the plantation bell
Calling us to another day.

Into San Francisco and New York harbors came the ships full of sugar: 400,000 tons from Hawai'i, 700,000 tons from Cuba, and more from Java, Mexico, and Brazil. In Louisiana 400,000 tons went into the refineries of the great sugar trust, while freight cars waited nearby to ship it nationwide.

New York cooked it into Tootsie Rolls. Farther upstate it found its way into boxes of Jell-O. Atlanta used it to sweeten Coca-Cola, and at the Wrigley's factory in Chicago it flavored Juicy Fruit and Spearmint gum. The New England Confectionary Company put it into gumballs, licorice, NECCO wafers, and the recently invented Valentine conversation hearts. Whitman's Chocolate Company in Philadelphia blended it into that luscious nineteenth-century invention, milk chocolate, and distributed the resulting product through its new nationwide marketing channels. The factories of Derry Church, soon to be renamed Hershey, Pennsylvania, in honor of the local manufacturer, poured their supply of sugar into the great vats that brought forth nickel chocolate bars. All these fed into the great river of candy—$400 million worth—that Americans consumed that year. As one contemporary noted, poor people indulged in especially large quantities: candy offered "cheap satisfaction" wherever the "standard of living is low."

And in New York City's Bowery district, Henry James sat in a darkened theater in December 1904 watching the audience around him eat candy and follow the action onstage. He searched their faces. He considered whether he himself, so long a wanderer abroad, belonged among them. He meditated on the United States they represented, so different from the nation of his childhood. He wondered what it all signified for the future of American politics, business, and culture, and for the peoples of the rest of the world as they either came to America's gates or found America at theirs. And while he thought, he munched his chocolate creams.

FOR FURTHER READING

All material on the Louisiana Purchase Exposition is drawn from Robert W. Rydell, *All the World's a Fair*, cited in Chapter 7, and from original guidebooks and reports. Especially helpful here is Matthew Frye Jacobson, *Barbarian Virtues* (New York, 2001); the quotation about Americans being "desperately provincial" is drawn from pp. 264–65. On other nations having to take the United States seriously, but not vice versa, I am grateful to Louis A. Pérez for ideas he presented in a lecture at Vassar College in April 2004. On the *Via Christi* books, see Patricia R. Hill's *The World Their Household*, cited in Chapter 8. For the analysis here I am also grateful to Kristin Hoganson for her paper, "Girdling the Globe: US Women and the Fictive Travel Movement, 1880–1920," delivered at the American Historical Association, Washington, DC, in January 2004. The section on Orientalism draws on Mari Yoshihara, *Embracing the East* (New York, 2003). On sugar and candy I have drawn on Gary Okihiro's *Cane Fires* and César J. Ayala's *American Sugar Kingdom*, both cited in Chapter 11, as well as George Thomas Surface, *The Story of Sugar* (New York, 1910).

The lessons one draws from any period of history depend, to a large extent, on one's choice of beginning and ending points. Those interested in such questions (whether or not they like the choices of 1865 and 1905 that have been made in *New Spirits*) might appreciate William Cronon's essay "A Place for Stories: Nature, History, and Narrative," *Journal of American History* 78 (1992): 1347–76.

Questions for Discussion

1. *New Spirits* tells, in brief, the stories of many famous and ordinary Americans who lived between 1865 and 1905. Identify two or three such individuals who strike you as interesting or compelling. What themes or ideas do their lives represent for you? Do they exemplify the era, and if so, how? Did you find any heroes in this book? If so, what qualities in them did you find heroic, and why?

2. The Civil War cast a long shadow over the decades that followed. Mark Twain called it an "ennobling war" (see the introduction), while José Martí described it as a "corrupting war" that bred a "habit of authority and domination" (see the introduction to Part III). To what extent do you think each of these views was accurate, and why? What legacies, both positive and negative, did the war leave for Americans who came of age after it ended?

3. Economic thinker Joseph Schumpeter famously described capitalism as a process of "creative destruction." In what ways did such processes operate in the United States between 1865 and 1905? How did they impact work and daily experience? Women's rights? Sexuality and family life? Religion and culture? Politics? In what ways do you see this "creative destruction" as having positive or negative consequences?

4. What kinds of violent conflict did Americans engage in between 1865 and 1905? What were the sources of this violence, and how did it shape relationships among Americans and between America and the world? (Note: a timeline of conflicts is posted at the *New Spirits* website, http://projects.vassar.edu/newspirits. It covers only public, large-scale episodes of violence; other forms, like domestic violence, were more hidden, but you may still want to take them into consideration.)

5. In the introduction, the author explains where the term *Gilded Age* came from and why she refrains from using it. Here and elsewhere she suggests alternatives, such as the "long Progressive Era" and the "paleotechnical era." She also employs several metaphors to describe the period, including fire in the introduction; Henry George's wedge in the introduction to Part I; and the telephone exchange in the introduction to Part II. Which of these terms and metaphors seem most useful? What would *you* call this era, and why?

6. Thomas Frank is one of many American commentators who have described the 1990s and the first decade of the 21st century as a "new Gilded Age." Does such a comparison make sense to you? Why or why not? (You may see no parallels—or see them in very different ways than Frank does—but for his comparison see "The

New Gilded Age," in *Commodify Your Dissent*, ed. Thomas Frank and Matt Weiland [New York, 1997], 23–28.)

7. *New Spirits* emphasizes the racial and cultural diversity of the American working class, which was drawn from the Americas, Africa, Europe, and Asia and included people of many colors, religions, and languages. What were the consequences of this diversity for the labor movement, for the economy, and for society and culture? What are its legacies today? If you have an interest in world history, you might want to do some additional reading and compare societies where the work-force has been largely imported (for example, Brazil and the United States) with those having highly homogenous, indigenous populations (for example, Japan and Scandinavia). How has immigration—whether forced or voluntary, or both—or *lack* of immigration shaped the histories of these nations?

8. Former US diplomat George Kennan, an iconoclastic thinker, has remarked that he has "a great distrust of the monster nations, where there is the exertion of political authority over millions of people from a given center. . . . I think they are danger-ous to themselves, as well as to everybody else. . . . You lose all real, intimate connection between the source of national power and the people themselves. For this reason, I feel that our own country has to be decentralized." Kennan proposes that the United States be divided up into "something like a dozen constituent republics." ("The Provocateur," *The New Yorker*, November 13, 2000, p. 100.) Using Kennan's idea, imagine a counter-history of the United States in which the Confederacy had maintained its independence and additional republics, perhaps starting in the West, had also broken away. Would the political, economic, and social results have been beneficial or harmful, and to whom? How might slavery have eventually ended? How might these "constituent republics" have responded to events in the 20th century? What relations might they have with one another today?

Index